MEMOIRS

OF A BIKER

To Jessica
Thanks For your Support!

By
KickStart

Vaughan

E-mail me! Panshovel54@Yahoo.com
Talk To you Soon!

PUBLISH AMERICA

PublishAmerica
Baltimore

ISBN: 978-1-60749-069-2
PUBLISHED BY PUBLISHAMERICA, LLLP
www.publishamerica.com
Baltimore

Printed in the United States of America

I would like to dedicate this to...
my loving wife, daughter, and son.
Also to my caring father who wouldn't let me down.

For all their efforts, time, and advice, I would like to acknowledge the following people:

My wife for her understanding and support.
Jamie D for all the professional hard work.
Thank you for helping to make it happen!

Table of Contents

MEMOIRS

OF A BIKER

INTRODUCTION

I invite you to come take a ride with me in the "fast lane" of the earlier years of the "Outlaw Motorcycle Clubs." You will travel with my Brothers and me, exploring the world of "One Percent Old School Bikers." *Memoirs of a Biker* is a true written history, based in the late sixties and early seventies, of the Outlaw Motorcycle Clubs during those early years of the California biker scene. It is a written history, of sorts, about a dying breed of men that today are all but extinct, watching from the background as a different, younger generation takes their place. We'll visit the days of the old "kick starter" Harley ridin' Outlaws of the early motorcycle clubs and its creators, all of whom will soon be forgotten; a dying breed of old street wise warriors that history book writers know nothing about. The early riders will all be soon be forgotten. Thus, I invite you to walk in my boots for a while and be subjected to what it was like in those challenging, turbulent, and dynamic days of sex, drugs, and rock and roll. Come, ride on the bike runs with me, go one hundred plus miles per hour, "splittin' lanes" on the highways. Attend Motorcycle Club parties with me and survive the bar brawls and fist-fights. Live for a while during Club wars and the day-to-day living in an often violent and dangerous world of days long gone. Experience what it was like, and what it took, to become a Member in the Outlaw Motorcycle Clubs world of those times; the Harley Davidson bikes of the times, and just what it took to keep our metal steeds ridin' down the road.

I wrote this book to basically document history, in my own sort of way, seen through my own eyes, from living the lifestyle myself. The history of man should never be forgotten, no matter what side of the fence one stands on. These pages tell the stories of some of my Outlaw Brothers lives, as well as my own. So come meet Stretch, Sidecar Larry, Salem Witch, Monk, Danny the Duck, Poncho, Rick the Rat, Pete the Reb, Red Neck, Gentle Jim, Teddy Bear, Dirty Rick, Chief, Hangtown Bill, Sweet Will, Fat Ray, Doc, Big Bruce, Big Moose, Big Red, Jungle Jim, Pie, Bergie, Slow Joe, Uncle John, Father Jack, Johnny B., Kanuck, Little Mike, Jim Jim, Harry the Horse, Kenny O., Spider, and many, many more.

BORN TO BE WILD

I was born in Northern California in 1954 in the Capital city, Sacramento. My Mother was born in England and my Father's Father came over on a boat from Poland to Ellis Island, just like so many did before them. Their marriage produced two children; of whom I, the blonde haired, blue eyed, *only* boy having the privilege to be born last.

I started riding motorcycles when I was ten years old, even though my Father forbade me so. I started going to my friend's houses and riding their bikes anyway, as I just couldn't stay off of them. Motorcycling would become my life long passion and inevitably, almost turn out to be my demise. From the first Moment I crawled on one though, I fell *in love*. From that Moment on, motorcycles and the world that came with it would be my life.

The first bike I got to ride was an old "tote goat" with the old flathead Briggs and Stratton five horsepower motor. We rode the shit out of those things, as well as mini-bikes, even though their top speed was only about twenty-five miles per hour. Then, a buddy of mine got a Hodaka Ace Ninety that was the most beautiful, fastest bike I had ever ridden at eleven years old. This was in the very beginning of the Japanese motorcycle invasion that would influence mine and others' lives. As kids we would sneak around on these small Jap bikes out on the back-country, paved roads of Northern California, just to see how fast we could get them to go! The law would chase us occasionally, but we'd just haul ass down our dirt trails and get away.

13

We also tried to ride those Cushman's on the roads, until Fast Eddie got caught, as they were to slow to outrun the law, even on the trails. But, they moved, and had a little throttle, so they were fun!

I couldn't wait to get a larger bike that would go faster (and *that* bug has never stopped throughout my life!). Then, one day at a high school charity benefit, my Dad won a Honda Ninety! He wanted to sell it but my Mom said to him, "If you want to keep your son around, you had better not!" Thanks again, Mom! So, as I was just turning twelve, that was my first motorcycle. It wasn't fast, but it was *mine*. It wasn't the Harley of my wet dreams, but it had two wheels and would do sixty miles per hour.

My Dad still made me work for him to pay for that bike, including a helmet that I didn't want. He said, "If I catch you riding that thing without that helmet, you won't ride it again!" Before I would take off, I'd get rid of it by hiding the damn helmet in the bushes on the edge of our property, so Dad wouldn't see me riding off without a helmet. I couldn't then and still cannot today, tolerate helmets. I've never worn them, and never will, even after forty years of riding and an almost fatal accident!

My early childhood was a little different than the average child's, as I had asthma pretty bad. I did eventually grow out of it, though. My parents sent me to a Lutheran parochial school from 1st through 5th grade. As a result I had religion stuffed down my throat all the time, from a very young age. I went through catechism and was confirmed and baptized in the Lutheran Church.

Starting public school at eleven was, as I recall, a significant turning point in my life, as I was suddenly exposed to the real world. My parents had moved us to a smaller town where, being the new kid, I was vulnerable and easily fell in with the more "unsavory" local kids attending the same school. My new friends and I started out early in life experiencing with illegal substances. We started out stealing our parent's alcohol and cigarettes, but getting stoned off marijuana quickly became our favorite.

We would mostly hang out in the woods at that time, getting drunk and stoned while smoking cigarettes. Around my thirteenth birthday is when we first started getting our hands on speed and psychedelics. We started fucking around with peyote and mushrooms at first, but, by my fourteenth birthday we graduated to good old world of LSD. You could buy a hit of acid at the high school for two dollars out of your lunch money. Drugs were easier for us to get than alcohol. We could also easily get "bennies" or "cross-tops," which were really Benzedrine, a highly addictive pharmaceutical form of speed. We never feared trying anything new; if it would get ya' high, why not? One of the scariest but most thrilling experiences I enjoyed as a young man was after dropping acid and riding my motorcycle for the first time. Back in the day, all my friends and I could not focus on anything, except motorcycles and getting high.

At that time the only motorcycle magazine around that I can remember now was *Cycle World*. The motorcycle revolution was just starting, with my generation taking it to the phenomena it is today. The Hells Angels and other clubs of the Outlaw bike world were just starting to gain Momentum. By 1966 the Red & White were just starting to make their presence known and recognized in California's society. They began getting noticed in the newspapers, where lawmakers and politicians spouted their disgust of them. It didn't matter to the clubs though, as that was the point, to get everyone's attention...

My first real exposure to the Hells Angels and other bikers happened when I was eleven. My Mom and sister and I all went to a thrift store in Sacramento to get school clothes for my sister and me. That's where we bought most of our school clothes, and my Mom would sew us a few new ones. We arrived there just as Lonesome and a couple other Red & White members showed up, riding in a pack. This chance encounter was the first time I got to see the Hells Angels Colors, sporting its famous death head insignia. The Members all were laughing and kidding around as we watched them and their girlfriends enter the store. My Mom told me to ignore them, though it was obvious to me that she and everyone else in that parking lot were watching and fearing them. In the store I observed them laughing and kidding around as they were trying clothes on. I noticed again how everybody in the store was staring at them out of the corner of their eyes, which only added to my youthful curiosity. Even at that young age, I *knew* these bikers must be special, to command everyone's sneaky attention like that. They bought some old fur coats and scarves and stuff. They were trying to look different, obnoxious, scary, and crazed. They put on these old lady fur coats, and then put their cutoffs over the top, and away they went. They looked like some real wild dudes and I fell in love with their chopped Harleys and their chicks with their low cut blouses and leathers. I noticed that after all that parading around the Members did, everybody still had their eyes glued on them, full of fear and curiosity, which impressed me more than anything! That was my first encounter with the Outlaw bike world, and one I would never forget. I knew right then and there, at eleven years old, *exactly* what I wanted to do in life. I would pursue that lifestyle; I would be my own unique individual, and live that life for the rest of my days. Six years later I would be introduced to Lonesome and become his friend.

SOWING THE SEEDS

I ran away from home for the first time just before I turned fourteen. Since I was already drinking, smoking dope, and experimenting with psychedelics, I felt older than my age. My fellow delinquents and I had heard all about the hippies' sex, drugs and rock & roll scenes in the Haight Ashbury District in San Francisco and Berkeley Ave in Oakland. My generation's counter culture of the turbulent sixties was in full swing and I didn't want to miss it. It wasn't that I hated my parents or anything; I just really wanted to see the world and couldn't wait to be old enough to do so.

So, my buddy John and I saved up our lunch monies and "borrowed" some more from our folks. We sold a little weed at school and did a little thieving; simply because it was the fastest way we could think of to get money. It was still safe to do so in those days, so we took off hitch hiking for San Francisco's Haight Ashbury district, as we didn't want to miss out on any of it. We left with the idea that we would be gone for good. The world was happening all around us, waiting to be explored, and we didn't want to waste any time not being part of it.

Arriving in the Haight Ashbury district, which was thankfully still full of hippies, we hung around for awhile, scored some good acid, and went trippin'. That's how we ended up in the notorious "tenderloin district," around Mission Street. As our seed money was starting to run out, we ended up eating at Salvation Army places and Missions that served food to the homeless. It didn't take long to learn how rough it was going to be trying to be free and live like adults, without Mom's and Dad's support. We soon realized that we weren't just going to be invited to live in some hippie commune and screwing hippie chicks for a living. That was really a big disappointment and made us realize that all we had heard about the hippies was pretty much horseshit. Free love and maybe a quick high were pretty much all you might find for free.

We quickly learned how survival was going to be hard without a money source. We were freezing our asses off at night which forced us to learn survival tips, like how to lie in tall grass and rob newspaper machines. Every night we would take a pile of newspapers and crumple up page after page and stuff them in our clothes for warmth. My Dad had taught me how to do that, as he had done it when he was a hobo during the depression. We were getting a streetwise education quick, for a couple of innocent, naïve kids having grown up in the suburbia of our time.

This was the first time John and I would meet drag queens and queers, as we quickly ran into them in the Tenderloin District, where we got a fast education! John and I were getting into a cheap hotel elevator when two beautiful women get in with us. One white girl and one black girl; the black girl looks at John and surprising to us, says in this deep, male voice, "How are you two young boys?" John looks at me as we both quickly realize something is radically wrong. As we start upward, the elevator door shuts and we hear, "You boys want to have a good time?" Right then, this black drag queen grabs John's dick and fondles him through his pants. "You boys come up to our room," the black one says, "and we'll take real good care of you." The white one coos at me, in a deep voice, "I would love to suck your young-ass dick." John and I look at each other in sure terror as the elevator door opens. We both run out the door with the black queen trying to hold on to John's arm. Now we knew what a drag queen was for sure!

With all our money gone after a couple of weeks, we quickly learned the street ways of hustling money; learning to panhandle for money was one of those ways. We did a few purse snatchings and made pretty good money at it. It was only when we were desperate did it get dangerous. Queers in Frisco were everywhere and would proposition us constantly. They would offer us ten to twenty bucks or more to suck our young dicks.

Once John told this one skinny fucker he would do it for forty bucks but he wanted to see the money first; when the faggot showed it to him, John snatched it from his hand and ran. The queer chased him for a while but gave up quickly. We figured he probably realized that he didn't want the cops to notice that he was chasing after a couple of juveniles. So, with that big score we went and had a big breakfast, as we were starving. Then we decided to ride the bus over to Berkeley and check it out for a while so we wouldn't run into that pissed off queer. Berkeley's Telegraph Lane was known as "The Ave," and always smelled of incense and petunia oil, just like the Haight did. When you walked in the head shops they were full of psychedelic posters, black lights, and paraphernalia. Free love, drugs, sex, and revolution propaganda by the anti-war protestors abounded, as well as the hippies that seemed to be everywhere then; but, they sure didn't help us on those cold nights finding a place to go and sleep safely and half-comfortably.

There was always talk of anti-war protests and coming musical concerts, speakers and seminars hosted by peace preachers, but we never saw any hippy communes to stay in. Berkeley College was producing young, bright minds, contributing to the positive future of my generation, but more important to me was that they were educating some of the best chemists of our time there. One old, hippy poster that I saw read, "Better Living through Better Chemistry," and that was what I would enjoy the most out of it all. The Osley Brothers were just beginning to produce some of the best LSD that would ever be made. We scored some hits of acid for a buck each and decided to go back to Frisco and sell them for three bucks each. One day we had scored some Christmas trees, which was a prescription speed drug that would wire you up for twenty-four hours straight. That was some dynamite speed as it kept us up for three days straight. We couldn't eat on it and got too loose and careless, which led to the law picking up my friend John for runaway charge. Without him, I only lasted a couple of days, having nobody to watch my back; so I finally decided to call my Dad who drove up with my Mom and picked me up. After about a month my first great adventure ended in living in the Bay area and that world. My parents chewed me out all the way home as they grounded me and put me on restrictions. The rest of that summer pretty much sucked.

MAKING MY BED

When that summer finally ended, instead of going to the local high school for my freshman year, my Mom and Dad decided to send me, their "runaway drug addict" to a Lutheran parochial school in Oakland, California; which would put me in the Bay Area where I wanted to be when I originally ran away. Apparently, my Mom and Dad had talked to our minister at our church for some guidance on what to do with their wayward child. He steered them toward a religious school, thinking that it would straighten me out, which is about the opposite of what actually happened.

The Missouri Synod Lutheran School was mostly a college, with a small high school for Lutheran juvenile delinquents like me at the time. We lived in a dormitory that had a cafeteria, gym, church, etc… One thing I noticed while there is that parochial schools enable a lot of parents to send their problems there, and this one was no different. I would say approximately half of us were there for that reason. The joke was on them, though, because now that they put a bunch of us troublemakers in one basket, the party was really on! Now I had the whole Bay area to play in, and that was the happening place at the time; ahhh, the Bay Area… It didn't take me long to find sources of pot, LSD, speed, and alcohol that were easily available to us. We could take a bus down to Berkeley to "The Ave" and buy all the drugs one wanted that were available at the time.

A required one hour daily class of religion was not only mandatory, but one was expected to show up at evening chapel as well. I will just come out and tell you right now how I feel about religion and God. My parents sent me to Lutheran religious schools from first through fifth grade. I am confirmed and baptized in the Lutheran church. The last time I had communion I was probably fourteen. I do believe in God and talk to him in my head when I feel the need. I do not feel I need to go to church to prove myself to him or anyone else. I prefer to feel him through the beautiful surroundings he has created for us. I'll be riding my bike through a beautiful canyon and I feel him, and it's enough for me. I know what is right and wrong, and have done more than my share of sinning. I have asked God to forgive me my sins and try to enjoy the life and the second chance he has given me. I am a God-fearing man, and I am very ashamed of some of the things I have done in my life. I feel his forgiveness and strength or I wouldn't be here. That is my religion.

By this time, down in Berkeley, the Osley Brothers were getting even better at making some of the best acid ever known to man, and sold it for two bucks per trip. All kinds of different assortments of crazy LSD was everywhere from a dollar-and-a-half to three bucks per hit of some good shit, depending on how much you bought at a time. A four-finger bag of Mexican weed was only ten bucks, if it was good. There was opium and hashish for the richer connesuirs. There were still all the hippie and head shops everywhere, around the Berkeley University campus, near Telegraph Lane. Nothing had really changed much in a year except the fact that the drugs were even more plentiful than before.

There was still that feeling and talk of revolution in the air! There was a change coming to America, a cultural revolution at the least. The youth then, my generation of baby boomers, felt that that this needed to happen. We felt that the key to making that happen was with our anti-war riots and demonstrations. Their cries of hope pleaded for free love and peace for everyone, an end to the Vietnam War, and, of course, legalizing drugs. My friends and I would get all fucked up and go down there to play in the peace demonstrations and riots; to party and get laid!

Once we saw some old surplus gas masks for sale at a pharmacy and thought it would be a blast to charge in with the tear gas at the next riot. The cops came in and cut loose with their tear gas and, thinking we were protected and could charge into the gas cloud and get away, us unprepared juveniles had to charge back out because the piece-of-shit masks leaked! I thought I was going to die from all the coughing and spitting that ensued, but all the hippy college chicks thought we were brave!

One afternoon we went down to a scheduled demonstration near the campus. About an hour before it was suppose to begin we dropped some acid. Just before we started to get off on the LSD and the demonstration started, we saw three Harleys come rumbling up. They all swung in and parked on the curb and threw their kickstands down almost in unison. It was the Hells Angels! I believe one of them was Zorro, an Oakland Member and Terry the Tramp. They got off their bikes and started harassing the war protestors. Everything quickly came into full swing when hippies persisted on chanting slogans and waving signs and shit. The arguing started to get out of hand when all of a sudden the Angels started shoving and punching on some of the anti-war activists and rioters. By then, the cops had their hands full with all the confrontations going on. Our high really started kicking in then, with all the commotion going on around us, and we were trippin' so hard. We had to get the fuck out of there! Unfortunately, fate had another riot planned for my future, later on the next summer, the "Summer of Love."

During that freshman year while living in the dormitory, I eventually got put on curfew, room confinement, and suspension. I didn't do very well following their rules. To me though, it was just fine, as if I had run away again to the bay area, but this time I had a place to live. I liked living in the dormitory and doing pretty much whatever I liked. When school ended they told my parents that I was smart but they did not want me back. When I got home, life was too slow and I had a lot less freedom than I was now used to. On top of that, I was away from the Bay Area drug scene, which was now my scene. So I decided to run away again to go back to Oakland and my friends there. I stayed with friends until I got a job on a golf coarse to support myself. I eventually left my friend's place and camped in the woods for a while near my place of work. I started dealing drugs a little to make extra money and hanging out on The Ave selling Reds, Crosses, LSD, and pot. I finally made a good connection and started selling some really good shit. My plan was to make enough money to by a Harley, the bike of my dreams. One day some buddies and I were trying to buy some White Lighting LSD, known to be the best trippin' shit there ever was produced. We all planned on buying some, but I wanted a hundred hits just for me, as I planned on taking it back home to sell and make some good cash. So the connect gave us a couple hits to sample, and we all took a half hit to check the product. It was some of the best I ever had. So we went back and the dude gave us a few more hits and said he would go get the quantity we wanted. We couldn't help but indulge and by the time the connect came back we were wasted. He said he had scored what we wanted but this batch had a little different color, although it seemed like to be the same good shit. We baulked at first but he didn't care. The shit was so good he could sell it to someone else easily. We didn't want to lose any of this good shit, so we bought it and continued peaking for at least twenty-four hours on the original shit. The dude knew we wouldn't be trying it for a while; the oldest con in the drug world. After we slept and waited a day we tried our "White Lighting" again. It was crap, he had burned us; but, we all agreed that the mind-altering trip we got off the sample of the good shit was almost worth it. Unfortunately we never found that con artist "connect" ever again. When you're that young in the drug business you better learn your lessons quick if you want to stay in business.

Later that summer I sat on "The Avenue," fourteen years old and a runaway hanging out and selling drugs. As people would walk by me, we would peddle our wares, whispering, "Reds, acid, Crosses?" I was selling some, but it had been slow that day. So I went across the street to a little store for my usual chocolate milk and cinnamon rolls nutrients. I wasn't paying much attention as I was munching and listening to other drug peddlers muttering their wares at other people walking by. "Reds, acid, Crosses?" I asked. All of a sudden this long-haired dude turns and grabs my arm as I could see another guy two steps away coming at me. I didn't know it at the time, but I had sold to a long-haired narc earlier that morning. He grabbed me by my arm and shoulder area and yelled, "You are under arrest!" I panicked and twisted my arm and pulled away from his grasp and started to run and his hold slipped but he was able to grab a hold of my shirt. I was pretty wired and scared so I was moving fast and dragging him as he held on tightly to my shirt. Finally the narc stumbled and fell to the sidewalk and I stomped on his finger with the heel of my boot. By then, his partner finally caught up to us and tackled me to the ground. The narc was screaming in pain about his finger as he handcuffed me behind my back tightly. At this time the narc car came screeching up abreast of us on the street. A big crowd was gathering around us watching this arrest go down; druggies, street people, college students, and hippies all gathered around. They watched as the police driver of the narc car jumped out and opened the back door of the car. The two arresting narcs proceeded to grab me up horizontally and head through the crowd to get me into the car. The crowd was trying to stop them while screaming and yelling, "Pigs, Pigs!" The cops purposely slammed my head into the open door, and then slammed me into the door-jamb between the doors as they threw me in the back seat. They threw me so hard that I hit the opposite door again with my head. I was rushing hard with that LSD flowing through my veins. I was scared to death as this whole bad scene came down like a nightmare. The narcs all jumped in the car, and, as usual for the street people of Berkeley, they started to riot. They were yelling verbal protests and throwing shit as they beat on the cop car. More beat cops showed up and tried to clear the people from around the narc car so it could drive off. Once we finally got going the narc with the hurt finger was pissed off and started yelling at me, "We got a real rabbit here don't we boys, I think we're gonna find us an alley on the way to the precinct and tune you up kid!" He was talking to his partner as if I couldn't hear. "How about that alley," he yells, "Let's pull in there so I can beat the shit out of this kid!" I'll admit, I was scared to death, as the whole thing seemed like a movie that I was just a character in. The LSD I took with my chocolate milk was almost pulsating through my veins now. I figured I was dead for sure, then the police radio went off and they said they were bringing in fire trucks to hose down the rioters and get them to disperse out of the arrest scene. The narc driver said, "Yeah, this kids nothing but a trouble maker, and it would be too bad if he tried to swallow all his dope and overdosed and died on the way, huh?" They pulled into this alley and stopped and I thought, "This is it for sure." They both opened a back door at the same time and came at me from both sides. They drug me out and padded me down again, shoving me back and forth roughly as they took all the drugs I had on me, including a bag of weed that I had stashed down the front of my pants. "This looks like some primo shit," old hurt finger said as he took my Buck knife off my belt. The other one pulled out his blackjack that he had clipped me with in the back of the head earlier and hit his palm with it several times. "Let's fuck this rabbit kid up," he said, as he glared at me. I was starting to peak on the acid and thought I would shit my pants. "No I don't want to do the paperwork, let's let the other prisoners have a piece of his sweet young ass," he said, as he shoved me into the side of the narc car. Then, they opened the back door and threw me back in, then got back into the front seat.

To my relief, they sped off toward the precinct and the next thing I know they're roughly pulling me into booking. They kept warning the others that they had a rabbit and to leave the cuffs on and, finally went so far as to put leg irons on me. I was still trippin' pretty hard; eventually, after being charged and interrogated, they got me over to the juvenile section, where they stated the usual, "Take us to where you got the drugs to sell and we'll go easy on you." After the preliminary hearing the next day, which my folks did show up for, I was released into their custody. I was originally charged with five felonies, sales of dangerous drugs, possession of dangerous drugs, assaulting an officer, resisting arrest, and inciting a riot. I knew I was in deep shit, but I also new it was my first arrest and I was a young juvenile. My folks drove me to court the next month, where a plea deal was agreed upon, agreeing that I plead guilty to two drug felonies, possession, and sales; all which I would get probation for. I have always been glad they dropped the assault charge because that's violence, which you don't want to have on your jacket. It was better to own up to the great social crime of drugs, because that assault charge would have screwed me worse later. I was sentenced to be a ward of the California courts and would be on probation until I turned eighteen. I met my PO and he said I was to see him once a week and was on house arrest, unless I got a job. He was a serious Motherfucker, as he would later become a judge and eventually sheriff of the county, which sucked, because he already knew me far too well.

I had a friend named Jim, whose Dad owned a Shell station at that time in Cameron Park. Since my PO still wouldn't let me off my old man's place, except to work, I had no choice but to get a job. I asked my buddy Jim for a favor and he got me a job at his Dad's Shell station. It was good just to get out into the public. I saved my money and started doing a little drug dealing again, because I still wanted that Harley Davidson real bad. Even doing that, after the rest of the summer the best I could do was sell the Honda Ninety and gather up all my saved cash for a new Honda. I found a used, chopped one, a Honda 350, which would have to do until I could raise a lot more money. Then, I had to stash the bike over at a friend's house because of my old man and my PO.

As school was about to start and business would be good, I hoped to keep working at the station and building up my drug business. It was then and there, at my buddies' Father's gas station, that fate would have in store for me my next encounter with the Hell's Angels. We were working on a Saturday morning and we had just gotten the gas station opened up. We just finished sneaking around the corner and blowing a joint. All of a sudden, we hear this rumbling coming off the freeway ramp as a huge pack of Harley Davidson's approached. We watched in awe as about twenty-five bikes came rolling into our station, flying Hell's Angels colors'. Tim wanted to just go back inside the office and hide, yelling, "My Dad will understand!" I said, "Are you kidding, I want to see these guys!" I ran out to the island and grabbed the premium gas hose and handed it to one of the Angels with a rag, as they all lined up in a row to fill up. Then, they all shut their bikes off almost at once, on queue, and started to fill up all their own gas tanks. I was glad they did so, because I didn't want to spill, or be responsible for any gas or scratches on their beautiful paint jobs. The leader, or the one who seemed to be in charge, came up to me and said, "Just keep filling them; I'll pay you for it all when we're done." I really didn't care if they paid, but I was thankful he did. As fate would have it, I recognized him as the same Angel I had admired years earlier, as a young kid. I would eventually find out that his name was Lonesome, as I would get to know him personally four years after that chance encounter.

In the meantime, my buddy Tim was busy doing the same thing at the other pump lane. We just kept handing them the nozzle and a rag. Some of their old ladies wanted change for the vending machines. I remember admiring their old ladies, all dressed in leather and denim. The Angels had fur coats on and swastikas, as well as other shit to look crazy. They had been there about twenty minutes or so when we just about had all the bikes filled up. Then here comes Johnny Law with what looked like the whole El Dorado County Sheriff's Department! Then who stepped out of the car but old Ernie Carlson himself, leading the Sheriffs and Highway Patrolmen like a posse from an old western movie. They all had their lights and sirens going, making it look like a circus. Old Ernie the Sheriff gets out with his old pearl handled single sixes strapped on his sides like a western gunfighter; this was getting good!

They had what turned out to be about every Sheriff, Highway Patrolman, Fireman, and Dog Catcher from the whole county that they could muster up to show. Lonesome walks out to meet the Sheriff, along with a couple more Angels. You could tell that the Sheriff, and all the rest of "The Posse" were scared shitless, but trying to be cool. Lonesome was as calm as he could be as I overheard him telling them that they were just riding through and did not want any trouble. By the characters involved, this all looked like a wild west scene being played out in the nineteenth century, except the Outlaw's horses were chrome, two wheeled steeds.

I was amazed at how afraid everyone was, including the cops of the Red & White. People were stopping along the road and across the street and at other business to see the show. About then, I heard an Angel behind me say, "Hey kid", so I immediately turned around and walked up to him. He says, "Hey kid, how much we owe ya?" I replied, "I don't know, but I'm not worried about it." But, the Angel said "No" and insisted on paying the bill and proceeded to tell me to keep the change. Finally, Lonesome came walking back over and made a little hand jester, and almost like a queue in a movie, they all started kicking their bikes back to life. Up their kickstands went, with some giving thanks as they filed by and rode off, with all the cops and posse right on their asses. This was my second encounter with the Hells Angels and as the first one was, I was inquisitive and it had excited me. They had over paid us almost ten bucks for the gas, which impressed us, and we figured we would go score an ounce of weed and split it up after work. Then, Tim and I went right back around the corner and blew another joint to calm down; besides, we knew the cops had their hands full and wouldn't be around for awhile.

I was fascinated as a boy by these "men of men" and their beautiful machines and lifestyle. They seemed so free and indifferent to society and its rules; people all seemed to fear them, or at least be curious about what they represented, which was freedom, non-conformity, recklessness, and lawlessness. They had no apparent concern for any of society's normality's. To me at the time, these Bikers and their machines were what set them apart from everyone else. These were the days, I feel, that Motorcycle Clubs were at the peak of their purity, of what had originally started the phenomena of Motorcycle Clubs.

Hollister had happened about the time I was born, which put the "Outlaw Bikers" on the public stage. The citizens bought into the story presented by Life Magazine, which was one of the first crafted from sensationalist journalism. The Hell's Angels became great headline makers, like the "rape of Monterey" did, and their lifestyles helped feed the fire. Hunter Thompson's book on the Hell's Angels in the mid-sixties would continue to feed that fire. Then the 'B' Biker movies started, in which filmmakers took their turn at capitalizing on the Outlaw Motorcycle Club's happenings, which in turn probably just multiplied the public's misguided fears. I remember going to the drive-in movies to watch them, afterward thinking that most of them were great movies. A couple of those that I liked were *Wild Angels* and *Hell on Wheels*. Although, the Outlaw Bikers portrayed by actors were phony, and nothing like what I had already seen myself. The real Outlaws Bikers of the time were different, as they weren't your normal people, but rather men that stood for what they believed in, the biggest thing being the freedom to live the way they wanted to. Thus, society naturally feared them, as they were non-conformists, but this also aroused people's curiosity. So, the paparazzi bullshit portrayals of Hollister and the 'B' movies' portrayal of drunken, drug-crazed bikers who were all killers and rapists were easily soaked in by society. These portrayals all had the Outlaw Bikers running around in gangs, preying on helpless citizens, causing mayhem and destruction of society's ideals and morals. Why wouldn't the public believe the movies and article portrayals of them?

As I turned fifteen, I saw one of the movies that actually helped guide my life, or at least confirmed my direction in it, which, of course, was Easy Riders. That was a turning point for me, as it not only reinforced my dreams, but made the method to get there very clear. I wanted a Harley and the freedom it would bring, and I wanted it as fast as I could get it. The eerie thing about it was that in the movie, Peter Fonda did what I had already planned and had been doing already, which was deal my way into one big dope deal to buy my dream! It was like déjà vu' to me; I just couldn't figure out how the writer of that movie could have known my plan. Selling dope wasn't new to me, and I had that same plan for at least a couple of years. Just sell enough drugs to get that Harley, invest and re-invest the money until I could buy that bike of my dreams; then, I would quit dealing and enjoy the freedom of riding my life away. It was the only fast way of fulfilling my "dream". In that movie, Fonda was acting out my dream and confirming my plan, so the movie just re-affirmed to me that it *would* work. I knew the risks, but was smart enough then to know that as long as I was a juvenile and didn't shoot anybody in the process, that even if I did get busted, I was under-age and, worse case scenario, I would only rot in jail until I was twenty-one. Recently, the judicial system has been getting tougher on juveniles and trying them as adults, if they do adult crimes. Back then, the gate was still left open, and I was more than willing to play the game and gamble my fate, as a Harley Davidson would be worth the risk and sacrifice of selling the drugs, instead of just taking them. The movie ends, of course, with the Bikers finding themselves lost in their dream of total freedom that the drug money had bought them. But, even with their bikes, drugs, and women, the money couldn't buy them total happiness in life. They were left with lives of little purpose and with society not allowing their total freedom they had dreamed of because of a jealous and fucked-up world. It was their love of bike riding and their non-conformity that really inspired me, though. To be an individual out of the ordinary, not the college graduate type robots that your parents wanted you to be. I just couldn't accept all that horseshit, as it wasn't for me. I dreamed, rather, that I would be just like Fonda and the Angels that weren't trapped in a wristwatch and suit, with society telling me what I had to do and be in life. I dreamed of being free from society's bonds of conformity. I would rather be an Outlaw, which has always sounded like the life for me.

I was fourteen and it was the summer of '68 with rock concerts, Vietnam, the summer of love, and plenty of drugs floating around, especially my favorite, beloved LSD. About half way through the summer, my P.O. let me off house arrest and curfew, which led to me being able to get out more to go partying and deal more drugs. My buddies and I took to taking LSD regularly, as an almost ritualistic, religious experience. I have heard people say that trippin' on acid was a spiritual enlightening, an escape from reality, and of coarse, mind expanding. Yeah, I guess some of that might be true, but fuck all that horse-shit, it just got me higher and more fucked up than anything else! We loved the shit and couldn't get enough of it. I knew some older dudes that dealt with bikers, so I had a good connection and sold a lot of it. I would buy it for one or two dollars a hit, then sell it for two to three dollars a hit. No matter how good it was, you could only take it so often. If you drop a tab one day, and then try to eat another one of the same the next day, you were lucky to get off at all. But, if you took two hits that next day you would get off the same as the first time; so, basically doubling your dosage was the nature of the beast. My personal record was about nine days straight. If you take one day off, then you can take one hit and you're flying like a kite again. We played with acid like this for a couple of years. So, when people tell me they used to be acidheads, I always ask them how many times they have dropped acid. Usually it's five or six times, then they always ask "How about you?" When I reply, "Oh, I guess 1,500 or so," their jaws usually drop open! I tell them I would still be dropping today if I could get anything that was worth a fuck! Then they usually ask you what the strangest trip you ever had was?

I've had a lot of them, matter of fact, my bags were *always* packed, I was ready to trip anytime, but this *one* trip was a *strange* one. One time, I was partying with a bunch of Miwok Indians I knew, and we had scored some four-way hits of Window Pane acid. Four-way means it's actually four doses on one tab, but in Window Pane's case it was some type of picture film material, made into real tiny squares. If you put a four-way hit into the corner of your eye, the high would come on twice as fast and nail you

30

twice as hard. In the meantime, we're all talking, smoking dope, and drinking beer and wine. I was talking to this chick and her face began to melt! It happened once in awhile if you over did it. I watched her for awhile, but before I started "blowin' it" (a term that meant busting out laughing, talking and making no sense; freaking out, or generally fuckin' up like some kid or amateur), I instead went outside onto the porch where there were about four of my buddies, all Miwok Indians, hanging out. They were sipping beers and passing a joint around. I sat down next to Rick, who was a childhood friend, as he turned and looked at me, and then passed me a lit joint. I took a hit and noticed he had turned and was staring back at this oak tree. I looked at the rest of them who were all staring at the same tree. I sat there for a minute, getting ahead of them on smoking that joint, as normally they would be anxiously wanting it. Then I looked up at the oak tree, and couldn't believe how fucked up I apparently was! The whole oak tree was covered with these little candy canes. I took another hit and nudged Rick, who took the joint and turned back to the tree, nobody saying a word. I looked back at this tree and, to my disbelief, the candy canes were still there! I couldn't believe this hallucination was lasting so long. I rubbed my eyes and looked again, but the branches were still full of candy canes. They just wouldn't go away; I remember thinking that I finally had over-done it. I had gone too far, taken too much, and was flippin' the fuck out! I mean peoples faces melting is one thing, I was used to that, but candy canes in an oak tree in the middle of summer; that was going to stick with me for a while! I took a couple long pulls of my bottle of ripple wine, looked back at the tree, and the fucking canes were still there! I nudged Rick again, and he turned and looked at me with these empty, wide eyes, then handed me the joint, which wasn't lit. I said, "Man, Rick, I think I took too much of that shit; I might be over-dosing!" He took the unlit joint back and turned to stare at the tree, saying, "Yeah, me too, but those sure are some cool candy canes in that tree!" Brian and the others looked over at us and nodded, Brian saying "But the way those fucking candy canes keep dancing around are great!" I damn near blew it right then, or, looking back, maybe I had lost it because I had never said a word about candy canes! How could we all be hallucinating the same thing at the same time? This had never happened to me before... We all were seeing the same illusion? I checked my sanity for a minute and in my head decided, "Yeah, this is some good shit!"

Biking for me right then consisted of sneaking around on back roads, as I still couldn't get my driver's permit or license because of my P.O. and my Dad. I had saved up my money I earned at the gas station until I finally had enough to start buying drugs in larger quantities, basically wholesale, and selling them to make bigger chunks of money than ever before to put in my motorcycle fund. I finally got enough bucks stashed away to buy a used 350 Honda at summers end. I had to hide it out in the sticks away from my Dad's house, so he didn't know about it. It would have been hard to explain to him, and my P.O., where I got the money to buy it. I just couldn't stay out of trouble though, and I was driving my poor Mother nuts with worry. Occasionally, she would find drugs in my pockets. She wouldn't rat me out to my P.O., nor to my Dad; she hated seeing the old man and I fight. I was getting a little too old for the belt beatings. One night, I was supposed to go to the basketball game at the high school. The plan was that I and my buddies would all drop some acid an hour before we were supposed to meet up, that way we would be all "getting off" when we gathered up. A good plan, if a storm doesn't show up. So I popped a hit and went in to say goodbye to the folks, who were watching "The Ed Sullivan Show" on the old black and white TV. While they were grilling me about when I would be back and shit, all of a sudden lighting and a major rainstorm started. They said I couldn't walk down to the high school a mile away in the downpour; I was trapped, and I had to take a trip on acid stowed away with my parents. Try "maintaining" while watching TV with your parent; that's a trip within itself. As soon as I could, I went to bed early and tripped all night in my room by myself. It never bothered me to trip on acid by myself, although I have known lots of people that freak trippin' by themselves. I have always found that people with higher IQ's are more fun, thus you can have funnier trips with them. I say that from experience and mean no malice by it. I believe they also enjoy it more. Stepping out of reality used to be my third favorite thing to do, ranking just under motorcycling and sex.

Fall came and it was time for my sophomore year to start. I went to the local public high school called Ponderosa High. My buddies talked me into playing on the Junior Varsity football team and we had a real good season, and even better, all the good looking chicks all wanted to date football players. Tim and I broke the Lake Tahoe's quarterback's leg, so they brought us out of the game for un-sportsman like conduct, especially after they heard us laughing about it. My best game I played was while on LSD; man, was that a trip!! I was so busy dealing and doing drugs, chasing women, and riding motorcycles that I really didn't care when I got thrown off the team. We would drop LSD on Monday, and take two hits on Tuesday, otherwise, like I have said, we wouldn't get off. By Thursday, it would take six hits to get flying again, even with the good shit I was dealing, that I really couldn't afford. So, we worked out a system, which definitely allowed for us to be high at parties and concerts. The system was really very simple, as all you had to do was skip the day before you wanted to get high. I dropped at all the concerts I attended up into the early '90s; to me, it was the only way to go. I am sure I've tripped on acid at least 1,500 times. The only reason I ever quit was, once again, the good chemicals for the production of it were gone because the law took care of them. I did get to trip at a lot of good concerts, such as Janis Joplin, Jimmie Hendricks, and Cold Blood, just to name a few. I also got to attend a couple three to four day concerts, probably the most famous being Altamont. That was the famous Rolling Stones concert that went bad. The Stones had hired the Angel's for security for themselves. The famous stabbing death of a black man was at that concert; he had been stupid enough to pull a gun in the crowd with full intent to use it. I missed the whole thing. A couple buddies and me had hitchhiked down there with our pockets full of LSD and other drugs. To tell the truth, I had over-indulged and remember very little of the concert. I remember more about rolling around in the weeds in a sleeping bag playing with some female more than anything about the bands. No, as I said, I never saw the stabbing, which is the first thing everyone has always asked me. That concert was one I remember the least of all, as I had taken way too many drugs.

I was dealing dope from my parent's house while I was on probation. If dealing drugs from there wasn't very smart, I was about to add to the problem. Down the road from my folk's house moved a man named Fat

Ray. He was an old school biker with a long criminal record. He was a drug addict and dealer, a thief, and a "professional welfare recipient," as he put it with pride. He had four kids and an old lady that loved the drug world, too. Ray did not like to work at all; as a matter of fact, he thought it was an insult if you even brought it up. He was a true street hustler and a very professional criminal. He was connected into the biker underworld of drugs, thieving, and fencing stolen merchandise, so he had all the connections. If you stole something and wanted to get rid of it, he was your man. His appeal to a few selected juvenile delinquents like me was his knowledge and hustle of Harley Davidson Motorcycles. To help support his ass, part of his hustle was to get our young asses into his crime school. Between the drugs and his vast knowledge and availability of Harleys, he would suck us into working for him. Once you were in his web you were part of his family, with really no way out. He got me going on a cheap Harley Forty-Five Trike Basket Case. Besides all the normal drugs he also got us turned on to Reds. Reds are a very strong prescription drug from the barbiturate family. The best ones were Lilly F-40's, although eventually Ray would get us going on Mexican made ones that were mostly just heroin, because that's all he could get. Ray would use them to party or sleep on, but speed was Ray's love. He would eat cross tops like they were candy. Once you start mixing them up, you were speed balling, taking Whites to jam and Reds to slow the speed down. So pretty soon you had gotten the habit, and of course, I got my friends and other kids into it so the profit would pay for my usage. This is when I first started to get into stealing and Ray kept me busy with learning the trade secrets. I would try and not party my profits away. I wanted that Harley Basket Case up and running so I could ride it to school and show some real class. We would do a burglary and go stash the stuff, then Ray would look at our score and start getting rid of it. Within a week, he would have most of it gone and would pay us in money or, more likely, drugs, which we didn't mind, as we could turn around and sell them and make even more money.

When your high on Reds you are pretty much fearless and just don't give a fuck. You do things you wouldn't really normally do. One time, my two buddies and me were high on Reds and decided to go make some money. So there we were, in this guy's Volkswagen, driving around, drinking wine, smoking weed and popping more Reds. So we spot this smaller house, off by itself on a back road. Without casing the place or anything, we decide that's the one. So, in the middle of the day in broad daylight we pull in front of the house and we all jump out. I walked right up to the front door and kicked the fucker open just like in the movies! Within a heartbeat, a huge German shepherd come flying out of the door with his jaws wide open, coming right at me. I instinctively drop-kicked the dog, square in the head while he was in mid-air; with a yelp he hit the ground rolling. He wasted no time as he rolled over and came up on his feet, hauling ass away from us with his tail between his legs! I probably couldn't do that again if I tried. We were all so wasted that we screwed around grabbing everything we wanted until we started trying to load it all up in the car. We obviously weren't thinking right; Volkswagens are not very good for this kind of work. We had had nowhere to put the guns, tools, a TV, a stereo, a chainsaw, and all kinds of other stuff that we had grabbed, so we did our best and loaded shit in every place we could, including the roof. When that didn't even load a third of what we had drug out, our brilliant solution was that we'd just have to make two trips. It took us forty-five minutes to drive to an old empty wood water tank near Ray's house where we used to play as kids. We unloaded the merchandise and drove all the way back and just pulled right in without even thinking about who, or what, could be waiting. Then we loaded up again, making another trip, making sure to stay high, and partying all the way. Someone should keep a record of some sort for the most people and junk stuffed into a VW at once. We stupidly made the third trip and still, luckily, nobody showed up. It probably took five hours to empty the place and we never did see that German Shepherd again. Looking back I realize, "How stupid can you be?" Pretty fucking stupid when you're on Reds. That burglary made me enough money that I bought my first Harley Basket Case from Fat Ray. I also got the boot from my parent's house that same week. My Mom's doctor told her she was ill because she was worrying about my drug use and me in general, too much. My Dad told me that I needed to get out of her life, as it was my fault she was sick; he would call my P.O. and, as I was a ward of the state, they would have to do something with me. My Dad would say, "It's their problem." So it was off to a foster home, which only lasted a couple of months. They were good people and unfortunately, they trusted me. I never burned them financially, but they went to bat for me with my P.O. and I fucked it all up after all their effort. This was another turning point in my life.

I didn't mind the foster home much, as I was still able to work at the gas station part time, which enabled me to keep my drug dealing business going. The one good thing was that my foster parents got permission from my P.O. to let me ride my 350 Honda to work and school on a permit. I had made a good connect for LSD through my older sister's girlfriend's older boyfriend. Barb was her name and she was my first older girlfriend and didn't mind using her "friend" to get me hooked up. Ray's source for it had gotten busted, so this new connect was going to make me some good money. Ray and I had cut a deal on putting my Harley together with my new-found wealth. My Harley dream seemed a reality as we were prepping the frame and tanks with bondo and primer. Soon, it would be painted and we would start bolting it together. Ray had a Wrench that was going to build the motor on a trade for 100 hits of acid. With my new 'unlimited amount' connection, that wouldn't be a problem. For once in my young ass life, I was the source of the dope. I was keeping my high school supplied and had sold a bunch of acid in the bathroom one day, like I always did. Actually, it was selling so fast that I hadn't brought enough of it, as I only had four hits left and it wasn't even lunch time yet. I contemplated cutting my next class and running to get some more, but decided to wait until after the next class. My P.O. was on my ass about cutting classes and told me he would violate my probation if I did it anymore. I liked my history class, as my young female teacher did drugs. We had run into her and her husband all fucked up at a Sacramento concert and hitched a ride home with them, smoking dope the whole way home. I was sitting in her class when the vice principal showed up at the door and came in and talked to her. Then, they both came over to me and he proceeded to tell me that I needed to go to his office with him because my P.O. was here to see me. I thought about the four hits of acid in my shirt pocket, and being Barrel acid they were pretty small pills. The hair went up on my neck though, because the teacher kind of gave me a funny look, but I saw no choice as I followed him to the door. When he motioned me ahead as he swung open the door, I knew I was fucked. I was trapped with the vice principal behind and two deputy sheriffs in front of me. I figured I wouldn't try and make a break for it this time and take my chances, as I thought that they were just picking me up for violation of probation. They escorted me to the office under that pretence, as they were saying my P.O. had violated my probation. I hoped that was it and that they wouldn't find the four hits of acid in my front pocket.

Soon, as we hit the office, the officers were all over me and found my stash. I was busted again for possession, sales of dangerous drugs, and violation of probation. They hauled me to the El Dorado County Jail where detectives questioned me. "We know you've been dealing and we can go easy on you if you give up your connections," the suit said. I laughed and told them to get fucked, that I wasn't a snitch. "So you want to be a hard ass huh? Well, we'll see about that!" They took me to an isolation cell that had nothing in it but a bible, no TV, no books, no pen and paper, absolutely nothing. The new juvenile facility was just being built so they had no place for us juvenile delinquents. So, after a night in the isolation cell in the jail, they paid a retired officer to transport me to the Auburn Juvenile Facility where our county paid them to keep their delinquents. 'The Auburn' was a privately owned place that was run by a Ma and Pa team. Some of my old Miwok Indian friends were there, so it was back to crime school training camp. The elderly couple that owned Auburn was ex-military and did not put up with any shit, whatsoever. They had isolation cells that had no windows, about eight feet by six feet in size, with a shitter/sink combo. These cells were used only for punishment and they were usually kept pretty full. The steel door had a slit they opened to give you food, and, once again, no paper, pens, pencils, nor clocks; just a Gideon's Bible in those cells.

When you first got there, they put you in for twenty-four hours, just to get your attention. The rules were simple; no noise or talking to the next cell or tapping on walls. Quiet solitude was the idea. When they served food was the only way of knowing what time it was. It's amazing how hard it is for some people to do isolation time like that; some just go nuts. After my first twenty-fours "on ice," they released me into the population with the promise of going back if I didn't follow the rules. Everybody was issued the same toothbrush, toothpaste, and comb. We used the combs like knives, as they would put a hell of a gash in somebody if you slashed correctly, and usually that was how we settled our differences. There was a women's side that was separate from the men's, except in the dining room area where you could see each other through some windows that separated us. I spent four months there going to court hearings on what to do with me. Like always, the Blacks had a gang, the Mexicans had a gang, and the Whites, Indians, and Chinks all stuck together. We all stayed grouped up in the recreation yard and the mess hall. The food was excellent except for one rule; you could eat as much as you wanted but you had to finish all that you took. Not finishing your food was punishable with twenty-four hour isolation for your first offence, so you quickly learned to watch your portions.

Brian was a Miwok Indian from Placerville that I used to party with on the streets, and we both got thrown in ice for forty-eight hours for fighting with some blacks. I had jumped into the fight to help little Brian. I could tell that Brian couldn't take the isolation, as eventually I would hear him start banging his head into the brick wall in the cell next to mine, trying to knock himself out. When he would regain consciousness, he would do it again to cope with the situation.

Time went by slow there while awaiting my fate, as I would get shuffled back and forth in leg irons and handcuffs to court dates and evaluations, etc… We passed the time by talking about drugs, connects, stealing, scams, and the how too of crimes. It was rare that we got a hold of any drugs in there, but occasionally someone would plan to get some drugs thrown over the barb wire fence in the recreation area where we could find it. One dude who was doing weekends smuggled some White Crosses in a tube that he had shoved up his ass. The tube leaked a little and kind of melted them a bit, but we ate them anyway. We gladly paid him in cigarettes and the following weekend he was going to try and do the same thing, but with LSD instead. We all anxiously awaited his "catch," but they caught him when they did a surprise anal search and busted him for what they found.

I met one white dude there that was from Auburn that I ended up sharing my cell with. He was a cool acid-head that was doing time for dangerous drugs charges also. We got along well and talked about dealing together when we got out, as he needed a good connection to supply Auburn. What was amazing was that he could play "Ina Gada Davida" by the Iron Butterfly band on his chest and stomach. It was great, as I would fall asleep many nights listening to him play. He was released about a week before my sentencing date, and as we parted as friends we promised to keep in touch and hook up on the outside and make some money. About a month later, I was in Fout Springs Reformatory when a mutual friend from Auburn told me the news I never received. This mutual friend proceeded to tell me that Dude's girlfriend was living with him and his Mom. They were tripping on acid when the Mom came home and found some of his acid stash and confronted him about it. They argued and she threatened to call the police, and he told her he would shoot the cops if she did. When the law showed up, he was up on the roof with his girlfriend and a loaded shotgun. The law's response to that was to send two more officers to the scene, and when they pulled into the driveway, they got out of their car and Dude shot them both down. The police then showed up in force, with TV crews showing up behind them. They tried to talk him down with loud speakers, but as soon as more cars showed up on the scene, he started shooting at them again. Finally, a police sniper killed him. He had previously told me that he was never going back to jail, and I guess he really did mean it. He was only sixteen years old at the time, and sometimes in my dreams I still enjoy him playing that song on his stomach, which was his favorite.

I turned sixteen years old on my way to serve three years in Fout Springs Reformatory, and that is what my high school diploma says on it. As juvenile joints go, I thought it was pretty good place to do time. It had no fences, as there was no need because it was so isolated that if you tried to run (as some did), they would usually find you dead from exposure before ever making it to civilization. Hypothermia, rough terrain, rattlesnakes, and navigation were the problems, so few tried it. The place was set up with a huge dormitory in the middle of the place. Inside were sections of bunks and lockers, all centered toward a caged guard area that was manned twenty-four-seven. Drugs and smokes were the real currency in the place. It was set up on a six day rotation of work and school, with Sundays being the only day off. The average day was five hours on work detail, then four hours in school, which was the only air-conditioned building the inmates were aloud in. If you did well you got points for completing your work. When you got enough points you would get a white scarf that you wore on your belt loop. Red being the next level, then the blue scarf, which was the highest ranking, and meant you were close to having enough points to get out. The higher your rank the more privileges you would get, also. If you fucked up, they would take points away, which would demote your level of privileges and time of release. Example being, if you didn't want to get up and go to work, you lost your points for that day. Plus, they could start subtracting your overall points if you bitched. I worked on one of the work crews for a week sweating my ass off digging rocks. Everybody bitched and moaned about going to school, even though it was worth one more point than the work details were, *and* it was in an air-conditioned school room. I quickly told the teacher how badly I wanted to learn and straighten my life out so that I could go to college and be somebody, I wanted to graduate. The head teacher liked me because I paid attention to his lessons. So he went to bat for me and I got to skip work and do school all day. I received two extra points a day for schooling, which meant I was in an air-conditioned room all day, and I loved it. The teacher made me head of the dark room for the photography class, so I made extra smokes on the side for making prints for other inmates. Plus, the blacks would give me smokes for a small amount of this one chemical we used in developing pictures so they could get high on it. All the teachers and guards thought I was a great example of an inmate trying to reform and used me in a research paper being turned into Youth Authority. I had a hard time keeping a straight face the whole time.

It wasn't long before I had connections in the kitchen and the office. I got extra food and drinks and had the kid taking care of the points books in my pocket. I traded photo work and cigarettes for what I wanted or needed, at first. Then, I finally got one visit and some help from my parents. I asked my Dad to bring me a Laredo cigarette-making machine with plenty of fixings so I could make cheap smokes. I would trade cigarettes for guys to make them for me, then barter off the rest that I didn't need. They weren't as good as store bought, but when you ran out of tailor made cigarettes, you came to see me. Then, I also had the old man bring me a portable evaporation cooler that you just add water to for cooler air. I set it up at the end of my bunk, since I had the only one I could charge whatever I liked. If you wanted to move that bitch over to your bunk and lie down and cool off, as it was such a hot Motherfucker, you paid me. My fellow inmates paid me with smokes by the hour for that scam.

The inmate population was over half black, and the rest, of course, were a slight majority of Mexican, with Whites next. A few Indians and Chinks and you had our gang. It was blacks against the rest of us, with each group having its own leaders. I eventually represented the Whites as a leader and the Mexican gang leader, named Ray, from Modesto, and I became good friends. We got along well, as the blacks outnumbered us, even with our combined members, so keeping the peace with them wasn't easy. I had this other friend, the leader of the Indians, named Chavez, a big Indian dude who we kept tight with us. I used to have some pictures we took that I had developed of the three of us smoking joints in front of the guard shacks entry sign that said "Fout Springs Reformatory," located at the prison entrance. There was also this old, ugly female cook that was a nymphomaniac that you could fuck, but she was too ugly for me. Things went along well for quite a while, as we all worked towards getting our releases back into the world. I was determined to not do my whole three-year sentence. I had it good as it could get in there, but I wanted my freedom back in a bad way, as well as motorcycling and women; in short, I wanted my life back.

The peace didn't last forever, as a confrontation with the blacks was inevitable. A big, black dude from the Bay Area had shown up, named George, and he was by far the biggest and muscle-bound man at that joint, and *knew* it. He had no brains, but a big attitude. With his size and physique he should have been playing pro ball somewhere. It all started over an eight-track tape by James Brown called 'Sex Machine.' They would play that fucking thing over and over and over, for weeks. Since we were all under the same roof and grouped up in rows of bunks, you couldn't get away from the music. We had had enough and tried drowning them out, but they had better speakers than we did. So one day, during work detail, the dammed thing came up missing. Well, the blacks knew as well as us that we did it, and the line was drawn. The guards put a call out to the nearest local and state law enforcement to come quickly, as we had us a race riot starting. The warden called the black leaders into his office first; then he called Ray, Chavez, and myself in, to talk. The warden explained that this whole thing could be diverted if we would just give the blacks back their 'Sex Machine' tape. We explained our unbearable side to the situation, and he did understand how the confrontation came about, but why does there have to be blood shed? I don't think the warden had ever listened to 'Sex Machine' twenty-four-seven for three weeks straight, or he would have better understood where we were coming from. We explained that we did not have the tape in our possession to give back. The truth of the matter was that it had already found its way to the sewage pond, where we felt it really belonged. He explained that we might be imprisoned here a long time more than we already had, if we had a race riot on our records that would put a blemish on his resume. He threatened us three with being sent to harder joints to finish our time, and he promised that he would get us all longer sentences. We all talked with the warden and explained that it was out of our hands and that nothing could be done except try to get it over fast with the least amount of damage. He said that he would take into consideration anything we could do to end this fast.

We figured we had to take out Big George first no matter what, but maybe we could use that asshole's conceded strength to our advantage. The blacks had gathered in the barracks and we did the same in the pool hall recreation area. We figured George would be the first one through the door to come right at Ray and me while playing pool, as he hated to see us two the most, which is exactly what he did, just as we had anticipated. George came right after me as he came through the door while I had been hoping he would go for Ray. As I turned to face him I broke the pool cue right across his head as hard as I could. The cue shattered, leaving about three feet of stick in my hand. I came right back across his face with it as he started to come back up. It bloodied his face, and as he came back up, he turned and came after me again. Just then, as we had planned, Ray broke his cue over his head again, from his blind side, knocking him to his knees. I turned to see Ray as he winked at me, when another black dude hit him from the side. Blacks against Whites and the fight was on. I jumped on top of George's shoulders as he struggled to get up onto his legs. I was scared to death he would get up and kill me, as I beat feverishly on the back of his head as hard as I could with clenched fists, shifting my weight as he would try to get up, causing him to lose his balance and drop back down to his knees. We had taken their biggest warrior down with our cunning!

It was total chaos as about every prisoner had squared off and was in a pinch. The next thing I know, somebody's got me in a full Nelson hold from behind, pulling me off of George. To my relief, it was a guard who had me, but his mistake was one that gave George a chance to get up. I was pulled backwards by the guard as he got up and flat on his feet in a blind, bloody rage and started coming after me again. Two other guards popped in between us to grab George and believe me, they had their hands full. George did just what we had figured and hoped he would, as he fired punches on the guards knocking the first one on his ass. That was it for him as three more guards jumped him and drug him outside with some other guards help, including the one who had pulled me off. They put him in the small barred cell to await transport to a Youth Authority maximum security prison. George had crossed the line by assaulting a guard. Later we heard that because of his size and violent record the judge sent him to an adult prison. As the guards were putting George away the whole thing had stopped while everybody watched. The riot was over as the guards directed everybody back to their bunks under threats of charges being filed against them. We were all warned by the yard speakers that cops were on their way and if we were not lying in our bunks we'd be arrested and hauled off to jail to face the court with assault charges. Everybody hauled ass for their bunks, trying to wipe the blood off themselves in order to look innocent. The reinforcements arrived as everybody was lying in their bunks with their halos on. The next day they hauled George off in a patty wagon with him screaming, and when he saw me he yelled, "I'll get you, you white Mother fucking honky because I know where you live in Placerville. I'll get you one day!" My first race riot was over and we had all lost some points. They also cancelled the weekly movie for a month, and they closed the swimming pool for two weeks. Things were back to normal before we knew it, and stayed that way until I was finally released. I did get into one more problem before that day, though. The kid that took care of the daily points had been cheating in my favor. I didn't figure anyone would catch on to a point here and there, every other day or so. I kept the kid supplied with smokes for his troubles, which was the same as paying him money, and I would let him sit in front of my cooler occasionally. But what I didn't know or foresee was that the kid would get greedy with the idea. He had a couple other clients that he was taking care of, and unfortunately, one of them got caught with a bag of weed his girlfriend had snuck in on a visit. So to save his ass, he gave up my man, who upon questioning and threatening by the warden, gave us all up. I had been there for about ten months and already had my blue scarf and figured I would have enough points by my first year to get an early release. I was doing extra work detail after school to get extra points, and that was legal, so I knew I would have made it.

The warden called me in to his office and told me what I already knew; that I had been implicated in cheating the Point system. "Don't try and deny it, as we all know how smart you are. I'm taking your blue scarf and taking the points that were gained by cheating and matching them with removal points also. You have been a leader and the hope of the teaching staff as a good example of success in their program, so we will try and keep this infraction quiet." I was really depressed and went back to my bunk and turned on my cooler and contemplated my bad luck. Ray and Chavez came over and tried to cheer me up and talked me into going down by the pool to smoke a joint and get high. I felt better and jumped back into my extra jobs and worked harder for extra points towards my release. A week later, to my surprise when I checked the newly corrected point sheet, it didn't reflect all the cheated points for extra jobs! I was elated and that only made me work harder. Soon I had my blue scarf again, and when my one year anniversary was about to come up, the high school GED test came up. I actually studied hard before the test, and one of the teachers that I really got along with helped me a lot by guiding me on what the 'important areas' I should study were.

When the results came out, I found that I had passed and all my teachers were proud of me. I thanked them all for their help and gave them the best line of shit I could think of. I told them I was anxious to get out so I could use all the new knowledge they had given me and turn my otherwise criminal life around. These reformers ate it with a spoon, plus with a stroke of luck I was being made out as a good example in the State Juvenile Teaching System's success report, or some shit like that. Anyway, they went to bat for me with the warden for an early release because I had accomplished three years of school work in a year's time, due to their great teaching, of course. Even though I was a little short on points, he agreed to cut me loose on two conditions. First, I would have to talk my parents into taking me back, and second, I had to have a job before I would be released and would also continue to report to my P.O. I talked my folks into coming for a visit and showed them my diploma. They decided they would let me come back if I would promise to stay off drugs. I talked a good line of shit and promised them and my P.O. that I would stay clean and away from my old drug dealing friends. They let me go home for a one week furlough so I could find a job. I finally found one at the A&W root beer joint in Placerville as a cook, as nobody wanted to hire a felon just released from jail. I went back to the reformatory and finally got my release two years earlier than my original sentence would have allowed. I was seventeen with a high school diploma and back on the streets.

I worked for about a week, saw my P.O., and kept my promise to everyone. Then, Chubby showed up at work and talked me into going out with him. I didn't know he had planned a party for me with a bunch of old friends and Miwok Indians that brought some party chicks. I got drunk and high with them and partied all night, finally getting laid, and had the best time since I had been busted. When I went home my folks saw right threw my bullshit excuses and knew I had just broken my promise. The cold shoulder went on and I kept going out after work and partying for the rest of the second week. On my Friday visit to my P.O., he questioned me out of suspicion, even though my folks hadn't given me up. That second

Saturday after my release, I was out all night again and said fuck it; I knew my P.O. was going to violate my probation and slam me back in jail, so I split. So much for trying the straight life! I paid a buddy to drive me down to Oakland to look up some old friends, with whom I stayed until one of them got me a job at a gas station he worked at. When I got my first check, I rented a tiny three room house for 50 bucks a month. I stayed there and kept working, and after I saved enough, I started dealing dope again. I took care of myself, catching the bus to work or hitch-hiking everyday in order to avoid the law. I couldn't get a driver license or anything, which was a real bummer. Then, I ran into one of my buddy's ex-girlfriends from the parochial school I had attended when I was a freshman.

She had been working as a model and had a car, and money, and eventually moved in with me. We were happy for about six months or so, taking a lot of drugs and partying. After an argument we had about having a baby, after dropping some good acid, I left her there and went to a party with a buddy. While she was their alone she had a bad trip and was crazed when I got home the next morning, and packed up and left. So I moved in a buddy to help pay the rent there as I couldn't afford mine anymore, and decided it was time to see if I could get my Harley Basket Case back. Fat Ray had gotten busted when I was in jail and was doing five-to-life in the joint. I finally got a phone number for Ray's wife in Sacramento from one of my Miwok Indian buddies. To my surprise, she had kept my Harley for me per Ray's direction, knowing that I would be back for it. She planned a trip up to see me and wanted to score some dope. She explained that Ray had cut her loose and divorced her and, although twice my age, she had always treated me like a son. We got all messed up on some good dope I had and, well, I woke up with her in my bed. When she left she offered to let me build my bike in her basement, saying that she still knew some bikers that could help me find parts and put it together. I kept saving my money and decided that I had to change jobs anyway, because I feared the law would find out where I was working because of my social security number. Besides, it was the best chance for me to get my ass on a Harley that I actually had. Then, I had two months to go before my eighteenth birthday, and I hoped the law would forget about my ass after that.

I immediately went to work on it, first rebuilding the transmission.

Then I started on sand blasting the frame again and then I bondoed the neck of the frame, and worked on getting the dents out of the tanks. Ray's old lady was flat strung out on speed at the time, which was relatively a new drug at the time. I would help her score it sometimes through my Gladiator connections. I didn't mind watching her kids when I was working on my bike, anyway. But she started going out partying more and more and disappearing for twenty-four hours at a time. I was spending too much of my bike money to hope to finish it without having to make some more. So I finally moved the bike and my ass back up to Placerville, to a welfare chick's house. She didn't mind if I dealt drugs, as she was a drug whore anyway. So I re-invested what was left of my bike money and started dealing and hustling again with my old biker contacts, Gladiators, and friends I had known and dealt with when I was younger. I stayed off the streets as best as I could, everywhere I went ducking down in the car seat, as I was known by sight by some cops and probation people who might recognize me, knowing I was wanted. I couldn't go to any public anything, dances, concerts, bike runs, restaurants, bars, etc… But it was good to be home and back around everyone in the bike world, when I *could* sneak around and visit. I had one hell of an eighteenth birthday party on some Reds and acid. One week after my party, Chubby and I had done a deal for The Gladiators and stayed up at Darlene's house out in the country all weekend. We woke up Sunday starving to death; Darlene had nothing to eat as that next Monday was welfare commodity day. So Chubby and I went down the street and stole a chicken from her neighbor's chicken coup as they were proably in Church. We cut its head off and plucked it and asked Darlene to cook it for us. She laughed and asked if we were kidding? She said it was gonna be tough and we told her we could eat the asshole out of a pig if we could find one, she said it would proably taste better. We couldn't even eat it as it was the toughest bird I ever tried to eat. That's when we found out what a *laying hen* taste like. Other than those few bites we choked down, that was all we had to eat that Sunday.

When we got up on Monday morning everyone was gone and we had to go take care of some business. So, against my better judgment, and encouraged by Chubby's prodding, we set out to hitch-hike. The plan was, Chubby would hitch us a ride while I stayed out of sight, and when he finally flagged a ride, I would pop out and get in. It almost worked, except when I popped out an El Dorado Sheriff pulled up exactly at the same time and threw on his lights. I thought of running, but figured I could probably talk my way out of it. The only problem was, even with my long hair and mustache, he thought he recognized me. He wasn't totally sure and asked for I.D. I gave him a friend's name and told him that I had lost my I.D. that morning, but I didn't think he was really buying it. He said he would do a warrant check on us and then we could get going. The driver who had pulled over originally had already driven off and the cop even said he was sorry we had missed that ride. When a back up patrol car showed up he walked over with more cops and arrested me. Off to El Dorado Jail I went again, but I consoled myself that I needed to get this behind me so I could get a drivers license and ride my Harley. I was tired of living in shadows and hiding. I was sentenced to six months in the county jail for violation of probation, but upon my release I was no longer a ward of the state. I was finally going to be a free man to live my life as I chose. Besides, a Harley Davidson was all I had ever really wanted. My release after my six months jail sentence would mean my total freedom finally, after four years of society's attempt to reform me, that didn't ever really work.

THE GLADIATORS

The Gladiators were a one percent Motorcycle Club based in the Placerville, California, area, in El Dorado County. We were a true one percent, three piece patched club, which means, we were Outlaw Bikers and lived the 'old school way.' Let me define one per centers; after the Hollister headlines about crazy motorcyclists, AMA, a straight organization of motorcycle enthusiasts back then, declared that the rowdies of the 'Hollister Riot' represented only one percent of the entire amount of bikers in the USA. That started that phrase and it still continues today. Only in today's world, it represents one percent of the Harley riders that fly Three Piece Patches, belonging to an Outlaw motorcycle club and whom are supposedly viscous Outlaws! Back in those early days there weren't any clean and sober, or religious, clubs with one-piece type Colors as there are today. All of the MCs in the '60s and early '70s were basically all Three Piece Patches that were all Outlaw One Percent Clubs. The entire Gladiators membership was a bunch of old 'kick starters', with lean and mean looking customized choppers of those early times. 'Kick starters' is a term for the old, mostly rigid frame Harley Davidson motorcycles of yesteryear sported.

Flat heads, Knuckleheads, Panheads, and some Shovelheads are all early model Harleys of that time that simply do not have an electric start and are kick-start only. The Gladiators never got big enough to have had any other chapters, with the average membership roster being around a dozen to 18 Members. The Club made extra money from selling drugs, mostly, and by living the then modern Outlaw's life of the times. But we did have some class, with over half of the Members having families, which included kids, and real jobs. The illegal money that was made was used for supporting the Club and taking care of extraordinary 'family' needs. So the 'fun money' always went to good times. Not just drugs, sex, and rock and roll, but also supporting Club bike runs and partying, as well as a little extra fun for the families, Members, and old ladies. We had radio controlled airplanes and shit for entertainment, for all to partake in. We would head for the local airport, throwing down the BBQ, with coolers full of Olympia beer. The old ladies would do some cooking and talking, while they helped the kids get set up so we could all play with our toys; in the meantime, the men would get drunk and bullshit. The Gladiators were a 'family Outlaw Club' of the times, that would set a standard in my life of what the lifestyle of a real Biker Brotherhood was, or should be.

The Gladiators were, what I feel, the best Brotherhood I was ever in. Neither of the next two Clubs in my life, or that I have met, would ever come close to being a true Brotherhood. The next Club I rode with, being the Hell's Angels, would eventually turn me to wanting to be in any Club again. I felt that true Motorcycle Club Brotherhood, as I had been a Member of, was gone forever. Like the hippies of the time, they would grow out of their innocence into something else.

It is hard to explain the Brotherhood of Clubs at that time. I guess to try to explain quickly, I would ask you if you have ever seen the movie *Rockie* with Sam Elliot, (my favorite actor), Cher, and Eric Stoltz; all great actors. They were superb in portraying a small Club's Brotherhood; the unity and feelings of those times were better portrayed in this movie than any I had ever seen before attempted on film. When you watch that movie, you see that it portrays the Turks, a factious Brotherhood, showing you the sacrifice, sharing, support, love, and caring of each other during their daily lives. Eating and partying together, attending bike runs, fairs, each other's family social events, and helping one another with their personal problems. That's the closest I have seen on film documenting what The Gladiators, Hell's Angels, or any other Club of that era were really like, as far as helping and caring as one, covering each others family members and own asses.

Although filmed in the mid 80's, the movie also has good examples of the Harleys of that time period, including all the chopped Pans and Knuckles, with the few new Shovelheads of the era. Nothing like the new bullet proof Harleys and aftermarket bikes of today.

Back then it was all about motorcycling and partying with each other as a family. Experimenting with new drugs and ideals in America's changing society, with our generation in the led. There were good and evil aspects paralleling the experimenting with drugs and dope, and its questionable affects of daily use, alcohol, and crime, but we took care of our own through it all, without any hesitation on doing what it took. Motorcycle Clubs were a society living within a society, having its own rules and needs. But back then it was all about Brotherhood, banding together to survive in the changing world at that time. That's how the Clubs in the early days started, not for any criminal purpose; that was just what the law thought up and wanted the rest of society believe. Rather, it was for survival, as there was so few Bikers back then. Bikers of those times banded together to defend their rights, and for protection. Thus, the Motorcycle Club phenomenon had started. The beginning of the '70s, though, would mark the beginning of the end of the innocence as far as Clubs were concerned, simply because they had lost some of their original purity. Just like the hippy / peace / communal movement, the Clubs all changed to being self-centered, drug addicted, with money and greed replacing most of the original ideals. The new, harder drugs of the '70s would change forever the new ideals of social change in the '60s. Like communism, it looks good on paper, but it can't work for long because of our human nature as a whole.

Asked by people what my experience was like while I ran with the Hell's Angels, I usually will ask if they have seen this other movie, *Beyond the Law*. Charlie Sheen plays the role of a real life cop who infiltrated the factious Jackals, which were based on the Dirty Dozen MC. I feel it shows somewhat of what the drug and gun dealing aspect of what the fast lane was like in the early '70s. The movie really doesn't show the whole crazy daily lifestyle of the Outlaws of that time and how they lived. But it does show how the more addictive meth and cocaine replaced pot and LSD.

Also for lack of a better example, the movie showed how Clubs were sought out and infiltrated by organized law enforcement.

Clubs had to evolve and change their bylaws to protect themselves as they have turned into more criminal organizations on a borderless scale. By the late '70s, they had lost their innocence of their beginnings as the modern day Outlaws, that just loved to ride their motorcycles and party. The only thing that stops any of the big modern Clubs from growing bigger and expanding their illegal operations is other rival Clubs. I rode in Bandito country for a while and they make Red & White look like real Angels in my book. The Angels, as a whole, are less ruthless to the general public. They're cold blooded against their rivals, but most of them, not all, would try and protect the innocents whenever they can. Like I say, you can have bad Members that get into any organization, and the Red & White are no different. But they are also the best I have seen at weeding them out of their ranks after they have been discovered.

The Gladiators began, and ended, there in Placerville, California. During their time, they owned that town, and as far as other bikers were concerned, that was our 'turf.' Turf being our place, or area, where we lived, made money, rode our bikes, and raised our families. We would defend our turf to the death, if necessary. When I was growing up in the Placerville area, The Gladiators were 'The Club', and we had all the spoils. Besides the Red & White visiting on occasions, we were 'it'. El Dorado County during that time had the highest crime ratio per capita in the State of California. I was helping to keep those figures up, I am sorry to say. But I would do some time for my crimes to pay my debt. Mostly married, or otherwise hooked up men with families made up most of the Club's Membership. They were all Hell's Angel types that could have easily belonged, but because of their families they didn't. To become an Angel most men will lose their families and jobs, and they just don't work out with being a member very well. For the most part, I was the only single member in our Club. We considered ourselves a family oriented Club. But The Gladiator's Membership definitely consisted of One Percent type bikers. Everybody always respected everyone's old ladies and kids.

I grew up on Placerville's main street. We would watch The Gladiators ride by on their Panhead and Knuckle head Harley Davidsons. All their bikes were chopped and chromed and looking cool, with colorful Members names like Stretch, Poncho, Sidecar Larry, Dirty Rick, Doc, and Gentle Jim on them. You couldn't help but idolize them.

The drug trafficking had been going on since before the hippy times back then, to those in the know; mostly Benzedrine, White Crosses, Reds, and evil Marijuana. The original operation was small, but profitable, with mostly drunk adolescent adults that didn't want to grow up, nor grow old. Some of them being disillusioned Vietnam Vets returning home to 'reality' and 'the real world.' They had survived witnessing too much death and destruction to go back to 'society's normality's'. My generation was preaching freedom of individual's rights, and the right to for one to be able to express themselves; questioning racism, invoking a sexual revolution, and wanting an end to the war. Although, mostly around El Dorado County they wanted free love and drugs, and I agreed with that. I didn't really believe in all that other political horseshit that most of my generation did; I just wanted the freedom of indulging in motorcycling, free love, and drugs. When the good LSD and drugs hit the market they changed my life as well as everyone else's. That's when the 'fast lane life' was more than a reality in El Dorado County; it would grow beyond anyone's expectations, and would eventually become Red &White turf, although not in the beginning. The Gladiators had their time in the sun and that's where I wanted to be. To me they represented the crazed freedom loving Outlaws of the times.

At 14 years old I idolized them, by 15 I had met one or two, and soon became somewhat of an on and off gofer, or just hang around for them. I was still mostly just a kid, shit, but I dressed and lived the part. After being in and out of jail, on the run until after I turned eighteen, I had gotten to know only a few of them. I would sell a few drugs for them or get some for them. If someone needed stolen shit cheap, to sell some drugs or fence some stolen items, I was probably one man who could help, if you know what I mean. I ran the streets with a bunch of crazy Sidewalk commandos, Miwok Indians, and your basic juvenile street delinquents. As I explained in another chapter, that was how the 'old school' process worked. This is the way I was able to become a Gladiator and later a candidate for the Hell's Angels. I finally became a Prospect for

The Gladiators, after I was 18, when I was released form county jail. I was living and working for Poncho who was a Prospect then, and soon got his Full Patch. Shortly after, I was at a meeting and got called inside. Poncho became my sponsor and I finally made my Prospect Patch for The Gladiators. I remember it being the happiest day of my life up at that time. I now belonged to the best Family and Brotherhood that I would ever belong to. I would Prospect for over a year before 'Patching out' at 19 years old, which was very unusual as you had to be 21 according to the bylaws. This would be the best years of my life. Unfortunately, there were dark clouds on the horizon that would end it.

Prospecting for The Gladiators was one of the greatest experiences of my lifetime. I did whatever was asked, without question. To their credit, it was nothing like the Hell's Angels. They treated you with respect, and never asked anything of you they wouldn't do themselves. I was a baby in the MC world, but they all nurtured me in the edict and ways of the Outlaws world. To some I was considered the son they never had and they would watch out for me as if I was their own blood. Most Members were at least ten years my senior. I was taught everything about wrenching on Harleys to how to behave with other Clubs and to show the proper respect. When to open your mouth and when to keep it shut. Lessons in shooting, knife throwing, as well as lessons on being proficient with fist fighting and bar fights; basic Street Survival Skills 101 for an MC soldier. They helped me survive my next 35 years of 'the life.' They made a wise Outlaw out of my young ass during my growing age, as groomed me into the man I am today. Brotherhood was what I was taught, like a child in class. I ran and did their errands, washed their bikes, pulled security, fetched them drugs or women as needed. I would know where everyone of them was on a daily basis, whether they were at work, play, sick, or visiting someone. I could usually tell you where they were.

This era was before cell phones. We were nothing less than a close family, as I knew all their kids and even some of their relatives by name. This wasn't because I had to, no; this was because I wanted to. There was nothing I wouldn't do for them, as they were my family that I loved. Our President's wife asked me if I could be nice to her girlfriend from the Bay Area. She explained how she had been abused by some bikers before.

"She's disabled with polio, but she's a real good person although she is really depressed," Ma said. So I agreed, and they invited her up for a weekend. To be honest, once you got past the skin and bones, metal braces, and hardware, she had a heart of gold. The physical thing, though, was the tough one for me, and I was embarrassed of how shallow I was. We went on long bike rides and I did do the best I could with the rest of it. Another time the same President's wife had another friend who went through a nasty divorce and was having problems finding another man. I volunteered for that one too, and to my surprise she was a stone fox! The things you got have to do for your Club as a Prospect!

The Hell's Angels relationship back then with The Gladiators was one of respect and business. They would come up for visits on occasions. The Gladiators would always host a party for them out of respect and take care of any Club-to-Club business needing to be done. Some drugs would exchange, of course, but really it was more like, "You've got to try some of this good shit!" They had some extra so that they could sell you some to party with them and try it. It wasn't about the money then, they weren't doing it for a profit, and those were the good days. The R&W (Red & White) respected us for our riding and partying skills more than anything. Riding high and drunk on our backcountry roads, few if any Angels could keep up with us on our bikes. We were known for taking curvy roads and trying to straighten them out. The Gladiators only rode curves one way, and that was fast. We also were known to know how to throw a party, with drugs, booze, and loose women. The Club had some mamas, Fat Vicki, Mary Joe, Lolita, and Judy K.

Fat Vicki wasn't always fat; she was riding with Sidecar Larry and he missed a curve and threw her out of his sidecar and down a hill. She broke her back pretty bad, but after that she never quit gaining weight or taking care of the boys. Lolita was one of my favorite sweethearts that was always after me for bike rides and my body. Lolita never wanted a steady old man. She used to tell me that she had tried it and found it too boring. Judy was a good-looking smart woman from a rich family that could have been anything, but she was way kinky. For her the more men the better, as she was a typical stereotypical Club Mama. She was very proud of that, and her affiliation with The Gladiators Motorcycle Club. It wasn't hard to impress the R&W with her as a party favor, as she would do any Member in our Club without any inhabitations. Usually a Prospect's duty was to nail her on the couch in the living room in the middle of the party we were having for our Red & White visitors to impress them. I know it was the most popular duty amongst us Prospects. As I've said before, "The things you gotta due for your Club are just terrible!"

Because of a possibility of an R&W old lady that might snitch on one of our Members to their old ladies whom they readily knew, Members wouldn't touch the Mamas at those parties. Gladiators rarely brought their old ladies to our Hell's Angels parties, as you never know what might happen. We always did whatever it took, out of respect, so the Angels would always have a good time when they visited us. Lonesome, Michael Mouse, Joe N, Teddy Bear, One Punch Steve, all famous Angels of their time. We did them some favors too, if we were asked. After the Gypsy Jokers War that the Hell's Angels won, they were the undisputed 'Mother Club' of California once again. That meaning that they owned the state as the biggest and baddest of the Outlaw Motorcycle Clubs. Thus, their will was what all MC's had to comply with, or face the consequences, which could lead to war if that's what they wanted. The Gypsy Jokers war, by the way, was a war fought for turf and who would run the state. When a war breaks out between two big Clubs going for absolute power, your Club better choose the right Club to buddy up with, or more important, hope it's the winning side you're backing up, as the lines gets drawn.

These turf wars are dead serious as they are fought with usually a lot of bloodshed involved. Members get killed and some go to prison, but that is how the game is played. Some of the other Clubs on their side may be asked for some help fighting, or maybe logistical help. If they asked us to hide some things for them that had been used in the war, there were a lot of deep mine caves in our area, so we obliged. If one of the Angels needed to hide out for a while, we would gladly help. The most famous, being the one that was involved in the Altamont stabbing at the Rolling Stones concert. The law never did get the right man while they tried to convict the wrong one! I guess they were supposed to let the guy shoot Mick Jagger. We had a good relationship with the R&W until they wanted our turf, then they would give us the honor of offering to let us join them.

Members would receive a Full Patch with a short probation period, leaving any of our Prospects having to hang around a while. I should have realized then that the Red & White was changing and this wasn't gonna be the same kind of Brotherhood that we all used to have.

Just before I turned eighteen years old, I'd been on the run hiding and dodging the law for more than a year. About a month after I turned eighteen, the law caught me with Chubby, who's Uncle was one of the Gladiator founders. Anyway, they picked me up and I had to go due six months in county jail for running from my juvenile violation of probation, and other offenses. One day, after being in that cell for about four months, a trustee slipped me a note from Poncho. He said he was doing 24 hours wino time for a speeding ticket. He was Prospecting for The Gladiators at the time. He said that when I got out, he would be there to pick me up, as he had some 'work' for me, if I was interested. So I sent him a kite back through the trustee saying, "Sure"; what did I have to lose? I watched that clock tick off the minutes, almost 24 hours a day; it barley moved. Then, it was finally time for me to get released, and I was going to be a free man again. I never figured Poncho would be there, but there he was, sitting in his 1970 Malibu.

We got down the road and I thanked him. I didn't know it at the time that how much he would influence my future. Poncho began taking me to finishing school for my crime education. I was tired of getting busted and doing time. We were heading downtown and he handed me a big fat joint, a jar of hot whiskey and a cold beer. "Thank you!!" I thought, as I asked where we were going; he told me that we were going to his house. He said, "I am taking you over to my pad to get you laid". "Thank you again!!" I thought, as I asked "by whom?" He said he had a house mouse named Door Knob; I thought "Who cares!!" House mouse meant that she belonged to nobody, except, while she lived at a Gladiators house, anyone could ask for some, and she would put out willingly on her own accord. She was a heavy girl and it didn't take a genius to understand how she had earned her nickname.

Poncho had a plan for my young ass. He had a lot of Harley Forty-Five parts. I had my basket Forty-Five Trike that was about half way done. I had it for about four years, but going in and out of jail, or being on the run from the law, I hadn't even gotten close to getting it up and running. It was hurting for some money and parts. He made me a deal, saying, "You help me move from my house, to my new house, and I will help you get your Trike going." Of course I said yes. Truth is, Poncho lived mostly off of stealing, drug dealing, and his white wife who had a job at the time. Later, after he threw her out, he turned to women welfare recipients to support him. After we got 'the pile' moved, it wasn't long before Poncho earned his full Patch in The Gladiators. I received my Prospect Patch after we got my Trike done. Then, Poncho got busted for rape. It was a bad rap, for sure. He was balling this chick at a party at her house, and the party was getting out of control, so the neighbors called the cops. This is usually what happened when you partied with the Miwok Indians because, as far as they were concerned, it wasn't a good party if someone didn't go to jail. The cops showed up and busted in on Poncho and this chick in the bedroom fucking and she reacted by freaking out about her now tainted reputation, and told the cops she was being raped.

Off to jail Poncho went, making the headline news in the local papers. "A Mexican Gladiator rapes a white woman," is what the headlines insinuated. It looked bad for him, as he was already convicted in the paper before he even went to trial. As far as the Club was concerned, they really didn't really care about the notoriety, but rather reveled in it. While Poncho was locked up in jail awaiting his jury trial, he tried to get his bail lowered enough so he could gain his freedom, but it never happened. We all tried to raise his bail money, but the judge wouldn't budge on lowering it enough so that we could. Then, a Miwok Indian biker named Robby started fucking Poncho's wife and slowly stealing his shit. Nobody, including Robby, thought Poncho would ever get out for a long time, but one thing I knew even then, was to never underestimate him. After spending a summer in jail waiting for his jury trial, it finally went to court. Poncho had turned down some plea bargain offers from the district attorney. Then, the unexpected happened, and the supposed victim-chick wisely recanted her story and told the truth, and, as bad as the law didn't want to, they had to free Poncho.

I got word of his release and showed up at our home, where he was waiting for me. He told me to jump in his car, as we had some business to take care of. First, he was pissed off that I had borrowed $75 of his bail fund that Red Beard, a member of The Gladiators, had been gathering up for him. I *did* borrow the money, because I had run into a screaming deal in Oakland on a brand new top end for my Forty-Five Harley motor. I explained how I almost had the bucks to pay it back, and I didn't figure it would matter until he got close enough to the bail amount he needed. I pointed out that we never raised even half of the ten percent needed to secure his bail. He told me that that was true and to forget it, but I still needed to pay the money back, which I later did.

Poncho then told me that Robby had been "Fucking his cunt." I tried to act surprised, but I already knew about it. I had shown up one day to work on my Trike, as I had been staying with a welfare chick in town. When I walked up and beat on the door, nobody answered. So I let myself in the shed where my Trike was, and Robby came out with some lame excuses. I didn't say anything because I knew it meant Robby's ass. Poncho told me to drive over to Robby's lair up in the mountains. We pulled up in his yard and Robby saw us and started to run, but Poncho was right on him. They ran through the brush, toward the highway. I drove the Malibu around on the road to the highway and turned the direction I thought they might come out. I spotted them and watched Poncho pistol-whip Robby a couple times to the ground until he was begging for his life. After Robby's confession and continuous begging for his life, he told him not only would he give back Poncho all his parts he stole, but if he would spare him he would give him his bike with the signed title and extra parts, too! "Please don't shoot me," he begged! I drove them both back to Robby's pad as Poncho kept his gun on him. On the way there Poncho would smack Robby in the head with his pistol a couple of times. Robby was bleeding all over the place, but Poncho wasn't trying to kill him or even knock him out; no, he was torturing the 'no good, son of a bitch'. Poncho took everything he owned, and I mean *everything*. We loaded his bike, parts, tools, guns, clothes, everything. Poncho then took his leather jacket, cutoffs, boots, sunglasses, *and* his belt and buck knife. He left Robby standing there in his socks, and told him that if he ever saw him again, he would fuck him up. Robby and I *both* believed Poncho's words.

On the way back to Poncho's house, he said, "I can hardly wait to beat my old lady for fucking around with him." I told him that he was gonna be watched more than ever by Johnny Law, cause they don't like to lose. I could understand Robby's punishment, he had it coming, but if he beat up his old lady even though she had it coming, he was asking for trouble with the law. Then, I brought up that his little girl would be there and would be freaking out. That finally calmed him down and made him think, and then he started planning on what he was gonna do next. I was just happy he wasn't going to kill or beat his old lady for her whoring offenses. Everybody knew the jail house code that used to state that if you were going to do much time, you might as well cut your lady loose, because she will be fucking around on you anyway. Then you just go nuts with jealousy, and you do harder time because of it, and it will drive you even crazier. I know, because it happened to me personally, that's why I used to have trouble trusting my old ladies. Poncho told me he was gonna fuck her in the ass for being the whore she was, and throw her out with nothing. He did, and she grabbed their daughter and ran down the street, happy to be alive. I always thought, "She got off lucky."

After beating a rape case and throwing his wife out on the street, Poncho found a cute, little, tough fifteen-year-old girl to shack up with him. Poncho did not fear anybody or anything, especially a society telling him who he could love. I knew this young, tough girl, as she was more my age than his. She may have been only 15 years old, but she was probably going on 30, so far as experience goes. My thoughts were, "He has just beaten a rape case and he moves in an under-aged girl; excuse me, but that takes big balls!" Everybody that knew Poncho knew that you don't fuck with him! He wasn't a very large man, but the type of man that you very well knew demanded one's respect. He lived by the code, and like most of us, was willing to go to jail or even die for it. He never rode his bike as much as most of us, but he was all biker in his heart. Nobody questioned his loyalties, and he would teach me enough to survive in the biker world that we lived in. He showed me how to hustle a living without going to jail. Poncho was a San Jose Chicano gangster in his younger days. He was truly an 'old school one per center,' and would live that life all the rest of his days.

After his 'young thing' had to move out, Poncho turned to his new scam, hustling welfare women. He would have one move in his room with him and he expected her to pay the house payment and provide food. They would gladly do this because he loved them and gave them rides on his bike, right? Then, he told me to kick the chick out I had staying there with me. He told me if I wanted to stay in my room that I needed to rent my room out to whatever chick that could pay. I did, and I know that sounds heartless; it was. We weren't hurting anyone really, as we were just trying to stay alive. We all ate welfare food while the girls made the house payments and paid the bills, as one big, happy family. We sold them drugs for money and conned money out of them for bike parts and shit. If you want to ride and live the life with me, then you had to pay, at least, someone did. These women were glad to have a biker and someone who would keep there ex-old men away from them. They wanted access to drugs, riding, and partying. So in my sordid reality, I justified using them, as I knew they were using me just the same. It seemed to work out for everybody involved at the time, anyway.

Unlike some white trailer trash Motherfuckers I've known in my time that would abuse these welfare-recipient women's kids, the Bikers I knew wouldn't think of doing that. To the contrary, they would protect them. So that's how Poncho and I survived for a long time. Poncho was also a pack rat and he never threw anything away. He was a scrounger, and very successful at it. He would see that somebody had some boxes and stuff piled up by a garage or something, and would walk up to them and ask if he could have it, if he hauled it to the dump for them. He would get rid of it, but only after he would go through everything. Once, he found this old antique vase that was worth thousands of dollars, he was a 'real hustler' who knew the values of exotic things. I kept my Trike up and on the road, mainly with Poncho's help, and some of The Gladiator Brothers. After I started riding with them, they would tell me to whose house or bar they were going to, and I would meet them there. My 750cc Harley was just too slow and had to go. I was getting sick of it, and they were too. Earl the club founder helped me put a real shiny paint job on it, for free. He painted a big swastika on each side of the tanks, then we put eight-inch slugs to extend the wide glide front end; it looked really radical!

The longest run I took my newly built trike that season was to

Calaveras County's 'frog jump' at Angel's camp. Hangtown had just got patched by the Hells Angels and had invited a bunch of us to go with him. We all grabbed some local woman and had a beautiful ride. We were partying hardy at some local chick's house that John R had picked up on. Chubby had come along in a pickup with a pocket full of reds and couple local underage red whores from Placerville. Chubby had bought a couple of bottles of sloe gin with the intention of turning out these two underage chicks. He had gotten this one young fine thing into popping some reds while drinking that red sloe gin to chase them down. He got her in bed and was nailing her when the chick went to spinning and ended up in the bathroom on her knees naked puking her guts out in the toilet. I came walking by them and heard Chubby screaming at her as he was making her pick the partially dissolved reds out of the toilet full of red sloe gin and puke in between her heaves. "You ain't wasting those dam reds you bitch," Chubby yelled! It was an ugly scene but what was worse is I agreed with him. Not long after that run we both ended up in the county hospital from seconal poisoning, plus we had the 'clap' which was one of my lowest times in my life. That was one wild all night party though.

I finally found some duck to buy my trike from me for 600 bucks, a lot of money in those days. I then bought an old retiring Member's Pan-head for 800 bucks, with the help of the Club who loaned me the 200 bucks that I was short on at the moment. The Member's name whose bike I bought was Dirty Rick, and like most nicknames, there is always a reason for it. Rick would get all fucked up on speed and go downtown to the bars and start drinking. He would go from bar to bar, getting wasted, and then he'd go home with some chick. The next morning you would see him being dropped off back at his bike which he left at the bar. Sometimes, you would see his bike parked down on Main Street for days. Many times, the local cops would call one of the Brothers and ask very respectfully if we would please take him home and clean him up. Because of his Membership in the Club, no one fucked with his bike. But his name fit not only him but more so the condition of his bike. Rick would do just enough wrenching to keep it rolling, and he rarely would wash it, if he ever did at all. He would ride it til' it broke down, or the tires finally blew. He didn't believe in maintenance, and could give a shit anyway.

Then, all of a sudden his life did a complete back flip, as he was trying to go straight with some broad he fell in love with and eventually married. The bike I was able to buy due to this marriage was this 1956 Pan-head, complete with its rigid straight leg frame, peanut tank, king/queen seat with up-swept dual exhaust pipes hanging over your head on a chicken bar; yeah, a real '60s chopper. I had a moustache and goatee, as that was all I could grow back then, and I had been hanging with the Club since I was eighteen in bars. I would walk in with them, and no one would say shit, as I looked old. I was truly having the time of my life. I had finally gotten the Harley of my dreams. I sold enough dope and stole shit, per customer's order, to pay the Club back, and was happy to do it. The bike of my dreams was mine finally. Now all I needed was enough money to party and keep my baby running. I remember thinking at the time that had I gotten this bike earlier, I wouldn't have had to do all that crime and jail time to achieve my dream; oh well, I had my baby now, and the rest didn't matter anymore.

One famous run we had happened when some Clubs rode over to visit us one weekend. The Devil's Rejects had shown up with about 20 Members. Tran and some of his crew from his Club had also shown up. Hangtown Bill, who was a Hell's Angel by then and a Prospect, came up with him from Vallejo having heard about the gathering. As everyone was partying hearty and dark was coming, they all decided to stay and just have the run at Poncho's house. Everyone spread out tents and their sleeping bags all over the hillside around the house. We built a huge bonfire in the middle of the camps. As always, everybody got all cranked up for an all-nighter. The combined Prospects made the beer run and showed up with about 30 cases of beer, and the party was on.

Somehow, a black fellow had shown up riding a Triumph motorcycle. Some of my Brothers and I wondered where he had come from, and who had brought him. Finally, Tran said he had followed them from a gas station but nobody knew him. As we're all massed around the campfire, this black, crazy fucker all of a sudden leaps across the fire. That got everyone's attention immediately, as we then started questioning him. He said he just wanted to party with us all, and we explained that we didn't want him there, and we didn't like him jumping over our fire. He started to get smart mouthed about rights and Gentle Jim tagged him and knocked him on his ass. He got beat and kicked awhile, until Hangtown yelled, "Let's hang the nigger!" The whole crowd was yelling "Hang him." The rope went over the tree, as some of the Rejects tried to figure out how to tie the Hangman's noose right. Then Poncho pointed out the fact if we hung him, what would he do with his body? "I'm not digging a grave for him!" he says. This colored guy's eyes were as scared as I have ever seen one's eyes before, as he pleads for his life, bleeding all over the place. So it was decided, against some hangmen's protests, to send him down the road instead, while Stretch and Jim pushed his bike over. Then, Stretch explained to him that he wasn't welcome there, and to never come back! Stretch then pulls out his gun and shoots a hole threw the Triumph's motor. They proceed to push the rider-less bike down the steep driveway, and let it go. Some Brothers then pushed and chased the black dude down the driveway, all running after the bike. Then, people started yelling, "And don't ever come back Motherfucker!"

We were all laughing when, all of a sudden we heard the Triumph sputter to life down at the bottom of the hill, on the county road. We saw the headlight come on as he started off back towards town, the poor bike missing and coughing with the headlight going dim and flickering on and off. Nobody could believe he got it started, as it was spewing oil out of the bullet hole in the motor. We all decided it would freeze up for lack of engine oil within a mile. Then we all gathered back around the fire while some of the Rejects were explaining their disappointment, as they figured since he had followed them they felt they should have been able to "hang the nigger!" Poncho then explained again that he was the one that would get stuck with the stinking body, and everyone laughed it off. The party went on until we saw the red and blue lights coming. Three Sheriff Cars rolled up with the lights and sirens going, and there in the back seat was the black dude. All the Sheriffs got out with their shotguns in hand, and walked up to us at the fire. As 50 or more Outlaws surrounded the six of them, you could tell they were scared.

The Sheriffs proceed to explain the complaint coming from the gentlemen in the car, and that he wanted to press charges, as we had ruined his bike and physically assaulted him, on top of trying to hang him.

We explained to the Sheriffs that the man was a liar, he had shown up uninvited, and fell down trying to ride up the steep driveway, hurting himself as he ran into some of our bikes. We further explained that all we had done was ask him to leave, and gave him a little push to help him get the bike started. While this was going on, Jim and Stretch were going after the black dude again, in the back of the cop car. One of the cops witnessed this and yelled, as the rest of the Sheriffs all retreated and defended the black dude in their car. As the cops were surrounded by about 50 loaded bikers and out numbered, they got scared and decided to split. The one cop said that the victim must have hit his head and was obviously imagining things, although he did wonder how the bike had an obvious bullet hole in it. "But with all you as witnesses here stating otherwise, it must have happened some other way!" He gave us that 'knowing look' and away they went. That 'hang the nigger run' was talked about all over California for a lot of years!

We had some good reckless times, as that what was happening everywhere. The Gladiators were the first Brothers to teach me the thrill of high speed riding, a bad habit I've never been able to break. The law wasn't dialed up to cope with what was happening yet. They would jack us up only if they outnumbered us. So if you were in a big pack, you felt pretty safe. Back then if you weren't falling down drunk they rarely busted anyone for a DUI. As a Club, we did everything together and always had a party. Once, we had a two day party because Red Beard had gotten his new tattoo equipment. He started giving out free tattoos to the Club Members to get some practice. He did a swastika on my shoulder for me. Then, Triple Jack decides that he wants 'Harley Davidson' across his chest, in big letters. We were all tweaking and drunk when he finished up. Jack had gotten all excited and was too busy showing off to realize, as one of the Brothers pointed out to him, that instead of 'Harley' his tattoo said 'Harry'. So he ended up with 'Harry Davidson' in approximately two inch tall letters across his chest!

We had some real crazed Members, like Sidecar Larry, in our Club. He told me this story about this time after he gave up prospecting for the Nomad Hell's Angels. While he was prospecting for them, they decided one night at a party (while they were all wasted) that they needed to teach the then active Black Panther Party a lesson. The Panthers had opened up headquarters on East 14th Street in Oakland. This pissed of the local Angels, as some were prejudice. Sidecar Larry had recently acquired a few hand grenades about then. Later on, he would do three years in the Federal joint for selling machine guns. So, in their partying state of mind, they thought they would drive by the Panther's place and toss a couple hand grenades through the front door. According to Sidecar, that's exactly what they did! He told me the way it went down was they pulled up just past the front door, jumped out, and to their surprise, there weren't any guards or anybody, so he ran up and tossed the grenade through the window and hauled ass away. He said they heard the explosion just as he jumped into the car. They drove off without a problem. He told me only two things pissed him off about it. One was that according to the news, nobody even got a scratch. Two was that, even after all that, the Angels still didn't make him a Member!

The Gladiators always stuck together no matter what. Once, just after I got my Colors, we all went down to the local dance. We were getting pretty fucked up all night long, and throwing our weight around on the dance floor. We pissed of all the local Dudes that were off us hitting on their women and such. After the band shut down, we were out drinking in the parking lot and the fight broke out. All the Members circled up as we fought off all the angry, drunk, young Bucks. Two of them jumped me at once; while I nailed the one Dude, the other grabbed me by my long hair and started pulling me forward. As he did that, I felt that handful of hair give, as it pulled out with what felt like my scalp. We were outnumbered at least ten to one. I pulled out my big Bowie knife and slashed the air at my assailants. My Brothers surrounded me as we fought our way out toward the parking lot, fighting side by side. That's when we heard the sirens that sent everybody running for their cars. That night I learned why we fought together, and that was to survive.

A bunch of my Gladiator Bro's and some 'Lone Wolf' type friends of the Club all decided to meet up in Lake Tahoe for a weekend run. It went on pretty much none-stop for over two weeks. It just kept gathering its own Momentum. We started out with our pockets full of Lily F-40's, otherwise known by the street name Reds. These powerful downers make people do about what ever they feel like, and mixed with alcohol, they make one hell of a party favor. Somebody brought some speed and someone else brought some good LSD. Of course, everyone had a bag of weed back then.

We rode our bikes over to the lake once everyday, in the morning, to sober up, bathe, and just go swimming. After a quick dip, we would start the party all over again; the party must go on! As more and more chicks and bikers joined in, we became quite a loose group. Danny the Duck picked up on a couple of biker chicks that had a four-bedroom rental. So we kept them buzzed on all the dope they wanted, so we could end up at their pad after the bars closed, sort of a home-base. So as more guys picked up more and more chicks, especially Duck, the nightly orgies grew. Within four days we had at least 25 bikes and numerous other vehicles in our entourage. The only thing that we figured could end this party was running out of dope. First, we started checking with the locals that we would meet and procured whatever good dope we could find. That helped, but there just weren't enough drugs there. So we gathered up, and Stretch explained that we had to start setting a limit on how many broads they picked up, especially Duck, or we were gonna run out of party dope too soon. Christ, Duck was nailing four a day, the guy was a pick-up artist; the best I have ever known. He was a crazy liar, con artist, thief, rapist, and eventually was convicted of murder. But we didn't know most of that when he first started hanging around.

When I first met D.L. Duck he wore straight clothes, had short hair, drove a brand new orange Chevy pickup, and didn't even have a Harley; he wasn't even a biker. Normally I wouldn't even know a guy like this, as he was kind of a straight citizen type that I didn't like. Since he had money though, I used him for a place to stay and eat and live off for a while. So I nick-named him 'The Duck' because in the beginning, I thought he was an easy mark for money; but instead of me hustling him, he was actually hanging around me to con me, and try to get in the bike world and get in with my connections in the Clubs. He had just gotten a divorce from a beautiful woman. He had fallen off a scaffold working in the labor union and broke his back. So, he had a monthly disability check coming in for his broken back and supposed disabilities. Duck was a thief that enjoyed his work. He had bought a brand new one-ton flatbed truck, which we used to steal everything that you can imagine. Let's just say that we kept the cops and insurance companies very busy.

One of Duck's favorite tricks was done at the bar. You would be standing there hitting on some good looking chick, when Duck would come up and fart behind you, then go down to the end of the bar to watch and laugh his ass off. Not only did he rip the rankest farts I have ever encountered, but could also fart almost anytime he wanted. He was one rude Motherfucker. Eventually he prospected for a while for the Gladiators, but he never came close to making it as a Member. Like I said, we were a family, and we had scruples, our own right and wrong according to our own laws, so eventually, like many others, he was weeded out. After he got thrown out, he moved to Sacramento. The Misfits MC ended up stealing his bike out of his garage. Their Member, Bergie, who stole it, only made one mistake doing it; the hacksaw he used to saw off the front fork padlock had his name welded on it. He forgot it and the cops found it. Years later, Duck blew a guy's head off with a 12 gauge shotgun. He got caught, and is now doing life in prison. Honestly, even though I liked the guy, and partied and rode lots of miles together, unfortunately, prison is where he probably belongs.

After the first week of our Lake Tahoe vacation, we decided to all drop acid one day. Then, we would ride over to Marklyville for a day ride and go down to the river and enjoy our acid trip. Well, the acid was a little better than we had thought. We were having a hard time riding our bikes, as we were beginning to 'blow it.' So, one of the local chicks riding with us mentioned that she had a friend who was recently divorced and had a big house. Off we went, and as we got closer, we pulled up to an intersection with a stop sign. Two of my Bro's up in front of me were talking to each other, and when they stopped, they both forgot to put their legs down, and fell over. It was like watching Laugh In on TV. We all started cracking up and laughing so hard that nobody even jumped up and helped them get up!

We finally got everybody rolling and made it to the divorcee's house in one piece. One of the Bros dropped his bike when we pulled into the driveway; it was getting hard to keep navigating and balance the weight of the bikes. Once the divorcee found out that we had possession of some Reds, we were welcome with open arms, and spent the whole night partying there. She had an excellent stereo system that we listened to as we drank all the alcohol she had, so we finally had to find someone straight enough to go to the store for more booze. The Duck didn't drop any LSD, so he was the one who went on the supply run. We talked one of the biker chicks into using her car to take Duck. So what does that fucker do? He brings 14 and 15 year old girls back to our party, then I ended up with one of them. Now we had some *real* underage chicks with us. People ended up crashing and pairing off in every closet and room, or corner of that house. We were running as loose as it gets, and having the time of our lives. A never-ending biker party; it seemed that luck would stay on our side. One night we heard about a local kegger party. We finally found it and rode up, throwing our kickstands down and jumping off our bikes. The party was big, with a lot of drunken jocks and their girlfriends, including a lot of high school-aged jocks as well. We were not digging what we saw, and would have left after a beer and however long it took to get organized enough to know where or what bar we would ride to next. There were about 200 of them to about 40 of us, and that included the woman on both sides. Immediately, these beefed-up football tackles and guards come right up to us and started talking shit. "You assholes need to get the fuck out of here," this quarterback yelled! We were all pretty fucked up, but it was easy to see that we were going to get our asses kicked. We all kind of got in a circle with the women and our bikes in the middle. I put my hand on my big Bowie knife to be threatening, like I was ready to use it. That's when Mike D undid his belt buckle and pulled out his primary chain belt from around his waste. "Let's get it on you stupid Motherfucker's," he yelled! Now, Mike was a big bad dude, one of the strongest men I have ever known. We all started to square off, with each side yelling at each other. "We don't want your kind here," Mr. Quarterback yelled! "We didn't invite you, you're crashing our party," one of their chicks yelled! Dudes and chicks alike, it looked like we all were going to give it a go. Mr. Tackle tried to throw a punch at Mike, which he answered with a chain across the side of the guy's head. Then, all hell broke loose. We all started mixing it up, men and women, with punches being thrown, and hair being pulled. But, the damnedest thing about these jocks was that they would run up and throw a punch and then run back into their crowd. We finally just chased them into the middle of their group and started fighting them all at once. At least their women were fighting one on one. It really had just gotten started when you could hear the sirens coming; someone had called the cops. Just as fast as it started, everybody turned and split. We hauled ass to our bikes and them for their cars. With the tall pine trees and multiple ways out of there, we never even saw the cops. We all went back to the biker chick's house to re-organize. Moral to that story is, you shouldn't fuck with people loaded on Reds, because their fearless and don't give a fuck! Or maybe, don't fuck with people's parties, no matter how bad you are?

Mike D with his blonde hair and blue eyes was a bad Motherfucker with a capital 'B'. We had been the best of Bro's for years. Mike had turned down offers to join many Outlaw Clubs like us, including the Hell's Angels, and the Misfits. But he never joined any of them; he just rode with them when he felt like it. Few would be stupid enough to argue with him. He wasn't the bully type, despite his size, but instead was very polite and well mannered, unless you fucked with him. He had a beautiful white, pearl painted Sportster that he truly loved and had put all the money in the world that he could muster up into. He had built up the motor big enough to carry his size. But he was so big that he dwarfed the bike; he looked funny on it. But, no one would tell him that to his face. Mike and I worked on a major forest fire together on the same fire crew once, and I swear, he could do the work of four men. Four years after I left California, he and John R. rode their bikes out to Denver, Colorado where I was living to spend a couple weeks visiting me. I heard years later that Mike came home and caught his old lady boning some Dude. The story goes as such; he told the guy to leave and walked back out to his garage. The guy walked in and shot Mike dead, in cold blood; the chicken-shit Motherfucker was that scared of him. The world lost a good man that day. I lost one of my best Bro's, and I will always miss him, but he will be one Bro that I look forward to seeing again and riding off into the beyond together

We had a few Gladiator Bros that rode up and stayed for a few days in Tahoe, or even a week, but then had to get home because of their jobs, and for some, their families. We had been there 11 days so far, and had closed the bar that night, heading back to the biker chick's house, where we had a little 'Church' to decide our final plans. Stretch, John R., Mike D., D. L. Duck, and I stayed the whole two weeks. Me, I could've stay as long as I wanted, because like always back then, I had no responsibilities, yet. Like always in life though, money became the issue, and of course, we were running out of drugs. The Clubs wild money for this adventure had been spent, and everyone's wild stash money was gone, so the 'boy's only' run was about to end. We had been operating off our own 'mad money' for the last couple days. We decided to pull out in two days so that we had enough money and drugs to have a good ride home. We also all wanted to take the long way home, as none of us wanted to really go home all that much. We hit the lake with everybody the next morning and started our day with some beers, a little speed, and a little weed. Duck took off for a ride, where I had chosen a dip in the lake to refresh my body for the day. Our big plan for that night in order to save some money was to skip going to the bar. Instead, we decided to have a bathtub party at our hostess's house.

The plan was to buy a bunch of 190-proof Everclear, which is almost pure alcohol, and you could buy it in Nevada. One of Ducks chores that day was to bring back a bunch of it. We sent some of the chicks out to get fruit and juices and shit to mix up with it in the bath tub. You fill the tub full of ice, poor the booze in, add your mixes, and stir. It's an economical way to keep 50-plus people drunk for a couple of days. We rode back to our hostess's house after a great drunk fest at the lake. Lake Tahoe is a cold Motherfucker if you have never been there, and a quick dip will sober you right up. The law had finally taken notice of our daily ritual and watched us at the lake for the last couple hours we were there, and it became apparent that we had worn out our welcome. The cops followed us back to the house, and just as we got there, Duck pulled up with the booze and three more chicks that he had picked up on his travels. The cops rolled on and the party started as we got the tub loaded up, and got the stereo rockin'. Everyone partied down as we drank straight out of the bottle of Everclear, with a guzzling contest going down. The party ended as usual, Bros scoring their lady of the evening in corners, couches, bathrooms, and closets. The beds are where you usually found the Duck, with at least a couple of women, having an orgy. Everybody was so high and drunk that they couldn't give a shit, and was just doing what felt good, and the Reds mixed with booze took away any inhibitions.

This orgy went on all night. After catching a little sleep while some of the booze and Reds wore off, I got up and hauled ass for the coffee. Stepping over couples passed out in the kitchen, I made my way to the stove. I heated up some of yesterday's mud, adding a splash of Everclear and headed outside to enjoy it, along with some wake up speed that I stirred into my Biker's coffee. As I went by a bedroom, as fate would have it, I heard Duck say, "Hey Bro." He was sandwiched in between three women, all butt-assed naked, in a double bed. "Hey Bro I need a favor, this chick needs a ride back to her house. Would you ride her over?" "I'll buy you breakfast if you do," this short hair girl piped up. I said "Sure, but not until I finish my coffee out front and wake the fuck up!" I gagged and almost puked on my coffee, but by the time it was gone I felt a whole lot better. She was a cute little thing and I thought, "How does Duck do it?" I got my scooter started and showed her where to put her feet on the pegs. We were both pretty quiet as she gave me directions to her apartment. The early morning air woke us both up by the time we got to her place. My coffee had kicked in as I started feeling human again. When we walked into her pad there was one of her roommates there.

Shari officially introduced herself and her friend before she grabbed me a beer and went off for a shower. She was done before I finished my beer and off we rode on my bike for breakfast. Shari asked me a lot of questions about the Club, just being curious, I thought. We hit it off pretty good, and I told her we were probably leaving the next day, so she asked if I would ride her around today. She said she was on vacation time and loved to ride bikes, and would pay for everything. Since I probably had only 20 bucks left in the whole world, I said, "Sure, why fucking not." After breakfast, we headed back to the party where everybody was up and starting to get back into the party mode. The bathtub was still two-thirds full. Shari offered to buy us something else to drink, so we went to the liquor store. When we came back we noticed the cops were already watching the house. So we took off again for a beautiful ride through the mountains before we got too fucked up. After that, we all did our best to kill the contents in the bathtub all the rest of the day and night. Shari and I got to know each other intimately and slept on the floor together. The speed and drugs were running out so people passed out earlier than usual. We got up and I did my coffee thing with Shari, and we went for breakfast again on my putt.

During breakfast, she talked me into taking her back home to Placerville with me. I told her I really didn't have a pad and I couldn't promise her shit. I had to admit that I was a bike bum and didn't work or have shit besides my bike. "No car, no house, and no money, I live out of my saddlebags," I told her. I figured that would discourage her. She insisted she had money and would take care of everything including buying a new seat for my bike as soon as we could, as it was killing her back. Normally, I would have taken offense about the seat, but it was trashed, so it was easy enough to say "Okay." So Shari ended up riding back with us after we went and grabbed a few of her clothes. Amazingly to me, she just crammed some make-up, underwear, a couple shirts, and some other shit in a large purse, and was ready to go. I strapped it all down with some bungee cords while stuffing some loose items in my bag. I could tell it was time to go home, as I smelled that familiar dirty clothes smell from my used up clothes when I opened my saddlebag. With all my socks and t-shirts being dirty, it was definitely time to find a place to do laundry. When we made it home, Stretch said we could spend the night at his pad. I think he wanted to cool off his old lady's questioning with a strangers presence. I thought immediately that I knew his old lady and oldest daughter would get my laundry done as always; now things were lookin' up!

The ride home the next day was fun, but clouded by a forest fire that was burning out of control. Highway 50 was closed because of the fire, but we were planning on taking the long ride around anyway. Shari bought us breakfast before we said goodbye to our beloved Lake Tahoe. As we rode through the mountain roads, I reflected on those two weeks with a smile and a promise to myself of doing it again, and I could hardly wait, as Lake Tahoe had to be Biker's Heaven. We stopped at a bar for a smoke and beer break. As we pulled back on the highway, I reflected on my love of the 'outlaw life' I had chosen, which put me in a good mood. Not knowing what lay ahead at the next turn was the way I liked it, along with not having a care in the world, a lifestyle of total freedom by choice. I reflect on what I had then, and I miss it. This lifestyle was dangerous and reckless, but on the other hand, it was the most exciting, carefree way one can live. While people from my generation were worried about money, family, kids, and careers, we were livin' the life.

I was living a life of total freedom with nothing to worry about except needing a few bucks to ride my motorcycle and party. Shari bought us all lunch and beers and we continued our beautiful ride through the Northern California Sierra Mountains headed home. We continued bar hopping through the mountain roads, wishing it would never end. While the Brothers were coming back down to the reality of families and jobs, my only concern was getting my laundry done. Money didn't seem to be a problem because this chick Shari seemed to have plenty, at least for a while. Until we parted ways, she could keep me going. I started wondering what kind of job or hustle this chick had going, as money seemed to not be a problem. She was being awful free with it, and maybe she wasn't bullshitting about buying me a new seat for my bike. Brothers waved good-bye as they split off from the pack headed for their homes, until we finally pulled into Stretch's house and our awaiting coming home reception. Ma was just a little pissed!

The next day I rode Shari down to Sacramento, to California Chopper Supply, the Hell's Angels shop, Lonesome's place. Shari bought me a new king/queen seat, along with a new matching chrome chicken bar for comfort. Of course, we talked her into a new chrome rear fender to mount the seat and chicken bar to, and as Lonesome saw the game I was playing, he suggested a new rear tire for safety's sake. Lonesome pulled me aside and asked me where I had found my new good looking sugar mama. I told him I had ridden her down from a Tahoe run, as she wanted to hang, and had money. He was very impressed with her. When we got back she wanted to ride up into the mountains and get some dinner, which we did at a fancy steak house. That's when over an expensive steak dinner, she dropped the bomb on me. She said she worked over by Carson City at a place called the Moon Light Ranch and had to be back to work in a week. She asked me if I knew about the place and I told her that indeed I did, that it was a famous whore-house. I didn't tell her that as a kid in high school we used to spend our lunch money there. She went on to say that if I didn't mind her staying that she would take a greyhound bus back to work. I told her I really didn't have a place for us to live, and she said, "Then lets go rent one, I got money." So that's how we shacked up, as she bought a bed, furniture, kitchen stuff, and clothes for both of us. The other Club Member's old ladies helped her. No empty promises or pledges of love or loyalty were ever said, as it was more an agreement of necessity between us.

I obviously didn't love her, and she didn't care, she just wanted to take care of me. She talked of having a pimp in Las Vegas and such in the past, and angrily said she would never do that again. She explained that her Mom was a whore too, and had taught her the tricks of the trade. Before she got back on the bus, we had a house right downtown, on the hill behind Main Street. To the lady's credit, she had money and did what she said she would do. All the Brothers, and even some of the Red & White Members that were around, were all jealous of me. Two weeks on, and two weeks off, that was hers and my working schedule. I enjoyed the notoriety of living off a whore like a king, and she enjoyed riding bikes with the Club and being part of that world. Word spread through the bike world of my good fortune and gave me some notoriety. So I guess we were both getting what we wanted? This went on for about six months, but living with a whore bothered me; in reality, I was no different than her. I figured if I wasn't her pimp, then what was I? I was making money by living with her so what was the difference? It was nice not to have to sell drugs, steal, hustle, and drift around, house to house. For two weeks out of four I could do anything I wanted, but I still missed my freedom that I had gotten use to. I wasn't ready for any kind of relationship, no matter how easy it was.

Shari and I *did* have some really good times together. What she enjoyed the most was my Club's close family ties, our constant good times, and doing things together as one large family. One of the good times was when the Club went to the county fair with all the old ladies and kids. We had ridden our bikes to it, and just as always, made quite the spectacle amongst the citizens when we arrived. We all started drinking beer right off the bat when we got there. I already had a good buzz going that morning on some Reds and wine that I had for breakfast. We went and played with the carnies first, winning toys and shit for everyone. We were putting on our usual antics for the citizens, fucking around and shit. We had their attention for hours, as the crowd of citizens followed us around keeping their distance and pretending not to be staring, nor paying attention. Then, we decided to get on some of the rides. That was when things started getting pretty loose. I was stumbling around wasted, handing my beer to the carnies to hold while I went on their rides, but only if I couldn't hang on to it. I mean this is back in the days when they didn't even really have cops at the fairs. You could drink back then and do what you pleased. Those were the days when society let people police themselves mostly, now a forgotten concept.

What happened next is possibly why they started having security and police at fairs. This was one of the stupidest thing I have ever done, but that always seems to go along with eating Reds. We all decided to get on the 'Twirl-A-Wheel' or something like that. It's like a round open drum, in which you stand and lean against the inside wall, which is solid for two foot or so. One person stands in each of these "cells". Each side has an opening of less than a foot or so, with cage wire covering so that you can't fall out, but you can see out. So anyway, it starts spinning at a fast enough rate that the centrifugal force almost glues you to the side. Stretch had given the carnie a few extra bucks to give us double the time of the ride. We all had our cans of beer and drinking as we were spinning. I decide in my drunken red induced state, that I had to pee. So I started rolling off to the side away from Shari and ended up with my dick out of the screened opening towards the crowd. We're spinning around and around and I'm just pissing away. Imagine the effect of urine flying over the crowd that was watching us and in the ticket line, it was like a giant human sprinkler affect. I thought it was hilarious as I said "Piss on them all if they don't like it!" Rightfully so, my Brothers decided it was time to get me out of there. Their old ladies wouldn't talk to me for a couple of weeks and I had embarrassed Shari, too.

I had it made for awhile, and I was used to using women for money, with Shari being my mark at the Moment. In a way, I was just a male whore. But for some stupid reason, it bothered me that she was a whore. It was hypocritical to the life style I chose, and also very arrogant of me to judge her with some kind of morality. All the Bro's wanted to fuck to her. Even Lonesome had made a comment at a Run, of his desires to do such. I didn't feel that I was better than her in any way, I was just too jealous of the fact that other men had her half of the time. When she first got home from 'work' each time, she would complain of being sore for the first few days. Shari said her Mom had taught her to use baby oil to help, which somehow made it all too real. Once, when we were alone and drunk, she opened up and talked openly of having to do guys no matter what. Legs or arms missing, ugly, or body odor didn't matter, as you couldn't turn them down because of the 'house rules,' she complained. I wish she hadn't told me all she did, because it turned me off and I couldn't get it out of my head. I was being very arrogant and immature about it. She had made it very clear from the beginning that her Mother was a whore and she would always be one too, as it was a family thing. Finally, I just couldn't do it anymore and broke it off with her. When I told Hangtown Bill I had left her, he said he was gonna kick my ass for being so stupid as to throw away a good living like that. After I had cut her loose and she was gone, I went back to living out of my saddlebags for a while, then realizing just how easy I'd had it, and how stupid I probably was for letting her go.

Being with The Gladiators, and living in the fast lane of the times, was full of experiences that shaped my life. One of those good times was right after I had gotten my Gladiator Patch and had healed up some from my Patching Party and wreck, I decided to go to Oroville and visit Herbie and The Devil's Rejects. I had picked up this petite, puppy love ex-girlfriend from my youth. She was so impressed with me being in the Club and shit that she wanted to go for a week long ride with me, offering to pay for it. So I figured Oroville would be fun, and we left early on a beautiful, sunny Friday morning. We rode on and had a blast. She bought us breakfast, we smoked some of her good weed, and life was good. We pulled in for a gas stop, where we ran into about 20 Members of the Bar Hoppers MC. I only knew one of them well, and his name was Bruiser, from Sacramento. I dropped his name and his Brothers told me they were on their way to meet up with him at a run that they were having, and I was welcome to tag along if I wanted to see him. What the fuck I thought, we had a sleeping bag and why fuckin' not, gotta go with the flow. We pulled into the run and I've never seen nor heard of so many Bar Hoppers. It must have been their national meeting or something. Bruiser came right up and jerked me off my bike as the kickstand barely hit the ground.

Bruiser was a huge dude, all muscle and not much fat. After a big bear hug, he took us over to his camping spot where he insisted we camp with him. We indulged in their hospitality and were treated like a royal family. They shared their drugs, booze, steaks, and everything there was to be had. That chick and I were having a blast, as I was the only other Patch there, besides the Bar Hoppers, and received some notoriety because of it; which was an honor. Or, I could be in deep shit, but I had always trusted Bruiser. The next morning I decided to keep rolling, and after eating a big breakfast that Bruiser had insisted on, we rolled up my bag and packed the bike. Everyone in the whole camp circled around to see us off, and I was a little nervous. The chick jumped on my bike behind me before I started kicking her to life. I normally would have told the chick to wait until I got her started, but everyone was watching us. So I got her up on compression stroke and gave her the big kick. The kickstand broke as I came down on the end of the kick pedal and we fell right over. The bike had fired and was running as the chick and I hit the ground. So there we are, lying on the ground with the bike running, with it lying on top of us. In a second, Bruiser jerked the bike up and held it up with one hand yelling, "Are you guys alright?" We got up, got back on my bike (still running), with someone handing me my broken kickstand, which I gave it to the chick to take with us. I thanked Bruiser again, and with a wave to all, we took off. That was one of the most embarrassing Moments of my life; why did it have to break right then?

I was always having the time of my life as a young Patched Gladiator, the best I would ever have. With a small, lucrative criminal business going, I did enough stealing and drug dealing that I didn't have to work. I had rented a place out in the country which became my home base for my operations. We held 'Church' out there, as it became our Clubhouse, where we held most of our meetings and had wild Club parties. One of my

Indian Bros, named Richard, had talked me into doing a burglary at this Dude's house, as a sort of a payback, for bringing nothing but trouble to his Mother. Besides the usual shit, we found a basement full of wooden wine kegs, all in various stages of fermentation. It took us three trips in a pickup, but we hauled off about a dozen of these kegs. Although we decided to throw a party, Richard and I decided we needed to get some food, too. Richard had worked on his Father's ranch and knew all about cattle, so he decided that we needed to go poach a cow.

So off we go to a remote ranch with two other Miwok Indians and Richard picked us out the cow he wanted. The plan was to use Richards's new 22 pistol so as not to make a lot of noise. While Richard was rolling a joint in the cab of the truck, we walked over to the cow and shot it in the head. It turned around and looked at us and mooed. We fired two more shots with the same success, and the dam cow started to walk off out of the spotlight. Richard finally comes running up yelling, "What the fuck are you guys doing, don't you amateurs know anything?" He grabbed the gun and walked back about twenty paces, turned, and fired at the cow. The dammed thing dropped like a rock, "You got to let the bullet get some velocity, you dumbasses!" Within five minutes he had us dragging hindquarters back to the truck. Next trip we had the front quarters and brought the truck back where Richard had the head cut off and we loaded the rest of the carcass. The whole thing took about fifteen minutes and we were on our way back to my house. We threw it all into the bathtub, and with the propane grill that we had burned with the wine we started cooking steaks, and drinking wine. It didn't take long for the word to spread about the free steak and wine. Some of my Club Brothers came and went as we partied for a week straight. Waking up to steak and wine for breakfast, and continuing throughout the day and into the night. Chicks would come and go all week long, some staying for the whole week as the nights would turn into a roman orgy. We finally ran out of our commodities, and the party came to a happy end.

The biggest bar fight I was ever in happened while I was a member of The Gladiators. We decided to make a Run over to Oroville, California. We were meeting another couple of Clubs and friends over there, one of the Clubs being the Devil's Rejects, and Herbie and Sidecar Larry. I am afraid to say that Herbie and Larry are dead and gone. I personally don't believe the world is the same, its missing two of the craziest Motherfuckers I have ever known. Sidecar was such an abuser of the sins, a speed freak, pothead; a drinking, smoking, snorting, acid head. That doesn't even come close to listing all of that man's appetites. I always figured Sidecar would definitely die before me. So long as that partying animal was alive, I had no worries because I *had* to out live him. When I first met Larry, I was a Prospect for The Gladiators. He told me "Don't ever let them make you a Member, stay a Prospect, its more fun!" One of the stories goes that after he quit The Gladiators, Sidecar started hanging around with the Red & White, waiting to become a Member. His first big party with them, he was being introduced to some Angels and he yells out, "Who wants to fight?" As all the Angels glared at Larry, he immediately started saying "Ok, you fight him and you fight him" etc... One of the Angels knocked him right on his ass for his out of place joke. When Sidecar bounced back up from the floor, another one dropped him on his ass. They didn't think it was very funny, but he definitely had some big brass balls. Despite his black eye, he had introduced himself and been noticed and talked about by just about every Angel at the party. Another one of their tricks that Herbie and Larry used to pull was taking firecrackers and clenching one by its end with their teeth. They would give you this shit eating grin and light the fucker. They would just keep on grinning until, "Boom," it would explode in their faces. They would sometimes end up with fat, bleeding lips. They thought this was the funniest thing. When they say, "Let's party," they meant it! Guess who was always the entertainment?

We were all supposed to meet up at Herbie's. I had ridden my Panhead up with my Club Brothers. We had a total of about eight Members make the beautiful ride with no breakdowns, which in those days that was close to a miracle. I was 19 at the time and had been Patched out for about five months. We had been partying since we left Placerville and had carried on all day as usual, consuming our usual volumes of beer and weed, with most of us speeding as well. The bullshit was flowin', as much as the drugs and the booze were. Then, like always, we all decided we needed to head for the bar. Some of the local Brothers were getting off of work and wanted to meet us there; after all, it was Saturday night. To this day, I don't know why Herbie picked *that* western bar. It was big enough for sure, but it was packed with rednecks; it was basically *their* bar. When we pulled up on our steeds, as soon as I kicked my kickstand down, I knew there was something wrong about this place. When we walked in you could feel the tension in the air. I guess they didn't appreciate a bunch of bikers invading their bar on a Saturday night.

We all started getting pretty loose, drinking and occasionally taken turns in the john with the crank bag. After about five hours the place was packed with people; about half of them bikers and the rest rednecks. I was sitting with my Brothers Stretch and Poncho. Poncho had fallen off his bike a couple of weeks before and had broken his leg. So he had a full cast on his one leg, and was hobbling around on crutches. Stretch was our President at the time. We were shooting pool and slugging down beers. We had held the table for hours, when a couple of the rednecks came over to challenge the table. Things started to go far south after that. It was obvious that the rednecks wanted to fight us more than shoot pool. Looking back I can see why they were getting pissed; this was their bar and we were the strangers that came in and took it over.

Some of the Brothers were hitting on their women, and purposely brushing shoulders with the men to provoke them; the same old drunk shit. But this was the good old days, when it was still just fists and knives, not many guns. Male egos and testosterone were flowing. Well, shit hit the fan when Stretch grabbed this one cowboy's hat off his head at the pool table. The guy immediately got excited and lunged for the hat, and then Stretch tossed it to me. The cowboy yelled at me, "Give me my fucking hat!" then lunged toward me. So I tossed it to Poncho, then he threw it back to Stretch. The cowboy throws a punch at Poncho, who dodges it. Stretch wasn't going to let this cowboy fire up Poncho, so he knocks him on his ass. The shit really hit the fan then, and it was all out bikers against cowboys. I jumped beside Stretch, as he was our Prez. A cowboy started to go for Stretch from behind, and I faked a left and nailed him with a right cross. He must have never seen it coming, because down he went. We had an instant advantage because of our unity and loyalty. I mean, we all reacted instantly to protect our Brothers and their old ladies.

You don't even hesitate for a second, you don't even think about it! That's what makes bikers survive, especially with the One Percent Clubs, which they all were then. We are a family and you don't let anybody fuck around with family members. We all started fighting immediately with anybody who wasn't with us, and whoever made the mistake of standing up got knocked on their ass. There are no questions of who, what, where, or why your family is in a fight, but we are gonna fight as one, or die trying to win!

There were probably about 25 of us and about the same, or more, of them. Everything just exploded! Everybody started punching somebody. Women screaming, tables turning over, glass breaking, men scrambling over chairs, just total bedlam. I saw Stretch punching the cowboy with the hat. I hit another cowboy that was coming up from the side, and then I thought for a second that I might have broken my hand as I felt a sharp pain run up my arm. He went down, so I started putting the boots to him. I turned and saw Stretch kickin' this other Dude in the head. He would slam into the wall with each kick, his eyes looking dead. Blood was splattering on the wall behind him, and with each kick blood also squirted out of his face. He would start to slide down and Stretch would kick him again and again. I was just starting to laugh when I got cold clocked in the side of the head. I already knew to never take your eye off your opponent or the fight, but I did, and by then, both men had gotten back up. Poncho came up behind them and nailed one over the head with his crutch, hitting him over and over in the head and shoulders while breaking pieces off the crutch, as Dude tried to run away.

I squared off with the other one and we exchanged some punches. He caught me with one above the eye, and I was amazed that I hardly felt it. I could feel the adrenaline that was flowing through me along with a lot of speed. I caught him with a good one to the side of his head, and as he slightly bent downward, I got in a good clean kick to his balls. He fell almost straight down to his knees, and I tagged him a good one again to the side of the head. He crashed to the floor. I turned and started to laugh again as I saw Poncho dragging his casted leg behind him as he chased this Hat with what was left of his crutch, which was getting shorter and shorter with each swing. Then, boom, I get hit in the back of my head! Once again, if you don't pay attention, you will pay. The blow knocked me forward enough to fall into Stretch, along with some tables and chairs. As I did, I saw Johnny, who is Stretch's blood brother, nailing this guy from behind. So I scrambled up to help Johnny put the hat, with the cowboy in it, on the floor.

I saw Johnny grin at me, and then I saw his face contort in pain. As he started to turn around, I saw over his shoulder, the cowboy who started the whole thing over the hat. I didn't see a knife in his hand, but later I found out that he had stabbed Johnny. Johnny started punching and kicking at him, when I saw another Hat coming from his side. I immediately went after him, attempting to kick him in the nuts, and missing and hitting above his knee. He let out a scream on his way down to the floor. I took advantage and jumped on top of him and punched him a couple of times, and then he was out. As I turned and scanned the bar, I could see bodies sprawled out all over the floor, mixed in with all the debris. I then saw Stretch again, kicking the shit out of the same Hat that started it all. Stretch could kick people better than anyone I have personally known. He is a tall man with long legs and arms; in short, a bad Motherfucker. I looked around the bar again quickly and saw that most of the Hats were down, or being finished off. I could see a couple of Brothers helping other Brothers get up. Stretch, our President, yells "Let's get the fuck out of here!" The bar was in shambles, as chairs, tables, drinks and bodies lay everywhere, all mixed together.

Women were scurrying around looking for their old men, and upon finding their knocked out bleeding asses, then started screaming and crying. We didn't really have but a couple of women with us, but everyone knew enough to start scrambling to get out to the bikes. As we hit the door you could hear the sirens coming. We split fast, and rode until we hit a stop sign a couple of streets away. I heard a yell, and Gentle Jim jumped off his bike and was looking at Johnny's back. "Johnny's been stabbed bad!" Stretch nonchalantly said, as he was too. His stomach was covered with blood. Stretch yelled at Herbie, "Take the lead and get us to the hospital!" When we got there and got Johnny into the entrance, you could see all the blood that was running down his leg and overflowing out of his boots. He was stabbed near his kidney. Later on we were told that it was a six inch blade knife, which they had measured by the depth of the wound. That wound was meant to kill. I then saw Stretch's stomach, and his whole front was drenched in blood. In the end of the fight, that cowboy con had seen that he was losing, and tried to do as much damage as he could, while he could, with a big knife.

I turned into a rage of anger, and wanted revenge. Both of my Brothers had been stabbed protecting my back. We all had been carrying knives, and a few guns, but the only weapons we had used were a crutch, chairs, and some beer bottles. We didn't use our knives, as to us it just seemed like a good old-fashioned fist fight, or bar room brawl, the old way of settling problems or just for the sport of it. I wanted revenge, blood for my Brother's blood. I turned to one of my best Brothers, named Go To, who was in another Club than I was at the time, though we were still close. I asked him to let me ride bitch back to the bar on his bike, that way I could get away by foot. I had my Buck knife with me and I had every intention of using it on some cowboys for payback. My plan was, after I was dropped off, I would go stab a couple of those Hats that we had left lying on the floor. Revenge would be swift and sweet, and then I would escape by foot. We could hear sirens heading for the hospital as we left the area. When we got to the bar it was too late, the cops were everywhere, complete with ambulances and shit.

We immediately started to turn around in the parking lot, when a cop yelled for us to stop as he came running at us. Another cop joined him and as they came up to us they asked, "What are you doing here?" We told them that we were going to have a beer but decided better of it when we saw what was going on. The one cop asked, "You boys weren't here earlier, were you?" We replied, "No, like we said, we were just coming by for a beer?" That's when one of the Hat's old ladies came running up, pointing at me, and said, "That's one of them that beat up my husband, you son of a bitch!" They asked her if she was sure, and would she would sign a complaint? "Oh, yeah" she said, and wham, I was drug off Go To's bike and cuffed. They asked her about Go To, and whether or not she was sure he wasn't one of them? She said "no" so they let him go. They grabbed my cuffs and pulled me to the ground, and Go To was told to leave, so off he rode. Some of the combatants and their old lady's started coming toward us, yelling and screaming insults and revenge threats at me. I yelled, "Go get fucked!" The cop told me to quit antagonizing them, as they put me in the back of the squad car to 'protect' me.

I watched the scene from the back of the patrol car, while the cops held them back, as they were trying to get at me in the car. I watched ambulances, more cops arriving, Hats, and women as it was turning out to be quite the spectacle. They kept trying to get to me as they pointed at me, screaming and shaking their fists. The cops still held them back. Then, over the cop's radio I heard the dispatcher say that there was another fight going on at the hospital, and for units to respond. Two cops jumped into the patrol car and off to the hospital we went, with the lights and sirens going. One of the cops turned and said through the steel cage between us, "Looks your buddies are at it again". Then, they told me that we had really kicked those cowboy's asses at the bar. I told him that I didn't know what he was talking about. So we get to the hospital and the two cops jump out and run into the emergency entrance. I am cuffed with my hands behind my back in the back seat. I realized these cops hadn't even had time to look at my ID, nor had they yet taken my wallet. All they had at this point was my Buck knife. I saw one of old ladies of our group going toward the entrance, and I started yelling at her to let me out, but she couldn't hear me.

I watched as other people from our group came in and out of the hospital. I kept yelling and screaming at them to let me out, but nobody could here me in the back of the patrol car. Then, cops brought out somebody else in cuffs and put him into another patrol car. My two arresting cops finally came out and back to their car, which I was still locked up in. Off we go headed to the Orville jail, as I had missed my chance of escape. The cops told me that a fight had broken out between three guys on gurneys that were getting treated for their wounds. The cops managed to get them all separated so that the doctors could do their jobs. They then told me that the one guy was under arrest, and would be hauled into jail for violating his parole, after his wounds were treated. "You guys tangled with a bad Dude; he was recently paroled out after doing five years for assault. His family and friends were having a Welcome Home party for him. Your two buddies, whom were stabbed, attacked the guy while on the gurney and started beating on him!" I told them that I didn't know who they were talking about. Of course, we were all wearing the same Club Colors, so it was obvious that I was full of shit, and they didn't believe me.

They booked me on assault charges, and threw me into a holding cell. Finally, they got me processed, and then put me in a large cell. I knew I wouldn't get bailed out until morning. I looked around the cell to see what I was up against. I saw about four Blacks that were still awake and playing cards. About eight more Blacks were sleeping in bunks. I'm figuring, at this point, that I'm gonna have some real problems in the morning. I noticed one red-headed white dude who was sleeping with his back to me in his bunk. I figured the safest place to be would be near him, so I took the upper bunk above him, hoping he would be my ally in the morning. As I tried to go to sleep, my adrenaline was still going, but the speed was still reeling my mind and my thoughts drifted. I thought about the month before, when I had been up here in Oroville visiting the Devil's Rejects.

I was out riding with their President at the time, named Gino. He was a real character, and one funny Motherfucker. He was always saying "hello," all the time. We were riding around in this all Black section of town, which looked to be their meanest block. There were Blacks everywhere, drinking cheap wine and beer, and listening to their music. We pulled up to a light and were sitting there on our bikes, waiting for the light to change, as I realize that they're all staring at Gino and I. I looked over at Gino and asked, "Why the fuck are we in this part of town?" He looks over at me with this shit-eating grin and yells as loud as he could, "Nigger Nigger Nigger!" I'm thinking, "What the fuck!" and look over at all the Blacks, who were momentarily in shock. Gino yells again, "Nigger Nigger Nigger!" grinning at me. I turn to see all these pissed off Blacks heading for us, with blood in their eyes. Luckily, the light turned green and we hammered it out of there, with Gino laughing his ass off and me thinking about what a fucked up joke that was. I couldn't help but wonder if any of those Blacks might recognize me, and my last thought was, "Ahh, fuck it, I'll deal with it in the morning," finally crashing in my bunk.

In the morning, I woke up and looked around, finally seeing all these blacks eyeballing me. I figured my best defense was a good offense, so I jumped down off my bunk and looked for the white dude I'd seen last night, hoping for help. The red-head dude was still sleeping with his back toward us, as he had been the night before. I looked at all the eyeballs glaring at me, and thought that I had better wake this white dude up for some help, quick. I shook his shoulder, and he rolled over and looked at me with the ugliest, blood-shot eyes that I think I have ever seen. I couldn't believe my eyes; it was Redneck, from the Devil's Rejects! I couldn't believe my fuckin' luck. The cops had booked him for assault in another bar fight that night, at another bar in Oroville. "Hey man, what the fuck are you doing here," Redneck asked? "Oh man, we got in this huge scuff with a bunch of fucking cowboys at this bar," I told him. We went on and exchanged war stories back and forth for a while. Then we both suddenly noticed all the Blacks staring at us, all at the same time. "What the fuck are you guys looking at?" Redneck yelled at the Blacks. They all turned their eyes and started talking, not paying us any more attention. I looked at Redneck, then down at myself, and noticed we were both covered in blood splatters.

No wonder they didn't want a piece of us. It's always been my experiences that if the Blacks don't out number you at least five to one, they will leave you alone. Mexicans are more like three to one, to their credit. I had learned these things the hard way, when I had been locked up in youth authority. The turnkeys showed up with coffee and breakfast, and I needed both. Redneck and I continued chatting over our breakfast, being careful to sit together on the bottom bunk with our backs to the wall. Just before lunch was served, they showed up for Redneck; someone had bailed him out. I was glad for him of course, but worried about my own ass left alone in the cell. He promised that he would go over to Herbie's house to find some of my Club Brothers, and let them know where I was and that I needed bailed out. "I'll do whatever it takes," he said as he walked out the cell door. Then, he turned and looked at all the inmates and said "You better leave my Bro alone!" They did, and my Brothers showed up about 3:30 that afternoon to bail me out, and man, was I happy to be out of that cell!

I thanked Gentle Jim and Doc as they drove me back to Herbie's place, using his car that they had borrowed. They filled me in on how everyone was doing. Johnny was gonna make it, although he had been stabbed in the back with a six inch blade. He came close to bleeding to death, until they were finally able to give him a transfusion, after the fight in the hospital got broken up. Stretch had been pierced with a three inch stab wound below his rib cage, and had been treated and released. He would later have Red Beard tattoo swastikas on each side of his scar. They said that unbelievably, that no one else from our group had been arrested. The cops apparently hated this guy, as he had hurt a cop years ago that he went to prison over, so they still had a hard on for him. They were happy about locking him up again, so we were been very lucky as far as the law went. There were mixed feelings about me going back to stab some of them fuckers. For one thing, I had almost gotten a Member from another Club arrested, Go To. Everybody understood my anger and rage, but I had been taught better, and should have known the cops would be there. When we got to Herbie's I grabbed a much needed beer as one of the Brothers drew me out a line of crank. We were going to get out of dodge as soon as we could grab Johnny.

His old lady had driven up that morning in Johnny's truck, to grab him and his bike. Stretch, the tough bastard he was, was riding his rigid frame Harley home. Being out of our town in a strange area wasn't helping anything. Bail bonds and all that took a lot longer in those days, which was why I had sat in jail so long. Some of the Brothers wanted to stay and get some more revenge on them cowboys and especially the Hat, but Stretch explained that he wasn't going to be able to bail out. Nobody would have given a shit if they hadn't stabbed our people. If the fight had stayed a brawl, without the stabbings, it wouldn't have been a problem. Actually, we would have respected them for putting up a good fight. But, when they decided to use their knives, it got personal. The problem was, it was the cowboy con that had done all the stabbing. He would be locked up for years, so we couldn't get our revenge until he was released or maybe by Club friends in prison.

I had to go to court weeks later, so Danny the Duck took me in his pickup. We both had major tequila hangovers that morning, so I tried calling the courthouse to reschedule the court date. They just said that if I didn't show up, they would issue a bench warrant on me. We drove like madmen, with the worst tequila hangover I think I've ever had. We sat there in court until they finally called my name. That's when the District Attorney stood up and said his witness would no longer testify. The Judge kind of eyeballed me, slammed his hammer, and the case was dismissed. Thus, ending for me the biggest brawl I was ever in.

TEDDY BEAR, THE NOMADIC WARRIOR

I am devoting a chapter of these memoirs to one of the greatest Hell's Angels of his time, Teddy Bear, a giant among men. The reasons are many, but mainly because he was an inspiration to me. He was the main reason I joined with the Red & White. Later on, he also would be part of the reason I would leave them. He is mentioned in these memoirs often, as he was a major influence in my life and to all those who knew him. To me he *was* The Hell's Angels, and everything I thought I wanted them to be. I have glorified very few men in my life, but Teddy Bear is one that I am proud to. He was one of those men that had such an incredible life force. He believed in the God of Odin. Being a Viking by blood wasn't the only reason he believed in the whole Odin thing. "Thor, the God of War" was his hero. His conversations about it were similar to a preacher trying to convert you to Christianity. Their warrior code was pure religion to him. He would tell all his close Brothers, "Don't you ever let them bury me without a sword." I mean, he was adamant about it. In the Nomad Chapter of the Red & White, he was the God of War, Thor-like all the way. He killed for his beliefs. He was a soldier turned captain, and a natural leader, while Ted was a major player in the Gypsy Joker war in the '60s. This war was fought for the Club's turf, and the spoils of owning it.

Just the same as all wars that men have fought, that are sanctioned by a government, which makes it a legal killing war. A government sanctioned war of any group of men fighting one another for their right to exist in the world, and to claim and govern their own choice of turf is legal, even if some of its citizens are criminals. Is it wrong when an Outlaw Motorcycle Club takes an area of land and population as their own to live and prosper in, and govern with their own people, if some of their business's were illegal? So that illegal part then makes it murder to participate in a war, right? Depends on what side of the fence you are standing on, in my opinion. The Hell's Angels went on to win their war with the Gypsy Jokers, as well as other turf wars in California, and would go on to live and prosper on those turfs. There would be more 'turf challenges' waiting for them in the future, for sure. Just like the countless wars of others throughout history. "To the winner goes the spoil," that's history. You've got to wonder what Thomas Jefferson would have thought. How big of a group of people does it take to make a war right? I guess Jefferson's group was big enough for their 'legal' war, or there wouldn't be the USA, but I do think the British thought different of it.

Teddy Bear was a very large man, and intimidating due to his size and appearance, which was sort of the same build as a good-sized bear. A lot of Bear's weight was in his lower end, like a bear's. He had a cunning disposition of outward friendliness, and was loveable to all, like a Teddy Bear, but instantly ferocious, like a grizzly bear, if provoked. He once told me that he was approximately 280 to 300 pounds. But that wasn't all fat, for sure. In his presence, you knew you were talking to a very dangerous individual that you had better show respect to. You knew he could rip your head off and shit down your neck whenever he wanted. He was a real nightmare for some people, but a real hero to others. He was one of the more original old school type Members that had the distinction of a Ten Year Club buckle, when I knew him. One of the few of those buckles you ever saw. Five Year buckles are rare too, and you don't see a lot of them, either. They are considered to be one of the higher awards you can get. Unlike some clubs that sport membership year pins. Like always, the Angels always outclassed them with their membership buckles.

A Hell's Angel's life span on the street is very short. Most end up in prison or dead, because the law or someone *will* get you. Whether a motorcycle accident, a rival Club shoots you down, or the law busts you as you're life's at constant risk. So when you see a Hell's Angel with a Five Year or more buckle, you are looking at a very cunning survivor. Hell's

Angels are some of the meanest, badass, toughest men to walk the earth. The world should fear them, and those that know them *do*. There was an old R&W hand drawn poster back in the '60s that had about five or six Club Members from the early days on it. They were all arm and arm, all fucked up and grinning. One of them was Teddy Bear. I believe Animal, The Pink Panther, and J. Witt, were on it. I use to have one, but lost it when I blew out of California. I haven't seen one in over 30 years.

Teddy Bear was a legend in his own time in the motorcycle world he lived in. Like Wild Bill Hickok, the famous gunfighter that was a legend in his own time, so would Teddy Bear be in our Biker world. Few men get to be famous in the world they live in during their own time, and most that find that kind of notoriety unpleasant anyway. That notoriety usually becomes their demise, as it would be for Bear. He was by no means a Heavenly Angel, but he was an Angel among Angels. Ted was a criminal in the citizen's world, but a hero in the biker's world. He had a tattoo on his shoulder blade that I never seen anywhere else. It read, "The only God fearing thing that God fears himself, is an Angel in the fast lane." I think that just about says it all.

The most famous true story about Teddy Bear goes like this. He and Uncle John were doing a big drug deal with a couple of non-members in Vallejo, CA. They had been doing business for a while with some long-haired citizen drug dealers, providing them with large amounts of methamphetamine and other drugs. This drug deal went bad, an argument started, everybody pulled their guns, and the shooting started. Both sides started blasting away at each other. Bear and John killed both of the drug dealers, but not before Uncle John took a shot through the heart with a very popular High Standard stainless steel two-shot Derringer's .22 magnum bullet. A small bullet, but lethal, especially if it's a hollow point and severs your main artery to your heart. Uncle John, a well liked and respected badass Hell's Angel, a large strong man, bled out because of that tiny bullet. He was mourned by all Members, and other people whom he knew, and had a big funeral.

Teddy Bear took two .357 magnum bullets in the chest. Then, he unbelievably crawled out of the house where the gunfight took place, and made his way out onto the sidewalk before he passed out, leaving a large blood trail right to where he drug himself. This triggered the neighbors to have enough balls to call 911, which would save his life. He was the only one to survive the gunfight, although it's hard to imagine taking two .357's Magnums in the chest. But if you knew Bear, you would have no doubt that he did! Bear barley survived, and it eventually took some of his inner strength away, but his legend only grew. In the bike world I lived in, this was our OK Corral shoot-out. You have two outlaw fractions fighting over making money, both in the same area. You throw in a little greed and jealousy, and men will fight for money, as well as a place to make it and spend it. These were the same exact things that caused the real OK Corral shoot-out. Money, power, and turf, are the same reasons why Angels fight for their rights, even today.

Teddy Bear told me this story himself. He claimed that the guys were a couple of greedy assholes that got wrung out on their own dope. The story on the street was that Ted and John were trying to burn or strong arm these two dealers, in order to rip these guys off for all their money and local dope business. Because they were R&W, they could get away with it. Who on the street would challenge them? These two drug dealers did, but the meth in those days *did* make you feel like King fucking Kong, and would cause its users to act without fear or rationality. The two drug dealers died for their bravado, or should we call it stupidity, or maybe it was just paying the price for the game they played. I don't know for sure which story is true, but I don't think it really matters, because the world had lost Uncle John. It was also the beginning of the end of Bears invulnerability. Both were good Angels.

Here is another famous exploit of Bears that was legendary. The story goes that during the war with the Gypsy Jokers, Bear, who was well known by them, managed to collect about 20 of their patches without firing a shot, or so the story goes. I never asked Teddy about this one, and he never brought it up. I heard the story many times, and will tell it the best as I can recall. Teddy found out about a chapter 'Church' the Jokers were having, about their confrontation with the Hell's Angels. Bear armed himself to the teeth and confronted their Security and Prospects at the door. He bullied and bullshitted his way into the meeting. He explained to them they had two choices. They could either give up their

Patches to him, or he was gonna kill every one of them, it was their choice. Now, when I told you that Teddy was a menacing looking Motherfucker, I meant it. He had a badass reputation and all, but he was just one of those men you meet in life that you know is deadly. When you walked into a bar with him, nobody took their eyes off ya, while doing their best to not let you notice that they're watching.

Amazingly, he walked out of that Joker meeting with their Club Colors and burned them. You can only imagine the brass balls this Bear had, and fearless for his own safety, as they should have killed him. But, with his bravado, he scared the shit out of them, so there was no fight. No one wanted to challenge his confidence and strength at the cost of fighting 'The Bear'. This only added to his legend and power amongst his fellow Angels, *and* with the whole bike world. In retrospect, he may have saved some of their lives, as he dammed sure might have saved some of his own Brother Angels too, just as he had helped end the war without as much bloodshed as there could've been. Bear was the Viking warrior of modern times, and believed totally in reincarnation. Like I say, he was a man among men. As for the Gypsy Jokers, they lost their war and retreated mostly up to Oregon and Washington, where they grabbed some other turf, or so the legend goes.

Teddy did live in the fast lane, and he helped create it, or was just it! He was, as I say, a fearless individual. He started out in a Club called The Ravens, and quickly went on from there. Drug dealing was his main gig, but whatever made money as well. It was said that he had done some contract hit work in his past. I heard of his immortality and fame before I even met him, as The Gladiators knew and loved him, before I knew them. They had drug and other dealings with him, including hiding some of the machine guns for him that was used in the Gypsy Joker War, or so the legend goes. The Placerville area was Teddy Bear's, as far as he and the R&W was concerned, so The Gladiators answered to him. That's how I got to meet him as a young Prospect for the Gladiators. The first time we met, I was told to get over to Dirty Ricks pad and do what I was told, we had a visiting Angel that needed to be taken care of. "Whatever he wants you get, no matter what it is," Dirty Rick had said. Teddy Bear was up bedding with Rick's young sister, whom we will call Shannon. Her and

Bear had a thing going since Shannon had been 15 years old. Dirty Rick introduced us and Ted said "Your kind of young for a Prospect aren't you?" I said "Yeah" and Bear says, "I sure could use some Reds." I was dealing them at the time, and told him I would be right back. I was only 17 years old then. I hopped on my bike and fetched some for him from where I had them stashed, and then, when I gave him the reds, he struck up a conversation with me. He was impressed with how young I was and that I was prospecting for The Gladiators. He told me that I reminded him of himself when he was young and joining The Ravens MC. He actually thanked me for scoring for him, and gave me a wink, letting me know that he would help me sometime. When I left Ricks, I don't think my bike tires even touched the ground, as I was so elated to meet the Legend! All the Red & White I had met before had always pretty much ignored Prospects from other clubs. They would fuck with you, saying "Go get me a beer" and shit. You weren't high enough up the social ladder for them to show any interest in you. When you are a prospect in other Clubs, you fetch and carry for any Patched Member from any club, but not if you are prospecting for the Angels. A Hell's Angel Prospect answers to nobody but them. Once you were patched a full Member in another non-Angel Club though, it was different, because then you had earned some respect from them. A lot of it was also just gaining trust with the Angels. They were very cautious of anybody until they grew up through the ranks. Call it a safety zone, but that's how they stayed alive and out of jail.

Teddy was different, though. If he liked you on first impressions, he would check you out. Dirty Rick told me later that after I left to go score for Ted, he asked what the story was on me. That flattered the shit out of me and began my gain of respect for him. When he would look at you with those piercing blue eyes as he talked to you, it was like they were looking right through you, straight at your heart. You were lucky if he liked what he saw, and *very* unlucky if he didn't. He was one of the most incredible individuals I have ever known. If he liked you, you would fall in love with his heart and his ways. I only had the pleasure of running with him for a little over three years, with my only wish being that I could have had the pleasure of more. Don't get me wrong, he *was* a criminal with a huge ego. He lived life as fast and hard as you can, and got away with it longer than most. He did evil as his lifestyle demanded, but had a good humorous side to him as well. There was something about him that you rarely see in people. A man among men, as the saying goes. If you had dealings with him and you were his friend, you would always come out square. That was hard to do with most Angels back then. We always partied with the best drugs, shared women and had fun. He is one of the few men I have had trouble keeping up with riding motorcycles and partying with. Ted *was* the fast lane! I tried not taking the money for the Reds deal, but Rick told him I had bought his old Panhead. Ted said, "You better take the money to put into your new bike. Knowing Dirty Rick, you'll need it." He was right. But I would have gladly given him the Reds for free. One of his little famous sayings I remember was "There's no sin in a little profit!"

I saw him once in a while at Rick's, or when the Angels came up to party with The Gladiators, or even when we would go where they asked us to be, and I would get a short visit with him. He would go out of his way to talk to me. Some of his Brothers, you could tell, didn't think much of that, or would look on with a curiosity, almost jealousy. I knew his reputation, and was warned by my Gladiator Brothers as to whom I was dealing with. "He is the *real* deal" Stretch said to me. It was funny, I knew I should have fear, but I didn't. I felt a trust for him that I would carry with me until his disappearance. I would have followed him into hell, if he would have tried to take me there with him. The Gladiators finally patched me at the illegal age of 19 years old (you were supposed to be 21, according to Club bylaws). From then on, Ted and I were more 'socially correct' hanging out. He would leave a message that he was coming up from Vallejo. We would take drugs, ride our motorcycles and women over, and party for days. We dropped some of the best acid and drugs together. Then, we'd go try to ride our bikes as fast as we could on Chili Bar Grade, which was a very curvy road. These were the best of times. The drugs were the best then too, and Harleys were fast enough to kill ya. Women were loose, and free love was still flowin'. The law wasn't too good then, as they had no real computers yet, so breaking the law was a lot easier back then.

I had met Mouse and Joe N. when they were in the Nomads, both eventually transferred to the Sacramento Angel Chapter. Both were legendary bad Motherfuckers, by their own rights. They were kind of cold until Teddy Bear asked me about whether or not I liked them. I shrugged and said that I really didn't know them personally. He insisted on going to visit them to introduce me. After that they treated me with a different respect. Same with Lonesome, Sacramento's legendary Chapter President. He was one of the first Hell's Angels I saw when I was a kid around Sacramento, CA. Ted always introduced me as a Brother, which was socially incorrect by the Biker's code. He should have said Bro, or cousin. You can't be a Club Members Brother unless you wear his Patch, or are related by blood. So every time he did this, I got nervous. It was showing me the ultimate respect, but in a dangerous way. I just knew one day I would get my ass kicked over it. I never did though, I just got evil looks. Sometimes they would frown at me, jealous of Teddy's attention he paid to me, except Ted's closest Brothers. They would just smile knowingly. It's like they knew, I was sharing their bond with Teddy.

At the time, I was living with a whore named Shari that worked up at Moonlight Ranch whorehouse, as I mentioned in a previous chapter. She set me up with a pad and all the fixings. She took me down to Lonesome's shop, California Chopper Supply. She bought a bunch of parts for my Panhead. That's when Lonesome told me I had to join the Modified Motorcycle Association. That was an R&W brainchild of the times that would grow into a huge bike organization of its own. I asked him what the MMA was all about and he said, "Just join it." I asked how many members there were and he said, "I think you would be the fourth one. Tell your entire Club they have to join also. It's only five bucks." My whore paid for it and the bike parts. After Shari left for Nevada to go back to work at the whorehouse, I invited Ted, Joe, Mouse, and Lonesome over to party at my house, while the El Dorado County fair was going on, and while my good fortune lasted. I also had a little 16 year old house-mouse chick for entertainment that would hang around while the whore was on her two week tour of duty (whores obviously don't work while they are on the rag).

Joe and a couple other members had their way with the house-mouse that night at my party, after the fair ended. I had Shari coming home that next morning. She was supposed to call me to pick her up at the bus stop, but one of my fellow Member's old ladies showed up with her, and had given me up about my party. I think she wanted me shut down because her old man was spending too much time over there partying with me while Shari wasn't home. So this whore, Shari, threw me out over the mouse being there, along with other girls, and my Hell's Angel guests. Then the brother of the house-mouse wanted to kill me over what happened. But we had a wild party that night, and I was actually glad to being kicked out, as I had had enough of being attached to that whore! Shari asked me to come back and I did, but it only lasted a month and I finally quit our relationship. Of course, after I left her and the news hit the street, some of my Brothers were over there that night trying to fuck her. It really didn't bother me much, because after all, she was a whore.

Don't get me wrong, I would have stayed a loyal member of The Gladiators all my life. I wish we could have kept our Brotherhood going. But history is what it is. At that time in my life, I was a drug dealer and a thief. After the whore, I moved my ass to a remote little rental house in a remote location. Danny the Duck and Poncho helped me keep it stocked with stolen shit. We had everything that was worth anything. We were running out of room to put it all. The Duck had a new one-ton flatbed truck we used. We would find someone who wanted some building materials and we would fill their order. We always tried to get rid of everything right away. Sitting on shit is a good way to get busted. When you're doing a burglary, it's like shopping, hard not to keep from picking the shit up. If the law had ever raided that place, I'd probably still be in jail. At the ages of 19 and 20, I just didn't give a shit about anybody or anything. You could say that I had no morals and that would be an understatement. We slowed down on the thieving after we got a message from above.

We had previously cased out a remote place to do a burglary. On a rainy, stormy night the three of us had stashed the one-ton truck and were walking across their field to make sure the owners were gone. It was pitch black, with strong winds, and storming all around us. All of a sudden, there was a loud BOOM, and a flash that blinded us and sent us to our knees. Lighting had struck right in the middle of us! It temporarily blinded us, as we rolled around in the mud trying to see and recover from the blow that had knocked us down. After a few minutes our eyesight returned, and we all decided that it was a message from someone to leave that place alone, and maybe slow down. After that incident the Reds started drying up on the scene, and it did my body and soul some good to slow down. My favorite motto back then was "It's better to rule in hell, than serve in heaven." Today I am not very proud of my stealing and drug dealing days of that time period, as I had no heart for most anything.

Like all good things, they come to an end. Teddy got busted on a machine gun rap. Sidecar Larry had introduced him to a Bro of mine we will call Tran. Tran was a fun loving Club Member who was a 1%, that just loved to party and ride on his motorcycle, as well as play with guns. He came from a family of four brothers who were all the same, as they all rode Harleys and partied with the best of 'em. I loved them all, and still do party and ride with the ones that are still alive. Tran had done some serious 'spook' shit in the Vietnam War. He got involved with the CIA doing some black ops flying, so he could get about anything he wanted state-side. Tran just happened to have some M-2 conversion kits that were for sale or trade, for some good product. The deal also involved some Sten machine guns that were George Wethern's favorites. Tran also sent along a special gift that was supposed to be given to 'the old man', a Ma Deuce .50 caliber. He told me decades later, that they were lucky that the cops didn't catch them with the hand grenades and dynamite.

You know how boys will be boys. The kits turned an M-1 carbine into a fully automatic weapon, which is one of my favorite. They are a US military weapon that are light, short, have high capacity clips, and as dependable as they get. These little carbines were produced during WWII by the millions. Before all the imported AK-47s and SKS rifles, they were very popular with the Old School Bikers, as a lot of them had used them in their military service. But the Feds didn't allow us to have the M-2 conversions to make them fully automatic. Ted was hoping that Tran and Larry were going to fight it. But their lawyers said that they didn't have a chance, and was trying to negotiate a plea bargain. Larry was looking at least three years, and Tran five, in the Federal joint. Ted was bummed out, because he knew what that meant for his case. His lawyer said that they had Bear by the balls, and intended to squeeze them.

Some how to me it seemed like Ted was untouchable, that no one could take him. You got that feeling about some of the Hell's Angels a lot, because of their lawyers. First, when they get busted, the Club bails them out immediately. Then, they have the top criminal lawyers on retainer. Melvin Belie and John Hill was a couple of them, back in the old days. So they would postpone and delay, and basically use every legal trick they had up their sleeve. These cases sometimes went on for years. Their code was you deny, plead innocent and then take it to jury trials, never copping up to anything. Dragging cases out helped a lot because of witness dying, or deciding not to testify, as they start worrying about their safety. Or, their stories would get vague, giving the lawyers more time to try and beat it. They would always immediately appeal every conviction. Of course, this was very expensive and drained Chapter coffers. One of the law's tricks was to arrest Angels on anything they could, to try to break down the R&W financially.

They also want you to cop a plea deal to lesser charges, so they can put you away later for being a habitual criminal. Sidecar and Tran might not have had the resources, but the Bear did, and was prepared to fight it all the way. So this was a seriously bad bust for all involved, and they were all facing Federal time. Ultimately, Sidecar and Tran got a high dollar lawyer and went to a jury trial, but the Fed's had an Ace up their sleeve. An Oakland Member, named Don Moore, rolled on everybody to save his own Rat ass. He gave them all up to the ATF and burned everybody's ass to save his own! Larry and Tran were finally convicted and went to do their time within a year. Tran pulled five years and Sidecar got three. Ted with his high dollar R&W lawyers would postpone and delay his conviction until his disappearance. That was the beginning of the end of Bear's era, in our area. Hangtown Bill, who once was President of The Gladiators, had joined the R&W Nomads. Simply put, Bill wanted Placerville's action for himself.

The methamphetamine market was really starting to boom and there was a lot of money to be made. With Ted's problems, he was losing his control over his Placerville turf, and soon it would be up for grabs. About then was when Hangtown called a meeting with The Gladiators. To our total surprise, he told us the Hell's Angels were shutting The Gladiators down for good. Either we join the Hell's Angels with full patches given to each member, or not. The only option we had was to go to war with the R&W, which was nothing more than a death sentence. Either way, The Gladiators MC was over. The vote to fold was unanimous, except for me. To fight them would have been suicide. Most of my Brothers had families, and didn't want to be R&W. Hangtown's plan worked very well, as he was able to take over the area's developing speed market. Hangtown held on to his turf until he died a wealthy man, with a ranch, Harleys, an airplane, etc... I was now no longer a Patch Holder and I would be bitter over losing the best Brotherhood I would ever be in.

This was about the time when Teddy started trying to get me to come down to Vallejo to join the Nomads. It was a life long dream for me, and so far I liked most of the members I had met. But the ones Ted introduced were the best. I was down there, hanging around at Ted's in Vallejo, when he decided we should go for a ride. We ended up back in Coloma in my old stomping grounds. He wanted to see Sidecar Larry to find out about how his defense was going on that machine gun rap that Ted and he were involved in. We brought along some good party drugs. I called a few party girls. Larry let us stay in his RV trailer. We partied hardy, indulging in all the good sins of the times, drinking, smoking hash and pot, eating reds and LSD, snorting crank and cocaine, and screwing these babes. As long as you fed these girls drugs and booze, they would do whatever you wanted. We used to call them "Roman orgies," trading the women back and forth. Then, we would work up to going for rides with the babes. I remember we rode up to Georgetown to visit Limey John's grave.

Limey John was another extraordinary Hell's Angel. His front end on his bike collapsed on him doing about seventy miles an hour killing him instantly. He was well liked and had a huge funeral. Limey used to always say, "Party all ya want, butcha gotta eat." When you were partying with him, he would always make you eat. Teddy always got real serious when we were at his gravesite, as he said he missed him. We rode our way back through the curvy mountain roads, back to Coloma. This guy comes up behind us in a new corvette. He tried to pass, but Ted wouldn't have it.

The race was on. To this day I can't believe we didn't crash. We were taking corners doing at least 100mph, I'm guessing, as we had no speedometers. The Vet finally dropped out of sight in our mirrors. He could gain on us on the straight-aways, but not on the corners, so he was ours. When we got back to Sidecar's place, Teddy said, "You ride as well as me." That was a compliment I have always held dear in my heart. Ted was one of the best, fearless riders I have ever ridden with.

That is when Teddy approached me about a score. Ted needed some money for his lawyer. He and another guy had devised a plan to rip off this Cat. He was a punk for a Rock musician. I won't mention his name, because I don't want to get sued, but his initials were J. T. This Cat let this guy suck his dick; whatever. I was introduced to this punk and went over and sold him drugs a few times so that I could case the place. Teddy's plan was simple. He would finance the U-haul truck under a phony identity, and fence the shit for his part. Ted's buddy and I would do the burglary. We would wait until we knew that this punk would go to visit his cocksucker sugar Daddy. Simple in and out, and we take everything. I mean everything, including guns, stereos, a TV, oak furniture, guitars, a drum set. Also, recording equipment, jewelry, camping and fishing equipment, everything. Everything went smooth, until this punk dude's house-mouse shows up unexpectedly. Yeah, he had some pussy on the side he was two timing on his sugar Daddy with, which we didn't know about. What was worse was that she knew me by face, and reputation. Here we were, in a hell of a spot. My partner in this crime thought that we should take care of her in a permanent way, saying "She's in the wrong place at the wrong time!" I told him that was crazy, as I knew her! We didn't know what else to do, so we threatened to hurt her if she told him we did it. Then, we told her we would tell the punk's musician that she was in on it if she did tell, and we would cut her in on some bucks if she kept quiet, so she agreed. We got the load down to Vallejo to Ted's house so he could get it fenced and turned it all into cash.

Teddy gets this phone call from a Sacramento Member who had been contacted by our mark. Obviously, the chick had to have given us up. The musician wanted his shit back, and was willing to pay us all a good price for returning it with no questions asked. I guess the guitars were priceless to the musician. In the end, we all made money without the cops involved, nor any retributions. They wondered if they could pay us extra to go ahead and deliver it. Sometimes, the power of the Patch even amazed *me*. To her credit, I guess the house-mouse got beat up pretty good before she gave us up. Once again, Teddy come out shining, and saved the day. The musician didn't want any trouble with the R&W. Even though he could have gone to the law, Teddy's reputation of sweet talking people proved true, and he had saved us again. I heard the musician fired his punk boyfriend.

After I was made a Prospect, I had a lot of members come up to me and tell me that I got the short end of the stick from Bear on that deal. Kanuck said, "Look at all the money you could have made," and he was right. I replied, "Yeah, I could have made about 10 times what I got. But, I didn't go to jail." Unfortunately, his fellow Brothers that were Bear's enemies used that fiasco against him. That was the beginning, I feel, of what was to come.

I remember my first 'Church' with the Nomads, after I had begun hanging around. I was staying at Teddy's house then. We parked our bikes in front of Luck's house. Chief handed me a hundred-dollar bill. He told me to go get some Bacardi Rum and coke, and six cases of beer. There were proably 20 members in attendance. I went outside to organize the liquor run, together with the other Prospects. I could put the rum and coke in my saddlebags. I learned while prospecting for The Gladiators how to carry three cases of beer on my bike; it was pretty easy, but four was my short ride personal best. So I couldn't carry it all and needed some help. We also needed to keep security at the meeting. That's when I could hear Teddy yelling at the whole chapter, "Fuck this and fuck that." Then, he called them all a bunch of pusses! There were a lot of bad men in there. Bear come storming out and said to me, "You had better stay here!" He jumped on his bike and did a burn-out as he split. That was the second time I fore-saw trouble coming.

I finally got my Prospect patch, along with a coveted California bottom rocker. I rode with Teddy Bear to the Bass Lake Run. That's probably the biggest California run of the year. Ted's old lady, Becky, hauled all our booze and camping shit in Ted's truck. We stopped at a bar that had about 50 bikes parked out front. I could tell by the paint jobs that there were a lot of R&W members inside. To be honest, I was a little nervous. Teddy kind of gave me a funny, puzzled look as we were going in. "Come on, lets go in", as he smiled. We walked in and the bar was full, shoulder-to-shoulder down the length of the bar with Hell's Angel Members. Everybody's all "Hey Teddy Bear, what's happening'?" Teddy's greeting everybody with hugs and back slaps and he had pretty much got everybody's attention. Then, he introduces me as his new Nomad Prospect. I got a few handshakes and "Heys", with everybody eye-balling me now. Ted's a legend to most of these Members. Even though there are a lot of egos, they all wanted to talk to Teddy, and I felt kind of out of place as I tried to fade out of the spotlight. Teddy bought me a drink as everybody else was buying him one. But, he made a point of buying me a drink in front of everybody. Then, he hands me the beer and says, "How come you hit me in the head with that wine bottle last night?" There was pure silence, as all these members just started eye-fucking me. I wanted to find a hole and crawl in, quick and deep! "I didn't hit you with a bottle," I responded. "Yeah, you did, and it hurt," Bear said as he started rubbing his head, playing it up. They all just looked at me in awe, as he says, "Next time we get drunk on wine, I am gonna pay you back." He wraps his big arm around me, and starts laughing. That's how Teddy Bear introduced me to these guys. They all just stared at me in disbelief, as I was pretty skinny then. I thought that one of them might light me up. Who was this new guy to hit their legend in the head with a wine bottle? Teddy put me in a spot, but it was his way of introducing me to a bunch of Angels and gaining their respect for me. He was also showing me to be fearless and bold. Also, it was a fast way of bringing me into his world. I admit it scared me. But I also got a lot of respect quickly for just being a new, nobody Prospect. You've got to have balls to play this game, or they won't even remember your name. You've got to put your life on the line, and believe in The Club. Being a Hell's Angel is a lifestyle of total commitment to their world. It's not a part-time thing. You have to totally commit yourself to the Brotherhood. Everything else in your life isn't important. If you have to die for the Club, so be it. If you have to go to prison, you will go. Your life becomes the Club's, as your Brothers become your only world, as you have sold your soul to it!

When Teddy introduced you to his special Brothers, it was different. They would instantly start a relationship with you. It was like the wall came down. They would expose their true selves to you and start an instant, knowing bond. Teddy and I rode down to the strip club in Vallejo one time, because he told me that he had a Bro he wanted me to meet. There, shooting pool was a huge Member from the Oakland Chapter, named Pie. He had a portable police scanner going. You could just hear it over the music. He says, "Hey, it's my Brother Teddy Bear, give me the big Bear hug." I could see that they were very close as Brothers, as they both tongued each other with a big sloppy Brothers kiss. I had heard of Pie, and by reputation, he was one crazy Motherfucker! He *looked* intimidating. He always carried matching 9mm pistols in shoulder holsters, under his cut-off. In those days, everyone had heard of Pie carrying his beloved UZI. He always carried it when he was doing security for Sonny, even if he was on his bike.

Unbelievably, he worked for Coca Cola since he was young, and made good money. After Teddy's hug and kiss with him, he turned and introduced us. "This is my little Brother," he says, and there was that socially incorrect intro again. He says, "Hey, my Brother how are you doing? Any Brother of Teddy's is a Brother of mine. This is the one you been telling me about." He then gave me this big hug. We talked and shot pool most of the afternoon. I did my Prospect thing, checking on the bikes every 15 minutes. The strippers were all over Pie. He was Samoan and Hawaiian by birth, a big, intimidating man. Everybody said "Sir" to him, because he was just one of those big, individual warrior types. I liked him right away. He started calling me his "Little Brother" from then on. He was one of Teddy's closest Brothers in 'The Teddy's Elite Club', as I used to think of it.

Prospect Chuck and other members joined us. We kept on for most of the day. We shot pool while we drank beer, snorted crank, and watched the strip-shows. Members, Bikers and Swabbies came and went. Teddy said he had to go take care something. Pie finally said he was gonna putt back to the Oakland clubhouse. He then asked Chuck and me if we wanted to ride along. Things had quieted down at the club, so what the fuck. Besides, the Members always told us to try to get know Members from other chapters. So we decided to ride back with him, as became a habit with us.

It was late afternoon and the weather was beautiful. We were on our way to Oakland when the California Highway Patrol jacked us up. They did the usual warrant checks, not very accurate, nor more than state-wide, if even that back then. They were only good for the main populated areas of California. They would call into the station on there radio, and wait while they were being checked. Not like today's units, that can find out the last place you took your last shit from their patrol car computer. Anyway, we were waiting for the call back on wants and warrants, and this young cop pisses Pie off. Pie says, "How old are you?" This young cop says, "It is none of your business." Pie says, "You asked me how old I was. How much money you make in a year?" "That's none of your business either," the young cop complained. "I bet you that I make three times as much as you," Pie replied. The young cop didn't know what to say as he just stared at Pie with his face turning red and the veins sticking out of his neck. Well I think this shit is getting funny, but Chuck didn't. Chuck had a Nevada driver's license, and the problem was that his last name wasn't Johnson, as the license said. Whenever Chuck got a ticket on his Nevada license, he had to go get a new one. Chuck had been doing this for years. I was also afraid that the cops would pat down Pie and find his guns. They didn't, and finally cut us loose. We finally made it over to the Oakland Clubhouse.

This was about that fateful time that Ted got busted on a large crank deal. He wouldn't normally have sold to a guy like this probably, but he was hurting for cash that he owed his lawyers for working on the federal gun rap. He was in deeper trouble now. His lawyer was telling him that he would proably get 25 years for what they had on him, between state and federal charges. He had enough priors that a conviction meant real time. Bear's back was up against the wall. He was cornered like a wild, un-tamed bear, about to be captured and put in a cage at a zoo. Prison was no different, if you ask me. Sidecar Larry finally got convicted and got three years, for just introducing Bear to Tran. Tran got five years, and this looked bad, as two of his fellow conspirators were both convicted for the same rap. So that just left Bear, who they had been wanting for a long time. No telling what they would give Teddy, but it looked like his freedom was coming to an end. When you get in that position, it is very stressful. I have been there, and I was only facing 10-plus years. You start worrying about everything. Your old lady, your Club, your Brothers, your bike, and everything else you own. You know your old lady's gonna find someone else. If you are going to due more than a year, you might as well cut her loose. Otherwise, it will drive you nuts when you are doing your time, and it turns into an even worse fucking nightmare.

Whether you decide to do the time, or go on the run, it doesn't really matter, because you have basically lost your life. Other options are death by suicide, or snitching, which can hold its own death sentence. Snitching means protective custody, and that is the same as being on the run, except with your family in tow, trying to hide them as well. Could you live with yourself for putting them through that? How do you turn your back on everything, and everyone you knew? How could you live with yourself, ruining your entire Brother's and their family's lives? If you have never been in this position, it is hard to imagine. Twenty-five years means you've lost everything, including your freedom. Teddy Bear was hard core, and true to the Biker Code. For Christ's sake, he helped invent it! I believe that he didn't even consider snitching, but some of his Brothers were worried, as he could easily take them out, as well as a whole lot of other Angels. Cookers and dealers with a whole network of methamphetamine production and sells were some of the people who he knew that could be taken down. I refuse to believe he would even consider snitching, to this day.

His lawyer told him that he was worried that they might try the RICO act on him, as he was in as deep as it gets. The law had finally cornered him. His lawyer told him to get some kind of a job to show how he supported his family. He told him to disassociate with the Club while he was getting ready to go court. He got a truck driving job for a couple days a week. That was the first anyone knew of Ted working. I had moved out of his house before all this came down. The cops had around the clock surveillance on him. Just going to see him or meet him was incriminating.

When I talked to him, he said he wasn't going to do the time, but was gonna run and figure a way out for his family to come with him. To do it with your family is really a pipe dream. To do it and get away with it though, you have to leave it *all* behind. Everything, including your old lady, kids, Mom, family, bike, Club, and Brothers would have to be left behind. Everybody would be lost to you, forever. I would face this, later on in my life.

As a matter of fact, it was 1989 and I planned on going to Alaska. I knew some Vietnam Vet Marines up there that would have helped me start over. I planned to never return home, nor see the ex or my children again, because that's what you have to do. I had my plane ticket in hand, and called my lawyer from the airport to say "adios." He proceeded to tell me that because of a technicality, the DA offered me a deal of no more than five years, and had continued the hearing. I began to realize that I would get out in time to see my kids graduate from high school, and be able to start over with them, in some way, and maybe be able to get to know my kids again. To me, it was worth going to the joint for five years. For ten years, I was gonna run, because my kids would hardly remember me by the time I got out. For ten years, I would take the chance and go rabbit and have to put it all behind me and start an entirely new life; but, that was just me. What would I do facing 25 years? I'll put it in a six letter word, and that's BYEBYE. Living in prison that long is worse than a death sentence for people like us, who have lived so free for so long.

So what does Teddy Bear do? What would you do? Teddy disappeared out of my life, and out of the Hell's Angels world, forever, and his family was left behind. What happened to his family? My Bro, Chuck, with whom I had prospected with had been patched just before this happened. After Teddy disappeared for a while, Chuck moved in with Becky, into Teddy's house, to help out. He sort of took Teddy's place. A hard pair of boots to fill, for sure, as he helped raise Teddy's little girl. Chuck is a good man in his heart, and Teddy always liked him, a lot. I did hear that Chuck got killed in a bike wreck a lot of years later, but I am still trying to find out for sure. Teddy Bear may have lost it all and ended up paying the ultimate price for what he believed in. An Outlaw trying to live in the wrong time was *his* sin. He lived in the fastest lane, as fast as one can, and eventually lost control and crashed.

You'll wonder what happened to him now, as I do. To my knowledge, he was never busted or seen again, and I believe he never will be. I like to believe that Bear started over in some other country, and is riding in the wind. If he is gone to see Odin, I only pray that he had a sword with him, because that's the way he would have wanted it. His legacy, exploits, reputation, and deeds, will only grow larger with time, as those of us still alive remember. His name and stories are still told in some circles, but those circles are getting smaller. I hope he now has a place in your heart, maybe a place in history, as I know that he would have liked that. I know he is dead, but his spirit is still with me, and I know that he has that sword! Teddy Bear was larger than life and got what he wanted, which was to be one of the greatest Hell's Angels that has ever lived. I believe that was, and *is*, his legacy.

HELL'S ANGEL BEGINNINGS

I lived the biker lifestyle and tried my damndest to become a Hell's Angel, which was a youthful dream of mine that I believed was my destiny. I believe the HAMC (Hell's Angels Motorcycle Club) is probably the hardest Brotherhood to join is in the world, and only a few men get the chance to join. As the saying goes, AFFL (Angels Forever, Forever Angels), that's the way it is. Angels, and other 1% Outlaw Clubs, believe they are the best of the badass people, and that theirs is one of the greatest societies in the world. Unfortunately, the law and the rest of society don't believe this, which means that Brothers will be persecuted, probably forever, for their different beliefs. But until you have been around that lifestyle, you really won't know what it is truly like, or if it is really for you. For most men, they just don't have the nerve or the balls to find out! The Outlaw world is for the brave and strong-willed, for those that have a sense of freedom and non-conformity born into them. I believe it comes from your gene pool, as some men just can't accept society's uneventful, mundane life of punching a daily clock that we are all expected to live.

True Outlaw Bikers probably make up approximately 30 per 1,000,000 people amongst citizens, and then there's Sonny B, whose type only make up about one in 1,000,000,000. These men of leadership, organization, and foresight are few and far between. Leaders and rebels of society's freedom loving non-conformists, they will live and die for a different cause than normal men. They live for their personal freedom and that of their Brothers. They want the right to be individuals within their own kind, and to do the things they love. They want the freedom to enjoy the thrills of riding their motorcycles 100 mph, of popping wheelies, and of getting high as their hobbies. They are thrill seekers that are not afraid to live on the edge of the fast lane, but also are willing to pay the ultimate price; men that want to take life to the very edge of death, for the thrill of it. I have known many Outlaws in my life. Most have died young, or are sitting and rotting in prison for the rest of their lives.

While I was incarcerated, I talked many times through the cell bars to other Outlaws that were serving life sentences, and not one of them would trade their lives in for a normal one. Of course, they don't want to be locked up, but they know that they couldn't live a normal life, either. As a Nomad Prospect, we each got a Hell's Angel inmate that was doing a long prison sentence that we were told to write to. Some were doing time for taking care of Club business, and other crimes, but they were not to be forgotten by their Brothers. They were referred to and thought of as more political prisoners, rather than criminals. These kinds of men, to me, were the beginning of the hard core Outlaw types; the ones that had really started it all. The beginning years of the MCs forming were the most innocent years of Club Brotherhood and Motorcycling, in the height of its purity. Men banded together then, to go on group rides that eventually turned into runs, to party together, and for protection against growing jealousy and animosity.

Motorcycle Clubs have attracted freedom loving men, some that had served their country and had seen a lot of action, and wanted to live life for the thrills. Like I said, Outlaws are that special breed of men that are not your robot type conformists, seeking the wealth of the world. As a matter of fact, in the beginning, most couldn't have given a shit about material things. Their only real earthly possessions that they cared about then were there beloved Harley Davidson motorcycles, their metal steeds of freedom, and the Old Schooler's way of riding them; this is the way of life they chose. One of the leaders that spawned from those early Outlaw years, that would take MCs to another level in the '60s and beyond was, course, Sonny. He would lead the Hell's Angels to becoming a national phenomenon. The Membership he led then was, for sure, made up of the wild and crazy motorcycle riding, freedom loving, fanatical Bikers that took no shit from society, and were all Members with un-dying loyalty. These were the true 1%er's in the beginning, not yet corrupted by the drugs, and worse, the greed that hard drugs brought.

The early '70s brought the new generation of drugs and fast money, where you could find power, and make a fortune fast, by dealing. The outcome was that these drugs would eventually affect a lot of this country's society dramatically as a whole, and especially the MCs. As it did with the hippie movement of the same time, it would become the major contributing factor of change in the evolving Outlaw's and MCs world. With the beginning of the '70s came change in the world, like never before. My generation started the movements that would eventually change the world for good. By the end of the '60s, the age of innocence was gone, for the Hell's Angels, hippies, and everyone else. The drugs were getting more powerful and were being produced in much greater quantities. What started out as 'turning on' people to drugs instead became a multi-million dollar underground business of selling to them. The hippie age of free love and awareness and peace through sharing drugs was losing its original innocence, which had started widely with pot and acid. The addictive drugs like cocaine and methamphetamine had come about and people, including hippies and Bikers, began experimenting with it and getting strung out on it.

This also was the time of the sexual revolution, as sex was finally out in the open in America. The Vietnam War was still a booming business, but the American people were getting tired of it, mostly my generation. The big, green war machine was coming under scrutiny. Racial problems were coming to a head, and the gays were 'coming out of the closet' with their own movements. The virginity and innocence of the Motorcycle Clubs, hippies and free love movements of the '60s was changing. It wasn't just pot, hash, mushrooms, and acid available any more. The '70s started with the use of the harder, addictive drugs that were around, and there were plenty of them. There was a lot of cocaine, some heroin, and the beginning of the methamphetamine scourge was starting to spread quickly. Some of the MCs were right in the middle of the meth epidemic, as Bikers were some of the first that started using it. Adolph Hitler had his German chemists develop chemical formulas that produced some of the first early amphetamines for his super soldiers, generals, and himself. Some say that is where the first chemical formulas used in the early production of meth came from.

The No Needle law of the Angels, that Sonny began, was a savior of the bike world that I belonged to. Addiction to snorting, drinking, and eating meth and coke was bad enough. All the MCs that I ran with had zero needle use, inspired by Sonny's stance in our bylaws that were strictly enforced. If we had all turned into needle hypes, junkies, or spikers, it would have been much worse, for both the Bikers and the rest of society. The meth quality was getting better and better, and there was more of it, while cocaine was becoming more the choice of the richer part of society. Meth was called the poor man's drug, although the quality was almost at its peak, as the chemicals used in the manufacture of it were of the very best quality then. I had some meth that was so good that it was often mistaken for cocaine, as some of it was real hard to tell the difference. It had no real chemical hangover as the shit they make today does. The original chemicals used were the best, and were less harmful to your body, as well as more user friendly. When our government figured out what the chemicals were that they were using, of course, they banned and regulated them until they were unavailable to the cookers.

Eventually the cookers found other available chemicals that worked, but were worse for and harder on your body. This cat and mouse game has gone on for 30 years, with the cookers being forced to try different variants of the chemicals that have not yet been banned. By 1991 the good meth chemicals that didn't fuck you up physically were completely gone, for good. Just like the fate of good LSD chemicals. When the U.S. Government found Marijuana crossing our border by the tons, they came up with a fast solution. Simply spray the Mexican marijuana crops with poison called parquet, which would poison the crop and the ground it was grown on, in order to stop any future crops. This only led to the poor, Mexican farmers poisoning America's youth. Just like the defecation of Vietnam, they fucked up Mother Earth's ecology along with all of us at the same time. You can always count on the U.S. Government to always take care of things!

When the quality was gone from speed, I eventually quit taking *and* selling the shit. But in those early years, I did participate and watch as meth became an illegal empire in the bike world and along with it came the massive greed. I snorted, ate, dealt, and transported the shit. It became the way I made most of my living; it ran my life like that, on and off, until my last big drug bust in the early '90s. Even after I left California, I continued to make a lot of money dealing meth. I would get it from wholesale dealers that I had grown up with that also handled some of the Red & White product, which in my opinion, was the best ever made. These old biker Bros that knew my story and knew that I did not want to deal direct with some of the R&W Members myself anymore, sold it to me for a nominal fee, so I could still get all that I wanted. I would then transport it to other states and sell it, sometimes to people who had never even had the chance to try it. Of course, I feel some guilt about turning people onto it. The quality of the stuff I was selling though wasn't that harmful to your body. The real guilt I feel is for the people who didn't quit it like I did, when the quality went to shit. Their addictive personalities kept them using, and ruining their lives. During my time of running with the Hell's Angels was the worst my addiction ever got, as I had used it a lot while I was prospecting.

Even though I was young and strong then as a Prospect, meth was the only way I could keep up with living in the fast lane. I had gotten moderately addicted to White Crosses (Benzedrine) as a kid, before I got locked up in youth authority. When I got out, Bikers were turned on to meth, in astronomical, epidemic proportions. Meth then was just too good and cheap, especially the Red & White's shit. When I left California on the run from the law, I was forced to get clean for a while and schooled myself on the perils of addiction, including my own. The Angels did not trust anybody new at all in the beginning. They had the advantage of being able to personally screen prospective members through the acknowledgement of other Bikers, and not having to rely on a computer's data. They could check a man out by talking to other Bikers of that area from where the prospect said he came from. When they started getting too big and growing too fast, they lost some of their caution and personal touch, and then they started to get some undesirables filtering in. Of course, in those early days, there were not as many Bikers as there are today.

You knew all of the Bikers that lived in your area that rode a Harley. Biker's being so few gave the MCs the advantage of secrecy and access to knowledge of people, even the old men with the garbage baggers to the stripped-down Harley bikes of the 1% type. The Bikers of that era knew each other, or knew *of* each other, criminal or not. You even knew the 'sidewalk commandos', which were nothing but wannabes that couldn't get it together enough to get a Harley, although they dressed the part of being a badass, greasy, leather strewn Biker. They were mostly drugged out jailbirds, dreaming of owning a scooter and belonging to a Club. As a kid dutifully selling drugs on the main drag in my hometown, I would stand in reverence and awe, as Club Members would pass by on the streets, flying their Colors on their beautiful Harley choppers. The only reason I went as far as I did so young in the bike world was just that. You almost had to grow up in the bike world to get the chance to join the Red & White. They all watched me grow up on the street, in and out of juvenile hall. They respected my selling drugs and stealing, and serving my time when I got busted, and not becoming a Rat. Because I had joined my local 1% Club, The Gladiators gave me an in. They still were cautious as I began Hanging, but they knew for sure that I wasn't a cop.

So by reputation and deeds is how you got to be known in the Biker and criminal world of those times. When you were young or new, you got to know some 'lone wolf' type Bikers as you went along, while they got you started in their crime school. They almost become my Father in a sense that they made me street wise, and became my connections. I would get my drugs from them, and fence my stolen shit through them. Burglaries would be set up with "Take this and that, and I will give you so many hundreds of dollars." They would get you hooked up on your first Basket Case Harley, selling it to you with your profits from working with them. At this point you were sucked in, as you needed them for bike parts and knowledge to build your putt. Fat Ray showed me a Basket Case 45 Trike. It had the frame with the rear end still bolted on it. There was an old, dented rusty gas tank from a Sportster, with the motor in pieces in a box, along with five or six boxes full of old transmission parts and various pieces of the puzzle.

I didn't care if it was in pieces, because it would be my dream Harley!

Ray had set the hook and I would be a loyal soldier, and he enabled me to build me a Harley. Ray continued to be my supplier and connection in my young life. Selling drugs and stealing became not only my living, but my chance for building my bike, as is what most 1% Bikers did, in the same capacity. That's why the older Members wanted you around, was for helping them make money. They held that dream of your Harley in front of you, in reverence. All you had to do was sell enough drugs and steal enough shit, and someday your Harley would be running, and be yours. It seemed the only way, as working a minimum wage job would take forever. No one even discussed buying a new Harley back then, not that I ever knew of, it just wasn't done or heard of. Just like everything else in my life, I wanted it all as fast as I could get it. When I got busted and did some jail time, my Basket Case Harley would be saved for me until I got out, by Fat Ray's wife. There *is* honor among thieves, sometimes.

So you joined the biker world at a young age, and at first had to prove that you could be trusted. You knew that if you got busted, you shut the fuck up, make no deals with the law, and take the bust on the chin. Say nothing and do your time, the code of silence cannot be broken. If you played the game, when you were released, someone would be there to pick you up and take you to a party that they would throw for you. It was almost like a thank you for not squealing on anyone, and you felt that you were part of something, that you belonged. The dealers and fencers all knew that you could have given them up, and done less time, so when you didn't, you gained their respect and trust. The criminal biker society watched you nurture. Then, you eventually got a chance to break into Hanging around the Club, and have the benefit of better contacts to do business with, someone higher up the ladder. The better your connections were, the more money you would make. Basically cutting out the middleman and making *his* fees as well on the deal. Sounds similar to any corporation enterprise, doesn't it? Sometimes your chance would happen, when your main man would go to jail for something serious and had to do a lot of time. Then, the guys above him still wanted you to keep making money for them, so they would approach you and you would climb another step up the criminal ladder. It was a structured criminal enterprise, and that loyalty and money making would be awarded.

At first, you would get to run and do business with one Member. Eventually, with hard work and day-to-day dealings, you got to know them all by their street names, not their real names. This was the Old School buffer, in case someone is spilling shit to the cops, or their phone was tapped. Nicknames helped confuse the law, and if your name was possibly dropped at the wrong place, it was a good buffer. Bikers would keep their eyes on you for years before you might even know their real name, if ever. After awhile of Hanging out and proving yourself on the smaller shit, you started to be able to do bigger business with a few more Members, and so on. The buffer system worked, as you were insulated from the main players as they were insulated from you. Then once again, one Member you were doing business with would get busted and do some time. Then another member would fill his shoes with you, like the mob, that's how you got to climb up the criminal ladder.

Eventually you would meet the President of your local 1% Club, in my case the Club was The Gladiators. Wild Bill, as he was called then, he knew my history and eventually trusted me enough befriend me at a young age. You sell their dope and fence your stolen merchandise through them. When it feels right, you ask one of the Members, "How do I get into the family?" They tell you that need to Hang round for awhile, and help out, so the Brothers can get to know you. At the next Church, if you were lucky, someone would bring you up as being interested in Membership. You have to ask them, they will not ask you, and it's not like in most of the movies. After Church, one of the Members will walk up and congratulate you, and tell you that your status is now one of an official Hang Around for the Club. If your name being brought up at Church was favorable, then usually the Prospects are told to start including you in on some of the workings of the Club. That's when you start helping out the Prospects, and this phase would usually take up to a couple of years, even if they knew you well. They wanted to check you out more, and also give you a chance to see if it's for you, as well. If things go good and you pass the grade, you then try and find one of the Members to sponsor you. Once again, you have to ask them, they aren't going to ask you. The Chapter Membership has to vote you in unanimously to become a Prospect. Your Sponsor is responsible for you, and in some Clubs his Patch is on the line if his Prospect seriously fucks up. God help you as a sponsor, if your Prospect turns out to be a cop or a snitch, because the Sponsor usually has to take care of it. If you have been in another MC of some respect, and if you left them honorably, then all this can all go a lot faster, mainly because they know that you already know the ropes, and have 'made your bones'.

I went to Hanging around the Hell's Angels Nomad Chapter, as some of their Members had invited me. I had already been a Patched Member in The Gladiators MC, which was a 1% Club. We had been an R & W support Club, and had many dealings and parties with them. Our ex Club President, who had quit our Club and joined the Hell's Angels, called one day to set up a meeting, and told us that The Gladiators were no more, and we had two choices. We could join the Hell's Angels with full Patches, or just shut our Club down. At our meeting we discussed going to war with them, which was voted down, as it would be committing suicide. Maybe call their bluff and see how far we could take this? But we had seen and heard of how this had worked out for other Clubs in the past. We discussed in length whether to accept to be 'Patch over', into a Chapter of the Hell's Angels, as offered. Although our Club was all old school One Percenters, all the Members were married and had kids. The feeling of The Gladiators was, "If I had wanted to join the Angels, I would have in the first place." By an almost unanimous vote, it was decided to roll it up and turn down the Charter that had been offered to us, me being the only odd vote. I wrote in detail of this in another chapter. This gave me a real advantage on getting a chance to join the Hell's Angels. To give you an example on how it was done by the old school way, I will tell you how it was done with me.

I remember one of my early rides with Teddy Bear. I had just committed to start as a Hang Around for the Nomads. We decided to leave Vallejo and head up to my old stomping grounds in Placerville, California. Before we left, Bear pulled out a vile of some real THC in brown tabs, the real good shit, the best I ever had. So we each popped a couple hits, and hit the road. On the way jamming down the freeway, not far out of Vallejo, a bike cop came up behind us, as we were pushing the speed limit. To say we were just feeling good was probably a gross understatement, for sure! Flying high and scooting down the freeway at about 85 mph, without a care in the world and stoned out of our minds, we didn't even notice him pull up behind us. When the bike cop lit us up, Bear took off like a bullet through traffic, with me right on his ass. Jamming now at 100 mph plus, dodging through traffic, to my disappointment, I see Bear pitch his vial of THC after we had passed and cut in front of a car where the cop couldn't see him. Bear then immediately slowed down and pulled over, with the cop catching up to us, complete with flashing lights and all. He was a nice, old, ancient H-D bike rider cop, and he bragged to us for awhile about how he had been riding the 'iron horse' for work and play, for most of his life. Then, he asked us why we had bolted out ahead of him? Teddy turned on the charm that he was always good at. Bear explained how he was trying out a new carburetor and was checking its high speed performance. The old man ate that with a spoon, and wanted to know all about the carburetor, and Bear was glad to bullshit him. Everybody, including the cops, loved Teddy Bear, hence his nickname. He was just a lovable big guy on the surface.

The cop said he was sorry as he cut us loose, with a five over speeding ticket, and an "I'll hope to see you guys again." We didn't feel the same way, but Bear had gotten us out of that one as easily as it gets. Down the road a bit, we turned around and went looking for the dope, with no luck. So we stopped at a bar in Sacramento to have a beer, and cry over our loss of some good shit. Like I said, that was the best THC I ever had, or ever hope to have. Not to be confused with Angel Dust, which was a PCP elephant tranquilizer the Angels had capitalized on in the late '60s. The real THC was very expensive to manufacture, and really kind of rare to find, so the synthetic stuff was more common. About our fourth beer in, Teddy asked me about my family and where they lived in the area. Then to my surprise, he said he wanted to go meet them, and I really didn't think about the implications of that at the time, as I was high. I told him that we really didn't need to stop, but he insisted, as he wanted to meet them, since we were riding right through their area. I hadn't seen them at all in the last year. Teddy said, "You better make your peace now, because you never know with our lifestyle how much time you have left. You're running with me, and we're going down the fast lane into hell!" That actually made sense to me, especially in my intoxicated state. So we rode up to my folk's house, with the famous Hell's Angel riding behind me. I had dreamed of doing just that, as a pissed off adolescent. I thought I would show them my success in what I was becoming; like I said, it had been my young ass's lifelong dream.

When they came out the door to greet me, I could see the both of them kind of go into shock; that, for some reason, made me happy. You could see the fear that Teddy's Colors caused in my parent's faces; I had gotten my wish. Teddy Bear, always the charmer, greeted them with warmth and started telling them how he had been waiting to meet them for years. "Your son is joining the best organization in the world," he tells them. He tells them that regardless what they may have heard from the cops and media, the Hell's Angels are really just a misunderstood group of motorcycle enthusiasts that takes care of their own. He then went on to personally promise them that he would take care of me, and protect me from any harm. He told my Mother, "There will always be an Angel looking over your shoulder, too" with his arm around her. Bear looked over and caught my eyes after he had said that, with a serious grin. That's when it hit me, right between the eyes. My Mother certainly got the point. That was the old school way of letting me know of my total commitment and the possible consequences of my actions with the Club. After my Mother died, years later, my Dad confided in me how much that incident had scared her, and it was all he could do to keep her from moving immediately, which she eventually did anyway. Bear had personally taken the time to make sure that I was who I said I was, thus confirming my identification for the Club with an unspoken threat of harm to my family if I wasn't loyal and true to our code. That's the personal touch of checking a potential Member out, that I feel is still needed in the Club world of today. Remember Teddy Bear, the true old school Angel that he was, had a tattoo on his back shoulder blade that read, "The only God fearing thing that God fears himself, is an Angel in the fast lane!" The fast lane is where I was riding in, and Hell is where I was heading.

This was the system in the days of old, and I guess it probably evolved out of necessity, as it was the only way to keep from being infiltrated by the cops, who then seemed to use mostly Rats and Snitches at the time. As you can see, back then, and still today, getting into a Club has to be a long and careful process, and to get into the Red & White, you had to have a lot of history. That, I believe, is what made them somewhat invincible to the law in the beginning. They all knew all about a potential Member through the old system, and it worked. In recent years, I have seen this system begin breaking down, with the huge growth in the motorcycle world. One Club starts patching a bunch of Members, getting bigger and bigger, then the other Clubs have to try to keep up with their Membership. What happened is that the old Membership screening system started getting more lax, using short cuts on proof of identification, and requirements to get in were loosened. Everything seemed fine for a while, but it really opened the door. It became much too easy for cops to infiltrate, and they soon did. The times also brought undesirable 'new bloods' applying for membership, that were in it for themselves and not the Brotherhood that came with the Club. Eventually, the Clubs would have to start tightening it up again, after being infiltrated by the law, and getting a lot of 'undesirable' Members that had to be dealt with, as they were bringing the Clubs a lot of heat and bad publicity.

In retrospect, the old school way of recruitment worked perfectly for a long time. The Biker world became bigger, though, and with more Clubs came growth. In 1969, when the Easy Rider movie came out, biking started becoming more popular than ever. With this boom and drug addiction, so started the decline of the old school way of recruitment that had worked almost perfectly, until then. There became more and more Bikers that wanted to join the elite, and with this growth, Clubs somehow lost their safeguards in the fast lane! This, along with drugs, would come back to bite the bigger 1% Clubs in the ass. Like I said, Clubs had begun to rely on computers and paperwork too much, as they had lost the personal touch. I have Brothers argue with me about this social security number bullshit. Yeah, you can find out what that social security number says, but isn't it only saying what 'Big Brother' wants it to? If you look at the recent infiltration of the Mongols, who patched an ATF officer named Queen, you'd see that he became an officer in their Club. That, in my opinion, took a lot of balls and means that he is a very brave man, but he should have gotten tripped up. In his book "Under and Alone," he talks about Red Dog, who obviously was raised in the old school way. Red

Dog was their Sergeant at Arms, who was in charge of investigating new Membership. To his credit, he would scare the shit out of Queens on more than one occasion.

Queens wrote in his book about how ATF had provided enough ID to cover any investigation, but Red Dog wanted his high school yearbook. He never got it and let Queens get patched anyway. ATF hadn't thought about a high school yearbook for his cover, which could have been a fatal mistake! That's where Red Dog almost had him, but didn't pursue it far enough. Be sure that the next ATF or FBI infiltrator will have one, like I have told my Brothers. If you send a Member to a Prospects hometown with his yearbook incognito to confirm the yearbook authenticity, and his pictured identity, you got something. His background could be checked with a current picture through his classmates and family members, as they can't all have been in on the rouse. Take the picture around to local bars and restaurants where you can find an old classmate to confirm his identity. It's not that hard, if you take your time and buy some drinks in his hometown, or maybe look up a woman from his high school class. This method can get you all the information you need to trip up almost any cop's planted identity. I have done investigating like this, and it does take time and money, but is well worth it! I am sure the Mongols would gladly pay whatever the price is, since they lost a lot of Members to the joint over the infiltration, some for life. I believe the only sure way there is, is the old school way.

I heard for most of my life that the Red & White had never really been infiltrated. Until recently that was true, because all they had before were Members turn Rat and roll over on them in order to save their own asses. George Wethern was really the first R&W snitch that I heard of. He also wrote a book about it that I've already mentioned. Then in the late '70s, it was Red Bryant, a Nomad (who actually was my sponsor in the HAMC), who did a lot of damage snitching. He went into the State Witness Program because he put some good Members into prison. Then in the mid '80s, it was Anthony T. that did lots of damage by voluntarily snitching, and writing a book on his Membership while working for the FBI. He was the first real undercover plant that I know of, to infiltrate the Hell's Angels. In the recent Black Biscuit operation against the Arizona

HAMC, a member named Mike K. rolled. I had met him way back in the Dirty Dozen Club years. He snitched to save his ass in a murder investigation, which is still pending in court. These are just some of the Snitches that are nothing less than Rats, who sold out their Brothers and their lifestyle to save their own worthless asses from prison.

Back where and when I grew up, snitching was the lowest, most unthinkable thing you could do. It was better to do life in prison than to become a Rat, similar to the Mafia's old rules of the code of silence. From the Moment you snitched, everyone in 'the life' would turn on you for good. Nobody, even women, would want you around; your previous life was over. I believe that is what helped in protecting bike Clubs from being infiltrated and snitched on. A trick the cops used was they would tell you that another one of your Bros had ratted on you, so why don't you get even and pay them all back? Just go ahead and rat on your whole world, but what they didn't know was our code. Rats are the lowest form of shit that inhabits Mother Earth. Are you gonna rat on your Brother? A Brother that has backed you up in fist fights, rode the highways with you for countless hundreds of miles at 100 plus mph, and will give you whatever he has if you are down. You eat, sleep, ride, cry, laugh, fight, and fuck with your Club Brothers. The cops think that you would give up your whole lifestyle and everything you have loved, trusted, and believe in, to save your ass from prison? I don't think so.

One Percent Outlaws in the various MCs live by a moral creed and oath given to each other that citizens will never understand. True Outlaws are a totally different type of humans that believe in their Brothers and the Brotherhood of their Club, above anything else. Would they give up their whole lifestyle and everything and everybody that they believe in and love? No way, Club Members are doing exactly what they want and are already prepared to suffer the consequences of their actions. Most have already tried the straight life and don't want any part of it. So what do the cops do to make you turn Judas? They lie like rugs to you, to try and turn you against your Brothers! Once, when I was fifteen, some detectives were questioning me about a burglary and used a different method of interrogating to me. A huge, older, Miwok Indian that I grew up with named Richard (who's involvement with me was doing a burglary and selling some of the stolen goods) had stolen this dude's bike, along with some tools and shit, from this guy who was a snitch, and had dropped my name to the cops. So that made his shit fair game.

We did a late night, tip-toe cat burglary in his garage. One of those that all you can hear is each other breathing as we tip-toed in and out, making off with his motorcycle, tools, and some other goodies. Richard had sold some of the tools, but the cops didn't have any serial numbers or marked ID numbers, all they had was the make and model of the tools that had been reported stolen. Basically, the cops had recovered the stolen tools and knew we had done it, but couldn't prove it. So when the detectives brought me in for questioning, they knew Richard and I wouldn't give up anything. The cops told me that I should rat on Richard, as he had already ratted on me, and they would let me off. I lived by the code as always, and told the cops to get fucked. "I didn't do it and I don't know nothing." Besides, if he had ratted on me then why would they give me a deal? I knew Richard wouldn't do that to me, or on anyone else. We had grown up together and both believed in the code. Then, they played a tape for me that really sounded like him ratting me off. They also tried the same thing with Richard. Because we knew neither of us would snitch on each other, even with their 'tapes', neither one of us were convicted of the crime. You have to have that blind faith in your Brothers.

Richard, some years later, would turn this young chick out at a party where he boned her, and then wouldn't let her get go until everybody who wanted some got it. Well, it turned out that she told her older Brother that was in a Bike Club, and whom didn't appreciate his sister getting raped. At a party one night at an apartment in Sacramento, a shot from a 30-06 rifle came through the living room window, and Richard's head exploded into many pieces. There is an unwritten code of justice, even amongst criminals. Through the years, I have known some chicken shit assholes that will trade in their Brothers and lifestyles. They are the Rats that simply won't do the time for their crimes. A few of these men fake their way into the Outlaw's world. They are usually the ones that are in it for the sex, drugs, and power, not for the freedom and Brotherhood. These hardcore criminal types that join a Club's Brotherhood are for all the wrong reasons. It is not about Brotherhood to them, but rather power and opportunity to make connections, and prosper illegally in the bike world. They wear their Colors so they can deal, rob, and cheat a living, but yet be protected by the Club's reputation. Their not into riding their bikes, they'd rather be driving around in a Cadillac. They are usually stone cold killers and thieves, and lie their way into Outlaw Brotherhoods. These losers are con artists that are good enough to fool the Membership into thinking that they belong in the Club. A lot get spotted as Prospects and kicked out, but some are cunning enough to con their way into the Membership. Then once they're patched, they turn into the monsters that you read and hear about in the media. By the time the Membership catches on, the damage is usually done, and the Club has a black eye. Like any organization, these men somehow sneak and bullshit their way in, unnoticed by all the background checks, etc... It happens in all organized groups, including the U.S. Government. They are the ones that make the headlines with their deeds, then the first to snitch to avoid doing the time for their crimes. They are the ones that give Outlaw Clubs the worst publicity, that have to pay for it by being stereotyped by these phony Member's deeds. It's a problem that happens to a lot of organizations, no matter how much you try to check people out. To their credit, the HA gets rid of these people as soon as the discover them. But the damage these criminals do is all the average citizen knows or hears about through the media. So the few bad eggs give a bad reputation for the rest of the Members in the Club. Like I have said, they are not all Angels.

So the trouble that Motorcycle Clubs have, and always will have, is the screening of new Membership. How do you keep undesirables, or law enforcement, out of the Membership? There is also another problem with new Members, and that is that when they first get patched, they get what we call 'Patch Fever'. This is a very serious disease that can cause more problems for the Club than you could dream up. Also, some Members, after they get an office of power in the Club, get power hungry, which can also decimate a Chapter, or even a Club. There have been many Patches that had to be pulled for these problems. With death, prisons, and old age whittling down your Membership roster, how do you keep the ranks full? I feel this is the problem facing Clubs' existence in the future, besides the continuous persecution by the law. The process of Prospecting has always been the only answer, and it is still the main tool used today. But even that doesn't always weed them out entirely, as I have explained. What else can be done? This question has been plaguing MCs since the beginning.

I've been in three 1% MC Clubs, with one that over the decades grew into something different. My last Club started out in the early '70s as a 1% Club, with old school types making up the Membership. Mostly drug dealers and hell raisers, that just love to ride motorcycles and make fast money, along with possibly playing with guns too much. That lasted for 25 years or so, until the survivors that were left had aged and matured, living through busts and changing laws, with their families and responsibilities growing. So the Membership shifted gears, into jobs and legal business, replacing drug dealing and crime to survive. In all three of these Clubs, they still have the same old problem, recruiting new Membership. As some of the old schoolers went to prison for life or died off, it has left a void for finding new Membership. Trusting a potential Member is the real continuous problem, and always will be a major issue for all MCs. The Membership is divided, as some don't want new Membership at all because they aren't old school enough for them, so you can't trust them! Others feel the same way, but want their Club to continue into the future, although clearly scared of child molesters, perverts, or even psycho killers that might sneak in. So everyone's got an opinion, but nobody has the answers for sure. Basically, trying to improve on the Prospecting process seems the only real answer.

My opinion on recruitment of Prospects is simple; go back to the old school way of screening them as much as you can. At present, most Clubs now do a computer background search to check out their Prospective Members. This has made the job easier than the old days, but damn sure not as bullet proof. Members brag "Give me a social security number and a few bucks and I can find out whatever you want to know about somebody on the internet!" Yeah, that's totally true, but I ask you, can that info be tampered with? Computers only tell you what people loaded into them, so how do you trust someone or something you have never met, or that won't even sign their name to the info they are giving you. Where does this info come from? A lot of it comes from our trusted friend and neighbor, Big Brother. That is who is always trying to destroy my world, not help it, or that's the way it seems anyway. Who loads this information into the net that you are basically staking your life and your Club's reputation on? Could it be the law, or Big Brother, who is always looking out for their own best interests? I personally believe that we have all been sucked into this computer age world because it's easy, and in the process we have lost the personal touch that's needed.

The Vietnam Vets are a Three-piece Patch Club that is made up of respected Veterans that served their country in an unpopular war. They created a sister Club as part of their own organization, as their answer to their fading Membership problems. See, the original VV bylaws states that you had to be a Member of the US Armed Forces, and that you had to have served honorably in the Vietnam War. Basically, a Vietnam Vet with an honorable discharge is what their qualifications stated in their bylaws. They are having the same problem, as their Membership is dying off because of age, disease and health, bike wrecks, and prisons, just like everyone else. Probably faster than most, due to some being exposed to Agent Orange, this causing a lot of health problems. So without new blood in their Club, their Brotherhood started to die off, like any of the other Clubs. You can see that their plight was the same as what's facing all the other MCs. To their credit, they wanted to keep the VV Club going, so they have created the Legacy Vets, which to me only made perfect sense. Legacy bylaws state that you have to be an honorably discharged Veteran from the service to join, period, which they feel will let their Club carry on to fly their Colors in the future. The Vets have always had an advantage in screening new Membership, in my opinion. The U.S. military has really done the job already, if they received an honorable discharge. I know in the Clubs I have been in, that when a prospect is being reviewed; he is always asked if he has had any prior military service. If he has, and had been honorably discharged, then it's a definite plus for him. Red & White will not let anyone in their Club if they have ever been in law enforcement, including military police. At present, we do pretty good background checks off the internet, easier than in the old days, but not as fool proof. This is a good way to find any criminal undesirables to reject. I believe this issue is so important though, that we go back to doing it personally, and really check someone out the old school way, as I have previously mentioned. I have made this statement many times at Church.

I believe that if Sonny had not gotten locked up in the early 70's, and would have been around, I would be a Member today or more likely in prison or dead. The reason I say this is that if Sonny hadn't been incarcerated, the leadership of the Nomads Chapter out of Vallejo, CA at the time, would have been kept in line. The drug and crime abuse inside the Chapter wouldn't have gotten so crazy and out of hand. They were mostly cranksters, with their Chapter Membership growing by the transferring of the craziest and drugged out Members that were in the Club at that time. Chief was our Prez, and loved his job leading these cranksters that were the kind of Members he needed, to build his drug empire. I do feel that the law has the wrong opinion about Sonny though, he has always kept the Membership in line, and he is their guiding force. He started and supported the 'no needle' law, which saved a lot of mayhem back then, believe me. PLEASE LEAVE HIM ALONE, AS HE KEEPS THE RED & WHITE RIGHT! The law has done its best to keep him incarcerated, and have won a few times. In reality though, they were really doing the opposite of what they were intended. I know that writers and authors have pictured Sonny as somewhat of a monster. To name one of many, in "Angels of Death" the author painted that picture. These people really do not know him, or the good that he *has* done. He is an individual, so that makes him an Outlaw. By saying that he is an individual, I mean that he stood up for himself, his Brothers, his Club, his family, and his rights to live and associate with whom he wanted. He has a God given right to be a free man, and to do what he wants as a free man. Riding motorcycles while partying on booze and drugs, society calls this a sin. In our society within theirs, we call this fun and having a good time. For that, Outlaws are hunted and pursued to be brought to 'justice', to be caged like a feared animal. For the crime of being different and not conforming to society's laws, you will be removed from society for theirs and your own good. Society knows what is good for you and what's not, all you need to do is ask them, they'll tell you. They have it all written down in their law books on what you can and can't do. This is all made right because they are the majority. Of course, this has all been voted on by our politicians, for what they say the majority has agreed upon. But what if you are in the minority? You lose and go to jail if you disagree. The United States is a democratic society that I believe is the best in the world. But if you are a minority, and there is no other option for you to vote on, you lose. That's when they brand you as an Outlaw, someone living outside of society's majority rules and laws. Yeah, Sonny is an Outlaw all right; he chose to live with his Brothers the way he wanted to, and not live by society's standards. I am surprised they haven't been able to throw away the key, although they are still trying. Sonny will live on in history long after he is gone, because he was an individual whose spirit couldn't be broken, no matter what they did, or proceed to do.

Hell's Angels are good people for the most part, and like any society, they have some bad people too, as I have explained. They have individuals that *do* deal drugs, but they have some that don't. Some Chapters may have some of the Members dealing, but not the *whole* Chapter. Everybody's standards of good and evil can vary a lot. But I suggest you don't fuck with them. The one thing they demand is your respect, and you best give it to them. When you wear Red & White Colors, even as a Prospect with just a Bottom Rocker, you feel almost God-like, and in some worlds, you are. In different areas controlled by large rival 1% Clubs such as the Outlaws MC, Banditos MC, and Mongols MC, it is the same. These Outlaw Clubs are made up of real individuals that stick out wherever they are. When you fly your Colors, people are always watching you, but carefully out of the corner of their eye because they are afraid, as they should be. Unlike the Mafia, who are able to hide, Outlaw Bikers who wear their Colors on their backs because they are proud of what and who they are. It's an exclusive Brotherhood that few men even get the chance to belong to. Citizens, which is an expression for the general public or anybody not in the biker world, are generally curious on what it is like to live this lifestyle. They can't ask of course, because they are too scared to, but they have fantasies of the unknown, of what it would be like. The drugs, alcohol, reckless danger, motorcycling, and of course the sex, are some of what they wonder about. I know this, because I *have* had some citizens ask me questions out of curiosity.

Living a lifestyle free of a job, no boss, no family, no responsibilities, just a carefree life, probably sounds perfect. Well it's not, really. Being a Hell's Angel, or riding with any 1% Club, is dangerous, to say the least. When you ride with them, you learn quickly how short lived and deadly it can be. They give out five-year buckles to Members that are lucky, and smart enough to survive that long. They also give 10, 15, and even 20 year buckles, and so on. But rarely will you see a lot of these, simply because it's hard to survive that long. So when you see a One Percenter, and he has a Club membership buckle on, he is a lucky, respected veteran of the lifestyle. If motorcycling doesn't kill you, the law or a bullet will! If you consider it an occupation, as I do, it would rate as one of the most dangerous occupations in the world there is. In the Outlaw Club world, you are talking about some of the baddest individuals that walk this earth, that are afraid of nothing, including death, which makes them very dangerous. They believe in their Brothers, which is their family, and the right to live the way they want to. Anyone who rides a motorcycle fast, and long enough, knows that they probably have a death wish, as it is dangerous. To live in the Old School way of life you had to give up any fear of death, which is waiting for you at every turn, and every bar. When you live like that, you can see how Outlaws become almost fearless in life, as they play with death constantly. You know your gonna get killed some day, and once you accept that, you might as well live for the Moment. I know that is fatalistic and insane, but it's the truth. I have seen many men meet their maker. I have been to more funerals than a man should have to have had. It just becomes an accepted part of it, and is a morbid reminder that you have sold your soul to a lifestyle in the fast lane to Hell!

I think you could best compare old school Bikers to Americas turn of the century Outlaws of the past. Their codes they lived by are almost the same as ours. They wanted the freedom to do what they wanted, when they wanted, and to live by their own set of rules as they pleased. Their loyalty to each other enables them to survive. They're non-conformists, that don't want to play by society's rules. These are fearless individuals that can't live normal lives as others, even as they have to live on the edge with one foot already in the grave. When I say fearless men that is what I mean. These men will fight at the drop of a hat, and die for their comrades. Today's Outlaws will go ride a Harley 100 plus mph down curvy mountainous roads, as would Outlaws of the past would ride their horse's full gallop, just as recklessly. Today's motorcycles are different than the Harleys of the past. In the early days, the Harley Knuckleheads and Panheads were a challenge to even keep running mechanically, which kept the number of Bikers in the old days so small. You almost had to be a mechanic to keep one running. Shovelheads came along with two little improvements. Going over 100 mph was dangerous on the old Harleys. We had extended front ends with slugs and shit. Raking frame necks, and hanging homemade 30" Girders, or Springer front ends, on these radical bikes. We experimented with motors and shitty tires, nothing like today's standards. Goodyear's high milers tires were what most of us ran then, as they were cheap and you got buku miles on them. Taking a corner at 100 mph plus on one of those was nothing but dangerous, and killed many a biker. You were actually riding on about a half inch of tread on the edge of the tire. If you got too low into the corner it would just drop you on the edge of the sidewall, usually causing the bike to slide out from under you.

I was riding with Pie, an Oakland Hell's Angel that had befriended me after I was introduced to him by Teddy Bear. Pie put his giant arm around me and said, "Any friend of Bears is a friend of mine." His nickname was Pie, which was short for Pineapple. His nickname fit him perfect, as he was a huge Hawaiian Samoan, and one crazy Motherfucker. A very large man who towered over me that I had to look up to talk to. Pie was also a very intelligent individual that feared nothing. For me our adventure started about noon as I walked into the Titty Bar and there was Pie and Chuck shooting pool. They had just put Teddy Bear to bed and they had decided to carry on. Pie had his portable police scanner with him, which he almost always had. He would somehow manage to find out the right crystals to tap in on the police channels of all the Bay Area Chapters areas. Pie gave me a big hug asking "How's my little Brother?" He gave me a big bump of product that got my eyes burning. We shot pool and drank beer as we wasted away another afternoon. They had done an all-nighter with Bear and were feeling no pain. I had gotten stuck on "Chief detail" that night, and figured he would be showing up soon, as I had left him over at a chick's house that early morning. So when Pie said he had to get back to Oakland, Chuck and I jumped up for that one again. Can't let an out of town Bro go rolling out on his own in our town, it just wouldn't be right. Truth was, we wanted to escape Chief. So we all jammed off on our bikes, all fucked up, as Pie took the lead, hauling ass as usual. I was behind him as we hit the freeways; rolling around 100 mph. Pie started splitting lanes, or center lining, through traffic, so we didn't even have to let off the throttle.

Pie was known to be a daring crazed rider that loved to ride fast and on the edge. So if that wasn't crazy enough, as we were starting to get boxed in by traffic, he passes this car in the fast lane on the left side, between the cement wall and the car. There couldn't have been but three feet between the wall and the car. Pie hammered the throttle as he shot around the car, without even losing any speed, and of course, I followed right on his ass! I admit, even being buzzed on alcohol, drugs, and the rush of adrenaline, my ass was puckered on that one, more than a little. I checked my rearview mirror and saw that Chuck hadn't followed us through the gauntlet of cars. I followed Pie as he kept up the insane pace, passing cars however he could, to get through traffic doing a 100 mph, for miles! If one of the drivers in the cars we had passed had gotten scared and flinched, or swerved instead of just freezing, there wouldn't be enough of us to scrape into a blanket, as I have seen before. My attitude was fearless in that I figured I would die bloody some day, might as well be then. I would have followed Pie into hell, if he had led us there. I sort of hero-worshipped Pie, as he was what I thought a Hell's Angels was, just like Teddy Bear, a Superman of legends and tales. We finally pulled off the freeway and were sitting at a light when Chuck pulled up behind us. I must have looked crazed as I looked at Chuck, as the adrenaline rush I was having had my eyes wide open, and what he described later to me as "A wild look with a crazed smile!" He looked at me and just shook his head as the light turned, and we jammed to the next light toward the Oakland Clubhouse, where we were going. Instead, Pie turned into a bar, and as we dismounted our steeds, Pie and I were congratulating each other on surviving the ride.

Pie walked into the bar and then Chuck pulled me aside and started chewing my ass. I told him I was just following Pie and doing what he did. "Yeah, but he's fucking crazed with a death wish, everybody knows that!"

I trusted Chuck and knew he was right, as I *had* been reckless. I told him that it's hard for me not to go for the adrenaline rush, if taunted on my scooter, especially when I was high and drunk. Chuck just shook his head and said, "It's your funeral, and I'll be there to put you in your grave!" It's hard to turn that kind of rush off when you got a Harley between your legs, flying it down the road at 100 plus mph through traffic; that is living on the edge! The physical speed of the motorcycle as the motor vibrates when you accelerate up to 100, and then almost stops as it turns into a smooth pulsating hum because the valves are moving so fast that they start floating. The road centerlines become a straight blurry solid line, as your eyes water and you feel the tears roll back across your cheeks. The bike just floats, as it becomes part of the air stream and you become part of the machine. There's nothing else in the world happening to you as nothing else matters, just you and your bike flying through time and space. Your mind tries to sense fear as you ignore it for the better sensation of flying, as the wheels don't even seem to be on the street. You become one with the machine as you fly down this ribbon of life, taunting fear and death to try and stop you. Knowing that at any second, you could both become a twisted, ugly, bloody pile of blood, bones, and metal. Now add alcohol and drugs to mix, with the adrenaline flowing fast through your veins, and you have the ultimate rush! Is this the ultimate thrill or simply a death wish? For some of my Bro's and me, I have known it as the ultimate rush in life. You are pushing life's ultimate end for the thrill of the speed, and saying "I don't give a fuck!" I got off my bike one time after a ride with a Bro like I just described. The first thing he said as we were walking into a bar was something I'll never forget. He said, "There's something about the taste of adrenaline in the morning, I don't know about you, but it makes me fucking thirsty!"

When you fly Red & White Colors, you can expect about anything. You've always got your biggest fans, the cops, watching you. You've got rival Motorcycle Clubs to deal with that can turn deadly at anytime, especially when you're riding your bike. Then you have your drunken sons of bitches that hate Outlaws Bikers for all kinds of reasons, including jealousy, or to prove their manhood. They will attack you in a bar, restaurant, or even on the highway. If you have ever been a Patch holder in any Club for very long, you know what I mean. You'll be at a bar somewhere and some assholes will want a piece of your ass. Maybe some Patch holder screwed his sister, or beat up his brother. Whatever Member did it, from whatever Club, doesn't really matter; all they see is that you are a Patch Holder. I guess we all look the same, no racial slur intended. So they want to take their vengeance out on you. It has been my experience that you have to constantly be watching your front, sides, and back in public. Then you just have the local badasses, who just want the glory of beating the shit out of you. I used to think it was fun in my younger years to enjoy a good fight. But as you get older and experienced, you find out two things. One is that anyone can get lucky in a fight, as there is always that variable. Second is no matter how bad you are, or think you are, somewhere there is someone badder than you. That, unfortunately, is a fact that you may not care to admit, but it doesn't matter because it is the truth.

These sometimes drunk badasses just can't help themselves. They may be proving their manhood and trying to impress their girlfriend that they are better than you, and could be you if they wanted to. That's one of the main reasons MCs started long ago and has been able to still exist. If they had not banded together to protect themselves, I am sure they wouldn't have survived in the early days of the bike world. All Clubs in the early days survived by one simple rule, that being if anyone hits a Member, he just hit us all, and everybody fucks them up. That's how they stayed alive in those days, and they still do. You may call it rat packing or even chicken shit, but I call it survival in the strength of numbers. It's like a rattlesnake, you fuck with it and it will fuck with you, with the passion of survival. Leave it alone and it will go away harmlessly, after it's made its threatening presence known. Outlaws are really the same way. What most people don't understand is that when you attack one of my Brothers, you are attacking my family, and me. They are as close to me as my family blood. It is an immediate reaction that you don't even think about, and I'll try to fuck you up before I give it a second thought. A good rule of thumb that I strongly recommend, that is a very simple rule, is "don't fuck with Outlaws!" Just like that rattlesnake, we will try to show you how mean we are first, but only if you won't step aside and leave us alone. We will strike you down with a vengeance!

There isn't a Patch Holder ever that hasn't had to fight to protect his Club. Now, when a situation happens, that feeling and physical response becomes instinctive and instantaneous. When it happens to you the first time with your Club, that's when you know you are in a real Brotherhood. You will immediately react to anyone challenging or fucking with your Brothers or their family's safety. You will instantly strike or kill, if necessary, to protect them, and that's what society and the law doesn't realize. When Citizens have to protect their families from harm, it is justifiable, but with Outlaws it's called brutal, senseless beatings, mayhem, assault, or murder. But we are just protecting our Brothers and their families, our own Society, our right to exist and live the lifestyle we choose. If another Club challenges our rights to live and do business where we have chosen to live, then we feel it is our God given right to fight them. That, in the media, is called biker gang, or turf, wars. I see no difference with that than when the United States is at war with another country. Our country's paid army's enforces our will and protects our rights against the rest of the world. It's legal if they kill to protect God and Country. But when another Club tries to takes over what is ours, and when we try to protect our family and society, it is assault or murder.

Outlaws have their own world they have chosen to live in. We're not asking for your help, just leave us alone and we'll take care of it. Have we ever asked for the Untied States government to save us from ourselves? No, to the contrary, we asked to be left alone. But that doesn't happen, because the greater mass of society wants to impose their rules on us. We won't let foreign nations do it, but we will let our government do it to our minority groups. How many people in one group does it take to make what they have to do to protect themselves or their turf, legal or right? Does it take 1,000 people, or maybe 10,000? One hundred thousand, no, let's make the rule 1,000,000 people, and all agree, and it's ok to do what they have to do to protect their turf. As we know from history, that doesn't work. Now you know why they call us different individuals Outlaws, as we live outside of majority law. If Adolph Hitler would have won his war, which thank God he didn't, we would still be Outlaws, because we all wouldn't want to obey all his laws and shit, either. Then, we would've been considered heroes by most, for our rebellion against that authority, which would not have let us live in our world, the way we wish. There have always been Outlaws, Jesse James, Billy the Kid, John Dillinger, Hickok, Sonny B… They were individuals that chose to live outside of society's laws. That is why they are idolized, because they didn't conform, they were different than the rest of society. That is what made them interesting and etched their names forever in the history books. I have always loved to hear or read about Outlaws since I was a kid, and I guess that's why I have always lived the Outlaw life. As my Father always told me though, "Might is greater than right." Society's majority rules will always be the way things are, but America still loves their Outlaws!

For most of my life, I have blindly followed Hell's Angels rules, or the Mother Club's rules of whatever area I have lived in. It doesn't matter if you are in a bike Club or not. If you are a true Biker, or associate around any bike Club and live the life, you are following Club rules. This is how it works. Say that you are a 'late life rider', or a newbie in the bike world. You start riding around, stopping by Biker bars or going to your local motorcycle shop. You meet other Bikers, and maybe ride with them for a while. Then you all decide to go on a bike run, as you start seeing local MC Clubs, and want to participate in their events. Bikers that ride together stay together; it's a family. You notice how this Club operates and how they have Hang Arounds and Prospects. You observe how they have respect, and dance around the Clubs Members. Unless you are a total idiot, you do the same, as these men have earned that right. You will learn one way or another to respect the Patch, or the Club's Colors, and the men wearing them. You should give all these people the respect they deserve, because you don't want to get the shit kicked out you. All you really need to do is be cool, mind your manners, and enjoy their hospitality and show respect.

One of the biggest M/C's laws states, "A Member is always right, no matter what." But like I have said previously, they to have a limitation on what they allow. These limits basically are simple, what won't hurt the Club, which is their family and society. With the law and society watching all bike Clubs, especially the HAMC, they have to be very careful. Believe me when I say again, they're no Angels. If they need to kill to protect their society and way of life, they will, in a heartbeat. But they also won't allow any senseless unsanctioned killing or mayhem. They have a sense of what is right or wrong, and besides that, it's also bad for business. Just like the United States government for instance, they have some of the same rules to protect their society. So they police their own, which is done very swiftly and efficiently. Club's laws also include snitching on the Club, a very serious offence. Being a traitor has the same penalties as U.S. Government laws, a possible death sentence. Believe it or not, there are so many laws of bike Clubs that are similar to that of the U.S. Government. The laws that protect their people's well being, beliefs, and their ways of life are some of the same. You cannot help but see some of the similarities. Clubs have an elected President, who names his own Vice President. They have their own security for their leaders and so on.

There is basically a limit to what the Citizen's society will allow their Outlaws to get away with, though. As the case of the Mongols and the Hell's Angels that got into a scuff at Harrah's Club in Laughlin, Nevada. That brought heat on both Clubs from the law. If they had fought it out in the woods with nobody around, they wouldn't have caused all the heat on themselves and the aftermath. You can't endanger civilians, as that's a big mistake. The Mafia learned this a long time ago. Public opinion against an organization can and will cause its eventual demise. History proves this over and over. Senseless killings or arsons that endanger Civilians scares society into persuading their branches of government to take action and protect them, using the law. If bike Clubs ever piss off the Citizens of this country enough that will be their final demise. That's what happened to numerous Outlaw gangs of the Wild West. The new terrorist laws after 911 have showed us all how quickly personal rights and freedoms can be stripped away if the public wants it, or if the government is allowed to do so. I know that after 911 the government, armed with new terrorist laws, immediately went after the HA Tucson Chapter in Arizona, and called them terrorists and put them on the terrorist watch list. That was the biggest bunch of bullshit and misguided power to take away individual's rights and personal freedoms. These "terrorist laws" took the handcuffs off for law enforcement, as all they have to do is say that they think you are a terrorist, and your life is ruined. We needed to enable law enforcement to combat the terrorist threat to our great country, I totally agree. But the law shouldn't be using these laws as loopholes to attack its citizens, either. That is exactly what happened after 911 when these laws were passed, and remains an issue today.

Recently a Red & White Member was arrested in the ATF's Black Biscuit arrests in Arizona. He was facing 30 years on some flimsy charges. But, he stayed with the Biker code of silence and plead innocent. He wouldn't accept any of their plea bargain deals, as he kept the faith for three years, when all charges were finally dropped. Being loyal to his Colors and the Biker code saved him a strike in his life. The Laws policy against Angel's and Bikers has been the same since the '70s. They follow you and harass you with all the tickets and charges they can give you. The good or bad busts don't really matter, as long as they keep that score card readily full. They will even drop charges down, as long as they get any conviction on the Members criminal score card. With the 'three strikes your out' law was enacted, the scene was further set into place. As long as they add up misdemeanors and felonies, eventfully they will put you away for life in prison. The Angels saw this coming before anyone, so their policy became to fight everything no matter how small, with the best lawyers available. I once got busted in Napa when I was prospecting and watching the bikes, for spitting on the sidewalk! Chief had to pay 75 dollars to spring me. The Chapters set up defense funds just for this kind of thing, with the best lawyers being put on retainer to be at any Member's call. When you get popped, you don't say shit except "I want to call my lawyer." It was rare for a Member to ever take a plea bargain, as it was always best to go jury trial, for you, your Brother's, and your Club's sake. They were able to accomplish this, as the Club developed defense funds for lawyer fees along with bail bonds to bail its people out. That way a Member could make bail and a long, procrastinating jury trial didn't leave him sitting a long time in the jail waiting for trial. With the Angels hiring the best lawyers of the time, such as Melvin Belie and John Hill to name a few, they had done the best and only thing they could've ever done. The Angels, and all 1% MCs, are ultimately being singled out to be persecuted into extinction by our government's law enforcement agencies. I watched the best lawyers around that can drag trials on for years and years! This is costing the government millions of your tax paying dollars. This was the only way the Angels could fight back against their unwanted persecution! One good example is when the RICO attempted prosecution of the Angels in the late '70s, which after spending millions the United States Government failed to get a conviction on. Of course they would try RICO again with the same results.

Another good example of these continuing persecution tactics took place at our Titty Bar in Vallejo one night. I was Prospecting at the time, when an incident happened with Mike K., a Nomad Chapter Member that I really liked and truly admired, which everybody did. He was old school for sure, and held a good job with the government. He didn't fuck with drugs much, but man did he love to drink his beer. I had been hanging out and riding our bikes with him, all day, popping beers and bar hopping. Around midnight, Chief came over to me and told me I had better ride Mike home. When we finally took off, he was wobbling quite a bit, but so was I. As we left the bar we made a couple quick turns, and had beat the cop's surveillance of our bar. We had just about made it to the freeway before we picked up some more heat. I saw the two city patrol cars in my mirror slowing down and turning around. As I looked over at Mike, he nodded.

We started to slowly accelerate until we saw the cop's light turn to flashing, as both cars finished flipping the bitch to pursue us. We looked at each other again and immediately made a quick turn down a side street, went one block, and turned again, as we accelerated from turn to turn almost drag racing, to beat the cops. I didn't know for sure about Mike, but I threw my gun first into some bushes as we rounded the second turn. I watched for the lights in my mirror down that block, as I got my switchblade out. If I saw the lights, I would take my chances and leave it in my handlebar. I got it out and didn't see the flash of light so I threw the switchblade too, and I heard it hit the sidewalk as the cop's lights lit our bikes up. Our experience taught us that you try to get the cops to pull you over as slowly as possible as you're putting distance between your weapons and/or dope you threw and the location of where you finally stop. The further you get, the less chance you have of them finding anything. I wasn't too worried, as I thought I was pretty sober, and I had managed to get rid of everything, or so I thought.

I was going through my checklist in my head, checking off getting rid of my gun and tossing the switchblade. I had no meth, except what was in me, and I was pretty sober, no warrants that I knew about, and I was cool, so what could go wrong? So we go through the usual cat and mouse game with the standard chitchat. "How you boys doing tonight, you weren't trying to ditch us were you?" "No I didn't really see you Sir, what's the problem anyway?" Mike K said. "You guy's rolled through that stop sign back there, let's see your registrations and licenses." We handed them our paperwork and they told us both to stand in front of the patrol car and keep both our hands on the hood! Then they asked Mike K. to do a sobriety test and led him off to the sidewalk, and told me to stand there. Then the one older officer eyed me up and down and asked me if I was carrying any weapons, I said, "No." Then he said he was going to pat me down for weapons, for his own safety. "I want you to leave your hands on the car and spread your legs as I am going to pat you down." He kicked my feet out even further and started at my boots, working his way up. When he finished patting me down from behind, he spun me around and stopped as he stared at my cutoff pocket. "What's that?" he says. I looked down at part of a baggie sticking out of my cut's pocket. It still really didn't register for a second. "I don't know food I guess?" I instantly flashed to earlier, how a Hang Around had given me a sample of some new green bud that he had just scored and was trying to sell. I remember jamming it in my front pocket of my cut at the bar, and honestly had forgotten all about it. He pulls out the sandwich bag with a big bud in it. I thought, "Shit, how fucking stupid." I couldn't believe I had forgotten that one. "You are under arrest for felony possession of marijuana," he says. Yeah, it was a felony then. He cuffed my hands behind my back and then locked me in the back seat of his patrol car. They continued with Mike's DUI test. He was still weaving a bit, but passed, and they cut him loose. He walked over to the car and told me not to worry about my bike or bail, as he tells me, "We'll have you out quick, and I'll make the call." He asked for my cut but they wouldn't give it to him, as it was now evidence. I wanted to wait to bail out, because if I waited a couple days, I would get to see the judge and maybe get released on my OR (own recognance). That way, I didn't have to pay the ten percent to the bail bondsman and owe the Club for it.

Besides I was pretty burned out from lack of sleep and wouldn't mind taking some time off from Prospecting to catch up on some sleep.

Soon, as the cops got me processed through booking and took me to my cell, I hopped in a bunk and fell asleep immediately. I slept straight through until the turnkey woke me up and said I had made bail. Chief was there with Brett, and as we walked out of the jail I thanked them while explaining that I was willing to wait until tomorrow when I would have seen the Judge and tried to get out on my OR to save money. Chief said, "How the fuck you gonna Prospect and be any good to the Club in jail?" "Yeah, you're right Chief, I really hadn't thought of it that way. I had to throw my piece and knife too, so I had better go try and find them." They dropped me off at my bike and I headed over to where it happened. I tried to be cool, pretending that my bike broke down and searching around for an hour or so, finally giving up as I was starting to get eyeballed by the neighborhood. Being it was nickel plated and shiny, I knew someone had probably found it, hopefully not a kid. I went over to the bar and Chief asked me if I had found it. When I told him that I had not, he went on to tell me not to get a nickel-plated one, it's too flashy in the night. Then he told me I better not try and take a vacation on him again! I was thinking how great it would be when Chief would finally crash again, so I could finally get some sleep again.

I finally went to my preliminary hearing and was told to be there one-hour before court. Chuck went down there with me early, as three Members and Luck would show up for court later. This suit finally walks up and introduces himself. It wasn't John Hill, so I asked where he was, and this underling apprentice gave me the stupidest look, "John only shows up if it goes to jury trial, so don't worry, it's not going any further than today!" That made me feel a lot better, although it looked liked he had just looked at my paperwork a minute ago. So he explained that he wanted to get the arresting officer on the stand, as he had to be there anyway, and he would take care of everything. By then, Chuck had joined Luck and the three Members that had shown up out in the audience.

The lawyer finally got the arresting officer up on the stand. He asked the cop why he had pulled me over that night in Vallejo. He stated that we had failed to come to a complete stop at a stop sign. He also stated that we began accelerating our bikes as we turned on the next block and were trying to evade him. The lawyer then asked how he had found this controlled substance on the defendant. The cop stated he found it while he was pat searching me down for weapons. My lawyer asked "Why were you compelled to do that?" "Well these guys are Bikers, you know, Hell's Angels, they are known to carry guns and knives all the time." "So if you were looking for weapons, how did you find the controlled substance?" my lawyer asked. "As I was pat searching him, I felt something in his leather vest pocket." The lawyer asks, "Did you think then that you had found a weapon?" "No" the cop says, "but I could see the top of a baggy sticking out of his pocket!" This old cop looks around the room all proud, like he was a good detective. "So," my lawyer says, "you thought this baggy was a weapon?" "Heavens sakes no, it was a sandwich bag," the cop kind of chuckles. The lawyer says, "So you knew it wasn't a weapon, but didn't know what was in this sandwich bag. I mean it could have been a pickle or a cookie." The cop gets all red in the face and says, "Of course it could have had those things in it, but these guys carry dope in them!" "Oh, I see, you didn't actually see that it was marijuana until you pulled the bag out of his pocket," my lawyer says. The honest cop said "Yes, I couldn't see the dope until I pulled it out, but I knew that it was, as they all carry marijuana on them in those baggies!" I saw the judge roll his eyes as he picked up his gavel and pounded it down. "In the interest of justice, this case is dismissed." I heard a whoop or two from the crowd as my lawyer walked me out a free man. He congratulated me on my freedom, but I told him he was the one who needed the congratulations, not me. He said "Keep them all this easy," and with a handshake was gone. I have always felt, to this day even, that I was very lucky then, as an honest cop had arrested me!

The point to be made is that if you have the money, you can get the best lawyers in the world, and usually stay out of jail, at least for a while. In the meth market there was a lot of money at stake. That little felony case of mine cost me almost $3,000, which would have bought me a brand new Harley in those days! Once again, I would be forced into crime to cover my debt with the Club. Their code is right, don't ever cop to nothing, and that's true today even in the DUI laws. If I hadn't have spent the money on a good lawyer, I would have had a public defender who would have gotten me to cop to some easy 30 days in the county jail. That would be just what the law would have wanted, as I would have another strike on my record for a felony conviction. Then the next bust or the one after that, they would go after you to be put away in prison because you are a habitual career criminal! They use that as an argument to put you away for life, as you are a proven habitual perpetrator against the helpless society that can't possibly tolerate you back on the streets. I have heard the DAs in court telling that to the court, "This man successfully completed his probation and continues to do crime. He has done three months here and a year there and that has failed to rehabilitate him. He's a career criminal and must be put away for good, as he is an endangerment to our society." Boom, in a heartbeat you're in jail with a life sentence and the law just won.

Are outlaws afraid of society's laws and its jails? No, but nobody wants to just waste their lives doing time in its prisons for society's rules that they don't believe in. Will they snitch or turn on their Brothers or their lifestyle, or beliefs, by betraying their own kind? Fuck no! That's what society and cops will never understand about Outlaw Bikers. We don't want to conform, because we don't give a shit about your society of safety, rules, or right or wrong! Living programmed lives to be filled with success, work, wives and kids, and to pay your taxes for the good of the internal bliss of society. To have to keep up with the Jones next door, with their color TVs and new cars. Yeah, you'll get your color TV and your safe, uneventful life until you grow old and die anyway. No fucking thanks, but that is what societies want to force on minorities and myself. Outlaws life's blood line is way beyond that shit, that's why societies choose to call us Outlaws. Living outside of their normality of their society, hence 'living outside of the law', explains it all. But what is so wrong about the Outlaw Club's society having its own rules and laws, beliefs of right and wrong? We are wrong because we are the minority, and because the majority wants us to live by their conception of their elected politicians of the great society. Throughout history, it is always the same, as the 'good will' of the majority wins over the minority's will. How do we threaten you and the rest of society? Oh, yeah…we are different.

THE USA RUN

I was planning on taking a vacation from the Club during the U.S.A. Run that year, as I had the year before when I first started hanging around in Vallejo. The Prospects used to whisper to me about the most talked about run in the Hell's Angels MC. Most were all a little nervous and full of apprehension to go. I had all kinds of plans for myself while the Nomad Chapter was gone. When you are Prospecting, or being a Hang Around, you really don't have the time to even take a shit. Not with the Red & White, it is a demanding real job, for sure. I was 20 years old at the time and I figured I would have to wait until I turned 21 to even get my Prospect Rocker, if I ever did. Their bylaws stated that you had to be 21 years of age, but so did The Gladiator's and I had already prospected and won my Full Patch with *them*. I often wondered how long I could keep up the pace of trying to make it as a Prospect. I had everything I owned in my saddlebags, and that's how I had lived, like a Biker gypsy or a Harley tramp, for years. So my plan was to head back home and hustle up some money, get my clothes pile up and washed, relax, and sleep for a week. Maybe go find a woman that I wasn't hustling to relax with. I was gonna enjoy myself. I knew the Club law was that you couldn't go on the U.S.A. Run unless you were a Prospect.

At the last meeting before the run, and much to my surprise, they called me in from the outside guard duty with the rest of the Prospects. That hadn't ever happened before, so I was shocked. I entered the room and right into the middle of the inner circle. Chief asked me what I was gonna due for the next couple weeks while they were all out of state. I honestly said, "I'm gonna take a fuckin' vacation." I heard a lot of Members chuckle. Chief went on and explained to me, "You think your gonna get left behind to go fuck off? You aren't getting' no fucking vacation on my watch! You just got voted in as a Prospect, so you're going with us on the U.S.A. Run." He then congratulated me, and informed me that my sponsor was Big Red. I knew him about the least of all the Nomads. Red, a huge Member, looked at me and asked, "Are you good with that?" I said "Hell yes," and Red said "Ok, but if you fuck up, snitch, or embarrass me, I will kill you. Do you have a problem with that?" "Fuck no," I said. "Ok, now go get me a beer!" Red, the biggest Hell's Angel in the room said. I believed he meant all of what he said. I couldn't have a problem with that. He was the hardest Member to get to know, mainly because of his personality. He dealt a lot of meth. He always had a gun within a foot of his hand. You could hardly start a conversation with him. He seemed to be the one to fear the most.

But I had noticed that even for his size, he didn't get a lot of respect from the older Members which looking back, I guess they may have had their suspicions of his loyalty even then. Big Red Bryant started in the San Rafael Chapter, which eventually dissolved into the Nomads. Red had the distinction of being one of the first biggest, baddest, ugliest Motherfuckers to ever turn into one of the worse Snitches the Hell's Angels ever had. He would go on to roll, putting plenty of his once Brother Angels in jail. He also testified at the later Rico Act hearing, but he was discredited for the Rat snitch that he really was. He was a chicken shit that wanted to play the big game, until it came time to pay and do his time. I hope he has enjoyed his protective witness time, and friends, and gets to read this! There's nothing worse in this world to me, than being a phony Rat fucking snitch like he turned out to be. Red being my sponsor was never really a problem for me at the time, except that he never really tried to help me as a Prospect, more like he ignored me. I didn't choose him, that was done by smarter men than I. Hangtown Bill gave me that knowing smile and nod I had gotten used to after Chief's announcement of my Bottom Rocker. "You have four hours to sew this rocker on," Red said as he handed me my California Bottom Rocker. Bear's old lady stitched it on for me an hour and a half later.

Teddy Bear was the first to come over and give me his famous big bear hug squeeze that always hurt like a Motherfucker. Then all the Members took turns given me shit and big hugs. To say I was elated would be a under statement, as I was walking on water. I had been accepted into the Nomad Clan, the baddest motorcycle Club in the world, the Hell's Angels. I was in the family now, not just a mere Hang Around! Not quite in the inner circle yet, but on my way to it. I didn't know I was taking one big step into hell. I was fulfilling my childhood dreams. I was a made man that all Bikers have to respect, whether they liked it or not. During that time, in our world to fuck with a HA Prospect was almost a death sentence. I also had made a commitment to the Club to give my life and soul for my Brothers at the drop of a hat. I was a 100% believer in Hell's Angels Forever.

This is what I had always wanted, and couldn't wait to get that bottom rocker sewed onto my cut. I had found what I thought would be true Brotherhood forever, in a Club that couldn't be taken away like The Gladiators had been. I didn't know at the time that I would never find that true Club Brotherhood in its true purity ever again. I was prepared to gladly give my life to have my Red & White family for the rest of my life, even though I had no idea how fast it all was changing in the bike world. The early days of Brotherhood would evolve into something different, as was the rapidly changing American society and times. I did not know that a few evil Members would try and take my soul to the darker side of hell, where there was no coming back from. A dark place that somehow I could not go, because I still had a conscious of sorts. There was still some good left in my soul. Though I was blinded by the Brotherhood, in the end I would learn to see again. Believe me when I say that I was as surprised as you probably are.

Besides the Bass Lake Run, the U.S.A. Run was the biggest run of the year in those times for the Red & White. I washed all my clothes and carefully packed them in my saddlebags. I had about four sets of the necessary two socks and t-shirts, with an extra pair of Levis. I also had my black leather shirt, pants, and jacket that I rolled up in my sleeping bag, putting it against my chicken bar so that I could lean my back against it for the whole trip. This created sort of a chair/cockpit backrest of sorts, for comfort on that rigid frame. I had my leather cut, with my Colors, and my beloved California Rocker on it. I was ready to take on the world with the biggest and baddest Motherfuckers known to man in modern times. Then Chuck, a veteran Prospect, and I set about to hustle up some bucks for our trip. We didn't have enough probably for the whole trip, but that wasn't unusual for us. Him and I proceeded to burn a scoot and got our usual $500 from our Frisco connect.

That burn went down like this. We borrowed one of Chuck's lackey's trucks and drove around until we saw this dude putting through town on his Shovelhead. We followed him to this grocery store parking lot, and watched him go in. Then like always, we drove up next to the bike, me jumping out and hopping up on the seat and trying the ignition. It was a new style Shovelhead, and so the ignition was locked. The owner had failed to lock a padlock on the front forks, the only real deterrent. I kicked it into neutral and stood it up, closing the kickstand. Chuck backed the truck up and then pulled up next to me. I grabbed the wing window bar of the truck while Chuck reached out the window and grabbed the handle bar. He feathered the clutch and away we went. We turned down the side street as we came out of the parking lot. We went a couple of blocks, pegging the bike with the truck, and then turned and went down a residential street. Chuck jumped out of the truck and we loaded it into the back, laying it on its side. An hour later we delivered it to our Frisco people.

It had gone off simple and easy, like always. I think that one was number 31 for me, and my karma has probably never recovered from that. Chuck and I were pros, at something we both hated to do, and promised ourselves after we got patched we wouldn't do anymore. Then we took that money from the bike and moved a few bags of dope. Then we 'borrowed' a few bucks from our stripper girl friends at our bar. I sold a hot pistol I had for 50 bucks. Which gave us a grand total of $850, and we were as ready as we were going to be to go. We all met up at our stripper bar as planned, with Hangtown Bill, and headed out for Sacramento to begin the journey. "Get your motor running," as we headed down the freeway, and our adventure began! That particular year the U.S.A. Run would be hosted by the Iowa Hell's Angels, with our final destination being around the Omaha, Nebraska area. At the time I had never been there, and it seemed a long way away.

Later on, I would end up hiding out from the law near there, on my Aunt's farm. On the way, we met up with some Oakland members, Duncan and Johnny B. By the time we got out of Sacramento, we had about ten bikes. We powdered up our noses and just kept riding on. We finally stopped in Winnemucca, Nevada, which was just a little short of our planned Salt Lake City first stop. Cross-country runs always look good on maps when you're all sitting around at the bar buzzed and bragging on how far you could ride without stopping. We found a smaller casino and parked our bikes around in the back alley. There were three Prospects, so we set up shifts to watch the bikes. Chuck and I took the late shifts like we always did. So since we were off duty as far as the parking lot was concerned, we went inside to watch out for the Members and sneak some drinking time in. Like always, we figured if we slammed some drinks pretty fast, we might be able to get a little bit of sleep before our shifts. We had been crankin' for a few days, trying to get our own shit ready on top of helping Members, with only about two hours sleep, if that was what you would call it.

As we went in I saw a black-jack table. I told Chuck I was going to play the two dollar minimum and give it a whirl, and get a free drunk out of it. I can usually drink faster than I lose. My Dad and Uncle taught me how to play when I was a kid. I kept getting lucky, stayed with the minimum bet, and slugged down the hard liquor as fast as I could get them to bring it. My lucky roll went on for a couple of hours and I kept slamming those drinks. Chuck had gone to try and crash as I kept on playing, getting about half shit-faced. You have to be careful on how fucked up you get, as it's a unwritten law that when you're a Prospect you're not supposed to be partying, but rather working 24/7 taking care of the Members. You can get away with it a little, but you have to be careful, and watch who's around when you do. Many a Prospect has gotten knocked right on his ass for exactly that. All it takes is for one Member to decide you're having too good of a time, or not paying enough attention to the Members, and

BOOM, you don't even know what hit you. I was keeping an eye on my mentor, Hangtown Bill, who was playing near me. Bill wasn't doing so well, so he came over and watched me play a hand or two. Then he leaned forward and whispered to me that my early morning shift was coming up soon, and that maybe I should get something to eat, and maybe a little sleep.

Hangtown was playing Father to me again, and I never minded that. Matter of fact, it probably saved me getting my ass knocked down more and a few times. I immediately took his advice and cashed out my chips, getting about $110 or so profit. Then I invited Bill and his old lady, and another Member who was still up, over to the coffee shop, and I would buy breakfast for all. We all ate and I still walked out of there with $90. I threw my bag out next to Bill and his old lady, along with another Member that had already crashed-out in the alley amongst our bikes. Chuck was still on watch, so I got a couple of hours sleep before Chuck woke me up at 4:00 am. He made sure I was all right and had the gun before he lay down. We didn't know it then, but that would be a good sleep compared to what we had coming in the future. I immediately grabbed some coffee and stirred some meth in it, known as Biker's coffee by us. I smoked a skinny joint for some entertainment as I started to get wired up, while I waited for everyone to wake up. I watched as Johnny Law cruised by about a dozen times. So everything seemed as it should be, with *some* normality.

As the sun first started cracking it hurt my eyes, which made them start watering and itching. I felt a weird sensation, as if I was home, like I always feel in Nevada. It's always been a deja'vu thing with me since I could remember. I would feel the same way as a kid, when my Dad took me to Carson City to visit my Aunt and Uncles. I always felt like I was at home and comfortable with my surroundings there, and still do. Nevada seems like my old stomping grounds to me, but that's another story. Everyone was up by 6:00 am, and went in for breakfast. So much for the "Salt Lake City the first day" bullshit. I decided to dump some more 'Drano' in my Biker coffee and felt ready for the day. I didn't need to eat as I was plenty full from our earlier breakfast. I usually ate only once a day then, anyway. Chuck came over and congratulated me on my winnings. He told me that everyone was talking about my winnings. Chuck and I were happy because we had added some money to our kitty, and might make it home after all. We thought that we may as well celebrate, so we smoked a joint for breakfast. I remember that we had to sneak off and be extra cool, because pot in those days was a felony, especially in Nevada, where it was still proably a hanging offence, and even worse if you were an unwanted Biker.

Just as we finished, a cop drove by, checking us out; whew, we were so glad he didn't stop, as we both stunk like pot. As the Members started coming out of the casino, the prospecting started. "Prospect, go get me some suntan shit," "I want a red handkerchief," "My old lady wants some lip balm, and hurry the fuck up as I want to get out of here! You don't want to hold up the pack," the Member said. I thought to myself, "I *am* holding up the pack; to get *your* old lady's shit!" We finally got the bikes fired up and away the pack went, "Head her down the highway!" We stayed on I-80 as we crossed the Salt Flats and Utah. We hit some of the worst, badass winds I have ever ridden in. We were all leaning into the crosswinds at what must have been a 45 degree angle, to stay up on two wheels. When we passed diesel trucks that had to move slowly, you had about a split second to jerk your bike back up straight, as fast as possible, because they blocked the wind. Then, as you passed them, you had to quickly jam the bars back down and bank back into the wind. At times, it felt like you were going to be sucked under the trailer. We had to pass hundreds of them, as their trailers whipped to and fro in the wind, which forced them to go slow.

In true Hell's Angel style, we never slowed down one bit, sticking to our custom of speeding down the highway. I thought it was pretty much a miracle that nobody went down that day. When we finally got to Salt Lake City, we stopped and gassed up and made a phone call at the pay phone. Before we could finish topping off our gas tanks, here come our escorts in force, the Sundowners MC. They were all decked out and waiting for us, as they had invited us as guests to stay at their Clubhouse. We followed two of their members as the rest got behind our pack, to show us their respect as they led us to their Clubhouse. It was the biggest MC Clubhouse I have ever seen; it easily could have been a whole city block. We were told it used to be an old hotel before they got it. At that time, the Sundowners were the biggest MC in Utah, and had Chapters in a lot of other states. The Barons MC was small then, and was the next biggest. Now, it's the opposite in Utah.

The Sundowners had *really* rolled out the red carpet for us. Free booze, rooms, drugs, women, anything you needed or desired; we were treated like royalty. They showed us Prospects to our own room to put away our bags, and told us not to worry about their own Members, as their Prospects better be taking care of their every need. When they walked out I said to Chuck "This is more like it; it's about time we are finally getting some respect and appreciation." We both laughed.

The drugs were flowing pretty well, and all the Members were having a real good time. That was good; it meant that we might not get fucked with all night. Chuck and I figured that we could possibly sneak off for a while and get a little R&R. More Angels started showing up from California and Nevada that were actually going to ride their bikes to the Run. With Chief and some of the hard-asses not there, things were better for us than ever. Chuck and I jumped up and did an early guard shift, and got cut loose for our efforts. Hangtown said to go have some fun, and we had to obey a Member. One of the younger Sundowner's Members took a shining to us and asked what we wanted to do? "Can I show you guys some bars and finer sights of Salt Lake?" "Hell yes, that sounds good to us," Chuck said. So we jumped on our scooters and away we went. We dragged raced around town while he showed it off. I noticed that the cops seemed to leave these guys alone. Then, we bar hopped to a couple big bars after about an hour of exploring the local tour.

There were chicks everywhere and this Sundowner seemed to know them all, as he introduced us as his Hell's Angel friends from California. It seemed we were very popular quickly, as we all had a chick on our bikes as we jammed from one bar to another, puffing on weed and snorting lines. We went by all the big Mormon churches downtown and shit, as this town was big, and we must have burned a tank of gas jamming around it all night. The Sundowner made the suggestion that we should go back to the Clubhouse to the party that was happening. Chuck and I knew better than that, the Members would probably steal our chicks and put us to work. We wanted to party too, and not just fetch the Member's beer and shit. AWOL was what we pretty much were, because we figured Hangtown had really never said how long we should be gone. We figured we would proably get our asses chewed for escaping the ball and chain for a while, but we also knew what was ahead. Well, at least we thought we did. We figured this would be our biggest prospecting challenge yet, or at least that is what the rumor was; and, how true it would turn out to be!

This young Sundowner seemed like he understood our need, proably because he had a shiny new Patch on. Other Club's prospecting duties back then weren't that different than ours; prospecting is prospecting. So he took us over to his place, and broke out all the party favors; so we did, too. He treated us like super stars, and this would be the bitchin' part of the whole Run for Chuck and I. At first, we broke out some un-cut crank that we had stashed in my handlebar. We could tell by what we had sampled, that this Sundowner and these girls didn't get the pure shit much, so we lit 'em up! The girls loved it to the point of constantly asking us what it was called, because they "Haven't had anything like this before, can I buy some?" We explained that it was just good old R&W crystal meth. The shit they got proably got stomped on so many times before it got to them in Utah, by everyone in between, that it proably *did* seem different. Like always, they all wanted to buy some. The Sundowner was trying to be cool in front of the ladies, but told us later that as soon as we could, he would love to set something up. Chuck said the right thing that "We would soon." Soon would be after we got Patched, which was when we'd be allowed to set up a deal, as we couldn't forget our place. So Chuck gave me a wink, and I knew exactly what he was thinking. They had been sharing their weed of a mediocre quality, so we broke out a joint of California bud from Chuck's handlebar. That crossed their eyes again, so the Sundowner finally broke out with his hybrid stash. It was pretty good, and he traded us a bunch to take on the road with us for just a little un-cut crank. We hadn't carried much weed through Nevada for the obvious reasons of going to jail forever, so it all worked out good. We partied hearty after taking advantage of all their hospitalities, including the bedrooms. Chuck got the blonde and I got the red head, as it was his turn for first pick. We always split everything, as fair as possible, down to the last smoke. We rode the girls back to the bar we had found them at, with the promise that we would look them up on our way back through in probably a week. A promise we would never be able to keep, and we never saw them again.

We knew we were gonna catch hell when we got back, and we did. We got the usual, "Where the fuck you been?" Sometimes you know why they call it prospecting more than at other times. It's a necessary ride you have to make to get down the road to full Membership. Some Members need attention all the time. "You and fucking Chuck go out partying again," is all Hangtown said while shaking his head. With that knowing wink our punishment was dealt out quickly, and they split us up going two different directions. I had to go watch the bikes all night and Chuck had to go wrench a Member's bike after he played fetch and carry up in the Clubhouse for most of the night. It was OK by me though, as I had a smile on my face and was wired to the gills. They couldn't take *that* away. Besides, I liked watching the bikes for awhile because you could get away from the Members. They came outside of the party once in a while for various reasons. A lot of times they come out to do a little bump and were normally glad to share their secret. Members are different to you in that situation usually, as there is much more one on one, and most are trying to get to know you personally. Without all the peer pressure and hype from the other Members, you usually got a friendly one on one conversation going. I used to always take this bike watching time to do any wrenching and cleaning up on my bike. If you were real careful, you didn't let a Member catch you, because if you did, that would give him the idea to clean or work on *his* bike. I got real good at dropping my tools or polishing rags quickly. You have to remember, these Members party hearty! I'm not saying that Chuck and I would play them, but I guess in a way, we did. Some Members saw this and would try their best to split us up. It all but died by 4:00 in the morning. I had put my tools and rags up and damn near fell asleep lying on the ground. I might have passed out for a half hour or so, as I needed to lie flat on the ground to straighten my back out. An early riser fired up his bike at about 4:30 am and caused me to jump straight up from my "back straitening exercise." I looked frantically, seeing that it was a Sundowner, as he acknowledged me with

153

a knowing grin. Yeah, he had busted me. I thought, "That's it", I got away with a nap and I wasn't going to get caught sleeping on duty by an Angel Member, especially with the Oakland Heavies with us, and while being punished for going AWOL. So I said, "Fuck it" to myself, and took a hit out of our stash in the handlebar. I didn't have any coffee so I just ate some, and had to gag it down. I almost puked, so I went and found somebody's half-empty stale beer from the earlier party and choked some down. There went the gagging reflex again. What I wouldn't have done to go get some coffee or water. When all else failed, I snorted it for fast wake up, because I was exhausted. I rolled up a dollar bill and just shoved it into the bag and up my nose, and huffed. I repeated that in the second nostril and my eyes crossed and started watering. I physically jumped around for a minute, as it burned up into my skull. I started focusing, finally, on the living, as the sun just started to crack.

That was pure shit all right! My mind reeled a bit as I collectively thought of how much of this prospecting I could do before my 20 year old heart jumped out of my chest, as it was trying to now!

In ten minutes I was wide-awake and ready to go on, and I had a feeling that it was gonna be one of those Prospector's Blues days. As always, everyone finally got up. It had been a long night for me. As Members started coming out of the woodwork, Chuck confided in me that he had gotten a little sleep. I told him what I had to do and he understood, and said "That's what we brought the shit for right, prospecting?" I finally got my coffee from a Sundowner Prospect who looked like he had gotten his beauty rest. Hangtown blessed my coffee with some meth for me, as if I really needed it now. If Chief ever caught you starting to physically or mentally nod, he would have a spoon of dope up your nose, BANG, as he cursed you for pussying out. To him, it was just snort more dope, fuck sleep and rest. Chief always said, "You're gonna have plenty of time to sleep when you're dead, why do it now?" I hadn't slept but for those couple hours in that casino parking lot since we had left. That new day's dawn looked to be the beginning of another long-ass day. But with the meth we had, you could run a week on it, as it was *that* chemically clean then, and we would do just that. This is was what it was like prospecting for the Hell's Angels, and they *all* have to go through it. We finally got organized and said our goodbyes and thanks to the Sundowners for their hospitality. I wondered as we were leaving if the Sundowners might be the next R&W acquisition.

Looking for adventure as we all lined up on the I-80 freeway heading for Wyoming, Duncan and Johnny B. were up front and rolling. I enjoyed riding cross-country with these famous, hard-to-know Angels from the Oakland Chapter. It was just one on one, as we gathered up, now about 40 strong. Most of the Angels we were riding with were some of the best of the times, which was as much fun as it was an honor. Some Members you can only get to know in a small group, and on a long run, while on the road. A lot of barriers and protocols begin to break down as you face the world all together as a group. When you see Members at big parties, clubhouses, and Runs it's different. That's when all their old Bro's are there and they really don't pay you much mind; you're just another Prospect. It's like you have to put in your time and earn their respect by your deeds and actions, before they will pay you much attention. Just because you get patched doesn't mean a lot to most Members, except that they respect the Colors you're wearing. You have to earn the rest. So it's a slow process, and that's just the way it is. Today's bike Clubs are very cautious, as they should be. It is their world, and they can't let outsiders or the law get too close and threaten it.

After we entered Wyoming, we stopped at the Little America on I-80 for fuel and a break. That's when Duncan bought a flask that had a leather cover over it. He sent me to get him a jar of whiskey to fill it up. Back on the road, we made it quite a few miles before we unluckily hit some road construction, and shut off our bikes behind the flagmen to wait. That's when Duncan called me over to where he and Johnny B. were leaning against their parked bikes, taking turns on having a pull off the flask. He told me, "Go ahead, have a shot on us, as Johnny and I want to get everyone to sign it that made the ride from Cali. That way there won't be any arguing on who did or didn't make the ride this time. If your name isn't on the flask, you didn't make the ride!" I signed it and handed it back over to Johnny, who took a pull as Hangtown came over and did the ritual and signed it. I was so proud to be with these men and have my name next to theirs. Before this Run, the only time Duncan had said anything to me was at an all night Club party in Oakland. I had been running with Jungle Jim for about three straight days of riding and partying, and was simple glad to be still alive. I was told to stay with him 24 hours a day, and not to let him out of my site. Jungle was a crazed, unpredictable Member with a serious drug problem that had been on a roll. He was an older Member, who had patched out from the Sons of Hawaii MC. The Club tolerated him when I knew him. He was a fuck up at times, for sure. As soon as we had rode up and shut off our bikes, I could tell there was a problem. A group of Members came up and jumped him, as I tried to get as small as I could and out of sight. I kind of knew what was going on.

I went downstairs and started talking to an Oakland Prospect when Duncan walks up to us and says, "Hey Prospect, what the fuck are you doing? You hiding down here or what? Get your ass in gear and take care of these Members!" I looked at the other Prospect, and then realized he was talking to me. "Yeah, I am talking to you, are you hiding or what?" Duncan asked me. I told him no. "Then get your ass going, go talk to a Member and see if he needs something. They are maybe gonna be your Brothers some day, so go fucking meet them and party with them!" Here's Duncan, the big famous Oakland Member who was at the time President of the Oakland Chapter during the time Sonny was locked up. I have to admit, I was being shy, as I was still pretty new at the time, and admittedly a little nervous. I also had been up for about three days trying to take care of Jungle Jim, as I had been told. I was cool with the Nomad Members that I knew, but not with the famous Oakland Chapter yet; they were like the other Gods in our world. To Duncan's credit, he was just being a good leader.

When we got to Green River, Wyoming we had news media car with us that had started following us along the way. So by the time we got to Rock Springs, they had the news vans with camera crews in them, following us. We were big news in Wyoming. They would pull up to the back of the pack and then pull up along side of us, with the cameras filming, trying to get the whole pack. Our standard policy at the time was to block them, so a couple of us pulled out to block the second lane. One of the Prospects flipped them off. They were determined to get the Death Head Patch on TV, even if that meant them causing an accident if they had to. They stayed right on our asses, and then tried to swing around us on the shoulder, so we swung out in front of them, again. I guess they finally got enough footage for the five o'clock news, because they dropped back behind the pack. We stopped for gas at some little shit-hole gas station, with the news guys following us. They kept their distance and filmed us fueling our bikes. When we left and got back onto I-80, I looked in my mirror and they were gone. We rode about 20 miles or so, with about 60 more to go to get to the next big town where there they were waiting for us, when we stopped.

They had followed us all the way into Rawlins, only this time they had pulled out ahead of the pack and were filming the Members in front; "Smart fuckers," I thought. We were celebrities now! There was a bunch of them now, and they were a lot braver as they walked right up to the Members and started asking questions. They refused any interviews, or to answer any questions that they kept asking anyway. I was topping off my bike with gas when one of them came up to me and asked me on camera where we were going. I told them "Nowhere I think, look around you," and I grinned at Chuck, who didn't say shit. Later on I got chewed out for saying that. "You don't say a fuckin' thing to nobody, Prospect," Hangtown yelled at me in front of some of our people. I didn't argue the fact that what I said was meant to be a joke. Later on that night, Hangtown pulled me aside and in his own way, said he was sorry for schooling me. We finally pulled out of that town and Johnny Law pulled us right over. The circus just kept getting bigger. I believe they had every cop, fireman, and dogcatcher all gathered up to confront the entourage.

I heard the one hot dog Sheriff say that our kind wasn't welcome in Carbon County, and we had better just keep moving on. One of the Members popped off, "Why would we ever want to stop here? Why would anybody for that matter, there's nothing here!" The one cop quickly said, "We like it!" Judging by the people lining up along the highway to get a peek at us go by, we were popular. There were cops and rednecks in their four wheel drives, with their guns hanging in the rear windows, all staring at us like they wanted blood. I couldn't help but agree with the Member; I mean this place was like Redneckville Heaven in Deliverance. We had gathered a lot of attention since the town of Green

River. I believe some of the redneck locals really wanted to see some Hell's Angels blood spilled, as it looked like this could get crazy real quick. We were proably the biggest thing to hit this area since the invention of TV. I have to admit that it was all a little intimidating. I thought how the Easy Riders movie had ended, and it was starting to feel too real, like it could really happen!

To show you how ironic life can be, my future wife of 20 years was watching the Hell's Angels on TV with her sisters in her little bum-fuck hometown in Wyoming. Her and her sister decided to all jump into a car and drive the 40 miles out to I-80 to sit along the freeway with some other curious locals, to wave at us as we went by. They all were just being nosey, wanting to see the famous rebels of the freeways pass by. So once on TV, and once riding by on the road to the U.S.A. Run would be the first of two times my ex would first lay eyes on me. As fate would have it, we would cross paths again at a large bike run in Colorado, called the Grand Lake Run, two years later. I would eventually marry her and Father my two children with her, as life can be strange.

We rode on and finally got to Cheyenne, the Capital of Wyoming. There we found more rednecks in trucks, cops, and curious locals, all trying to get a look at us. It was starting to get dark as we pulled into a Holiday Inn with cops tailing us. As some of the Members started to walk in, Johnny Law finally got brave enough to pull in behind our pack and turn their red & blues lights on. Duncan, Johnny B., and Hangtown all went over to talk to them, and I heard the same old "We got the right to ride through here like anybody else." The cops countered with the old "We don't want any trouble here in our town, were just trying to defuse the situation." They wanted us to keep going and we refused to leave, telling them we needed a place to crash for the night. I don't know how they struck up a deal, but the pack got the sign to fire it up. So a single cop car leads the pack back to the interstate with the rest of the cops following behind us. They slipped us off the freeway at the far edge of town at the last exit. And lead us around a little road to an out of the way hotel. The two cops got out and talked to our leaders, while the rest of them watched from their cars from a distance, and finally they all split. We had finally ditched the circus with the law's help, which was a damn good plan. I spotted a cop car with two Deputies pulling into a parking lot a little ways away. That kept them pretty much out of sight and they were able to keep an eye on us all night. There weren't enough rooms for all of us, even if Chuck and I could afford one. So we just threw our bags down between our bikes and made us a camp; we were gonna be out on guard detail all night anyway.

Hangtown come over and gave us our pep talk, "You guys need to pull a shift tonight and keep watch over everyone, and the bikes. We need you guys to stay on your toes all night, watching for any rednecks or citizens; the cops warned us about it and said to watch out. They don't want any problems, and we don't either. So stay here and keep a low profile!" After he walked away, Chuck said "Oh well, it doesn't look like any bars or local pleasures for us tonight." I told him I didn't get any sleep last night, so I wouldn't have been worth a shit anyway. Then a Member comes over, "Hey you guys need to get everybody's food order and make the run for the liquor store, too. Try not to lead any company back over here!" Chuck and I were waiting in line for the food at McDonald's when I asked Chuck, "What do they think this is, the Easy Rider movie all over again?" We got back with the food and the booze and got everyone fed and happy. Then, Chuck and I grabbed a bar of soap and casually slipped into their small pool for a quick deush. We tried to keep the suds down, as it sure felt good.

I got about three hours sleep that night, as my shift was the last one. I loaded up on some Biker coffee and had to get down behind my bike as I chased the coffee with a small joint. I saw the cops watching us change shifts too, so I kind of nodded at them to acknowledge that I appreciated them being cool. I was wide-awake as people started getting up and coming outside, milling around. I was told to pass the word to get our shit together as we needed to get the fuck out of there. The word was that we would make it to the U.S.A. Run by tonight! We stopped at a diner for breakfast and everyone went in to eat. I had to watch the bikes but my Bro Chuck brought me out another coffee, which I loaded up. I wanted to stay standing anyway, as my ass and back was hurting from all the miles we had ridden. Even though I was a young buck, I'm not gonna lie about my ass, I was sore; even with stuffing an extra piece of four inch foam pad under my ass that Chuck and I had brought along to help. They actually make them now out of space foam or gel, but ours were the forefathers to that idea, as we had cut them out of a chick's waterbed pad. She had gotten really pissed off about it, too! We finally got gassed up and everybody fired up and got back on the road, and left Cheyenne behind us in my rear view mirror, as we continued on for Nebraska and "what ever comes our way!"

As we proceeded along riding through the day with just quick fuel stops, we finally crossed the Nebraska state line. Our pack just kept getting bigger as we picked up a few members here and there, as the seemingly endless miles rolled bye. We were 60 strong by now, and kept on rolling. I was ready for a little break personally, but our Road Captain didn't think so. Finally, when I was convinced my ass would be totally numb for the rest of my life and I was pretty sure I wouldn't be able to walk ever again if we did stop, we pulled into a rest stop for a small break, as we had spotted some Nebraska Angels there. With some backslappin' and hugs, they decided to take a break and have a few beers. I knew what that meant for us, "Prospect go get some beers!" Chuck and I were back in the saddle and on our way back to a liquor store we had passed about five miles back, in a little town. We unloaded our sleeping bags so that we could haul more before we hit the road. We scored the booze and proceeded to use our experienced expertise, as we had to tie five cases down as best we could. We made it about half way back when I had to motion Chuck over, as one of the cases against my chicken bar had started to slip. I lost a case off my bike once and didn't think I would ever hear the end of it.

We slowed down and pulled over off the edge of the road and towards this dirt ditch. I started re-tying this beer down, when over Chuck's shoulder I saw what looked like a dream come true. There in this cornfield along this drainage ditch, in-between the corn was all these beautiful pot plants! I mean big, budding cannabis sativa plants that looked to be at least eight feet tall. Chuck and I looked at each other in total disbelief as we agreed that we had hit a big score this time! "Wow man we hit a fucking gold mine, how did this beautiful shit get here anyway", I asked? "Who cares," Chuck yelled, "Lets load up as much bud as we can. We can probably get rid of most of it at the Run man, and make a killing; we'll be fat!" Out popped our knives and we went to work. We cut all the buds off, and I threw out socks and t-shirts to empty one side of my saddlebag. We finished filling it up to the point I could hardly get the buckle to work in the last hole. I started to cram all the stuff out of that bag into the other and thought fuck this shit, if I fill that side up too, I can buy all new socks and shit I wanted with all the money we were gonna' make. So I emptied it out too, and filled it with more bud. Chuck saw what I did and was doing the same thing. We were speeding and were working fast for a bunch of reasons. First, we had a whole bunch of thirsty Hell's Angels waiting to have a cold beer, and they weren't getting any colder in the sun. Second, we felt like we were stealing and if the cops showed up, they probably would figure that we had grown it somehow.

"Well, let's haul ass," Chuck says. "Yeah, we better get man, but look at all the bud we are leaving behind," I said. "Well we can roll some up in our jackets, too," Chuck says. We jumped on that, and quickly had them stuffed and tied back on after re-packing the beer. We were finally satisfied that we had taken all that we could possibly find a place for. "We'll remember the mile marker and if we sell all this, on the way back maybe we can rent a u-haul truck and load our bikes in it and take a pile of this shit home," Chuck said, as we threw up our kickstands and pulled out. We had ingeniously stuffed bud into every pocket, even in our tool bags. I mean, we had it stuffed everywhere on those two Harleys! We kept looking over our shoulders and going as fast as we could to haul ass back to the pack. We didn't want to get our hands caught in the cookie jar. We caught up to where the pack was, and they were just getting ready to send out a search and rescue party to find out what the fuck happened to us. We knew they would be pissed but figured if we passed around some free bud all would be forgotten. So while we were getting our asses chewed, Chuck pulls out a hand full of bud with this big shit eating grin and his big, brown eyes glowing. "Look what we found," he announced!

I will never forget the gleeful excitement on his face. One of the members grabbed some and asked us where we got it? Chuck told them the story of how we found it, and that there was plenty more in the cornfield if they wanted to go get some, too. This Nebraska Member busted out laughing and asked us if we had smoked any yet? "No we haven't had a chance to yet, we just stole it and wanted to haul ass back here before the beer got warm" Chuck said in our defense. "You two dumb fucks, that's no *high* weed, it was grown around here during WWII to make rope for the military. If you smoke the shit, it will give you a bad fucking headache is all," he said with a giggle. Everybody, including the few old ladies that came along, all started laughing their asses off, as we started unloading all our 'money' into a garbage can. We told Bill after we unloaded it that we were going to be leaving to haul ass back to get our shit back. "Sorry, but we're leaving in a few, and you guys can't hold the pack up by going back," Hangtown said. Now we had no clothes and no money. That's a true story, as much as I hate to admit, it really happened.

Following our Nebraska Brothers, we un-eventfully rode through the rest of that state for a while. We seemed to have lost our news media coverage back in Wyoming; good riddance. As we rode on, I couldn't believe how much corn was being grown. The country was flat, and hot, which made for a boring ride most of the day. The good thing about riding through Nebraska is getting to the other side, and we finally did. We were "Born to be wild," and more Members kept joining us as we approached Omaha, with our pack being well over a hundred bikes by then. We didn't know it, but the cops and the news media knew exactly where we were going, and were waiting for us. All of a sudden, they fell in just behind us, as we entered the outskirts of Omaha. All I could think of was "here we go again," as the cops edged up behind us Prospects at the back of the pack with their sirens and lights going. There must have been at least 30 cop cars, and some media mixed in that rolled upon us. They were two abreast with their cars one in each lane, which then blocked both freeway lanes going in our direction. We were riding two abreast in the inside lane, which was a little out of the norm of our usual "running in the fast lane."

In the outside lane a cop car inched up until he was across from us, when the cop in the passenger seat started waving at us to pull over. After a half-mile or so of all of us ignoring him, they started honking their horn, and then used their PA system to tell us to pull over. We all just looked at them and shook our heads no, and pointed up towards the front of the pack. This went on for a couple of miles when the cop car started to merge into us. We just scooted in a little and held our lane. That seemed to piss them off, as they had about ten rows of cop cars behind us with them all two abreast, waiting. None of the Prospects would budge, because we didn't want to get our asses chewed out for breaking formation. This went on for five miles or so, and we were getting closer to downtown Omaha. Finally, the cops got the idea and punched it and hauled ass up to the front of the pack, with their line of cars in tow. They had a row of cop cars next to us, from the front of the pack to the back, all with their sirens and lights going. There were TV camera crews jockeying for position in this parade. It was quite the spectacle, as we all watched this whole procession going down the road for another couple miles.

The Members in front were shaking their heads no and refusing to pull over. I was beginning to think that we might get away with it by not pulling over. Finally, Duncan and the leaders pulled the train over. Then the fucking circus started as they all jumped out of their cars and approached us. They checked our licenses and registrations and tried to match up the hog's case numbers and called everything in. They were hoping to catch some of us on warrants, and thank God they didn't have the computers of today's world. This all went on for about an hour and a half. We pulled a old California trick on these country bumpkins. We would stand in small lines shoulder to shoulder as they checked out our bikes and call us up one by one while eyeballing for weapons or drugs while examining our paper work. Behind our backs we passed our guns and stash back in forth to avoid detection, worked like a charm. TV cameras were going, with the reporters crawling around trying to get interviews with *any* of us. Word spread down the pack that we agreed not to stop until we got through Omaha, if they would let us get going. That was our plan anyway, as we were just trying to get to the Run to see our Brothers, not party in Omaha. We all finally got to put our paperwork away and fire it up again, moving the whole parade as we rode through Omaha. As we came to the outskirts of town we all pulled into a large truck stop for fuel and hopefully a break, as I desperately wanted a beer!

The Nebraska Chapter of the Hell's Angels was sponsoring the U.S.A. Run that year. They had snagged some land in probably the only tree laden area of the state, which must have been a challenge from what we had seen riding in this flat-ass state. We finally had left Omaha with the Nebraska Members still leading us, in a pack of what must have been 150 bikes. What seemed like a five hour ride, as my ass was totally numb, was probably half of that. The Run site was definitely out in the sticks. Thanks to the cops and the news media, we were arriving after dark. We finally hit the main gate, which already had a bunch of Prospects from all over the country manning a makeshift security barricade of sorts. As we finally got to dethrone our horses of steel, my legs wouldn't work for a minute. So I hung on to my handlebar until blood started flowing back into my legs. Everyone started backslappin' and throwing out the "How you been?" "You rode all the way from California?" another asked. "No Shit," another Member commented. Electricity was in the air and you could feel it. It was like you knew something wild was gonna' happen, like at a Jimi Hendricks concert, or something. Hangtown finally came over and said he wanted to get down to the main Run area so that we could try to locate any of our Chapter Brothers who rode in the Chapter's U-haul and set up camp. We fired up our bikes and left the rest of our road trip companions behind.

We had to ride around awhile to locate them, as our fellow Nomad Chapter Bro's had camped amongst other Bay Area Chapters. The big 32' U-haul truck my Chapter had rented to haul the majority of our Member's motorcycles to the Run was parked under a tree. Harry the Horse had been in charge of that, with Sweet Phil's and Big Moose's help and Chapter monies paying the rental, gas, etc… The rest of the Members had come up in their personal cars to meet us and their bikes there. If it weren't for Hangtown Bill's intervention on Chuck's and my behalf, we would have been stuck in the Run truck. Bill had talked them into letting us accompany him on the road trip, thank God! We weren't gonna' have the same luck on the way home. Our camp had two huge trees that they had spread out under. That's where Chuck and I decided to throw down our bags and what was left of our shit, kind of under the big U-haul truck, to make camp. This, like always, would later be a mistake, as we ended up needing to use the truck. This would be our tent and home for the next four days.

Glancing around it was hard to believe how many Angels were there.

My God, it seemed like an entire city was encamped here. At the time, it was the biggest bike run I had ever been to! There were some lights set up through the trees and a lot of campfires going, with one main fire in a staging area. I was taking in the site when Harry came up and asked Chuck and I "Where the fuck have you guys been?" I explained how we had just gotten there, and we were setting up our camp spot. "Then are you through fucking around yet?" Harry asked. I wanted to say, "I am not the one that hauled my bike across five states instead of riding it, I rode mine!" Instead, I answered, "Of course, what do you need done Harry?" "Well, we want our bikes unloaded, what do you think?" Harry responded. "Of course, what was I thinking," I exclaimed! We immediately went over and pulled out the ramp. It took us awhile, as we were tired and had to untie each one and roll it off. We finally finished, and I was exquasted.

Thank God, right then Moose comes walking up and says, "Prospects, you're with me!" We strolled out, away from the camp, when Moose asked us, "How was your trip?" I gave him some quick details, excluding our pot find, and explained that it was one long-ass ride. Chuck briefly filled him in on the Wyoming and Omaha news media thing. "I will try and cover for you guys so you can get some sleep, because you look like you both need it. If any Members come up and bother you guys, tell them to talk to me. We'll tell them that you need your sleep, as you both got guard duty tonight. Now go crawl under that truck and get some sleep," Moose said. I thought to myself, what an Angel, literally. I was beat and wanted to go check everything out real bad, but I know when you get a chance to get some sleep when you're a Prospect, you're a fool if you don't take it. So I was asleep in about five minutes, and only the magic bag could have awakened me. Chief woke me up in about two hours and Chuck was already gone.

"What in the fuck do you think you're doing hiding under this truck," he said. "Ah, I think I was sleeping Chief, Moose told me I could before my guard shift," I said, probably a little sarcastically. "I don't give a flying fuck what Moose said, here Goddamn it, get your fucking act going and quit embarrassing me, and you're at the U.S.A. Run for Christ sakes!" He handed me a bag of crank and a knife. "Fucking get tuned up will you,

you're not going to embarrass our whole crew, Goddamn it. If you even think you're getting tired, you come find me and get some more. Keep that bag on ya', and keep Chuck up too. Where is he anyway?" "I think he went to take a shit," I lied. I did a double barrel snort, right out of the bag, and was up and running in about a minute. Once my eyes quit bleeding, I focused on Chief. "Hey Chief, I'm sorry I was sleeping, I don't know what I was thinking, we just rode in a bit ago and unloaded everybody's bikes. How was your drive, anyway?" I knew I was asking for it with that smart-ass comment, because he was our leader, but I rode and he drove, and I was beat because of it. I paid for that one right away. "Ok smart ass, you get on your fucking bike and ride up to the front gate and I'll see you in the morning. Where's that fucking Chuck shitting at anyway?"

Yeah, I guess I was a little cranky and thought fuck it, I'll pull fucking guard duty all night, at least he gave me a bag. I got up to the gate and there was a lot of action happening there. Everyone was wound up tight with excitement and anticipation of the next five days. Things were looking good, as the Prospects of Omaha were my kind of Bros, as they had a cooler full of ice, beer, and sodas. I figured that this wouldn't last long, but it was nice for now. I asked for a beer and was told to go ahead and help myself to some all weekend. So I slammed the first one and then immediately popped another; I needed that! They had placed some chairs and tables around that made it comfortable. I tried to analyze the situation, which was probably unnecessary. With all these Angels here, who would be stupid enough to try and steal or fuck with anybody? What exactly were we guarding and who from? I guess we *could* get a full blast frontal assault, or be attacked by the Outlaws, Pagans, or maybe even the cops…

We did have a good walkie-talkie system going so that we could warn the main body of any coming attack or disaster. I finally admitted to myself that I was doing my job and Chief would fuck with me one way or another. The Members all took off for the main camp and party, and that left a half dozen of us Prospects on the gate. They had radios at the two other entrances; one at the back gate and the other one at the side entrance. We all got to know each other and shot the shit about everything. The sun finally started cracking and finally I could see real well. I wondered when I might get relieved, when here come Chief in his borrowed Cadillac. He and Big Moose jumped out of the front, and some young stranger got out of the back. "Everything cool," he asked? "Yeah, Chief, it's been slow the last couple hours," I said. He broke out a bag and a little spoon and, after indulging, handed it to me. "Good, this is Terry and he's a Massachusetts Prospect that I wanted you to meet. He's gonna' come back on his bike because I have asked him to show you around, so that you can show the rest of our people.

I shook Terry's hand and noticed that he was a long-haired, younger guy like me, but seemed awfully nervous. They split, and I sat down and drank a beer and smoked a joint with another Prospect. Terry pulled up on his bike as we were finishing the joint. He jumped off his bike and strolled up and grabbed a beer. We drank a couple pretty quickly then jumped up on our scoots and rode around and through the whole Run. We cruised through the various camps, from one end to the other. Terry showed me all the entrances and where we had security shifts going. It was an impressive site, as there were Angels from all over, with all kinds of Prospects around, which made me feel better. I was starting to like this Terry character, as he was cool enough to let me know everything. "If the cops raid us, we'll try to slow them down or stop them, while we call on the radios to warn everybody inside. If another Club shows up, we alert them by radio and send someone back to warn them. Then we'll shoot the fuck out of them with these." He walked over to a small car and opened the trunk, and there was an arsenal of shotguns and assault rifles, all loaded and ready to dance. "Or, you can just stab them like me," and with a blink of an eye Terry had his stiletto out. "Can I see yours?" Terry asked me. I made my fastest draw as best as I could, which was pretty fast. "Yeah, it's a Rigid," I told him with pride. "Nice, but it's too big," as Terry went on to tell me the finer points of knife fighting, how many people he had stabbed, and how he couldn't wait for the next victim. Terry was a likable guy, but I could see one flaw in his character, and that was he was a psychopath. Over the next four days while working side by side with him, I would get to know this lanky speedster too well. No wonder Chief liked him, as they were two of a kind for sure. I kept noticing the entire back-east Prospects shying away from him like he had the clap. This Terry took a real shine to me for some reason, but looking back it's not hard to figure out why. I had learned a long time ago in jail that you don't shy away from psychopaths. You're better off to absolutely show no fear at all, and if at all possible, make them think you have the same thoughts and desires. I couldn't really get rid of him as he stayed close, and his own Members seemed to think he was crazy enough to just let him do as he pleased. But in this place, I would use him for protection, as I wanted to survive.

Bikes and more bikes came in and out. The walkie-talkies worked just great enough to keep us Prospects running. When we caught up with Chuck, I introduced him to Terry. Chuck kind of gave me that look like, what the fuck? So Chuck joined us as we toured the rest of the run, and we saw this long line of Members. I asked what they were doing and Chuck said he had checked it out earlier, and they were getting branded! We watched as they put the red-hot glowing branding iron to one Member's arm, and you could see the smoke and smell the burnt flesh. I almost gagged on that smell. I saw Big Moose there in line; he was drinking on a bottle of Blackjack whiskey. Our eyes met and he gave me this smiling, knowing nod, as he took another pull off the bottle. It looked to me that you would need more than whiskey for that one, because this made tattoos look like child's play. The branding rod emblem was simply the letters H. A. There were at least a hundred Angels in line waiting their turn to be branded. I had never heard of branding humans before. As we left there, we got pulled over when we went by our camp. There were a couple of Omaha Angels there, and some others I had never seen before, all talking with Chief. They informed us that the Prospects needed to get more firewood, as they had burned it all keeping the fire going last night. "You've got to get organized and leave some Prospects at all the guarding locations, and take the rest that you can to go get wood," Chief ordered.

So off we rode to stop and gather up every Prospect we could find, and tell them to meet us up at the main gate. We decided on who was on guard detail and who would go for wood. We were scratching our heads and trying to figure out how we were going to do this, when one New York Prospect says, "We can all just ride out to the woods and tie some on our bikes." Chuck and I got a chuckle out of that one, when Chief comes strutting up. "What we need is a big truck to get a big pile of wood" Chief said. Then he told Chuck and I to get our big U-haul truck from Harry the Horse, and go pick everyone up at the front gate. "Don't come back without a big pile of wood, Goddamn it." Obviously, Chief had just woken up. On the way in I didn't remember seeing any firewood, as it was all flat farming country, because after all we were in Nebraska. The only woods I had seen were where we were camped, so I thought this might become a real bitch. Terry, the Massachusetts Prospect was still hanging with us and complaining, which would prove to be a habit. "I don't know why the Omaha Chapter didn't have this already taken care of. They're sponsoring this Run, so it's their job and we shouldn't have to do it." He kept muttering how unfair it was that we had to do their work. "And, if that one don't quit grinning at me, I'll fucking stab him," Terry confided in me! He was referring to an Omaha Prospect. I could see that this was gonna' be a long Run. When Chuck, Terry, and I got to camp, we found Harry all fucked up. I didn't blame him a bit, because he just got branded. "Yeah, go ahead and take the truck, but you get them fuckers to fill it up with gas." We finally made it to the gate and crammed about three Prospects up front with us, and three more hopped in the back. With that, we told the rest of the Prospects that we would be back and to have fun on security. I felt relieved for the first time in days as we drove away from the gate. It was like a monkey had just crawled off my back. We drove somewhat aimlessly looking for wood on back dirt roads, as we listened to Terry explain the art of stabbing people, with three of his own personal stabbing stories. I looked over at Chuck as he rolled his eyes during the last story. To be honest, nobody had the balls to tell him to shut up, as he kept ranting and playing with his stiletto. We found a couple broken limbs here and there, and a small, dead tree, but had neither chain saw nor ax, but we were able to push it down with the truck bumper and load it. This wasn't going to be enough, and would take forever and cost a lot in gas. We spotted an old wooden fence and tore it down, and loaded about a dozen of the fence posts.

We drove back and backed up to the bonfire area, and started to unload our find, when a couple of Members walked up. "Is that all you got," one of the Nebraska Members asked? One of their Prospects spoke up in our defense to the fact that was all we could find. We got our asses chewed out because there was no way that would be enough for even tonight. We got the same old story on how worthless we were, and how "Back when I was a Prospect, it was a lot different!" Same old shit and you *have* to stand there and listen to it. I watched Terry's eyes darting around, at attention, and could only wonder what was going on in his mind. I was beginning to think that we were fucked, as we were told to go back out there and fill the truck up, and not to come back until we did. We stopped at the front gate and explained to the Prospects there our problem, and nobody had any bright ideas. The Nebraska Prospect said there was a good-sized town about 50 miles away, and if we pooled our money maybe we could buy some. "We're going to buy the wood for the next four days? We don't have that kind of money," I commented. We all agreed we needed to do something fast. We told the Prospects on security that they had better just stay where they were, as we didn't know how long this was going to take.

We took off driving and eventually ended back in the cornfields; I thought, "This is going nowhere". We were on a remote dirt road trying to find a place to turn the 35' truck around, when we saw a house with a for sale sign at the bottom of the driveway. We pulled in to turn around when it hit me, "Look, there is a barn and a fence we could steal." This place was sitting out off the main drag, off a dead end dirt road, and with nobody living there or within eyesight. We got all the Prospects out of the truck and held a little pow-wow. I asked everybody what they thought about tearing down the fence and maybe chiseling on the barn a little to get a full load. Terry was the first to speak up, "Fuck it, let's steal all we can!" We all decided that we had no other choice because we needed a lot of firewood, and there was no other place to get any. I broke out that bag of dope Chief had given me. We calmly passed the bag and knife around, and we all got to know each other a little better. After passing around some joints, someone coughed up that we were ready to get started. We got the corral and fence first, and the hard part was that we had very little tools. We found the truck's lug wrench that we used to pry boards off. Then someone found a couple of old leaf springs and some axles, in a pile of what looked like old tractor and farm machinery parts. At first, we were looking over our shoulders, waiting for the cops or owners to show up. So after a hustling our asses off for the first hour, we had all calmed down to the point of laughing and joking as we worked. With those simple tools and eight guys, it didn't take long and the first load was ready to go. Everybody's spirits seemed to pick up, as we knew we would impress the Members back at camp.

Four of us remained behind to start tearing down some of the barn for the next load. I went in with the first load, and we drove right up to the main bonfire area and started a pile by this tree, to kind of hide us. Members came up and were impressed with our progress as we quickly unloaded. We had driven by the cops on the way in, as they were watching us at all the entrances. They were taking pictures and writing down bike's license plate numbers, trying to bust us on a warrant or something. With that 35 foot truck that was totally enclosed, they didn't have any idea what was in the back, so we felt safe. On the way back out, we stopped here and there, as we all wanted some beer and water to take back. When we got back to the scene of the crime, we were happily greeted, as they were all thirsty from their labors. It took us most of the day to get the first three loads, taking turns on who stayed and who got to go unload. The corral and fencing were long gone, as we got started on the barn. It took a lot of kicking, beating, and prying as we disassembled it.

We finished taking off the lower part of the barn's board siding and took a break, passing around a bag of crank for energy. Then we backed the big truck up to the barn and got on the roof of the truck to work on tearing the roof and trusses off. We were on another beer break, and as we sipped some beers and passed around a couple of joints, we were looking at a chicken coup. We figured, fuck it, it's going too. We kept it up even after it got dark, and felt safer, as we could see anybody coming. We rode a couple bikes over to use their headlights to see as we worked and loaded. On the one run in just after dark, they had to stop and gas up the truck in town, so we had them stop and get burgers and beer. I went on a delivery run and was impressed by the size of the bonfire as we backed up and unloaded some of the wood directly into the fire pit. The party was on, with a band playing on the stage and Members drag racing there bikes here and there. There was still a line at the branding fire. The whole scene reminded me of a big carnival, with everybody having a blast. We got back to the scene of the crime and told everybody what was happening, with everybody feeling some jealousy. So we took a long break and got a good buzz going ourselves. The truck arrived back at about sunrise, and they said it was slowing down some, and it looked like we proably had enough wood for the next night.

We kept it up all day, changing some Prospects with others who had been doing guard duty. We all knew we were racking up good points with the Members, as we were all working hard and doing our jobs. I got pulled off firewood detail late that afternoon and was told to help on one of the re-supply runs. When we got that done, I was told to go pull a security shift at the front gate. I watched the U-haul truck come and go all night, and when I had a break I rode back to camp and saw the huge pile of wood they were accumulating. I figured the barn must be totally gone by now. On the third day, I got to ride escort with my bike for another re-supply run. On the way back, I decided to swing by the firewood operation and see how they were doing. To my surprise, the whole fucking house was about gone! They had almost torn the whole thing and took all the wood. Mostly all that was left was old plaster and shit that couldn't be burnt. I thought about how you can't stop a bunch of motivated Hell's Angel Prospects with a bag of crank from not doing their job. Then all of a sudden it dawned on me, and I kind of panicked and got the fuck out of there. Someone was going to be pissed! I have always hoped that they had plenty of insurance on that old place; but we had solved our firewood problem! When you're prospecting, sometimes you have to have an imagination to make things happen.

When I got back from the supply run and checking out the house that was no more, I didn't even get through the front entrance and was back doing security again. Chuck was there, so we snuck off to blow a joint of that crazy Sundowners shit. My finger was all cut up from the firewood detail, as all I had were fingerless gloves. I could hardly hold the joint. I mentioned to Chuck how I couldn't remember my last tetanus shot, and would proably get a fatal infection going. Chuck started cracking up laughing, and said, "I wouldn't sweat that Bro, look where we are! If this doesn't kill us, our ride all the way back home probably will!" He was right as always, as we were definitely in harm's way and far from home. We went back to our post and sat down and told Terry and another Prospect that it was all clear over there. Chuck and I changed our socks, as we had picked some up in town because we hadn't changed them since we had thrown all our clothes away. The old ones stunk so bad that we threw them in the garbage can. I was watching Terry playing with his knife when a car with Massachusetts plates pulled up, full of Terry's crew's Members.

They called him over and talked a minute, then let a girl out of the back seat. He grabbed her by the wrist and walked her to his bike. She looked pretty roughed up, but not a bad looking gal. The phrase, "rode hard and put up wet" came to mind. I immediately knew something was wrong with this picture. Then Chief and a couple of Members came riding right up to us. They apparently knew what was going on with this chick. He told me to go with this Prospect, meaning Terry, to town, to help him with her and cover his ass. I told him, "Sure," although I wasn't sure what "help him" meant. Off they rode, and Terry said to me "Let's go!" What was going on was this chick was that she had been 'turned out' as they had 'pulled a train' on her at the Massachusetts camp. She had been either innocently baited, or knowingly came, to this Run. I have seen many women end up in this position for many different reasons; some actually enjoy it and some hate it. She was being coy, but I could tell she obviously had had enough. Somehow, she had convinced them that she needed some medical attention, and smart enough to convince them that she wanted to come back for more. Using some medical condition as an excuse to plan her escape, she had been damn convincing to talk her way out this far.

Terry put her on his bike and off we headed for a nowhere, Nebraska town. We followed the hospital signs through town to find this little hospital. We parked the bikes under a tree at the curb. Terry jumped of his bike, pulled his knife out, and got in this chick's face and started yelling at her. I figured she must have been pleading with him during the ride over to let her go. I could see the sheer terror in the girl's eyes. He told her that if she didn't do exactly what he said, or try to get away, he would stab her. He had this crazed look in his eyes, and I belived that he meant it, as did she. He was all pumped up and angry. I don't know if it was the drugs, alcohol, or lack of sleep, but he was very convincing to me that he was a truly a madman. Since I had met this guy, he seemed pre-occupied all the time with stabbing people. This Terry was definitely on the edge of his sanity, totally an evil man. I thought, "Why would the Hell's Angels want this crazed motherfucker in the Club?" This was one of those times that I had to question myself about being a Prospect for this Club.

What was I doing here with this psychopath of a human being? Had I crossed the line of no moral sanity, like this Motherfucker? She kept sobbing and begging to please be let go. She promised that she wouldn't say anything to anyone about anything, if she could just go home. I couldn't help but notice that she had a few marks and bruises on her, and I could only imagine what she had been through already. She probably got into this willingly, as a fantasy, or to get back at her parents or guardians, maybe drugs; whatever the reason, obviously she had had enough. But, she didn't understand that it was easy to get into her position, but even harder to turn a bunch of partying Outlaw Bikers off. They are not used to being told no, and rarely will listen to reason. Terry had been told to take her to get whatever medical attention she needed and to bring her back. That was exactly what Terry was planning to do. He told her that if she said anything, or plead with the doctor, or tried to run, that he would stab her right there. I could see the fear in her eyes as she quit sobbing; she believed him, and so did I. He asked me to watch the bikes and said that he would be right back. I watched them as they went threw the glass doors at the main entrance into the little hospital.

They were gone for a while, when I decided to go sit on the steps and smoke a cigarette. I couldn't help but feel sorry for this chick and tried to convince myself that this wasn't really my problem, or any of my business. The chick had gotten herself into this, and my Club Brothers could do whatever they wanted to. Somehow, I had this feeling of guilt that I didn't understand. Right then, the door opened and she came running out, and as she went by me, I grabbed her. She immediately started pleading with me to let her go, that she would do anything for me if I would just let her go. I knew that I had to help her. I just didn't want to get caught by the Club, or stabbed for it. What if the law picked her up, or she went to them for help? I would be implicated, probably for rape, and maybe even kidnapping charges! All sorts of possible scenarios were going through my mind. If I were to go to prison for my part, I would be a dead man amongst the population for going against the Club. I didn't want any of this, and was risking everything, but I knew in my heart that I had to help her escape.

I grabbed her by the shoulders and looked into her eyes and told her to run, and not look back until she found a place to hide; stay there for a while, then go home. I told her, "Whatever you do, don't go to the law, because you don't want to get involved in that, or you'll be hiding from the Club for the rest of your life!" She looked at me with those wild, terrified eyes, and promised she would do as I said, then ran off around the corner. I would like to say that she gave me a dramatic thank you, but she didn't; she looked at me with wild, scared eyes and then ran for her life. About a second later, Terry came busting out the door, yelling, "Where is she?!" I told him that I didn't know, and turned it back on him, "She was with you!" "Well, she had to come out this door," Terry yelled. "You didn't let her out of your sight, did you?" I queried back. "Well fuck, they took her into the exam room and said I couldn't go in, and to wait in the lobby," Terry said with panic in his voice. "Well, there must have been a back door then," I said. "You guard this door while I run around to the back door and check out the inside again, as she must be hiding in there," he yelled over his shoulder as he ran around the corner. I prayed that the chick had done what I said and ran to a good hiding place, because there was no telling what Terry would do if he caught her!

It took awhile, and I was relieved when Terry came back out alone, saying he couldn't find her. He was real nervous and said, "We have to get out of here now, I think there calling the cops!" I could believe that, just by looking at this crazy motherfucker and imagining what he said and acted like in front of the doctors and nurses. We fired up our bikes as fast as we could, and jammed back for the safety of the Run and our own kind. On our way back, I pondered what was going to happen when we got back without the chick. It wasn't my fault that she got away, as far as they knew. I could see the cops showing up with her in the back of the car, pointing out her assailants. How many Members might be busted for rape or kidnapping? If she gave up that I had let her go in court, my ass was dead. This was the first and only time that I had gone against the Club, my own kind. I was playing with fire; for that matter, my life. I had broken the Club code, and my conscious would let me feel nothing but shame and guilt.

When we got to the turn to the front gate, Terry stopped and jumped off his bike and I was sweating bullets. Then he said nervously to my relief, "I'm gonna' tell them that she must have said something to the Doctor, because they grabbed her and wouldn't give her back, ok! I never let her out of my sight, right?" "Yeah, you didn't, you did just what you said, and I'll back you Terry, because I like you!" I was glad that he hadn't tried stabbing me. "Ok, man, you had better back me," and he jumped back on his bike and we rode up to the gate.

I sat there on watch at the side gate that evening, waiting to see if the cops would show, and wondering if she had made it without talking to them. Chuck could see that I was in deep thought and was leaving me alone to my thoughts, and talked to the other Prospect that was there. He and I knew each other *that* well and always gave each other respect, as we were together sometimes constantly. I contemplated on what would happen to me if she had talked to the cops. I was praying that she made it, and could hardly believe what I had done. If that crazed Terry ever found out, he would stab me, for sure. I checked my strap on my knife sheath, thinking that I would put up a good fight. I wasn't going to give that psychopath Terry a chance to stick me in the back. He had been bragging on how many people he had stabbed. I always figured a woman would be my downfall, but I never figured it would be one I didn't even really know. I didn't want to fall in love with a chick, because I didn't want the responsibility of it. But, here I might have blown my whole life on a woman that I didn't even know. I popped open another beer, as I contemplated the possible fate that my stupid actions may lead to. Finally, I decided fuck it, what was gonna' happen was gonna' happen, and there was nothing I could do about it. I went and joined the others, talking and partying.

We were there all night, which suited me just fine. Unlike the constant traffic at the front gate, the side one was relatively quiet for the most part. So Chuck and I devised a scheme to each get an hour sleep. I would cover for him as he would go 'walk the perimeters,' but really go lie down in the bushes until I would wake him up. He took his turn first and then I had mine. Then we watched the sunrise together. Some other Prospects came to relieve us, and told us to report up to the front gate.

We were doing our time at the front gate and stopping everyone who wanted to come in. The cops were still manning their position, watching us. I was enjoying the warm sunshine on what turned into a beautiful day. I was trying to keep that chick out of my mind. Then, here came most of the Nomad Chapter, all riding their bikes. They pulled up and threw down their kickstands, and Chief walked over to us. He told Chuck and I to get our putts, as we were going for a ride to go check out the town. He told the other Prospects there with us not to worry, he had a replacement for us on the way. For some reason, it cheered me up that we were going for a ride. Then Chief pulled us aside and handed us a bag after he took a whiff, and we packed our noses with him, while he muttered something about us going to sleep on him. He always did that after about the third day of no sleep and running in the fast lane. I don't know if he had gotten any sleep driving his Cadillac to the Run, but I knew he hadn't since he got here. Waiting for Chief to go to sleep was a waste of time, because he rarely did. He liked the idea that there was "Plenty of time to sleep when you're dead!" He's been catching up on his sleep for a long time now.

It actually felt great to get back in the saddle again, even though at the time my ass was still sore from riding through five states in three days on a rigid frame. Of course, riding with a mean bunch of drugged-out Outlaw Bikers seemed like the best thing in the whole world. I always liked the riding part better than the stopping part, because nobody fucks with you when you're in the wind, Prospect or not. That and I could always sort out my feelings and problems better while riding. I felt a lot of guilt and fear, mixed with a strange feeling of a conscious, for once. My fate was like the wind in my face, unsure with an unknown direction. I thought to myself that things just couldn't get any worse; or could they? The next thing that was about to happen would change my life forever; something I will never forget. I still wake up with nightmares about this ugly, vivid memory. I am sure now, looking back at it, that the fatigue and drugs probably enhanced what I remember about this.

We rolled into town and Chief picked out a bar where we could see other bikes at. I was glad it wasn't next to the hospital, and praying that we wouldn't run into her. Chief ordered a round of drinks, while Chuck and I waited outside, watching the bikes. I was relieved, and Chuck wanted to count how much money we had left, to see if we had enough for a couple new t-shirts. Our money was getting low and buying new clothes wasn't helping; fuck it, we had to have new t-shirts. We calculated what we thought it would cost us in fuel, and figured we could at least make it to Nevada if we were lucky, and didn't eat much. We knew that we could borrow some coin from Hangtown or Father Jack, and make it up by selling some dope when we got home. That's when Prospect Terry came strutting down the street with some of his Chapter Members. My heart almost stopped even though I had meth pumping through it. They stopped and Terry introduced us to his Members; one of them was the Salem Witch. I had heard of him from Bear talking about him. I liked him right away because he seemed real, as he looked you square in the eyes and shook your hand, and Bear said he was a good Brother. I don't even remember the others names, as they acted like the usual stuck up, Patched Members you always meet.

We all bullshitted a little bit about California, Massachusetts, the U.S.A. Run, and the trip home. To my relief, the chick was never brought up. We talked of our mutual Bro Teddy Bear and his misfortunes, "If you see him again, tell him the Salem Witch says high!" I enjoyed our brief conversation, and as they started to leave, Salem told me that when I got patched, to come on out for a visit and he would show me around. If not, he said, "I'll see you next year" as he handed me his card with his phone number on it, and saying to keep in touch. This was pretty much out of character for a Member toward a Prospect. After they walked away, Chuck came up and said, "You guys really hit it off." I told him that if Bear liked him, you could figure him on being good people. I didn't know it, but that would be the first and last time I would ever talk to the Salem Witch, but not the last time I would see him. Everybody started coming out of the bar and we were told we were going to hook it up. As fate would have it, we had to wait on one of the Member's old ladies to get some film.

As we were fired up and idling at the curb waiting to pull out, my eyes were darting around looking for that chick. I noticed the Witch was riding by us heading back out of town towards the Run, riding in the front. He gave us a wave as him and his crew, including Terry following behind their pack, came by us. A couple more cars come by and we finally pulled out. I thought that if we were lucky, we might catch the Witch and his crew at the front gate, and I might get a chance to talk to him some more. Salem's group was probably a hundred yards or so ahead of us. We came upon a long, straight stretch of road. I saw another group of maybe five bikes heading toward us that had just came around a corner and into view. You could tell that they were hauling ass, as they seemed to appear so fast. We were doing about 75 mph or so, so that meant that they had to be doing a hundred plus. I watched as the lead rider of the oncoming group was just about to pass the Witch's group, who the Witch himself was leading.

At that split second as they were about to pass, the lead rider of the oncoming group just kind of floated up and drifted over, just crossing over the centerline. At the last second, as they crossed paths, he slammed right into the Witch. It was like time froze for an instance, as I saw a flash of sparks and a splash of red, misty color flash as it exploded in the air, with a loud boom and pieces of debris flying in every direction. Our pack almost ended up in the middle of it. Both packs of bikes and other traffic all hit their brakes at once. You heard this load screeching everywhere, and saw smoke as everybody locked them up and went into a skid, trying to stop and avoiding colliding into each other, or the accident. I still can't believe no one else collided, as by the time we all stopped, both lanes were blocked with bikes, and vehicles behind us. The Salem Witch that I had just met an hour earlier had literally exploded in front of our eyes. The flash I saw was blood, bone, and body, in a flash of red, as the Salem Witch disappeared. There weren't enough pieces to gather up to call a body. In a matter of a split second, he had vaporized and disappeared forever. We had skidded and finally stopped almost in the accident scene, as we jumped off our bikes and ran up. The biggest pieces of both bikes were mangled together, making the bundle almost one bike. Witch's bike was not recognizable at all.

Monk, a very big Member from the New York Chapter, was lying in the road trying to get up, but couldn't. He was in deep shock as we all gathered around him in a circle. I looked down at him and he was lying in his own pool of blood. A Member yelled "We got to get him an ambulance now!" I saw his Levis that were almost torn completely off his bad leg. There you could see that above his knee, half way up his thigh, was a huge slice missing. He started yelling, "Let me the fuck up!" He just kept screaming that and trying to sit up. Someone behind me yelled "We have to hold him down because he's bleeding to death!" All of a sudden, I'm kneeling down by his bad leg, and a Member says, "You hold here and push down and stop the bleeding" as he directed my hands just above the gash. I focused on just his leg, as I had to push harder because his thigh was pushing my hold up, and the leg just stayed there, showing the separation. I could see that it was literally cut off, with just skin or a little muscle holding it from totally separating. I could feel his warm blood squirting on me, as I pushed and tried to squeeze the stump that was left of his leg from squirting blood.

There were at least six of us trying to hold him down. He just kept trying to get up and yelling at us to get off him. It was like a nightmare with the yelling and screaming, as I watched him lose more blood and starting to get paler. I don't know how long this went on for, but I couldn't see one spot of him that wasn't fucked up real bad, with blood everywhere and chunks missing all over. I couldn't believe how strong he was, as he at times would almost lift us all up as he struggled to rise. It seemed like an hour, but were actually minutes, before an ambulance arrived, with the Members yelling at the two Ems, telling them to hurry. The lead guy looked like some farm boy dude with glasses that must have just left the farm. He was terrified with the Members yelling at him all at once, in their despair. When he saw Monk and pieces of the Witch, he turned fucking as pale as Monk was. I thought he was going to puke on us as he started babbling to his assistant. Monk was fighting less, and growing weaker and paler. A Member shoved the geek with glasses to get him moving, and he just started babbling again about how he had to call a doctor for something like this. "Fuck, you had better do something now!" a Member screamed at him.

These two country bumpkins were going into shock themselves. Then another Member yelled, "God damn it, there's no fucking time for that you fucking idiot, you have to stop the bleeding now!" I looked down at

Monk and all the blood and pieces, and felt desperation for him and helpless. I continued squeezing as hard as I could. I believe it was Kanuck that yelled, "He's bleeding out," and grabbed the EMT by his shirt, screaming as he lifted him up. "Do something to stop the bleeding, get a tourniquet and some bandages on him now!" I heard someone else say, "These guys are gonna' let him die!" I could see that blood was everywhere, from both men.

They started to react finally, and the EMT was getting stuff out of the van. I still had my hands clamped around Monks leg, above where it had been all but severed off. I continued to keep all my weight on it, but I could feel Monk getting weaker. Then the EMT was all of a sudden kneeling next to me with this cloth leg cast looking thing. I heard someone behind me ask, "What the fuck are you going to do with that fucking thing?" He started mumbling that he was putting his leg into it so it would stop the bleeding. I'm no EMT, but as soon as he started putting the lifeless leg into the leg cast, right where it was severed it started to come apart. I know that he did more harm than good.

Blood started squirting at us more as he got the lower part of Monk's leg into it. The EMT told me to let go. I looked up for just one second, and Kanuck nodded yes to me, and I let my grip go. The EMT slid the bandage quickly over the gap and the rest of the whole leg. I watched Monk's face contort a little and turn paler. I continued to watch, and what seemed only a second later, his face went totally white as his heavy breathing and mumbling stopped. I stupidly tried to put my hands back the way I had them over the bandage. It was all over, Monk had passed.

I remember we all stood up, looking down at him lying in his Hell's Angels Club Colors, in a pool of blood. I wished I hadn't let go of him then, for his sake and my own, as that would be my nightmare. A Member grabbed the EMT and slammed him against the ambulance, "You killed him, you worthless piece of shit, I should kill you!" The fucking sirens finally showed up as two farmer cops jumped out of their patrol cars. They took one look at the bloody scene and I thought they were going to puke, too. I looked down at myself and the blood all over me, and my first thought was that I couldn't change my clothes because they were all in a ditch in fucking Nebraska. I was in some kind of shock myself. Little did

I know then, that almost exactly thirty years later it would be me lying there, trying to get up with people and EMT's trying to save me from bleeding to death?

I really didn't have the time to go into shock, because Chief confronted us and told Chuck and I to "Go pick up the remains of the Salem Witch!" You can always count on Chief. "Fuck man, he's gone Chief," I wearily said. Then Charlie spoke up, "What pieces, he's all over the place, fuck, he's gone Chief!" "I want every piece of him picked up now, were not leaving one piece of a Club Brother here on this chicken shit road, motherfuckers!" When I reflect on it now, I have to respect Chief for what he did and said. We did need to police up our own, as it was the only measure of respect we had left to give him. In a way, we were picking up ourselves! We all somberly spread out a few feet apart, and walked the entire scene. We did the road first and then the ditches on each side of the road. As we did find him we gathered him up. One bone fragment here, maybe with a piece of flesh on it, or maybe just blood there. A piece of mirror here and a piece of unidentifiable chrome there, even pieces of Levis and shreds of his Colors; we picked it all up. We just kept walking back and forth and continued picking up the pieces, like robots. This went on for a couple of hours, as I felt stunned and chain smoked one cigarette after another. The funny thing was that my hands were calm and I never shed a tear.

Police cars and ambulances came and went and they took a lot of statements from the eyewitnesses. The best account of what happened that day by those who were there, was that Monk, a New York Member, was in the lead of a pack of Angels as he came around the corner and into the straight stretch, doing 100 mph plus. Monk, along with some other Members, was headed for town to check it out. The Salem Witch was leading his Crew back to the Run, doing about 75 mph. Both groups were riding two abreast, as is the standard. Right where the two packs would cross each other, the road had a long dip on Monk's side of his lane. When he hit the beginning of the rise, he traveled threw it, and into the dip he lost some control. At the high speed he was going, his suspension system flexed enough that his bike sort of rose, and the momentum made him float as it came back down, putting him across the double yellow line. It was just enough to cause an almost straight head on collision between the two bikes. The force of the impact was tremendous, but more devastating on the Witch, being the slower moving object. Witch just disappeared into a red prism and his death was over for him in the blink of an eye. Monk suffered with his fatal wounds for how long, I really couldn't say, but too long, for sure.

Monk was a very large Angel in size, and the younger of the two involved in the accident. I was told that he had a good reputation as being one wild and crazy dude. I never was introduced, nor had the chance to meet him before the accident. I had seen him at a distance waiting in line on the first day with other Members, for his turn to be branded; that didn't hurt anymore. My hope is that the Salem Witch didn't feel anything, and I'm sure that was all right by him; I know it would be for me. I feel that the irony of it all is here are two Hell's Angels that risk their lives everyday to be the individuals that they want to be, with a war going on with another Club that's out there trying to kill them. You face crazy motherfucking drivers out there trying to run over you. Then, you have the cops constantly after you, with a permanent jail cell just waiting for you. So how do these two Hell's Angels come to meet their fate like this? There is no reasoning to it, there's just fate. An old saying back then that was said to have originated back in Vietnam was, "When your time is up, your fucking time is up, and there's nothing you can do about it!" Maybe in Vietnam that seemed true, but this was fucking Nebraska, on a two-lane, back-ass country road. What kind of a fucked up epitaph is that?

We are talking about proud men here that taunted death against all the odds and previously survived! It broke my heart then, and still does to this day. These two Outlaws, in my opinion, deserved more, and maybe their story won't be forgotten now. This incident was one of the saddest days of my life. I could go on, but I won't out of respect, and re-living my nightmares that I try to forget. I have tried to forget the sight of the pieces of poor Witch, and the dreams of the men that were scattered everywhere, along with the bloody scene of Monk dying in my hands. Even after thirty years, it is still vivid.

We finally made it back to the run where Chief stationed me at the front entrance. A bunch of Angels were gathered there, seeming lost and dismayed. Everyone just felt so down and helpless. For once, there was no one to blame for our tragedy. There was nobody to go fuck up or kill to set it straight, for what had happened to two of ours. Everyone was just bummed out over our loss.

I was at the biggest Biker party of my life and it had suddenly ended. Angels may argue, hit, fight, cheat, or fuck-over a fellow Brother, but that's all just fun and games to them. The death of a Brother hurts, and two at once was just way too much. This is the only weakness that Outlaws really have, is losing one of their own. They have their own creed they live by that outsiders can never understand. The hardest part about Monk and Salem's deaths was that they were so pointless and unnecessary. Their deaths would have been easier to understand if another Club would have shot them down in the street, or maybe a drug deal had gone bad. This wasn't some old gray hair running over two of our own. There was no one to blame, other than our crazy, reckless lifestyles. No one really believed that anyone could have saved Monk; he was as dead as Salem when they hit, it just took him a little longer to go. Angels know that they have an early destiny with death, and you accept that when you put on the Colors, which has a Death Head on it. Do they truly realize that they are ultimately playing with their own lives and deaths? Absolutely, Outlaws live for the moment of one more bike ride and party. They know that they have to pay the ultimate price for their wild lifestyle. It's just a matter of time until it happens. It's like you know you have it coming, but please not yet, I'm having too much fun! This is true of all the old school Bikers that have lived and died in the fast lane. Death could be around the next corner, and that's part of the juice of living this kind of lifestyle. Their deaths were just a reminder to each Member they were just as vulnerability of a premature death. Remember what is on their backs, their beloved Death Head. When they wear that Death Head everyday on their backs, they're showing you who they are and what they are all about. On this day it felt like our protective shell had been broken, like we were exposed. Everyone there was bummed out, no games, bike races or brandings were happening anymore. The party that I thought would never end was all but over.

I came back to our camp after I had been relieved, and was amazed at what I saw. There was a hush that had fallen over the entire camp, and everybody had grouped back up into there own Chapter campsites. The constant laughing and joking was all but gone. There wasn't the constant roar of motorcycles revving up and riding around amongst the group. I hung with our Chapter for a couple of hours talking with Members about what happened. I was glad when I had to go pull another eight hour shift at the front gate. Chief came over and packed my nose for me before he sent me, as I'm sure that I looked like I needed it. I was numb and exhausted from lack of sleep. I rode up to the gate and parked my scoot. It wasn't the busy place it had been before, with people coming and going. I smoked a joint and drank a few beers with some of the other Prospects. I was trying to forget what happened, and that wasn't going to happen because they all wanted to know the gruesome details of the accident. I was trying to avoid it, but they kept asking questions, so I finally explained what happened in a whisper.

We then all speculated on what would happen when the sun came up. I explained that our Chapter, I was told, would be heading home in the morning. Then, we all drank and smoked ourselves into a better mood. To try and forget, we got to talking about who was in the great firewood caper, which kind of cheered me up. Who tore down what, and who cut his hand, and "I wish I could see the look on the owner's faces when they discover it; man are they gonna' be pissed off!" "I'm surprised the cops haven't been here yet about it," I said. I needed the chitchat to get my bearings straight again. I was still feeling guilt about letting the girl go. I knew it was the right thing to do, but for the first time I had turned on the Club. For once I had showed some morality and it scared me! Hopefully she had made it, and it sure looked like I would get away with it. It would be a big relief to a lot of potentially serious problems whenever we *did* leave. I just wanted to get back on the road and leave the wreck and that chick all behind. I used the beer and weed as a crutch to get me through the night, along with the meth, and to do my job.

The sun started to up and the light cracked through the clouds, and as I felt the warmth from it I felt better. I was living the life with the family I had chosen, and convinced myself that everything would work out. Another Prospect showed up and said he was my relief, so I fired up my bike and headed back to camp. When I rolled up it was pretty quiet, and I saw people already packing up their shit. There was still a reverence and quietness in the air. Chuck and I were told to go start loading up the Member's bikes that were ready to go, Next to the U-haul truck. First, we had to unload their damn bikes, and now we got to load them back up. Oh well, no sense in bitching, such is the life of a Prospect. In between Members finally bringing their bikes to get loaded, we policed the area for trash. All we did was picking and tying for a couple of hours. Both Chuck and I started getting tired and sleepy, so we dug into our magic bag to keep going. Some of the Members came up and said their goodbyes as they headed back home in their cars.

We asked around and nobody seemed to know if there was any group riding back to California. That kind of bummed us out, but then we thought of what a great trip it would be since it was just the two us. "Man, we could stop in Utah and visit the Sundowners again," Chuck said. Then Chief came up with his bike to load and tells us to load ours, too. Chuck saw our opportunity come up, and asked if we could ride back as we had planned. "No, you two fuckers aren't taking any vacation; you'll stay with the bikes and help the Members get back home," Chief yelled! You just couldn't get one by on old Chief. We waited and loaded the others first, so that ours would be in the back, just in case. That would mean we would be accompanying Harry the Horse, Sweet Phil, and Big Bruce back to California. All the Members, except for Hangtown and us that rode all the way down, were relying on the Chapter's gas and rental truck to get their bikes back home. So that made it TCB and we couldn't get out of it.

We spent a couple hours saying our goodbyes to everyone, as most of all the Chapters were leaving, too. The wreck had ended the U.S.A. Run and not on a very good note. When we pulled out, Chuck and I unloaded the last of the garbage out of the back of the truck into the dumpsters. When we pulled up to the front gate where I had spent a lot of the Run, it was a real cluster fuck. Different Chapters all leaving and stopping to talk, exchange phone numbers, goodbyes and shit. There were cop cars hanging out and watching one group of them that were talking to some Nebraska Members. I immediately wondered if they were inquiring about that chick or the missing house, but figured it was proably about the accident. Chuck and I would probably be riding in the back of that truck most of the trip, and the Members would take the front, as that would be more comfortable. So we had left a space for spreading out our sleeping bags down for somewhat of a bed. We used some of the Member's gear to make a sort of couch out of their rolled up bags. We got it ready and then went out and drifted through the Members and Prospects, saying our goodbyes. Everyone was still bummed and kind of quiet, talking and being respectful. With our goodbyes done and finally getting our turn to pull out, we were on our way home.

I felt a big relief that none of my fears about the chick or the house had come true. In the back of that truck it was hot, noisy, bumpy, and smelled like gas and exhaust fumes. We thought that it might be hard to sleep, but after being up for about a week and having got almost no sleep, it was a snap. We both stretched out and I was out in about ten seconds. The Members up front didn't wake us up and we slept strait through across a couple states. They finally stopped and woke us up at the Bonneville Salt Flats. It was hard to believe that we had slept that long, but obviously we had needed it. We wondered why they hadn't woken us up, because they usually always fuck with you. It turned out that my buddy, Big Bruce, had talked the others into letting us sleep, that we deserved it. The big door had suddenly rolled up and slammed up to the ceiling, which caused us to jump up. There was Harry standing there grinning and yelling, "Wake your asses up!" We asked where we were and he told us, and then we asked why they hadn't woken us up before. "Because we didn't want to feed you, nor listen to your whining asses," Harry says.

As we were crawling out Bruce was there. He winked at me and pulled a bag out of his cut, as he handed me a big sub sandwich and a bottle of our mutual favorite, Ripple white wine. Chuck and I split the sandwich and washed it down with the wine. We brushed our teeth using the wine to rinse, as we had no water. Big Bruce was a friend, and liked me and always looked out for my best interest. When we had first gotten to the U.S.A. Run, he had pulled me aside and said, "Scary isn't it? Don't worry, it's my first one too, and I will help you all I can!" He was like that, and he is one Member that I truly miss.

The sign read, 'The Bonneville Salt Flats, home of the land speed records'. I was still trying to grind the shit out of my eyes, when Sweet Phil came walking over and handed Chuck and I a cup of Biker coffee. Whew, that got us up and back on the job again! It was hot and dusty, with a constant wind. We figured, fuck it, and climbed up on top of the 35 foot U-haul truck to watch the show. Harry had parked parallel alongside of drag runway, so we could see the whole thing. The Members had thoughtfully bought some beers and had iced them down in a cooler. Chuck and I knew from experience that it would be best if we drug the cooler up onto the roof, because after all, we were professional Prospects and knew our job. All of a sudden, a jet car made a fast, noisy run, blasting down the strip with the announcer calling out speed and time. Then, a drag bike made a sub-sonic dash run down the strip. The speed demons made it very exciting with their dangerous quests for speed records in their respective classes. Then there seemed to be a brake in the action, as nothing appeared to be running. Finally, we saw this little dot moving and as it got closer, you could hear this faint buzz. We all kept watching, as the dot got bigger and the buzz louder. We were all straining to see what the fuck it was. Then boom, it was in sight and gone in less than thirty seconds.

Some guy was walking behind our truck as to avoid us seeing him. I yelled down, "Hey sir, do you know what the fuck's going on?" "It's the small engine motorcycle class, I believe sir!" he timidly answered. Everybody looked at me like I had broken a rule or something. Then we all started laughing our asses off at what it was. It took almost ten minutes before it finally went by, and seemed like another ten before it was gone. It was a Honda 50 or something like that, and we all got a good laugh out of it, as we had no clue. Thus, we found out that they had land speed records for almost anything with wheels. I guess we all thought, who would care? This seemed to break the spell of the Witch/Monk incident for us. After our first laughter since the accident, everybody seemed to go back to themselves. We all joined in a toot of meth and pounded down some more beers. Chuck broke out some of the Sundowner's shit, and we kicked back and enjoyed the show. It was one of those times when you're more one on one with the Members, and actually get to know them more personally. We had all the bikes right under our asses, locked up in the truck, the beer was right there in the cooler, and you couldn't get a better view for security; we were doing our job. I think the only prospecting we really did that day was going to get some more ice, and I needed the stretch anyway. Nobody really seemed to see the need to crawl down off the truck to piss, as nobody wanted to miss any of the show. Everybody would just stand on the edge of the truck with their backs to the crowd and let it go. I noticed that not long after we had arrived and passed around the drugs, the crowd all moved a distance away from us, anyway. It was a great way to forget what we had left behind us.

We got out of there just before dark, which left Chuck and I all wired up in the back of the noisy U-haul truck. We decided fuck this, and started slamming beers and smoking weed until we could finally lie down and get some more much needed sleep. We probably weren't even asleep for more than an hour when they pulled over and woke us up. Two of them decided they wanted to lie down in the back and get some sleep, as their buzzes were wearing off. Ok, fuck it, we let them pack our noses and jumped up front and started driving. We talked about the Run and shit, and everything that had gone on. Chuck brought up that Terry dude from Massachusetts. We figured that he must have gotten some real shit over losing his Chapter's turn-out they had brought along. I didn't say anything, and Bruce joined in, "Yeah, I heard about that, and I *was* gonna' try to get some of that." How in the hell did you guys lose her anyway?" I pondered how I was going to answer that one, when we heard someone beating on the back of the cab behind us. I was saved by the bell. So we pulled over and opened the roll-up door, and out the two Members jumped. "Fuck this, how could you guys sleep back here with all the noise and vibrations?"

So we had to exchange places again with them, and off we rolled. Fuck, now we were all wired up again, and there was no way we would get back to sleep for a long while. We left the roll up door partially open because it helped with the heat. As we talked, we decided to see if they would cut us loose in Winnemucca, Nevada, as we couldn't stand this all the way back to Vallejo. At our next gas stop we jumped out and asked them if we could bail out there. "No, Chief said he needed the both of you guys back home," Harry said, like a robot. We plead our case, and the best we could get out of them was they would cut us loose in Auburn, California. That town is right on I-80, and near our old stomping grounds. We promised that we would be right behind them after we picked up a new primary chain, and some money in Placerville. We told them that I would have to make the trip as soon as I got back anyway, and we weren't going to make it in the back of that truck that far. That is how we conned them into it. So they did cut us loose there in Auburn, but it took us three more days before we got back. Chief was pissed, but it was worth the ass chewing we got when we got back. We had gotten some true R&R time of sleep and worldly comforts that our souls really badly needed.

Looking back at the U.S.A. Run, I reflect on some great men that I had shared the road with, and an organization that at the time was my young life's dream to become a part of. It was a bike Run really beyond measure and an experience of a lifetime that I cannot ever forget. I went from a Hang Around to a Prospect, becoming part of the family which not only felt good, but protected you. I also got my first taste of the notoriety of being with the Hell's Angels. Being part of 'the family' gave you the feeling of invincibility, as all you meet fear you. I had a lesson of the life and death reality of being with the Red & White organization. But, I also had betrayed a trust, as I had let my conscious override my blind loyalty to "the Club is right no matter what."

For the first time, my soul was in a fight between good and evil with a conscious guiding my actions. Even all the drug and alcohol abuse, and the quest for the ultimate thrill, couldn't seem to override it. For the first time, by my own actions, I was questioning my life's dream. It wouldn't be until Yosemite that I would see the good try to surface again from within. I had always been taught to believe that your Brother was right, no matter what he did. But, I would find out that there were some things that a few would do that I couldn't go along with. Many times I had seen evil and had remained loyal to the Brotherhood, right or wrong. I had belonged to another 1% Club and had been living this life for a while. This was the life I had chosen, so what had happened to change my blind loyalty? Was it the carnage I had seen that went on to haunt me, or my inner conscious, or soul? I had found out something about myself that would go on to influence my life's future. Some of the scars I still carry today. The U.S.A. Run was over, and thanks to the law, there would never be another one for me.

BOOTS AND PATCHES

Boots and Patches is a term that a Hell's Angel Prospect doesn't want to hear. If you were ever at an Angels Run in the late '60s or early '70s, you will never forget that scream to order, "Boots and Patches!" The Prospects cringe, as the Members and old ladies scream with joy and let the games begin. It's the Olympics time for the Prospects, only these games are just a little different. When "Boots and Patches" is screamed out, everybody gathers up, including the Members, old ladies, Prospects, Hang Arounds, and any fortunate guests. Then designated Members get all the Prospects together and tell them to strip down to just their boots and patches. So there you are, standing there with nothing on but your boots and sleeveless vest with your bottom Red & White rocker that says 'California'. There you stand, bare-assed with your dick hanging out, naked as the day your Mother had you. That's when a couple of Members proceed to tell all the rules of the first game. At the Bass Lake Run, as an Angel was explaining the rules, I glanced around at some of our Chapter's Nomad's old ladies, and they were just staring at us and giggling amongst themselves behind their old man's backs.

The first game was similar to the old biker weenie bite game, with a few added variations of motorcycle skills. They had hung about twenty strings along a wooded path to the trees overhead. It was about 300 feet long, with the strings somewhat evenly spread out. They had tied hot dogs on the ends of all the strings that hung from the trees. It was like a regular weenie bite game, except there is more than one string and they swing the hot dogs back and forth. Usually, you are packing someone on the back of your bike to go for a bite of the hanging stationary hot dog; that is the conventional game. The Angels version of the game is just you and your Harley and a lot more skill. Two Members manned each string as they would start them swinging back and forth across the path. The hot dogs were all hung about two to three feet higher than your head if you were sitting on your seat while riding your bike. So you had to stand up on your foot pegs to get a chance to take a bite of one, while trying to ride as slow as possible on your bike. The rule that you cannot touch the hot dogs with your hands nor arms, only your mouth, was simple enough. So you had to keep both hands on your handlebars at all times, as you rode your bike down the path as slow as you could, to try and get a shot at one. You keep riding back and forth until you get a bite of one, and then you can't swallow, drop, or even spit it out. You have to carry it in your mouth the whole time as you ride over to the Members in charge. They would check you out to see if you really had a bite of one. If you were lucky, they would tell you "You're done," then you could go ride back over to you're clothes and put them back on. The tricky part of the whole thing is standing up on your foot pegs to the right height, while going as slow as you can go without falling down. Then you had to time the thing swinging back in forth with your speed and travel, to try and get a bite as the hot dogs are swinging back and forth, with most of them bouncing off you, so to even try to get a bite of one is tough. This went on for over an hour or so, as it is a lot harder than it looks. The only part that I really didn't like, in the beginning, was all the Member's old ladies watching me ride around with my dick flopping around and my ass bore to the wind, while standing up on my foot pegs. I was waiting in line on about my fifth pass, when I saw the women all staring and shit, and I thought, fuck it. I am not the only one out here doing this, so it really shouldn't be bothering me.

After the next pass I got lucky and got a bite out of one, basically because a Nomad Member, Big Moose, had cheated and swung one right at me with perfect timing! I finished riding the course in line and kept the dog in my mouth, and as I pulled over to the Member Judges they reluctantly told me that I could go get dressed. I would like to think that Big Moose did it as a total favor, but I found out later that he and some others from our crew had bet money on me against other Chapters. The game was very challenging to your bike skills, and I thought it was a lot of fun, for the most part of it. I pulled into my Chapter's area and threw my kickstand down and jumped off my bike. Teddy Bear's old lady Becky came running over and brought my clothes over to me with a smile. She said blushingly, "I saw you and you did real good!" "Thanks Becky, I did my best," I replied. Great, I thought, so was she meaning the game, or my dick bouncing around; which one did good? I felt like I had made it though, and hopefully had passed the test with flying colors! The worst was about to come, though. I sat down naked on the grass, took my boots off, and put my underwear and pants back on, thinking that this isn't so bad. I contemplated on Boots and Patches as I watched the others trying to get their bite of the elusive hot dogs.

The other phrase that represented an order that you could hear in the old days of the Hell's Angels Motorcycle Club was the "Condition Red" alert being yelled. It means one of two things and neither of them was really fun. If you are sitting around in the Clubhouse or a bar, and a Member yells "Condition Red," that means grab your shit and let's go. Shit being your Club Colors and your gun and knife, dressed and ready to do battle. Condition Red also means that it's a life threatening situation or the Law, both viewed with about the same reverence. You are taught on that command to expect trouble of the deadly confrontation kind, so you go in to protect the Club and go into your own survival mode. But at a Club Bike Run, it was like a family reunion party. So condition red meant to get ready for the fun and games to begin again!

When we had first arrived at the Bass Lake Run, I had noticed this large pit that had been freshly dug. It was full of water and mud and stunk, as I had noticed some Members pissing in it and laughing. That went on all day Friday after we had gotten there, and all that Saturday morning, with a Member filling it up with more water and turning the mud and shit over with shovels. Whoever had done the original work with the backhoe had done a fine job. By the afternoon it was getting riper, by now full of beer and soda cans, food scraps, urine, and all kinds of disgusting shit! I saw the old ladies throwing shit in there, too. I finally asked Chuck what the pit was all about, and he just rolled his eyes, "you aren't gonna' believe it!"

Then all of a sudden, "Boots and Patches" was yelled, and we all stripped down again to our boots and Patches; I was at least getting used to it.

They split us up into two teams, with Prospects from the different Chapters being divided up equally. They put Oakland, Nomads, and Richmond on one side, then some other Chapters on the other side, until they got the two sides evened out. They went on to explain to us all that this was a tug-of-war, and the losers would be drug through the pit. "If any of your teammates start to lose and go in, then you're all going in. If you think of dropping the rope and walkin' in, that's not going to work, as Members will be there to throw your asses in, no matter who you are! There is absolutely gonna' be no ties!" They stretched out a big rope between us and lined us all up, making sure it was even, and then a Member announced that this was the "TUG OF WAR!" They shot a gun in the air and the war was on. We all started pulling our asses off as if our lives depended on it! At first, we all kind of just held back a little, because we had whispered between ourselves before the start of the war that we needed this to go on for a while, for some good entertainment. We knew that if it went too fast, they would make us do it again, and none of us wanted to go through this twice. On it went, back and forth for awhile, then we went into the real thing, as some of the Members started to figure us out. That's when we began to lose, as we started plowing up dirt with our feet. Some of the Members were betting with each other. We finally got pulled right up to the edge of the pit. I figured we had all had it as we started slipping into the entrance, and looking down into that pit of shit was scary, and I didn't want to go in!

I believe everyone on our side must have felt the same way, as we all dug our heels in deeper. Ronnie, a Nomad, was one of the ones out in the front, and one of our biggest boys, who almost had his one foot down in the pit. This was as physical as it gets, and we forgot all about being naked with our dicks hanging out and flopping around, or at least I did! I am sure mine was shrunk beyond sight as we got to the edge of that stinking shit-pit! We held them at the edge, to my surprise. But after what seemed like 30 minutes, we started to drag them poor bastard's right back towards that shit-pit. Someone let out a war cry, along with some pleas of encouragement from the crowd, as we drug them poor bastards right into that shit-pit. We didn't stop until we had them all in up to their necks. I mean, they were swimming in the shit. We all got a big cheer by all the onlookers in the crowd. Our Members came walking over with their old ladies running ahead to congratulate us all. We all went for our clothes and started getting dressed while they all watched and continued their congratulations. I looked over to see all the losers who were trying to get out of that damn pit. No one wanted to get any of that shit on themselves, so no one wanted to help, as they were laughing too hard to do so anyway.

Finally some Members grabbed the end of the rope and told the losers to line up and grab back on, and they started pulling them out of the pit. Towards the very end of the line, they had the bright idea to let go, causing the last two to tumble back in. After the laughter died down they got all of them pulled out, then they lined them up and hosed them off. It sure felt good not to been in that mess of shit. Their boots were full of shit, and they'd have to try and get their cut cleaned and dried off somehow, in order to wear for the rest of the weekend. Man I felt sorry for them, but better them than me. It did cross my mind to carry an extra pair of Levis on next Run, just in case. Believe me when I say we had to give it our all, because nobody wanted to go through that disgusting shit-pit. I had once again gotten really lucky, as we had the Oakland Chapter's Prospects on our side, which had a fairly hefty lot. Chuck, Luck, Ron, and I had sworn to each other before we had started that there was no way we were going through it. Luck even said that if we let them drag him through that pit that he would "Personally shoot all of us." I do believe that he had meant it too, as we all felt that same way. That was some of the entertainment at the famous Bass lake Run!

My second California Run with the Hell's Angels as a Prospect, besides the USA Run, was at the River Run. The whole Nomad Vallejo Chapter was supposed to meet up at Luck's house at 9 am. This was earlier than anyone was really used to, as we were night people mostly and wouldn't get up before noon. We had the usually late Members come in and Chief, our President, chewed their asses as they came straggling in. He then told Chuck and me to ride our asses over to our Vice President Kanuck's house, to "Go see what the fuck is keeping him!" So we dutifully fired up our bikes and scooted over to his house. When we pulled in, he was sitting there on his bike, waiting on his old lady. I could see that he was getting really pissed off at her. About eight kicks later his putt came to life, and he looked at us and smiled. He then yelled his old lady's name out, and after about ten seconds, he yelled her name again, then said to us, "Bye, bye bitch; come on Prospects, let's hit the trail!" Off we rode without her; I guess she should have known better. Angels demand their Old Lady's to be compliant, especially in front of their Club Bros. Generally speaking though, if their lady helped support them financially, which would be about 90% of the case, Members would be a lot more tolerant.

We got back to Luck's house as Chief and some of the boys were inside, getting tuned up with a bag of speed. As we walked up to hear what was next on the list and hopefully get a whiff, Chief told Chuck and me to have a line. "You motherfuckers need to wake the fuck up," Chief barked at us. You just couldn't do anything right by Chief, no matter how hard you tried. "Now get the fuck over to Pete the Reb's house and see what the fuck is up with him; if you were thinking, you would have stopped by on your way back from Kanuck's place." We really didn't give a shit about what he said, because we would have been wrong either way. If we *had* stopped, we would have deviated from his orders and gotten yelled at for that; but, that's Chief. We got to Reb's place and he was sitting there on his scooter with his old lady, and had his bike all packed and ready to go. You could always spot Pete the Reb in a crowd, because he wore an original Nazi swastika arm-band that he would center on his forehead and use as a bandana. We pulled up and Reb asked us, "Where the fuck you been, we're going to be late thanks to you guys! Hurry up and give me a push so we can get going!" I was wondering to myself how it was possible that this was our fault. His old lady was just staring at us, with her mouth open and that zombie look on her face, like always. I thought it was too bad that it was too early in the morning for flies.

The lazy fucker probably only kicked his bike twice trying to start it, if that, and then gave the fuck up. It was easier to wait and get us to push-start his ass, as he knew they would send us to get him. He was the laziest biker I have probably ever known, especially for one that was strung out on speed. He wouldn't even do his own fucking drug deals, as he would make his old lady do all the running and collecting, if he couldn't get us to do it. It also would have been a lot easier if we could have gotten his old lady off his bike while we pushed him around. We pushed their asses about a block and a half before his old Panhead sputtered as it reluctantly came to life. Away he went after it started, and didn't even bother to wait for us. When we finally got back to Luck's, all the Members were firing up their bikes to leave, because Reb didn't want to shut his bike off. He and his old lady were just sitting there on the bike with it idling, and his nose in the bag. I thought to myself what a weekend this was gonna' be.

Chief got everybody all lined up in his pecking order. Some Clubs do it a little different, but mostly the Road Captain is front, left of the pack with the President on his right. Other Officers line up next by rank, with the Members lining up next. Sergeant of Arms, or Security, usually follows them, bringing up the rear of the pack. Then you have your Prospects and any Hang Arounds bringing up the very end of the pack. Some Clubs position the President in the second row to protect him, but usually it's the Prez's choice. Chuck and I were bringing up the rear of this pack, along with Ronnie and Luck, our other two Prospects at that time. We had made it about 55 miles without a break-down, which would turn out to be a record on this run. Then, we stopped along the freeway at a gas station. The Peanut, Hummer, and Sportster gas tanks used in those days didn't go very far on a full tank of gas, but they looked really cool!

Reb shut his bike off so that he could do a line up his nose and then filled his gas tank. So when it was time to leave, of course, it wouldn't start again. That meant all of us Prospects had to push him and his old lady around again to get it started. After numerous tries, the fucking thing still wouldn't start. The four of us Prospects were panting in the summer heat, as pushing bikes is a bitch! It's especially hard when it's fully packed and his old lady's ass sitting on it, but he's a full Patched Member so we can't say shit. Reb calmly looks over at us and says he needs a battery. I thought really, who could've figured that out? Chief overheard that miraculous statement of fact, and jumped dead into Reb's shit. "Why the fuck don't you wait until we're out in the middle of fucking nowhere to decide that you need to replace your fucking battery! I want to get to the Run today," Chief yells! Reb looked at the ground as he was being scolded. "We all aren't waiting two fucking hours to go back to Vallejo to get you a new fucking battery! Why in the fuck didn't you get one yesterday?" Chief asked. "I didn't have the cash," Reb said solemnly, like it wasn't his fault. I was told that he was just like this as a Prospect, and got his ass yelled at then as he still was that day. I wasn't diggin' this one too much, as Chief yelled, "Prospects, lets get the fuck out of here, peg him!"

If you don't know what pegging is, then let me explain. First off, it's very dangerous, with a capital D. Be very careful if you ever want to try this one boys and girls, as I have seen a lot of blood spilled doing it. The idea is to get one bike's power to push the broke-down bike. You accomplish this by pulling along the left hand side of the broke-down bike, pointing forward with what we'll call the power bike. The power biker puts his right foot on the broke-down bike's left foot peg, which means he just lost his means of braking, unless he cuts the broke-down bike loose. Half of us didn't have front brakes in those days, as they were too heavy and ugly. Then, the rider on the power bike has to lock his right leg stiff. The broke-down bike rider then grabs your right handle bar with his left hand (this was easily accomplished in those days, as everyone had pullbacks and Z bars). The power bike rider has all his controls working, except that his right leg can't use his rear brake. The broke-down bike has all his controls except the use of his left arm, thus on most bikes he loses his clutching abilities, which isn't that important if the bike isn't' running anyway. On a jockey shift set up, he loses his ability to shift gears also, but he can use his left leg to clutch. So if you both are experienced enough, the broke-down rider brakes when necessary to slow both of you down. If it needs to be a fast stop you cut each other loose, then you both can hit your brakes and gears. It's not too bad once you get through shifting and get your speed up so that you're rolling down the road in high gear, which was fourth back then. Usually, unless you are really good as a team, you cut the broken down bike loose to come to its own stop or turn. For a turn or a light, you can come up from behind and hook up again while he is still rolling, which is easier than taking off from a dead stop again. It works, but you better be good at it, as it either saves the day, or ruins it just as quickly. The tricky part is getting there in one piece, especially if it's far away. It's hard on your leg to keep it stiff enough for very long distances.

One trick is, if the broke down rider holds on hard enough with a strong left arm, and someone gives you a little push when you're taking off, it helps a lot. Once again, believe me that it takes a lot of practice, and some brass balls really help. Back then, in our crew, if you were a Prospect you got plenty of practice! That day, it seemed all we did was take turns pegging "broke-down Pete," which should have been his nickname, and his old lady down the freeway. Of course, I got lucky and drew the first shift. Chuck and Luck gave us a shove, and with a little wobble we were off. Once we got going straight down the freeway on ramp, I shifted through the gears and finally popped her into high gear, and down the road we went. Naturally, the pack didn't slow down a bit, as we were running the Hell's Angels speed limit, which is fast!

After 50 miles or so, we needed to pull off for another stop. I cut him loose when we got off the freeway and onto the off ramp, so we could both coast and have brakes to stop at the oncoming stoplight. I had waved Chuck up into my position as the power bike, so that after the light turned green, Chuck pegged him into the gas station, as my leg was on fire. We all gassed up, with me limping, and then clustered up for a needed break. The powder bags and a few joints were broken out and passed around. Chief had sent Ronnie and Luck to go find a liquor store for some beers; remember this was the old days. Chief started talking it over with some of the Members about Pete the Reb's bike problem, not really including Reb in on the conversation, who sometimes got treated like the child he was. Someone remembered a scooter shop that was about ten miles out of our way. They decided to send some Prospects to save the day, as always, and go buy a new battery for Reb, while everyone else would sit around and drink a few beers.

Chief picked Chuck and me and told us where to meet them, which was another 60 miles down the freeway, where they would be turning in the direction towards the Run. "Haul ass and don't fuck around," Chief ordered as he was giving us the money. At least it would be Ronnie and Luck's turn to peg Reb the rest of the way. So we split, without even having a beer, and eventually found this little scooter shop. When we stopped, Chuck brought up what a pain in the ass Reb was, and I told him that I couldn't agree more. "Babysitting these fuckers all the time, I get sick of it! When I get Patched we're gonna' take a long vacation, you and I, without any of these guys," Chuck commented. I told that him I couldn't wait, because it sounded like fun. Chuck was getting a little tired of the shit, as he had been prospecting for about 14 months at the time. He had talked about transferring as soon as he could to the Sacramento Chapter. He said, "At least we got away from them for awhile." At that point I was pretty new, and couldn't really understand why he would say that. I thought it was cool to ride with the pack; but, by the end of this Run, I would be agreeing with Chuck. It was like Chuck had always said, that this was more like baby-sitting, with some of the Members, like Pete the Reb.

I tied the battery to my seat and chicken bar, as I didn't want to get any battery acid on my clothes and the shit in my leather saddle bags. After all, I had everything I owned in there. We hauled ass as fast as we could, and they were waiting for us when we got there, at the gas station. Luck and Ronnie had already gotten the old battery out and we slipped the new one in. Then we started kicking and kicking, then Luck asked us if the battery was even charged? All the Prospects took a turn kicking, except Luck. When it was his turn, he got up on the seat and says, "This fucking thing is dead!" Luck was always the more knowledgeable one, with his smart-ass humor, but he always thought things through, and was usually right. "It hasn't even let out a puff once," Luck said. Like always, he took the easiest route, using his intelligence and wanting to avoid the use of physical exercise. We all agreed and decided to take a break. The bag and knife went around, enhancing our already vast knowledge and wisdom and worldly things, and we discussed our next move.

You could always count on the meth then to get everyone's brain rolling again. It took a few minutes for your eyes to un-cross and the watering to stop. I always preferred to drink it or eat it, although the effect takes a little longer to kick in, but I was ten years younger than everybody else and wanted to try to save my nose for awhile. Coke never bothered me much, but some meth would make my nose bleed after extended daily abuse. Anyway, with our now accelerated thinking, we finally came up with the next logical move and checked the fire at the spark plugs. After-market parts were just coming out then, and of course, Pete's coil was one of them. I hate after-market parts with a passion, as they aren't as good or as reliable as good old H fucking D parts! "So now we need a new coil; fucking peg it," Chief yells! Chuck took the lead as the main pegger, and I was his back up this time. I helped give Chuck a push to get them rolling, and then jumped on my bike and took the backup position behind him. Chuck pegged him for about 40 miles or so, and then I picked up Reb at the bottom of the freeway off ramp. I pegged him into the gas station parking area and cut him loose so he could roll in.

Now you can see how this works. As the backup man hangs behind the two bikes pegging, he then takes over when the lead pegger lets off to stop at a freeway exit or a stoplight. The bike then rolls on its own, slowly braking up to the stop, hopefully being able to roll through the stop. It's up to the broke-down rider to look for cops or cars, and decide whether or not he has to come to a complete stop, or take the chance and keep rolling through. If that's the case, the backup man rolls up and hooks up while the broke-down rider is still moving, to go again. If he has to come to a complete stop, the two riders next in the pack jump off their bikes to give him a push, to get him going again. Off you go to the next turn or stop, back and forth until you get there. You can do it without a backup man, but it's faster if you have one. Slowing two bikes down at the same time isn't too bad, just tricky. But, coming to a complete stop is too difficult and rarely done. One bike can slow down easier without his pegger hooked on. There are a lot less crashes if you follow the rules. Enough for your education; you'd better be a really skilled rider to try this, and I'm warning you that it's fucking dangerous!

I was beginning to think we weren't going to make it to the Run at all, thanks to Pete the Reb's fucking bike. We broke the tools out after first visiting the bag again, to get all wired up and motivated. Luck and Ronnie went for a new coil this time. Of course they had to pay for it, because Pete was broke already, or so he said. This all took about another hour, so Chuck and I got to slam a couple of warm beers down. When they finally got back, we wrenched the new coil on. Then it was back to kicking, kicking, and kicking. We checked the fire to the plugs again, and no spark. Chief was getting pissed, as he wanted to go, so then he threw a big fit, cussing and throwing shit. We just kept our heads down and our hands wrenching. We finally found the real problem. The hot wire to the coil was broken, one of those that you can't see, but you can feel it through the plastic wire covering. It had been intermittently shorting out for awhile, until the vibration had finally separated it enough to finally break the continuity. Unfortunately, we didn't have those little ohmmeters back in those days. So we replaced the wire, which was easy, because most everybody carried enough wire and ends to rewire their whole bike if they had to. I personally only fried all my wiring once on my 45 trike, and once on my Panhead. Then, you start learning to put a few more fuses in when you "chopper wire" your bike. So in those days, you carried plenty of everything. Reb's bike finally popped and sputtered to life.

Whew, what a pain in the ass this Run was starting out to be. We all patted each other on the back on how smart we were, and passed the bag and knife around again. Everybody got all fired up and away we went. Chief kicked us hard in the ass as we hauled ass for the run. Just before our last gas stop, Reb pulled out of the pack and came to a stop. All of the Prospects stopped while the main pack went on. Pete says, "Peg me". Off we went again, until we finally caught up to where the pack had pulled over to wait for us. Chief was just pacing, which he did a lot. We borrowed the gas station's battery charger. After we got it going, we popped the cover off the voltage regulator to look at the points, and they fried, of course. So we filed them enough to stick them together with a rubber band so that we could roll on. Off Chuck and I went, to find another voltage regulator. As we were leaving I could here Chief yelling at Pete, "Do you ever wrench on your fucking bike! This shit always happens to you." We found an auto parts store. Chuck started chuckling, and I asked him what was so funny? He said, "Oh, I was just thinking about how much I enjoyed the ass chewing Pete was getting!" I couldn't have agreed more. We caught back up with the pack and pulled over to put the regulator on. The old Panhead fired right back to life. We were finally back on the road, after replacing most of Reb's electrical system. Reb would end up getting someone to haul it home after the Run.

I don't think people know how much trouble it was in those days to keep a pack of bikes running. A lot of our pack Runs back then were just like the Run I just described. In today's world of Evos and twin cams, it would be hard to believe. But let me assure you, it was a real Bitch, with a capital B. Running Knuckleheads, Panheads, and the newer, supposedly improved Shovelheads, was a constant problem. You carried so many tools, wire, nuts and bolts, points, chains, oil, and extra parts. I had one side of my saddlebags full of this shit. I had a tool pouch roll filled with tools, usually strapped onto my chicken bar. You just couldn't carry enough mechanical stuff. Between everybody's shit, there wasn't much we couldn't fix. We all were at least some kind of mechanic. A lot of the problems were just the nature of the beast, and also from shitty wrenching and lack of maintenance. In the days of the rear chains, you had a transmission chain sprocket, the rear wheel sprocket, and the drive chain. You put on a new chain, but you don't replace one of the sprockets, or both, that have worn out teeth. What happens is, you ruin the chain prematurely, which leads to more wrenching, because you have to adjust it more often, as it is prematurely stretching the chain out. If you were unlucky, the chain would snap and wrap around your tranny, cracking the case in half. I was only unlucky, or stupid enough, that it only happened to me once on my Panhead, when I popped a wheelie. Then I learned, and listened to the Old timer's advice, and changed out my sprockets when they were bad, along with a new chain. Then I had no more problems for a long time, if I kept the chain evenly oiled and didn't pop too many wheelies. The whole bike was like that, in the early days of Harley Davidson. Notably, the kicker assembly was another one that you had to replace everything all at once. If you replaced all the worn out parts at the same time, used lock-tite and aircraft lock nuts, plus kept up on maintenance, you could avoid a lot of constant wrenching and breakdowns. I went through the constant break-down shit for awhile, until I noticed that the old guys didn't seem to be having that many problems. I finally listened to them and did what they said. I had a pretty reliable Pan/Shovelhead that I rode for 13 years. Back then, being the bike thief that I was, I would snag a new bike for the parts to rebuild mine. I put an almost new set of the first '66 Shovelheads I had ever seen on my Panhead's lower end. We went and stole the brand new Shovelhead an old man had bought in our town, used the parts I needed, and then traded the rest for fancy paint and transmission work.

How I procured the first set of Shovelheads I had ever seen is a story. Danny the Duck and I happened by this brand new Shovelhead on our way to a party. From a distance we oohed and ahhed at this new bagger, with its funny looking new Harley motor. We were already pretty buzzed on that day, and decided to go get Duck's truck and steal it, as we had to show the Brothers this new machine. We figured the old man had insurance and would get a new bike out of the deal. We went and told our plan to another bike stealing Bro, as we needed a third man we figured. It was a good thing we did, because this other Brother knew about Harley's new alarm system that had come out on the '66. Basically, it was a mercury switch in the license plate frame. When the bike was moved, the mercury would flow, setting off an alarm that was guaranteed to wake the neighborhood! But, according to a Misfit Member that our Bro knew, all you had to do was freeze the mercury by spraying this Freon shit on it. The bike was parked on the street in front of the owner's apartment, on top of a hill. Our plan was to park the truck one block away, at the bottom of the hill. One guy would wait there with the tailgate down and a plank set up, so we could roll the bike right into the back of the truck. We would lay it on its side and cover it with a tarp, and drive off for the mountains to strip it down.

The two of us boldly go up to the bike at 3 am, and Duck sprayed the Freon shit all over the plate bracket. We immediately took our 4 ft. bolt cutters and snapped the padlock off the front end. I jumped on the seat and pulled her up off the kickstand, as Duck started pushing to get me rolling, with the plan of him carrying the bolt cutters and jumping on behind me to ride it down to the truck. The first thing that went wrong was we got going too fast too quickly, and Duck almost dumped me trying to hop on. So, he's running behind me as I'm riding down the hill. Nobody thought of how long the Freon would work, as this was our first time experimenting with this technology. About halfway to the truck, this un-Godly alarm goes off, as the mercury had thawed. Neighborhood lights were coming on as I made it to the truck. Up the ramp I went, a little too fast, as I crashed into the back of the cab, breaking the rear window. Duck caught up to us as I squirming to pry myself out from under the bike and glass, as the bike had fallen on its side, with me on it. We panicked and skipped the tarp, and just drove off, with this alarm blasting away as we drove out of town and into the mountains. That's how I got my first pair of Shovelheads at 18 years old.

My personal best of trouble free Panhead riding was 50,000 or so miles of doing nothing but changing the oil and adjusting the chains. That was a real record in those days. I had almost two years of trouble free riding. That was the best I ever did. You just had to listen to the old school boys, and hustle enough money and steal some parts to do it right. Unlike then, riding is easy now, in the days of "bullet proof" Evo bikes, and better yet, the Twin Cam Harleys. You push a button and ride, not kick and kick and wrench. You don't wrench your way there, as we did in the past. Evolution in technology has let anybody who wants to ride a Harley be able to do so. You just go down to the "Thousands of Dollars store" and pick out the one you like. You hop on, hit that starter button, and away you go. With some bikes now, you don't even have to turn on the gas. It wasn't like that in the old days at all. I believe that the evolution bikes were responsible for what started the biker boom. The need of the old school training was gone. You no longer had to be a wrench or have extremely fat pockets to ride. In the early days, you had to really want to be a biker. You then had to take a lot of shit in order to learn from the boys how to keep the bike running. The reason they called us greasy bikers then was because we were; it was the nature of the Harley, the oil puking beast.

The tricks of the trade, so to speak, no longer apply to these new bullet proof Harleys. In the early days, you better have had some mechanical knowledge and talent, or the old schoolers wouldn't give you the time of day. Citizens looked at us as dirty greasy bikers, but what they didn't realize was that you got that way by wrenching on your bike as you rode. That and just the chain oil being slung around in a pack, was enough to give you that greasy appearance. I started learning to wrench and keep bikes running back when I was a kid. My uncle was a mechanic and he would show me things. When I was a juvenile delinquent I had learned from Fat Ray. After 17 or so, I had Poncho and other Gladiators showing me how. The point is that it took a long time to get where I could keep a Harley Davidson Panhead going. These bikes took a lot of work. The Shovelheads from 1966 on were wanted, top-end improvements, a rework of the old basic design, but nothing close to the Evolution. That re-engineering of their motor and tranny is what I believe started the unbelievable biker revolution. You just push the button and go! You rarely need tools, as the days of constant wrenching your way somewhere are over. You no longer have to have a mechanical talent to be a Biker. The new designs and engineering has made it easy to be a biker, and you can now become one almost instantly; the down side is, so can cops!

We finally got to the River Run late that afternoon, in the summer of 1974. This was a big annual HAMC Run. It looked like every Hell's Angel from California was there. The Nomads grouped up under a tree. We Prospects helped everybody get settled in. "Prospect! Help my old lady set up my tent. Prospects, you guys need to make a beer run, now! Prospects! My old lady wants this kind of wine. Prospects, I need three packs of Marlboro cigarettes! Prospects, we need a Styrofoam cooler with ice! Prospect, we need a fire pit! Prospects, you need to get some firewood!" Prospects that, Prospects this, I want, I want, that's all we heard for hours. You make out lists of shit members wanted at the store. I've had to procure some weird shit in my time, from tampons (had to be supers), underwear, prunes, condoms (fluorescent orange), A-200 (crab & lice shampoo), and all kinds of other weird shit. We found another Chapter who had their shit together enough to have a chase truck. You begin to wonder if some of the Members have ever taken care of anything for themselves. Then you have Members that really have their shit together and hardly bother you at all. The only comfort you have is the knowledge that someday, you'll be a Member, and of course, you won't be so lame then. We hitched a ride in the truck with them to the store. It's not easy packing Styrofoam coolers on a rigid frame Panhead. Although we have done it before, it takes a lot more trips and time on a bike. We went and found everybody's shit. The other Prospects didn't seem to have to find as much shit as we did. Their Chapters must have had the bright idea of coming a little more prepared. I knew we had Father Jack coming in a vehicle later. He came prepared to camp, but I would find out later the shit he was bringing for everybody wasn't just camping gear. Cagey old Father Jack was bringing some of the Chapters arsenal.

The River Run, besides the Boots and Patches games, was most famous for getting some target practice shooting with your Brothers. They all got to try out some new weapons; Angels like to play with guns, and I always have, too. My Dad and Uncle taught me how to shoot since I was a kid. Only at this Run, I wouldn't be shooting. I would be the gopher, and gophers we would be. We got every Member everything they needed for awhile. Then we got the campfire pit ready and we scrounged up some firewood for the night. Finally, we had time to look around a bit, and bullshit with some other Prospects and Members. We all had a meeting to get the security and watch schedules ironed out. Chuck and I asked to pull a guard shift together, between two and six a.m. We always tried to pull the same shifts. Chief used to catch us doing that, and throw a fucking fit, but he was gone packing his nose with Kenny O. and some members from Oakland. Chuck and I just trusted each other, and would cover each other's backs. We also enjoyed each others company, and always wanted the late shift for a couple of reasons. One reason is that it was always entertaining as hell when the last fucked up members went to punching each other out, or chasing each others old lady's around. You could always count on at least one or two good drama scenes, old ladies getting schooled up, or a Member too fucked up to find his own bag. I don't just mean sleeping bags either, but go fast or pot bags, also. You had Members arguing over some of the finer points of matters. Some of the best entertainment though, is late at night you could hear Members getting laid or getting a blowjob. Moaning and groaning and guttural noises, it was all good quality entertainment when you had nothing else to do. Some of these girls really put on a show; sometimes it was hard to look them in the eye the next morning without busting out laughing. We would argue over whether or not we thought it was a real or fake orgasm. I know we were pieces of shit for listening, but we had nothing else to do; anything to relieve the boredom and stay awake on your shift.

Why didn't we just bring our own women to keep us company? There were a lot of reasons. If you liked them at all or were hustling them for money, you didn't bring them. You didn't have enough time to pay them any attention, as you are busy prospecting. The golden rule of thumb was, as a Prospect, you just didn't bring a date unless you just didn't give a shit about her or wanted to "turn her out" to make points with Members.

That, plus every single Member there would be either trying to fuck her, or actually be fucking her, before night's end. You could bring them to a Chapter party if you were married to them, or had already went through all the shit of telling all the Members that she were special to you because she was how you made your place, meaning you were hustling a living off them and living at their house. Members would respect that, as it was your living. We all hustled a living one way or another. Members from other Chapters didn't know you well enough to know that a woman that's yours. Even if that wasn't the case, they were still kind of up for grabs by other Members from other Chapters. Even if you took a loyal date to a party, you probably would have some Member banging her before you got back from your first beer run. As soon as you hit the door, some Member would be over there charming her shorts off. That would last about five minutes and then she would be asked, "Do you want to do a line?" Then more bullshit until the blast up her nose takes effect, then a drink. Then it's more bullshit for a while, another drink, and then here, "If you are amping too badly, here, take a few of these Reds, they will straighten you right up." All the while, they're telling her what a great Prospect you are and what good buddies you are. After about a half-hour, she's spinning, and they tell her how she can help you to get patched by doing them a favor. Or, they'll say, "He won't mind, he and I are Brothers, we share everything." When you get back from your hour long beer run, she's flat on her back in a bedroom, with at least the second Member mounting her by then. You can try to protest, but you'll get, "She isn't your old lady or money maker, let the Brothers have some fun, she's enjoying herself, you gotta learn to share with your Brothers." The worst part about this was that she was probably so fucked up, she was having a good time at first.

They will keep her on Reds for as long as they want their little party to last. After the train has been running awhile, most women will start protesting, as they hurt. That's when it gets ugly. I have seen this scenario happen many times. That's why you don't bring a date to a Red and White party when you are a Prospect. This is true of most other 1% Clubs, too. I knew a Member of the Dirty Dozen MC from Arizona that reveled in this scenario. I mean he was proud of it. He said they would get all these wannabes at a party with their old lady's. Then, he said they get the old men all wired up, stoned, and drunk. Then they would get them to pop some Reds. With a little instigation, they would have all the men outside, fighting each other. That's when most of the Dozen's Members would be inside fucking their old lady's. Slow Joe said it worked every time. He couldn't believe how stupid the Prospects were. Scenarios like this one are why they are called One Percenters.

When I was still prospecting in the Gladiators, I was really young and naïve to One Percenter's ways. The Brothers were having a party over at Doc's. The party was rolling with Reds, speed, marijuana, whiskey, and beer. I had been out riding my bike earlier in the day and had run into a foxy chick I had known in high school that I hadn't seen for a while. She had been a cheerleader and wanted to go for a ride on my bike. So I took her for a ride out to Coloma and Georgetown. We had a good time smoking weed, and surprisingly to me, she asked me if I had any speed. Well, she had been kind of straight in school, the cheerleader type and all, but we had always wanted to fuck her, so it took me by surprise. I said, "Sure," and pulled some out of my handlebar stash and gave her a bump. She told me she had started taking drugs lately and really loved to party. Now, this seemed a big turn around, as she was a straight A student, and straight laced in school. The evening was approaching and I told her I had to go to a Club party. She got all excited about my Club, and had always wondered what it was like, and begged me to let her come with me. Not really knowing any better, I invited her. When we got there, unfortunately, all the Club Brothers were downstairs in the party room without their old lady's, partying down.

After a bit of time, I was told that I needed to take a bag over to Triple Jack's place for the Club. As I couldn't do the dope deal at Jack's with her along, I innocently left her behind. So I told this chick to enjoy the party, and I would be right back. Off I rode to take care of business, and returned as quickly as I could. When I finally walked into the party, all the Brothers were sitting around partying and this chick was on her knees giving one of the Bros a blow job. They had given her a bunch of Reds and booze, and had told her that if she would give everybody a blow job, she would be helping me get my Patch sooner. Later, as she making her rounds, she came over and sat in my lap, slurring her words and saying how she had gotten me my Patch, all proud like. This and her breath now turned me off, but I did in those days think that it was pretty funny that Miss Goody Two Shoes had been duped so easily. I mean, she wasn't my old lady or anything. It did make me popular with the Brothers, as they thought I was sharing my foxy prize of the day with them. I didn't change their thinking on that one. I just figured she was another whore at heart anyway, as it only took only a few Reds to get her guard down. She kept coming back around and bugging me to go on Runs and to parties; she had become a Club Mama, and was enjoying it. But eventually, one of the single Bros fell head over heels in love with her and made her his old lady. After he was killed on his bike, she went back to Club Mama status; like I say, we were One Percenters.

Everybody at the River Run was getting wired up and ready to party hearty; you could smell it in the air. The natives were starting to get restless, as Chuck and I threw our bags down over by a tree. Amazingly, all the Members were so excited partying with each other that they were leaving us alone. So we tried to get a little sleep before our shift. We lay there and passed a joint back and forth. We drank a pint of whiskey to try and help slow the speed in our veins down. You get so wound up while your snorting meth, that it makes it's hard to get any rest. You can knock your wired buzz down with some downers easy enough, but as Prospects, downers weren't really allowed. What seemed to me only an hour later, another Prospect woke us up and said to hurry up, as it was our turn. I had really just closed my eyes and lay still enough to rest. I would do that for my body's sake, because my mind wouldn't turn off. Chuck had told me that he always did the same thing. Then Chuck said sarcastically, "Wow its 2 a.m. already, we had better get to our watch quickly, now that we have gotten at least one hour of rest." We jumped up laughing and went over by the entrance.

The Prospects that were on duty were in a hurry to split, but they did leave us their chairs. We kind of sat there for a few minutes, focusing. Chuck asked, "Do you want to do a line?" I told him, "Hell yes, I thought you would never ask. Then, let's smoke a joint." We were still a little buzzed from before, but it was gonna' be a long wait until sunrise. We always used meth to stay awake on guard duty, as it was usually pretty boring, so we would smoke weed and drink, too. No matter what though, you did not want to be caught sleeping, as that was the cardinal sin of sins. Such was our lives as Prospects, as we couldn't wait to be Members. We snuck over to another Chapter's cooler we spotted over by a tree, and "borrowed" some beers. We stayed there for a bit, as we listened to a couple having what sounded like an exceptionally good time. He was grunting steady like a pig, with each stroke. She was keeping pace also, with this high-pitched shrieking noise. We ended up drinking about three beers as we waited to hear this gal's final orgasm. Chuck won our bet, as she let of this loud steady scream like she had been stabbed!

We hurried back to our post, as we were laughing and didn't want to get caught listening. We then kicked back and discussed the day's events, and how Pete's bike kept breaking down. We discussed how funny it was when Chief had yelled at him, and he just looked down at the ground like a little kid being scolded for misbehavior. We discussed the fine art of chasing everybody's shit as Prospects. But in reality, we were really just venting each others frustrations and boredom with our jobs. Chuck started talking about the next day's events, as he had been on this Run the year before. He told me we were going to be gathering up cans and bottles for the Great River Shoot-out. "They are gonna' have us digging through garbage," Chuck said, "looking for cans and bottles to be used for targets. We put all the targets in garbage bags and go up-river. Then we start throwing them out into the rivers current. You'll hear the guns going off down-river; this will go on for some hours until they run out of ammo." I asked him if we got to shoot, too. "Hell no, I wish we did, as it sounds like WWII going on." He also explained to me to stay close to him, because he knew from last year where to be and where not to be. "You don't wanna get shot by one of the wasted Members," he added. I totally agreed with that. "If we stay far over to the right, we'll be safe, because some of the Members get pretty loose with their guns!" There's my Brother Chuck, always looking out for me. You can see why we tried to hang together, mainly out of necessity and to try to survive our commitment. It gave us stability, and a good chance of getting through all of this alive. We dreamed of both getting our Patches and being able to go and do what we wanted. We just had to get that Patch, no matter what, because then we would have it made in the shade. We talked and talked, until we watched the sun start cracking light; it was gonna be a beautiful day. I didn't really know what lay ahead that day, but I trusted Chuck and I knew that he would help me get through it all, somehow.

A few Members just started getting up after our shift had ended. We were shootin' the shit with some of them. Best to talk to them early, before they start getting all fucked up, as they're more themselves then. Then a few more got up, scratching the last night's party out of their eyes. If you are looking for a free toot of go fast, this is a good time, as most of the Members break out their bags to wake up and get rolling again. It's a sight to behold, as they all start crawling out of their tents. The old ladies won't look you in the eyes, until they brush their hair and get some make up on. Like all women, they were always thinking of their looks first. I saw one of Rick the Rat's old ladies emerging from his large tent. Then the other one come out, and both got started cooking breakfast for their old man. I always wondered how he kept the peace between them. Most Members had trouble keeping one old lady, but not Rat, he had two. He was a special temperament kind of a man. I always enjoyed talking to him, as he always had his shit together.

The first time I met Rick the Rat was when I was a Gladiator Member, and I had wrecked on the first big MMA Runs ever held in California. Rick, Hangtown, and their old ladies' were sharing a big tent. I showed up all bloody and half knocked out. I had wrecked on a tight corner, as I was going too fast, racing to the bar in town, and slid and rolled with my bike. I rode back to the Run in a daze, with a friend of mine who had been racing with me. I stumbled into the Red & White camp and found them, where they made me a spot for me in their tent and they had their old ladies bandage me up. Since I had hit my head, they all kept watching my eyes for signs of a concussion. They decided the best thing to do was give me a line of crank so I wouldn't go to sleep. I was given the royal treatment all afternoon, and as my head finally quit spinning, I started feeling a little uncomfortable and self-conscious at being the only Member from another Club camping with the Hell's Angels. I tried to leave, but they insisted I stay for dinner, which I did. I had lost my wallet when I ground the back pocket off my Levis on the asphalt, as I had slid through that corner. So I told them I was gonna' go back and try to find it. Hangtown insisted I take twenty dollars from him, in case I didn't find it, for traveling money. They were the greatest to me, and you just don't forget shit like that.

The whole River Run was having a good, quiet morning. But like always, it had to come to an end, and it did when Chief came walking up to us. "What the fuck are you two up to? Now go get some bags, and fill them with bottles and cans for the shoot out; and, I want a bunch!" Chuck had this part right. After we walked off, I looked at Chuck and asked, "Should we do a line and have a beer for breakfast?" "That's probably all were gonna' get, so let's sneak a joint too, ok," Chuck replied. We went over to the dumpster area where no one could see us and did our thing. Afterward, we filled a couple bags, and that first beer had tasted so good, we had another. I looked out around the other camps and I could see other Prospects and Hang Arounds doing the same, filling up bags. Misery always enjoys company. It took us about an hour or so and there weren't any more 'targets' to be found. Chief, our tireless leader, sent us over to a dumpster he had found, where some citizens were camping. Now we were going through other people's garbage, as they eyeballed us like we were nuts. All the Members were up and fed, and had gotten their highs going. Some started drinking and smoking that morning's 'kick off' joint, while others were doing biker coffee or lines.

Everybody finally woke up and started heading over towards the river, as the shoot-out was about to begin. Luck had hustled us a lift for our 'targets' in a truck. Father Jack let us fire up his rig, and we threw some more bags in there, and he drove us down to the river's edge. After unloading, Father Jack walked over and asked us to help him with something. He told us to take the rear bumper off on his Volkswagen truck. He handed us a couple of wrenches and screwdrivers, then showed us a hidden panel to take off, and we went to work. Hidden in there was a bunch of rifles and pistols, along with ammunition. We helped him put all the guns carefully on a blanket in the back bed of the truck, along with all of the ammo. The Nomads weren't fucking around, as they had come prepared to shoot. Father Jack told me that little hidden compartment had made him a lot of money in the past. He said he used to run drugs and guns across the Mexican border for years, without getting busted, using this same stash place. He was a very honorable, cagey old bastard that had transferred over from the Richmond Chapter that I liked and respected; he was an Angel, all the way. I used to wonder where he got them jars of Mexican Reds I used to sell for him. I had used the money I was paid to rebuild my bike's transmission.

We headed over to the river where Angels were all lined up along the bank of the river. All the Prospects had hauled all the 'targets' around this bend and upstream. We all got the nod, as about half of us started throwing bottles and cans into the water. You had to flip them out there, to where the current would take them around the bend. We figured there were enough of us that we could take shifts doing it. That's when all hell broke loose; Bam, Bam, Bam, Bam, holy shit! I could see why Chuck had positioned us on the far side of the bank for throwing. My only wish right then was that I had some earplugs; we ended up using cigarette butts. We sent a Prospect over to the firing line to see how we were doing with the amount of 'targets' going by. He came back and said that they said to just keep them coming. Then he mentioned, "You wouldn't believe how many targets they are missing. Most of them are getting away!" We all got a laugh out of that, because with the amount of gunfire going off, you wouldn't think they'd miss shit.

Everyone had pistols, shotguns, and rifles, with them all blazing away at the floating targets. A lot of .45 autos, 9 mm, .22s, .223 Rugers, M1 carbines, 12 gauge shotguns, just to name a few. I told Chuck, "After about an hour of this mad minute shit, I think with all the lead that is going in this river, it will probably be changing its course." Chuck hit the ground, laughing. We had just passed around a couple of joints. We all actually were having a good time, flipping shit out into the river. The pile of targets was starting to get low. We were hoping not to have to go find more. Bam, Bam, Bam, Bam, it went on and on. I went up to check on them when it was my turn. I watched for a minute. Chief was blazing away with his full auto pistol he always had. He had some extended clips for it, but I still didn't see him hit one fucking can which made me chuckle to myself. It was if he had eyes in the back of his head. "Prospect, get your ass over here and start loading me up some clips, would you!" I kept on loading the 9 millimeters as told, watching him scarring the hell out of the cans.

The sound was deafening, with all the yelling and gunfire. Angels love their guns, and they love to shoot and play with them even more. Most of the targets were getting away though, as they floated out of sight. I remember thinking that I didn't think the Outlaws MC had too much to worry about. "I hit that one," someone yelled. "If they don't sink, they don't count!" someone else yelled. Finally, they started running out of ammo. The shooting came less and less, then Chief was about out, too. "How many bullets I got left?" Chief asked. "Make sure I got enough left to fill all my clips." I filled them all up and told him he was about out. He gave me a small clip and told me to go for it. I got lucky and sunk three out of nine shots, when Chief just grabbed his gun back. "Fucking smart ass," he said. The great shoot-out was over. I could only imagine the people downriver seeing all this trash going by. Everybody went back to the campground and the party was on! The bullshit was flying about who had out-shot who, and who was the better shot. That was the main topic of bullshit for hours and long on into the night.

All the Members kept on partying hearty, as they all were still laughing and talking about the games. We didn't have to do a lot for a while, just the occasional "Prospect, get me a beer!" But, we had gotten everything everybody could possibly need on the last beer and supplies run. I don't know if they all felt sorry for us after our day's work, or for the fun and games they had put us through, and were giving us all a well deserved break. No, I would find out later that was never the case. No real incidents came up as we kept security up and, amazingly enough to me, no cops had shown up. Chuck and I talked our way into the late shift again. We never got any sleep, we just stayed tuned up with our friend, meth. A lot of drugs and alcohol was being passed around. We hung around the entry area where our main security station was, as I pretty much had a feel of that area from the night before. We bullshit there for a while, and then wandered off, walking the security perimeter. We ran into a Richmond Prospect I knew and he asked us if we knew that his Chapter was turning out some chick in their main tent. He told us it was good pussy and she was diggin' it, too. We told him no thanks, we were on our shift until morning. He told us that there was a pretty long line anyway, and every time it was his turn, a Member would cut in front of him, until he gave up. I shrugged my shoulders and said, "What are you gonna' do?" He agreed and went on about when he got his Patch, he wasn't gonna' treat the Prospects like that. I told him I bet every Prospect there ever was probably says that and when they get patched, they soon forget all about it. "Not me, I won't. Well, if you hear a lot of noise later on coming from our area, especially the big tent, I wouldn't bother anyone about it." I thanked him for the advice and said I would let the rest of the Prospects know. "Hope we get patched soon," and with that, he was gone. We stopped and chit-chat with a few Members on our way back over to the security area. I told them what the Richmond Prospect had said. "I wouldn't touch that chick with your dick," one of them said. I agreed that in that case, I wouldn't either.

That's when our luck ran out as Chief had found us. He was amping, as usual. "Now I don't want you motherfuckers going to sleep," he said, as he pulled his big bag of dope. "Here, wake the fuck up," as he handed me the knife. We obliged him, as usual. We stood there for 10 minutes, hearing the usual speech. "You got your fucking guns?" As we showed him, I couldn't resist saying, "Really shot the shit out of those cans at the river today, huh Chief?" "Oh shut the fuck up, you smart ass!" I could hear Chuck gagging next to me as he tried not to laugh. Chief ranted and raved about the sights on his gun, and then scolded us for another few minutes on us doing our job, and then split. Chuck said, "You know, you shouldn't piss him off like that, I thought he was gonna' have a heart attack." "I know, but I couldn't resist, besides Chief really can't hit shit with a gun," I explained. Then I told him that I thought the Outlaws MC was probably safe enough, which Chuck agreed to as we busted out laughing. "Some day, I ain't gonna have to put up with that shit anymore," Chuck said. He had been a Prospect for about 11 months before I received my bottom rocker, so he was getting really tired of all the bullshit.

Other than the Richmond tent, everything was getting kind of quiet by about 4 a.m. Chuck and I did our rounds with our flashlights, came back, and smoked a joint and popped a couple of beers. We were both wired to the teeth still from Chief's dope. His was always the purist shit, because he got it direct from the cookers. We kept on bullshitting until the crack of sun came through, bringing us a new day. I welcomed the warmth on our souls, as somehow it seemed to purify the happenings of the previous night. My rear chain needed adjusted, so I broke out my tools and got it where it needed to be, then sprayed some chain lube on her. I hurried and put my tools away as I didn't want to get stuck wrenching on any Member's bikes. I had learned my lesson on that. They catch you cleaning or wrenching on your putt, this gives them ideas about theirs, and you will be busy. By 8:00 a lot of Members were stirring. I figured that they must have been getting hungry, as was I. That's when Father Jack came over and told me to come with him. I couldn't figure out what this was all about. We walked over towards the Richmond camp, which sort of made sense, as he was originally from that Chapter. I figured he wanted to introduce me to a Member or something.

We went through their camp, stopping to say hello to a couple of Members that were up early, and he motioned me to keep following him. We walked down to this creek area just out of sight of camp; now I am starting to sweat. Then I see this chick lying in the dirt, with most of her clothes torn off. "There she is," Father Jack said. We walked over and kneeled beside her. Her face was all swollen, with black eyes and a bleeding lip. She was pretty out of it. "No more please," she kept saying. Jack was pushing her matted up hair out of her face. "What an act of kindness," I thought. I was feeling bad for this chick, as obviously she had been the turn-out the Richmond Prospect had mentioned. They had roughed her up, as she had all kinds of bruises, and you could see some from fingers squeezing her. She was a real mess. She was slurring her words pretty badly, so I figured she was fucked up on Reds. Jack said her name and asked her if she knew who he was. "Please, no more," and "I have had enough" is all she kept muttering. I thought of how cool Father Jack was, and that we were going to help her. Then, Jack picked up her arm and there was a turquoise bracelet on her wrist. He took it off, along with the rings that matched, and then he put them in his cutoff pocket. He kept saying, "You're going to be alright." He took the rest off her other hand, and it was all beautiful Indian jewelry. He stood up and said to me,

"I know who she is; she has been through this before. Every six months or so, she comes around for more. She likes a lot of men and she likes it rough, so the Richmond Chapter obliges her. Good looking whore, don't you think?" "Yeah, I said." "Did you get some of this?" he asked. "No," I replied. "You should have, its pretty good stuff, as I've fucked her more than once. She gives good head too man, are you sure you don't want some now?" "No thanks," I replied. "Come on, let's get out of here then," Jack said. "Should we do anything for her?" I asked cautiously. "No, one of the Richmond Prospects will take her back," he answered. We walked a different way back to camp than we had coming in. About halfway there, Jack turned around and faced me, saying "You don't tell anyone about this, ok?" "No, I won't," I said. "I mean no one, understand? Do you want one of the rings? "No, they look like a matching set to me," I said. "Yeah, one of my girls is gonna' love these," Jack said. I asked Jack why a good looking chick like that would want to put herself through all that. He stopped and turned around and looked at me as if I was his son asking a stupid, innocent, adolescent question. "The story I heard was that her Mom died and her Step-dad used to do her with all his buddies when she was young. If she tried to resist, they would rough her up, and it kind of fucked up her head real bad. She's a good, hard working whore, but she won't have anything to do with having a steady old man. Believe me, a lot of Brothers have tried, but she doesn't want even a Brother as a Daddy. She could make a man a lot of money, what a fucking waste. Think of the possibilities of all the tricks you could charge money, with a good whore like that. She's a fucking gold mine and believe me, I have thought about this for awhile. She could make more money than most any whore. She just don't trust any man though, and I guess I don't blame her." As we walked back I thought of how much of a heartless bastard Father Jack really was, but I admired that he never missed a chance to make a buck; what a cagey old fucker. I had seen women like her before. They all have two things in common, they were all usually abused as children, and they always picked out patched bikers as their tool to show the world their feelings of hate. I guess for them it showed God and everybody their pain, in a tormented physical statement. For sure, 1% bikers were more than willing to oblige, that you could count on, with no questions asked.

After the River Run, the Nomads sort of split up, with some heading home, and a few others wanting to go to Yosemite National park. I was tired of prospecting, but to go with a small group sounded like a vacation to Chuck and I. It didn't really matter where you were, you are always prospecting anyway. We said our goodbyes to Chief and the rest of them, and Chief said to find him as soon as we got back to Vallejo. Our group headed for Yosemite, which was a short ride away. When we got there, Luck and another Member picked out a camping spot. I threw down my bag next to Chuck's, under a tree. We took care of all our prospect duties, beer and shit. We all gathered around and sat at the picnic table. We passed the knife and the bag around, and Chuck turned down the meth, mentioning something about just wanting to get some damn sleep. Then Chuck and I lit up some weed. We all drank beer and passed around the joints. There were some campers around. They could see us, and could probably smell the weed, but so what. When we entered the park, the ranger lady at the booth that took our money was wide-eyed and really checking us out. We were used to getting a lot of that kind of attention, so it didn't seem like anything different. Wherever the Hell's Angel Patch goes, it always causes a commotion.

We didn't pay anybody too much mind, as we just sat around smoking and drinking and relaxing after a long weekend. That's when Chuck said he was going to lay down and get him some needed sleep. I was wired up and decided to take a putt down to this gas station, restaurant, bar place that we had stopped briefly at on the way in. I had seen a good looking bartender girl in there that I had made bedroom eyes at. I was tired, but still running on a full nose of meth. So I rode over and went in there and sat down at the bar. She said, "I was hoping you would come back," with a smile. "I couldn't resist," I told her. I ordered a beer. There was just one old couple at the bar, and she went and checked on them. When she came back, we started talking, with her asking the usual questions about the R&W MC. "How come you ride with them? What is it like being so famous and being watched all the time? Are you ever scared?" The same old questions, but she really seemed interested and intelligent. "You have a beautiful bike," she said. That's the quickest way to my heart, and of course my response was, "Do you want to go for a ride?" "I have almost two hours left on my shift, but I would love to." I told her no problem, I would just hang around and drink some beers, as I needed to relax and was off duty for a while. She giggled and said that would be great. She had never been on a ride on a Harley before. I explained to her that she was really missing something, but were going to fix that right away.

There was something about this girl that I can't really explain. I was attracted to her right away. We both started talking about everything and anything, as she was so easy to talk to. Besides being young and beautiful, she had this certain innocence about her. She was 22 years old, a little older than me. She said she had been going through college, and had been doing some traveling. I asked how she ended up here. She said she had been seeing the sights and asked for a job so she could stay around the area for a while. Her parents lived in San Francisco. She asked me where I was from, I told her I was living in Vallejo right know, and then her eyes lit up and she told me that her Grandma lived there. We talked for what seemed like four hours, and then finally some dude showed up to relieve her. We had actually just talked for less than two hours. We went outside and she put her stuff in this brand new Beamer sports car, and I said "Wow, that's yours?" "Yeah, my Daddy bought it for me." "Yeah, I figured you didn't get that as a bartender, but you sure got a nice Daddy." "Yeah, I know, but he's good to me, although I probably appear to be a spoiled, rich girl," as she jumped on the back of my bike. I actually had to show her where her foot pegs were, and away we rode. This is some beautiful bike riding country, but she made it even better. She loved the ride and told me it was thrilling, as we rode on, and that she had never felt so free before. That's when I explained to her that that's why we do it.

The meth was starting to wear off some and she invited me over to her place. It was a beautiful little cabin in the trees. We sat at the kitchen table and I asked if she smoked weed or did drugs? "I smoked marijuana in college, and I still do once in awhile." I broke out a joint and we smoked it. I asked if she did any hard drugs, and I was glad of her answer, which was "I tried cocaine once, but I didn't really like it." Normally, dollar signs would be in my eyes and I would be talking her into doing a line, as its better than cocaine. But I couldn't do it; what was wrong with me? We laughed and talked and she made me a sandwich. I asked her if I could borrow her shower, as I really needed one, and she agreed. We ended up in bed and I finally went to sleep. I was out for probably a couple of hours and woke up in her arms. I knew I should get up and go check on everybody at camp, as I'd probably catch hell for being gone too long. But I felt happy and relaxed, and couldn't remember how long it had been since I had felt this way.

We made love again and laid there for an hour or so, and then we got up and took a shower together. I explained to her that I had to go back and check on my crew, but she wanted to come with me. I wanted her to go, but I didn't want to bring her around my people, as I was afraid the ugly would show. Then I realized that she really wouldn't understand or fit into my world, as I wouldn't hers. I told her what a gypsy that I was, all I had was a sleeping bag with the ground as my bed. She then explained that she didn't really care about that, as long as we would be together. I knew I shouldn't take her, but I thought of who was there and I was sure I would get away with it, or I would somehow get her out of there if I had to; I didn't want to let her go. "Ok, let's roll, but you gotta' do exactly what I say, I mean that." She agreed, and we rode by the bar and checked on her car, and then rode into the park and into camp. Everyone but Chuck hardly noticed or paid any attention to us, as everyone was hanging onto some young chicks having fun; this was great for me.

Everything was cool, as Luck and a couple Members had picked up some young chicks and were getting them high and partying. So we kind of slipped in, and I sat her down next to me at a picnic table. I introduced her to Chuck, who stopped building a fire and walked over to greet us. I could see Chuck being taken by her, as he was being extra polite, to the point of being out of character. Chuck and I had been through a lot together and had talked about everything in the world. We knew each other's feelings about a lot of shit. We both never trusted woman, for various reasons. We always talked about meeting a real woman instead of the drug whore sluts or welfare recipients we always met. We had come to the conclusion that if there were any decent women left out there, we would have to wait until we got patched or there wasn't any point in trying. Because, as a Prospect your life really wasn't yours, you could hardly sneak off long enough be normal with anybody. We chalked this up as what it takes to become a Hell's Angel, as we would have plenty of time after that to find these real women, if they really existed. As I have mentioned before, you can't bring women around as a Prospect, or at least around the Nomad crew. Chuck gave me a wink to confirm what I already knew. I had two choices, one was almost natural, to just go ahead and hustle her for the money and do what I had always wanted since I was a kid, join the Club. The other was to give up something fresh and respectful, a different kind of life, something I never thought I would really consider or ever find then, a real woman. This was a real crossroads for my soul. Do what I was trained to do, use her for money, house, and support. I could get her into the meth trap and live off her and her family for years. I could get married to her and get Daddy's money when they step in and want me to divorce her. That's when you get a big chunk of money, is when they pay you to get out of her life. This is almost an unwritten rule in hustling, and a very easy and profitable scan. This was totally different than the whore I lived with from Nevada. The problem was, in a few short hours I had grown to like her, and strangely also wanted to just be with her. This wasn't going to work out very well in my world with the Club. I had dreamed of an easy mark like this for years, but somehow I knew I couldn't do it to her. As we talked, I was thinking that maybe I could keep her straight, and a secret, or at least away from the Club somehow. I could see that I was trying to talk myself into it. I mean, what the fuck was I thinking, this would be easy money, a place to live, and the way she looked into my eyes, it would be a piece of cake. But that was the problem, when she looked deep into my eyes!

We laughed as we talked with Chuck. We had a few beers and a joint. I asked her if she wanted to go for a walk. Actually, I was doing my security perimeter walk, TCB again, taking care of business. We talked and talked, checking out the scenery as we walked. She asked if we could go for another ride, as she loved my bike. I kidded her and said that's why she was hanging with me, was so that she could ride on my beautiful bike. She reassured me that was not the case, but that it was a nice benefit, though. This was all going too easy, I thought to myself. It looked like Luck was having an orgy over there with the others, so I figured this was a good time to get her out of there. We went riding, and it was just sunset time as we rode though some beautiful scenery. I tried to talk her into going back to her car and going home, and she said she wouldn't unless I went with her. She didn't have to be to work until 11:00 the next morning. We rode back to our camp as I didn't want to split up with her, either. It was pretty quiet when we got there, and Chuck was tending the fire, and it looked like things had slowed down. I didn't see Luck and our crew and Chuck said he hadn't either. Chuck jokingly said I owed him, as he had taken care of my end of helping with the fire detail. We drank and smoked until we decided to lie down, as I was getting tired. I didn't know how we were both going to fit into my sleeping bag all zipped up, but with me on top of her we did, and I passed out after we made love, as I was exhausted.

The next thing I know, we were being woken up with bright lights blaring in our eyes, which lit up the whole camp. Yelling was coming from bullhorns everywhere, as we struggled to get up and out of my sleeping bag. The loud bullhorn speakers blared, "Don't move, get on the ground with your hands behind your heads, we are federal officers!" "Do not move or resist, you are under arrest, stay on the ground, you are surrounded!" We had managed to sit up, but all I could see was the trees coming alive with movement in the shadows of the night. We fell back to the ground, with the bag about half unzipped. We scampered to get dressed as best as we could, still halfway in the bag, as I looked in every direction and saw nothing but lights from around the trees, moving toward us. I knew they were cops by the way they yelled. "Oh, fucking shit, lie flat on the ground and do not fucking move, they might shoot us," I told her, as she was trying to button up her blouse and I was trying to get my pants on in the bag. They approached us in teams and they pulled her then me out of my bag. Then they pinned us to the ground and put our hands behind our backs and zip tied them together. As they pushed our heads back down towards the ground, I told them we didn't do anything. Like robots, they just kept reciting the same thing, "We are federal agents, get down, you are under arrest, don't move, put your hands behind your head!" I thought they were acting like fucking drones in a training film. I was looking at her shocked face, as she lay on her side just like I was, on the ground next to me. Then one of the officers said, "Yeah, I don't think this is one of them, you two just wait here and don't move!" Where in the fuck were we going to go, I thought? I looked at her and figured that my decision about our future had already been made.

We laid there for what seemed like hours. I kept apologizing and reassuring her, and she kept saying it was all right, but she *was* a little scared. The officers finally got us up and let her slip her pants on in the sleeping bag before they got us completely out of the bag and sat us on a picnic table, the same one that we had been sitting on earlier. They pulled a transport van into our camp amongst all the cop cars. I watched them loading Luck into the van, with his hands handcuffed behind him. There in the back of one of the cars, were those two young chicks, surrounded by their parents and cops. It looked like they were identifying their "assailants" for the feds, and I figured the rest out. They were questioning Chuck, and I told my little rich girl to tell them that she showed up with me and we went right to bed, and she didn't meet anyone or see anything. I could tell that she was scared, but she smiled back reassuringly. When they interviewed us, it went perfectly. They told us that the girls had said they had not even seen us that day. They cut the zip tie cuffs off and they took all our info, and said that we might be called for witnesses. I told them that we couldn't have witnessed shit, as we hadn't been there. They said they make the decisions and we would be informed.

Chuck was still a little stunned, as he came over saying, "What a fucking trip." The wreckers were hauling off the other bikes involved in the crime. If they had searched our bikes they would have gotten us too, for drugs. We had our crafty little hiding places and they really hadn't been using drug dogs much then. We couldn't believe that they didn't search us, as they had searched everybody that was arrested.

We all started calming down after they finally left. Chuck had been cool and polite as we were in the presence of the law. He knew how to play the game. He had stayed away from the others with the under-aged girls, and thank God he had. "Those were federal agents, they must have driven here from the Bay Area to make this bust," Chuck surmised. We figured the parents must have gone to the law right away to report their daughters were with Luck and them, and were partying with them, as they were minors. Luck and the crew had a bunch of felonies to deal with now, with the United States Government. Being on federal land meant federal bail, too. Shortly after this arrest, Luck got his full Patch. He never took the charges very seriously, but he would be part of other crimes later that he did have to take seriously. He was still quite the smart ass towards the law, but they would end up putting him away for life in prison. I had prospected with Luck, and I basically liked the guy. He was always good to me, as I had stayed at his house for a while. I knew he was Hell's Angel all the way, as he lived for it. I know that because I did then, too. Chuck said we had better call Chief right away, and then he winked at me and said he would do it. "I'll make up something about you, to cover your absence," he said. I rolled up my bag and fired up my scooter and we went to pick up her car. The bar was closing, so I bought a bottle of wine and followed her back to her cabin.

We stayed up pretty late drinking, smoking a little weed, and talking. To my surprise, the bust and what she was put through didn't seem to change her feelings a bit. We talked about her moving to her Grandma's place in Vallejo, as she had a big place and a smaller house detached from the main house. I told her I wasn't so sure of how my living with Grandma would work out. She assured me that I would hardly even have to meet her, and there was a nice garage for my bike. There were two two-bedroom houses, with each place separate from the other house, so Chuck could stay if I wanted him to. She told me it was located in a rich, exclusive neighborhood where no one would bother us. This was a hustler's dream. I could see it all unfolding in my mind and it looked good. I explained how I wouldn't bring her around the Club until I got my full Patch. She agreed, after what she had seen that night, and said that would be fine with her. We fell asleep talking about future dreams, and how we could make it work. I couldn't believe I had finally found a lifelong hustler's dream, and it was all coming true. I hadn't taken any meth that day, so I slept like a rock.

We woke up and picked up Chuck and went to breakfast. He said Chief was pissed, and that we were supposed to ride home last night. "I told him you were having bike trouble and we would be there as soon as we could. He said he didn't give a fuck if I had to peg you, to get our asses back there," Chuck said. I was starving, and ate like a pig, and with no meth in my system, my appetite was back. Chuck was itching to get as many miles as he could from Yosemite, and I didn't blame him, with Chief being pissed and the cops watching the camp all night. He said that when we had left that night, a set of car lights lit up after we pulled out and probably followed us to her place. He figured that they were trying to drum up some warrants on us, and Chuck always sweated that Nevada license he had. Once, Chuck and I had ridden over to San Francisco to pick up our money from a stolen bike deal from a few weeks before. On our way back, we got pulled over on the Bay Bridge. The highway patrolman walked up to us and asked for our driver's licenses and registration. Chuck handed him his license and asked him what he pulled us over for. The cop looked at him and threw Chuck's license off the bridge and into the ocean. "No driver's license," he nonchalantly said. I kind of hesitated when he reached out for mine, and he just glared at me, so I handed it to him, and he smiled. I didn't say a word and got mine back after he ran it. That's a true story. After the cop let us go, Chuck said, "Their goes my half of our money for another fucking trip to Nevada for another license!"

We finished breakfast, which she insisted on paying for, even though it was pretty expensive do to some Bloody Marys we had, then we went outside. I pulled her aside and said my goodbyes. I promised I would call her that night when I got back to Vallejo, and she said she would give her notice at work that day. As we left, I had feelings that I had never had before, as I was both elated and feeling guilty at the same time. I couldn't explain my feelings even to myself. Chuck motioned me over after 40 or 50 miles on the road and said, "Let's do a bump." I agreed, but for once in my life I was wondering if I should, as I needed to think things out. We stopped and I pulled my left handgrip off my handlebars and pulled out our stash. Chuck said that I was acting funny. "You ought to be happy as shit, scoring that chick; looks like you finally got it made!" "Yeah," I told him, "I should be." I explained to him that I sort of hated to ruin this chick's life, I mean she was so innocent and cool. "Oh Christ, don't tell me you found a conscious all of a sudden; God, man, she's the score of the century," Chuck said. "I know, I just hate to fuck her up with our shit. Don't tell anyone about her until I figure this out, ok?" "Bro I won't, I thought she was cool too, so innocent and beautiful, but worth a lot of money, with a rich Grandma already living in Vallejo; and, did you see that fucking expensive car? You know Luck might be right about you, because you are thinking way too much for your own good!"

We fired up our bikes and headed back to our world. I thought as we rode that Chuck was right, I couldn't believe I didn't want to use this girl. I thought of all the different ways I could maybe do this, but I knew that every one of them right now would be dangerous, and using her. If this was a conscious, I better lose it fast, because it wasn't allowed in my lifestyle. I realized that I couldn't have something that nice in my life because I would ruin it, leaving an ugly mark on something good. Or, was I afraid that she might change me and my dreams? I felt like I had during the USA Run; I was committing a foul against the Club and my lifestyle and what I believed in, as they were my family, and my life's dreams and ambitions in life.

When we got back to Vallejo, we got our ass's chewed off. Why were we so late, why didn't we do something about Luck's beef? We had to tell them exactly what had happened and what we had seen. After I finally got away to a pay phone, I called her and told her that I had gotten away as soon as I could, and told her something had come up and I would call or come see her in a week or so. She explained that she had already talked to her Grandma, and the house thing was all set up. She said she talked to Daddy and he was going to send her some extra money to move to her Grandmas with, besides her normal allowance. She said that she had mentioned that she had met me, and that she hadn't mentioned anything about me being in the Club. I told her that was all great and I was sure this thing wouldn't take too long up north. She said that she loved me, and asked me to be careful with whatever I was doing, that she was behind me all the way and would be waiting for me. When I hung up, I couldn't believe it; this was the perfect hustle. My newfound conscious was tearing at me, as it wouldn't let me do it. My soul was changing for the good, I guess. To my surprise, I never called her back, and I wondered how much that decision had changed my life, and hers. I look back at it as a good thing, as things were beginning to change in my world with the Hell's Angels, and it probably saved her. If I had moved in with her, would that have made me stay? I wouldn't have had to do that fucked up drug deal that would force me to leave the Club and California. I guarantee one thing; I know I would be dead or in prison today, if I had stayed.

This chapter, along with The USA Run and Running With the Devil, should give you a glimpse of what Club Runs are like as a Prospect. Everyone joining the Club has to go through shit like this. Now, you might be asking yourself why grown men would go through this kind of deprivation and humiliation. The answer is very simple, as you want that Patch more than anything in the world. Why would the Club want to do this kind of thing to its prospective members? For a lot of reasons… It shows that this man would do anything for the Club, without hesitation. No matter what position he's put in, he will do what it takes for the Club. Even if it means personal embarrassment, disgust, or pain, he's gonna play anyway. When you think about it, what better test could a Club devise? They are putting you through a secret ritual of sorts. This tests a Prospect's bike riding skills over a period of time to see if he's a good enough rider. This is when the members can get to know you, and see if you are what they want. To test a man to see if he is willing to do what is asked of him by the Membership, no matter what it is. They find out if you will fight for the Club. The getting naked part shows his loyalty, response, and reactions, the commitment to fulfill any task given to him by the Club, even if requires his giving up his personal dignity at his pride's expense. You have no secrets from the Membership, because you have exposed yourself naked for all to see. It also shows that they accept you as you are. I believe this event was very important in the growth and security of the Club. It's a test in front of the entire Club, for them all to see. I don't know if this is still being done the same way as it was to us, but it should be. Being a Hell's Angel isn't for everybody, as it's really only for a select few. It is a very elite man's Club that compares with none in my humble opinion. In my day, the Angels were a warrior's breed of men that feared nothing. There was no disgrace allowed, nor any test of honor that they could fail. They are proud of who they are, and of their honor. This explains a lot of their ways of schooling and testing their Prospects and potential new Membership. I often have heard members state, "We won't ask you to do anything we wouldn't do ourselves." I remember looking around and thinking that didn't leave out anything. They will kill if that's what it takes to preserve their Club, or their way of life. Look at the Laughlin, Nevada incident, as an example. As I have said, the Hell's Angels live by their own set of rules, in their own society, not yours. They don't ask you to live by their rules, so why would you as a society ask them to live by yours? That's what is always going to be the problem. Big Brother is big, and they will win someday. But if you don't leave them alone, you'll have big trouble. The law machine probably will take them down someday, but society won't!

RUNNIN' WITH THE DEVIL

The biggest man I ever fought, or I should say helped to fight, was with four Nomad Members from the Hell's Angels MC. We were out bar hopping one afternoon, waiting on a drug deal to fly. It was just another typical day in the Red & White life. We had gone to a bar, which we usually never did, because it was close to where the deal was to come down. Just doing our thing, taking care of business, and as soon as we walked in I could see why we hadn't come in before. I was the only Prospect that was there that afternoon, as all the rest of them had dodged it, or were truly busy. I was with Chief, our President, and three other Nomad Members. One who was there was Brett, who had transferred over from the 'Frisco Chapter. He was a very arrogant man that acted like a lawyer while being a total crankster; a very intelligent man, but I don't think he shit like the rest of us. He was another stone cold meth addict, and also one of the crazed motherfuckers. He would talk of killing for the Club anytime, just for the pure enjoyment of it, and you could feel his sincerity.

That day should have been nothing but shooting pool, snorting meth, and drinking some beers while waiting on a drug deal to come down; a somewhat normal afternoon for us. But unfortunately, there were some black dudes in the bar too, with one being one of the biggest black men I have ever seen. He was a huge man, shooting pool and drinking beer and acting tougher than the others. Well, Chief really hated blacks a lot, but then again, most all of the Angels of the times that I knew did, too. I had plenty of trouble with blacks when I was younger in the Bay Area, so at that time in my life, I was predacious myself. I could see when we hit the door that trouble was going to happen. We all ordered beers, except Chief's rum and coke, then we started playing pool, as usual. It didn't take Chief long enough for me to finish my first beer to get the fight started. "You niggers need to leave," Chief yelled! "Well, we were here first and got the right to be here too, and who you calling nigger, white boy?" the big, black dude responded. Chief answered him with a "You mother…" and finished his response by breaking a pool cue over the big guy's head, and the shit was on!

I guess that was going to be Chief's and the rest of ours only response. I had a pool cue and immediately went to work on the one man standing closest to me. We had knocked the three of them down pretty fast with the cues. We had them out-numbered and used the pool cues first, giving us the advantage all the way around. I'll give them credit though, as every one of them put up a fight and tried their best. It's been my experience that in a situation like this, when you're facing Hell's Angels with pool cues, most men would cut and run from their friends. These men fought together as a group, which surprised me. I beat the man in front of me and took one pretty good shot on the side of my head, and to his credit, the punch spun my head for a minute. They put up a good fight and have my respect for their bravery. That's when I noticed Chief and another Member still beating on the big dude. I think he could see that he wasn't going to get any help from his buddies, so he was trying to fight his way out the front door and into the street. Brett had gotten one down in this booth on the floor, between the table and the seat. He had his hand up on the divider and was putting the boots to this guy. While I could see that the guy was done, hopefully not permanently, I yelled and pointed out the door, "Chief!" Brett looked and gave one more kick and went for the door yelling, "Come on, let's go get that big fucker!" We had knocked the rest of them out, or at least they weren't moving anymore. Brett and I ran out into the parking lot and we all turned our attention to the big guy, as we definitely had him surrounded and out-numbered. The big guy had no way out, but he was ready to fight to defend himself. I came up from behind him and kicked him as hard as I could in the balls. I had steel-toed engineer boots on, which I always wore in those days. That was an old chicken shit move I had learned the hard way; my balls still don't hang right since I got kicked just like that. My foot went perfectly right up between his legs, and it was a very solid kick. That would drop most men to their knees, as it did me. Instead, he just reeled around with a half-assed swing at me, which I easily dodged. I could see that he was bleeding from all kinds of cuts. I mean, this guy was squirting blood all over us. We had him surrounded and kept punching and kicking him. He just kept spinning around, trying to take shots at all of us. I was beginning to have some respect for this giant fellow, as he could take a savage beating better than most I have seen, and he just would *not* go down.

We heard the inevitable cop sirens in the distance, as I heard one of the Members say, "We got to leave, now." Brett started to try and pull Chief off the guy, with no success, as Chief was enraged by now that the big guy wouldn't go down. We wouldn't leave our President, no matter what. So Chief pulls his pistol out and aims it at the guy's head, and yells, "Fuck it, you're going down nigger!" At that second, Brett pushed Chief's arm straight up as the gun went off. The bullet *just* cleared his head! Brett yells, "Not here, its not worth it, damn it!" Chief brought the gun down right on top of the guys head, and pistol whipped him. The guy staggers, but he's still standing there bleeding. "Let me shoot this fuck; he needs to go down!" Chief screamed. He hit the guy with his pistol a couple more times, with all of us hitting him from all sides, as we kept bouncing blows off of him. The sirens were almost there, and Brett yells again, "Let's go!" We all make a dash for our bikes, and for once, my baby kicked to life on the first try. As we jammed away, I look back at the guy, and he's still standing there with his fists up, bleeding all over the place and swaying, but still glaring at us and still standing. We barley missed the cop cars by turning on a side street and hauling ass to get away. When we pulled up to a stoplight, we all laughed and agreed that we had never seen a man take a beating like that and stay standing. Chief wasn't laughing, as he was pissed at everyone for not letting him shoot the dude in the head. He kept saying, "It isn't right, at all." Brett said, "Did you want go to prison for shooting his big, black ass?" "Yeah, I would, Hell's Angels don't leave niggers behind like that. I am gonna' find his ass again and shoot him," Chief said. That was the kind of Angel Chief was, and I believe he would

238

have killed him, and maybe *did* eventually, as he always held a grudge and never would let shit go!

My life with the Nomads in Vallejo was a day-to-day, real experience of the lifestyle of life in the fast lane. Prospects spent most of their time delivering dope and shit, or working on Member's bikes, or getting parts for those bikes. Also, protecting the Chapter's President wherever he goes; that also includes when he's making business calls, day or night (I hated that one); We spent a lot of time running errands, moving drugs, babysitting (a term used when a Member wants you to hang with him to party and keep him company *while* he is partying), picking up court papers, making deliveries to bail bondsmen, moving money, and trips down to the Titty Club to pick up or deliver. Prospect's responsibilities also included taking out of town Members around town, or to wherever they needed, to visit other Chapter Brothers or go get them lined up with some local pussy. "Run over to Richmond and pick up this, go over to the Frisco Clubhouse and see so and so, bring me back whatever he gives you right now, and don't stop!" You rarely knew what you were hauling, but you could guess by the package that it was illegal.

Sometimes, it was fun accompanying a Member to protect him wherever he was going, whether to a party or to a drug deal, as they would always keep you buzzed on the product. Members always had uncut shit. If Members drank or smoked weed, or whatever, they would usually share with you. Not all of them partied all the time, so it would vary with each member. You would be with some of them that would be short with you, or even ignore you and treat you like shit. Others would be cool and you would enjoy being with them. The majority of Hell's Angels of those times were good Members that had jobs and partied on drugs or alcohol, and loved to ride their bikes, but not the Nomads! Prospecting for the Red & White was a 24/7 job back then, and I believe still is today. Actually, it's more than a full time job. There were times, even as young as I was, that I didn't know if I could make it. Sleep deprivation will drive you nuts, especially doing it all the time, and would at times make you pray for just get a few hours of sleep, somehow. Even with speed to help you to try and keep going, it was the hardest thing I've ever done in my life!

Even after you get patched and become a Member, it is still hard to be a Hell's Angel. When do you get to let the badass part down, or can you? The truth is, when you are wearing the Patch you have to be a Hell's Angel all the time, and never let your guard down. That's true for about almost all Patch holders from any three piece 1% Outlaw Club. Rarely, and only with a few of your closest Brothers, can you let your guard down. Flying your Colors is pretty much a full time job. Some Members handled being human better than others. Some were just hard asses all the time to you. Some would relax and let you get to really know them personally, after some time. I always enjoyed the more personable ones, and would go out of my way for them. They weren't all Teddy Bears or Hangtown Bills, to say the least. But you had no choice, as you had to take the good with the bad, without question. The few evil, crazed cranksters were the worst for me though, as I couldn't stand the evil they generated, and you never knew what would happen next.

Like I said, you don't really have the time for a regular job when you're living in the fast lane. I knew I had to do more hustling to be able to play the game full time. I felt that I had no choice, as this was my one chance to earn my Colors and get patched. One example of what it is like in that fast lane life is when I got busted riding Mike K. home one night from the Club's Titty Bar in Vallejo, which story is in another chapter. But because of that illegal bust, I had to pay the Club back for bail, and a high dollar lawyer. Back then, marijuana was a felony bust that would give you a strike, and if convicted of three strikes, you are out. If you wanted to stay out on the street with your Club, you had to fight all your busts. It is common knowledge that the law's ideas of getting Clubs off the streets were to bust the Members with everything they can. Traffic tickets, domestic charges, and any busts they could warrant happened, to try to wear you down by taking yours and the Club's money, so that they could weaken the organization as a whole. That's why Angels rarely take a deal from the D.A.'s office for a lesser charge with probation. The cops try to make it a sweet, easy deal so that you plead guilty to something. When they finally get you on your third felony bust, or accumulated misdemeanors, you then are considered a habitual criminal and sentenced to life in prison. To be caged like an animal for life, they might as well give you a gun with a bullet in it. That's the law's plan, to use the tax payer's money to put us away, for the citizens well being of course, no matter how much it costs. So this was happening to me because of this bust, and I had to come up with the extra money somehow to pay the Club back. So I did more crime, to get the money to stay free, and so the circle went, with everyone doing their part. The cops bust you, and then the bondsman bails you out. Then, you do some crime to have the money to pay the lawyer and bondsmen to try and stay out of jail. This becomes the routine of your life, and the reason why Members would get into drug dealing and crime to have all the money they needed to live their life in the fast lane.

We all had our scams and hustles to make money, but it was harder for the Prospects, as you're so busy all the time prospecting. If you did get something good going and certain Members heard about it, well, let's just say that you're better off keeping it to yourself. For God sakes, you never want to brag about it if you want to keep it. Chuck and I had our stealing scooters and selling hot parts gig, selling dope, living off women's favors, anything but work! You really just didn't have the time as you were kept busy all the time. Rick the Rat had two old ladies that both had jobs and took care of him, and they were stone foxes. They all lived together as one big, happy family. Rat's old ladies would go to work every day, and he did what he did best, be a Hell's Angel. Welfare ladies with kids and child support were referred to as the real California gold, and were very easy prey. You could always hustle food, a place to live, and get a small allowance from them. Sometimes, you could have two, or even three, going at the same time, especially if they were doing meth. The point is to make a living and not work because you already have a job that takes all your time; you're a California Hell's Angel Prospect. Sell a little meth here, turn a quarter pound of weed there, or just get a welfare chick dealing for you, because that's easier money yet. You do have to lean on them once in awhile to keep them straight.

Stolen property is another lucrative business, as you really don't have to steal anything, you just trade meth addicts for your merchandise, so you get shit so cheap, and you don't have to steal it yourself. Although, I have to admit, I used to enjoy the juice of tip-toe crime. But it was easier to turn a profit on the dope, and then you also made money off the hot shit you traded for dope, sort of double dipping. The problem I had at first was that I was from a different area, so when I moved to Vallejo I lost a lot of my connections. In the beginning, after I moved there, I constantly had to go back to my old stomping grounds in El Dorado County to turn a buck. That's when Chief would get mad because I wasn't running around with them, as I would head home for a couple days every couple of weeks to make some money.

After awhile I got things rolling in Vallejo. The world just doesn't turn for anybody without the almighty dollar. Up until then I had only held two straight jobs in my young-ass life. The first job, I had to get so that I could get released from Youth Authority. With a job on the outside as a waiter I could get released early from Fout Springs Reformatory, as soon as I passed the G.E.D. test and graduated from high school. This all happened just after I turned 17, as I had already been locked up for 18 months. My parole only lasted two weeks, as I violated it when I quit my job and said fuck 'em. The second job I had only lasted about three months, which was driving a truck. I just didn't have the time because I wanted to ride my bike and run with Clubs. I admit that I was a hustling criminal, because selling dope and committing burglaries were more my main forte. The point is that you had to make your money illegally, because you were just too busy with the Club Prospecting, and trying to stay out of jail!

I remember when gas was only about .38 cents per gallon for premium, and cigarettes could be had for about .59 cents per pack. A complete Big Mac Attack with fries was like .59 cents, and a quart of Ripple wine to wash it down with was only .69 cents. Shit, I would only eat a Big Mac once a day, so I could live on twenty bucks a week. I started chewing Skoal smokeless tobacco because my lungs started hurting from smoking so much dope and cigarettes. Plus, you could get a roll of five cancer cans for less than two bucks. Life was good enough, as my dope was free because I sold it. I had one old steady sugar mama back home that was religious about sending me a twenty spot once a week. All I had to do was drop by once in awhile and life was good! She was divorced, with two little girls and worked as a beautician. She made excellent money and received regular child support payments from her rich ex. Her parents were from an old rich family, so bucks weren't a problem. She had never been on welfare; her parents were way too rich for that.

There was a 28 year difference in our ages. Our relationship kind of reminded me of the Maggie May song by Rod Stewart. I never loved her or even said I did, and she wouldn't either. I was her young, bad boy biker that she could show off to her rich friends. I was more of a conversation piece than anything else. She would buy me clothes, jewelry, and all kinds of shit, and then give it to me in front of her friends at her staged Christmas parties and shit. I would go some place for a three-day weekend vacation with her and one of her rich couple friends. I would be uncomfortable until I would get a good drunk going, as her nor her friends did many drugs. For me, it was just an easy hustle. I didn't care when people would stare at us due to our obvious age difference; fuck them, this was easy money. It was pretty much plutonic and we were just good friends. I saw a lot of places I wouldn't have otherwise, and drank and ate at some very expensive restaurants. Whenever I got back into town, I had it made, and would stay there with her. It was a sweet deal, as I could come and go as I pleased, and as long as I checked in once in awhile, she would help support me.

One rule we did have though, was that I would never bring around any of my friends nor Brothers, as she was terrified of them, and wanted to protect her kids. When I told her that I was going down to Vallejo to go Red & White, she didn't approve and was sad, but supportive; that was the deal. She bought me my new leather vest that I eventually ended up putting my bottom rocker on, and included a custom made leather shirt, and pants to match. She also bought me my expensive Bowie knife when I first met her, and I carried that knife until I left California. If I needed some quick cash to get my bike running again, I would tell her I couldn't come over because I had no wheels, and she would give me some of the money I needed. She hated the Clubs I ran with, but ignored all that. When we got drunk once in awhile we would get in an argument, and I believe it was just for her friend's sake. Something for her and her friends to talk about; I was the bad boy toy who had to play the game. I know I was nothing more than a male whore, but it didn't bother me a bit at the time. She was a pretty good friend through it all, and fortunately for me, an even better hustle.

Sometimes I also would have a welfare chick or two going when I had to, especially when I lived in Vallejo. All at the same time, you just traded a little love and an occasional bike ride once in awhile for a living. By a living, I mean that you get a place to eat, sleep, borrow a car on occasion, and get your laundry done for free. All valuable perks that are needed to survive and not work. Most of them had two to three kids from two Fathers, which was the average. The golden rule was that you don't fall for them, because if you did, you would end up working your ass off for the rest of your life paying for them and their kids. So you should never let yourself have feelings, or get puppy love. You had to pretend that this relationship was forever and you were the shining knight of their dreams; you are going to rescue the damsel in distress. You were gonna' change their miserable lives and make their ugly existence beautiful again, as their shiny white knight in black leathers, riding them on your steed of metal and paint. The reality was that you were going to use them for everything you could, and leave them. I felt like a predator at times, and didn't have any feelings for these women. My only problem, usually, was leaving the kids. I would school them up on their behavior, and then I would get a soft spot for them, so I had to watch that one. All they wanted was someone to love them, and most of all, just pay attention to their young lives. You had to be heartless and detached of their plight, but at times I would get depressed over my shallow feelings, a hollow spot if you will, in my soul, along with a very empty feeling of regret.

I had learned from the best to be cold and cruel, empty of any feelings, to always be conning these women for support, them being the by-product of the more "free" society of our generation. You have to remember that for me it was a living, not love or personal passion; you had to have a very cold heart of stone, and I did! Tell them what they wanted to hear, and use them for every dime you could get out of them. This was one of the main biker hustles in those days, as we called it "The California hustle," or "California gold." Life wasn't too hard with their help and support though, as I was a real low-life motherfucker in those days.

When my bike needed rebuilding, I would go rip another one off. Then I would use all the parts I needed, and then sell or trade the rest off for motor or transmission work, or whatever I needed done. If we were going on a bike run, Chuck and I would go burn a late model hog and run it over to Frisco to collect our traveling money. Then we would split the $500 that we made and that was a lot of money in those days. Like I said, I would resort to burglary on occasion, but that was a lot like work. Moving heavy shit, renting trucks, fencing the shit, then you sometimes had to move it again. The profit really wasn't worth all the work, usually. Now, moving a bag of dope that fits in your pocket and pays off better for almost no labor, that's easy money and we did all the dealing we could. Getting the dope was easy, because we were the connection. Large quantity deals were the best of course, as it was fast money with no street exposure, but even selling only mass quantities had its dangers. Narcotics officers always wanted to set up large quantity deals, in order to bait you with the fast money. One thing I learned fast was that if a dude you don't know real good wants a mass quantity, and doesn't argue for a cheaper price, eight out of ten times, they are cops. The idea was to make a living without working, and stay out of prison, and we were damn good at it!

I was shacking up (as was called it then) with this divorced welfare chick in Vallejo. I had been staying at Bear's at first when I moved there, but then accidentally run into this unhappy home. I met her at a stoplight on the main drag as four of us were out riding our bikes over to Bear's house to go on a four day out of town bike run. I was in the back of the pack, where I belonged as a newbie, in sync with the pecking order of the pack. All of a sudden, this chick jumps out of the car that pulled up behind us, and runs up to us. "Who are you?" she asked me. I told her and then she asks, "Are you staying here?" "Yeah, I just moved here," I said. "Well, I want to take you home with me," she yells over the noise of the Harleys. "I can't go now, as I am going on a bike run for four days," I explained. Then the light turned green and as we started to pull out, I yelled at her over my shoulder, "I will look you up when I get back!" "I know where to find you, so don't go anywhere else," she yelled back. We stopped a couple of lights down and I pulled up next to a Buick, next to Luck. "Hey, you wouldn't believe what this little chick just came up and said to me." "Yeah, I can, that's Sharon; she's a Patch chaser," Luck said. "Wow, I'm kind of liking Vallejo already," I responded. Luck said, "Don't worry, she's a welfare bitch that you're not going to be able to get rid of!"

When we got back from the run I went to stay at Bear's house and try to get my shit together to move out. Bear's old lady Becky came back from the store. "Hey, you got a real admirer," she told us. She had bumped into Sharon, who told her that she'd been calling all the girls in the Club looking for me. "If you're interested, I can get a hold of her, if you want to talk to her. Please call her though, because she's been hounding all the old ladies, trying to find you!" "I forgot all about meeting her, looks like my luck has just changed for the better," I said. I asked Becky if she new any history on this chick, and she said that she did. She filled me in on all the news about her first husband, and that Pete the Reb used to date her, etc… Becky handed me the phone along with her number, so I called her. She wanted me to come over, so I did, and I ended up moving in with her that night, which isn't very hard to do when everything you own is in your saddlebags on your bike!

Sharon had two kids, which is two more than I would have liked; even one that was still in diapers. I'd been *here* before. It's been my experience that these kids are generally just looking for attention, and want you to become their friend. With a little schooling and some candy for rewards, they'll do just about anything for you. The Mothers usually appreciated the guidance and discipline, but for me I just wanted some controlled behavior and peace when I was around and maybe for them to fetch my beers, but I always grew to have a soft spot for them.

I wasn't the first biker from the Club to live with her, and I am sure I wasn't the last. One dude was a Hang Around that didn't make it into the Club. Then, there was Pete the Reb, who had just been using her on and off for financial gains, until he got patched and went on to better hustles. Pete would turn into a big problem for me with Sharon. He would later try to get her insurance money from her that she wanted to give to me. Sharon was an ok gal, and she liked her meth, but mainly just the weed, and would rarely drink. Unlike most of the women then, she wasn't a full-time tweaked out, drunken whore, which was one of the few things I liked about her. She would keep beer in the fridge for me. She always got up and cooked me bacon and eggs for breakfast, which was my favorite meal, and she bought the food with her food stamps. Hell, that alone was saving me seven bucks a week, and beat going to McDonalds, as I only ate once a day then. I didn't give her much meth, as I didn't want her to get strung out bad, because of her kids. Normally, assholes like me would get her strung out on meth and then get her working down at the Club's Titty Bar for cash, so she could still collect welfare. You give them more dope, collect more money, and then give her a little more time to get strung out some more. A year of that and all the dope she can use, and then you have a first class drug whore, having graduated to the top of their class. Then, if she was even average looking, you could get them doing tricks at the bar, or better yet, you could send them up to one of the Ranches in Nevada, and keep them flat on their backs, making you even more money. Once they were worn out and the drugs ate their looks, you discard them, as that was "The System." I couldn't do that to her, or to her kids, as my conscious wouldn't let me.

Sharon had a carport that I parked my bike under, and after being a bike thief myself, I had to get set up with some security for it. I had the normal chains and locks and shit. I had learned a good trick from Fat Ray. You get a small steel cable and hook it through the rear wheel and frame, and then run it through your bedroom window and fasten it to your bedpost. If they try to roll it off, it wakes you up quickly. I was Ray's protégé as a kid, and it was hard enough to hold on to your bike in those early days, especially if you weren't associated with a Club. Once I was a known Red & White associate, I didn't have to worry any more. I traded some dope for a hot AKI reel-to-reel stereo system and a colored TV from the same burglary. I set it all up, and it made Sharon's place a real comfortable pad for all of us. Sharon was happy with that, as the other guys before me had just stolen her stuff and sold it all for money. She had an old Chevy Impala which I helped keep running for her, as I would occasionally borrow it once in awhile to take care of Club business, TCB. She had been in a pretty serious car accident, and her ex-husband had given her this old beater for the kid's sake. I had met him once and he was scared of the Club, as he should have been. Sharon had a lawyer that had been working on getting her a settlement for her accident, for over a year now. This whole situation was working out well for me, as all I had to do was hustle enough to keep my bike running and attend to everything.

Thanks to Sharon, I now had a residence in Vallejo and was an official Hang Around for the Nomad Chapter.

Unlike some Clubs, the Red & White always had Church every week, either at the Clubhouse or at a Members house. The Nomads had lost their Clubhouse before I got there. When Teddy Bear was President, it was always at his house, which was a white house with painted red trim, how would you figure? It didn't matter much; cop surveillance would always find us anyway. They would use Luck's house often, even though he was a Prospect. It was a big place with a lot of garage space, as Luck had a radiator shop there for a while. Luck also had a couple of successful legal businesses before he hooked up with the Hell's Angels. He was also a good framer and carpenter, and was making big bucks when he needed the money. So his house/business became our place of business, and home to an all-the-time Clubhouse. He let all of his legal business that he had going then gradually go, with him and his wife seeming not to give a fuck about any of it. There were people there all the time, coming and going. About then was when Sweet Will transferred out from a back East Chapter, and moved right into Luck's extra bedroom. The doors were always open for the Club, as Luck and his wife were going Red & White all the way! He was rapidly getting into the illegal enterprises of drug dealing and prostitution. When I knew Luck, he wasn't a real heavy dope user, but wanted more to get into the fast lane all the way, and make money at it. Things would have been a lot different for him if he hadn't met the Club, as he was a very intelligent man that could do almost anything. He always criticized my actions a lot, along with all the other Prospects and Hang Arounds, as he was probably too smart for his own good. He would go on to become a rich drug dealer, among other things. After he was patched, he quickly gained a lot of power in the Club, and lots and lots of money. He's currently doing a life sentence in prison. So, back then, an average morning usually included a trip by Luck's place, for one reason or another. We would work on somebody's bike there, drop off some parts, gave a message or a packet to a Member, or just visit and hangout with each other, checking out the scene. Then, we would always end up in the afternoon at our Titty Bar, drinking beer and partying while we shot pool.

Vallejo was a naval port that had all kinds of shit going on, especially during Vietnam, so there were plenty of swabbies with money that the girls could hustle. We would go shoot pool and hang out with our Members, or with visiting Members, and always keep an eye on our moneymakers, in a bouncer type capacity. We had police scanners that we would monitor to keep an eye on things, and on any Members that might get jacked someplace else in our town. We gave the swabbies full reign, and kept the others away so the girls could make money. It was our bar, and the girls made sure everyone knew who they worked for. Most of the members had at least one of those chicks dancing and hustling for them, as this was always a very lucrative hustle. When I first came to Vallejo, Chuck had a chick we used to call Scar Face. She had a great body, but had been in a very serious car accident and had to cake on the makeup. She had a good attitude, but just had to work a little harder to support her habit. Like all the girls, she was addicted to methamphetamine. Chuck had hooked up with another one and dumped her, and then offered her to me, which was like handing me some money. All you had to do was supply them with dope and they would take care of you. They didn't care if you lived with or loved them, all the time or not, because their true love was that bag of dope and the rush it would bring. So you supplied them with whatever drugs they wanted, and hustled a place to live, and could love them if you wanted. Besides the money you made off the dope deals, they would give you some money for protecting them and being their Daddy. This was very easy money that helped keep our machine running 24/7. It's not all crime, there's a lot of riding bikes and partying, too. Just like everyone else, you have to have the basics; a place to shit, shower, and shave, just like anyone else.

People always wonder what Outlaws do all day, but generally are afraid to ask. First, remember what being an Outlaw biker meant, simply that you are living outside of the law. The Hell's Angels are like any 1% motorcycle club; they live by their own rules and in their own society that they have created, and believe me that it does truly exist. They have their own laws and creeds, constitution, standards, by-laws, judges, jurors and enforcers to uphold all this in their society. They believe in honesty and loyalty, and they also get phony infiltrators in their society that they to have to deal with. Does this sound like countless other countries, societies, and governments that make up this world today? How many people does it take to have your own legal government and society? People say that by having their own society, Outlaws are breaking "society's" rules, and so they can't... Wait a minute; they have their own rules and laws that they live by, although different than yours. Different than yours for sure, but don't we have the right and the freedom and liberty to chose our own rules to live by, as we don't persecute you for living by yours of choice? There are more of you than us, so might is greater than right, right? Thus, Motorcycle Clubs are like any oppressed group of people that are forced by prison or death to live amongst others and obey their laws. Yes, it is happening right now, as it always has in the past and throughout our history. I am glad though, that a Rebel named Thomas Jefferson was around to challenge the existing authority of the time, or we would still have a King and Queen to bow down to right now. I have never met an Outlaw biker that didn't love the U.S.A. as a country. I do believe that most of them would die for it, and some of them have. Many Outlaws, if not most, have served their country, and with their sacrifices have defended our country and our rights of freedom. They are not against it, but rather for it, and would rather be left alone to live the way they want to. But this society's majority wants to end the MC world and put them all behind bars, in a cage. Bikers are just trying to live in this world the way they want to, and with freedom. Unfortunately, I believe that the majority of our great society will succeed one day soon, and end what freedoms we have left. To me, it is amazingly and painfully clear on what that outcome will be.

Here is one explanation on what belonging to an Outlaw 1% Motorcycle Club is like to a citizen. You see all the time on TV and books and such about the camaraderie and bond that military troops have from serving in a war together. Men serving in any war, whether it was WWII, the Korean War, or Vietnam, it doesn't matter, they form a feeling for the Brothers in Arms while serving with each other. These men are put together and live a daily routine with each other, but more importantly, they're watching each other's backs. They become a family of men that become very close as they play the ultimate game of staying alive in a hostile environment. They have a common enemy to protect each other from. When they get into a fight, they survive by watching each other's backs and sacrificing themselves for their Brothers in Arms. This unexplained bond has been happening since anyone can remember; documented thousands of times throughout modern history of soldier's willingness to self-sacrifice themselves for each other. It is almost a phenomenon. Citizens can't possibly understand this loyalty, or how this could be. How can relative strangers be willing to give their life for another? Medal of Honor winners, in every conflict, have thrown themselves onto a hand grenade to save their Brothers in Arms. This amazes the average citizen, as they have never felt anything like this in their lives. Maybe they have been part of a sports team in high school, but they wouldn't die for each other. The military camaraderie is the same as being in a true, old school Motorcycle Club Brotherhood. The unexplainable willingness to take a bullet for each other are what citizens can't, and will never to be able to understand. The willingness of one to risk his life and limb for others is incomprehensible to most citizens. When asked, that is my best comparison of what its like to belong to an MC Brotherhood.

Even some street gangs experience this, but the one thing that corrupts their Brotherhood is, like everything else, money and drugs, which causes greed, thus destroying the Brotherhood. Its similar to cancer, as it slowly eats away at its membership, and ends up being the Club's demise, with no real way to stop it. That, and sometimes jealousy, power, and arrogance will destroy true Motorcycle Clubs. I remember when Luck was a Prospect and he came back from visiting in Oakland. He showed me a U.S. brass button on his cut, a military button for US Army personnel. Luck explained that some Oakland Members had given it to him, as he was part of their little group within the Club.

Another one of these inner groups was The Filthy Few, which Bear and Pie belonged to. Chief, whose real name I was told was Dennis, was the Nomad's President in 1973. I also heard he had been called Dennis the Menace, and also Crash, as he wrecked his Harley a lot when he first came around the Club. Luck told me that in a whisper, because that was before he had made President of the Nomad Chapter, and he hated

Crash. He was a real crankster, that is, a gangster and a methamphetamine addict. His only care was being a Hell's Angel President and dealing meth; that was his life, as worldly possessions really meant nothing to him. When he drank it was Bacardi rum and coke. I know that because as a Prospect, you fetch all the booze for the Members, so I knew what everyone drank. Before meetings, Chief would flip me a hundred dollar bill and say "Ice, Bacardi, coke, and whatever the fuck anyone else wants, and hurry!" He always had at least one gun on him, and was one crazy, psychopathic motherfucker, for sure. He was Red & White all the way, with guns, meth and women, which is all he lived for; and, Al Capone was his hero. He was not a very big man by Hell's Angels standards, with our kind of lifestyle. He was really kind of thin, but with an all muscular build. He had one of the biggest sets of brass balls that any man that size I have ever known had. I remember a Church we had in the Santa Raphael area at Big Red Bryant's. Chief showed up on his chopper, arriving late for Church. All of the Prospects were outside the house doing our security thing. He got off his bike and walked right up to me and asked if I had my gun. I said "Yeah", and told him that we had a sawed off twelve gauge, double barrel shotgun hidden in the bushes, too. Chief said that he had just ridden over from Frisco and he thought the cops were following him. He instructed us all, "Do not let anyone near my bike, and I mean nobody, or it's your ass! I don't give a flying fuck if it's the cops, or who the fuck it is, got it!" I told him, "No problem." This was kind of a strange order to be given, even from Chief, because the cops were always following him. Luck and Chuck kind of looked at me with puzzled looks; could this be a mud check I thought. I looked at his bike and there was a square shopping bag all bungeed down on the front end of his bike, just below the headlight. If you took a brown, paper shopping bag and fully opened it square, that's about the size this bundle was.

After Chief walked into the house, Luck and I concluded that this was indeed strange, because we had both seen a plain clothes cop car go by us, checking us out while we were still talking to Chief. I waited there, nervous as shit that the cops would come back and we would have a shootout. After about half an hour, I got called into the meeting. "Prospect, I want you to go get me that package off my bike, and bring it in here right now!" Chief ordered. Away I went from the front door, trying to walk instead of run. I unstrapped the package off his front-end and remember thinking how heavy it was. I walked back into the meeting and looked at everyone around me, staring back at me and the package. "Put it on the table," Chief told me. I did, and nobody told me to leave, so I stood there as Chief and Big Red started opening the package. They started telling everybody as they worked that they were gonna' love this shit! It was pure, uncut methamphetamine, and a lot of it. This was the good uncut shit like he always got from Jim Jim, or Kenny O (who is serving a life sentence in prison for cooking meth). They cooked the best shit that I ever had and were the best in their trade back then. In those times, meth was being made out of the best chemicals, then the law outlawed them and the quality of the stuff has gone downhill ever since.

Chief started passing the blade around and everyone walked by in turns, dipping into this huge bag of meth. After some of the Members at the table were done, they handed the blade to me and I walked up and took a blast. The blast immediately crossed my eyes and tears started rolling down my cheeks; good shit! Chief had been talking business as soon as the bag opened, and then all of a sudden, he looked up at me and said, "What the fuck are you still doing here Prospect? Go back fucking outside and shoot anyone who tries to come in, got it!" Then he kind of giggled, with his eyes on fire; he was in his element. This was as good as it would ever get for him. Chief *was* methamphetamine; it was his life, and besides the Red & White, it was all he had or wanted.

If I were to guess, I would say that there was thirty to forty pounds of meth sitting in that paper bag. I couldn't even guess the street value, being an uncut product, but it was definitely a *lot*. That crazy motherfucker had rode over from San Francisco with that big bag of dope strapped onto his bike out in the open! I couldn't believe it. The cops would follow Chief around all the time, but no one would have ever expected that, not even the Members! I had been transporting and selling drugs a long time, but nobody I knew ever had the balls he had when it came to drug dealing. Chief never feared anything, not even his own death. That was the way he was. When I first started hanging around, he came up to me and asked me where my gun was. I used to carry my big custom Bowie knife on my side, as I always did. It made people nervous, it was legal, and that was the weapon I always carried. Being a felon, of course, meant that guns were a no-no. I patted my knife and told him that was all I usually carried. He said he didn't really give a fuck if I carried my knife or not, but if I was hoping to become a Prospect in his Chapter, I had better get a fucking gun. "You don't bring a fucking knife to a gun fight. Make it a throw away, too. I just don't believe you young guys!" A throw away is a stolen gun that's not traceable to you. "What if we run into some Outlaws, you gonna' throw that knife at them?" Chief barked. I felt a little embarrassed, as Members and Prospects were listening to us. My answer was that I would throw it, because I was pretty good at it. I realized right then that I was in the big leagues now, and they were packing guns to stay alive, not just for show.

As soon as I could, I got a hot one from my old stomping grounds. About a week later, Chief walked up to me again at Church, "Let's see your gun." I proudly handed my .32 automatic to him. He looked at it and told me to get rid of my pea shooter, and get at least a 9mm. "Until you do, let me see that one," he said, as he brought out his roll of his special tape and wrapped the handle with it. This tape would stop any fingerprints from sticking to the handle. Then he carefully wiped the whole gun down for prints before handing it back. He mumbled something about amateurs.

You were supposed to keep your pistol in your belt and handy when you were riding for obvious reasons; we were at war. But many a time, I would have to throw it before I got pulled over by the law. This was an old trick; something about felons not being allowed to carry guns. I also used to carry a switchblade stiletto in my handlebars on my bike. If you pulled the rubber grip off, it would slide right out into your hand. I ran Z bars or Pullbacks back then, so the angle was perfect. I also carried, like almost all bikers of my era, a vest pocketful of nuts and bolts. Anything from a quarter inch to a half inch worked fine. Besides also being handy for breakdowns, they were like carrying a shotgun on your bike, only legal even for us felons. When you're cruising down the road and somebody comes up behind you and starts fucking with you, no matter truck, car, or bike, you just reach into your pocket and grab a handful of nuts and bolts and flick them over your shoulder. What happens to whatever is behind you is they get a shotgun blast of steel! At 55 mph, it's worse than a 12 gauge of buck shot. Those babies rip holes through radiators, windshields, car bodies, *and* flesh, no problem! Who's to say that you didn't accidentally hit a bump, and they fell out of your pocket and oops, they hit something Hardly pre-meditated murder. There are no ballistics and no fingers prints, and are only traceable to every hardware store on the corner. As a Prospect riding in the back of the pack, if somebody started tailgating us, or the pack, or a rival Club came after us, standard practice was to start tossing nuts and bolts at them while cranking the throttle. I heard many stories about bikers saving their asses by doing this. One biker I knew was riding home from the bar on I-80 near Rock Springs, Wyoming, when some jealous rednecks from the bar tailed him and tried to run him off the highway at about 90 mph. He claimed that he hammered the throttle, but the truck stayed right on his ass and was about to hit him, when he tossed a handful of nuts and bolts over his shoulder. He said that he saw the radiator and windshield explode in his mirror, as the truck went sideways and then launched off the side of the highway. I feel that they got what they deserve. He felt that trick saved his life that day, and it probably did. About a year later, near Green River, Wyoming, a lone biker was run off the same highway, and is in a wheelchair for life. It wasn't always easy being a biker in the old days, when we were few. Personally, I have seen windshields explode, and steam and smoke blow out of radiators as they exploded. Every time, they locked up their brakes and you didn't see them anymore; if any of them died, I wouldn't know. You're the most vulnerable thing in the world on a motorcycle with literally no protection, so you have to do what you have to do to survive. I still carry a pocket full of them today, so stay off my ass!

Chief lived by the gun and would die by it, and if you knew him at all, you knew that would happen some day. He was totally running on the edge of the fast lane, as hard as a man can, if you wanted to die young. He was a true, fearless, crankster Angel, all the way. You couldn't help but admire him, as he was totally living the life he had chosen. When he would go to make his constant phone calls, as a Prospect it was one of your jobs was to go with him, to protect him. He had this trick black box that Jim

Jim had given him, that would take at least a half hour of cussing in a phone both to get it hooked up and working. Depending on how many days since he had last slept would usually tell how long it would take, then he would go on for hours making his calls. All of us Prospects thought it was some of the worse duty you could pull, and I tried to dodge it, always. I hated that job, as you would stand there for hours with your hand on your gun. Chief was as deep into the drug dealing world as you could be, with everyone playing for high stakes. It really wasn't a matter of *if* he would get gunned down, but when. He always gave you a blast of meth when you were guarding him, muttering something about keeping you awake and on your toes. That usually just made me more nervous, as I would be concentrating hard see see it coming. All you could do was stay alert and be bored out of your mind. Oh, the first few times it was exciting, but then it was just like being a guard or something, because thank God, nothing ever happened. He told me how this black box was fool proof. You could call anywhere in the world for free, and it was totally untraceable. He loved the idea that nobody could monitor or record anything, as it would scramble it. He was really proud of it, and how well it really worked, I'll never know.

One night, we were at our Titty Bar doing the usual night of cranking and drinking. Chief and Brett were on a roll, as they were nearing the end of one of those three or four day, no sleep, snorting all day, drug runs of theirs. Brett, as usual, was where the dope was, as he was totally addicted to meth. He was a very intelligent man, and talking to him was like talking to a lawyer, but he was very much a wigged out, scary, crazed personality. Pete the Reb was trying to catch up with Chief and Brett, and Kanuck had joined us earlier that evening. Chief and Brett were bragging about some dope deal they had pulled off. Kanuck suggested that we go over to his place to continue the party after the bar closed at 2 am. We sold the girls their bags of speed that they so desperately needed to keep hustling, so they could pay their "old man" and to keep going at their job, just to buy some more speed for tomorrow. This was their endless cycle of self-abuse they lived.

So off we rode at two o'clock in the morning, doing burnouts in the parking lot, showing off for all the Brothers and dancing girls that were getting off work, with a few of them still hustling some swabbies. I remember that it was a cold ride through town that early morning, but it felt good as it sobered me up. My nose was packed and I had gotten about seven hours sleep the night before, which was a miracle in itself. We pulled up in the alley, parked the bikes and looked about. I then took my piece and stuck it into my waistband behind my back, as I usually did. Chief and Reb started playing some grab-ass, and Brett decided we needed another blast. We all got in a circle and passed the bag and the knife. I must admit, that blast spun me around and I passed on my second turn, as I was plenty wired and had enough speed in me. Reb fired up some Humboldt county weed that we passed around, which neither Chief nor Brett wanted any of, because that is some badass weed that can spin you for a loop if you've been up for days. By now, I was really spun and almost regretting my own indulgence.

Kanuck's house was set in, off the alley a little, and there was no real driveway to it, so you had to park in the alley and walk in. Pete's house was close enough that you could hit it with a rock from Kanuck's. Luck's house was just down the street about three houses down; this was our block. We started to walk up Kanuck's porch stairs, when something moved or something, and Chief yelled, "Get down it's an ambush!" We all hit the ground and dove for cover, pulling our guns out as we did. "Where the fuck are they," Brett yelled, sitting up a little and pointing his pistol. "Fuck, they're right fucking there," Chief yelled. I looked over towards Pete, and he was crawling for cover towards his house. That is when Kanuck stood up with his pistol drawn and started up the stairs, as Chief did the same. I stood up with my gun in my hand, shaking a bit, covering the guys. They cautiously opened the door and went inside as I followed up the stairs, looking into every shadow. Kanuck popped his head out and said, "Its okay, Brothers, nobody's here!" That sure woke me up and we continued partying until the sun came up. Chief told me I did pretty well, but they all kept kidding Pete for his crawling off in the wrong direction. He claimed that he was just trying to flank them. He said that he had been in the army and these were new tactics, and everybody just laughed at him. I was just glad that it was a false alarm, but of course, they sent me out by myself to watch the bikes.

I contemplated what had just happened and how sleep deprivation was gonna' get somebody killed. Uncle John had been shot two houses down, and the blood still stained the sidewalk where Teddy Bear had crawled out to the street with two .357 holes in him. Like I said, this was our block and it had a lot of blood spilled on it already.

One of the funnier things with Chief was this thing he had going with Kenny O. It had been going on for a long time, and you never knew when or where it would happen next. The first time I saw it happen was at Hangtown's house, when I first got to Vallejo and was just meeting everyone and hanging around. We were partying all evening on the usual substances and Chief had been up cranking, probably for about his third day. We all had a good buzz going, and stayed the night there as we were too fucked up to leave. At about four o'clock in the morning, Chief wanted to go outside and have a "pow wow," as he put it. He started to explain to me about my duties as a Nomad Hang Around while he was pissing on some bushes, and I really think he just wanted company. I listening to the rules and the laws with great interest, and happened to look down at our bikes down on the street, which was lit up by the streetlights. That's when I noticed something on the chicken bar that I hadn't seen when I had been checking on the bikes earlier. Chuck and I had been taking turns watching them all night. Chief was telling me about how important our jobs were, as the Club had many enemies. He went on about, "Those fucking sneaky Outlaws, I want to kill every one of them wormy bastards, we just can't find them." He was going on and on, and I was waiting for a chance to say something about the bikes. "When you are riding with us and you see a fucking Outlaw, you kill him, you got it! Cause if you don't, he'll kill you!" After what seemed an hour of schooling, he finally zipped up his fly and reached into his cut and pulled out some crank. That's when he finally took a breath, as he was snorting some product of the end of his buck knife. "Chief, there is something on your bike," I said. "What the fuck" he said, as he spun around and spilled a bunch of meth off his blade. He dropped the Buck knife and immediately pulled out his gun and ducked down, pulling me down with him. To his credit, he had that gun out and cocked as fast as any of these modern day Outlaws I ever ran with. And of course, he didn't drop the bag of dope. "You see them; who the fuck is it," he asked. "No man, it's just something hanging on your bike," I told him. We finally stood up and walked on down to where the bikes were, him with his gun drawn. There was a big ass logging chain woven through his rear wheel, then through the frame and out the chicken bar. On the end of the chain and lying on the street behind the rear tire, was this big steel wrecking ball off of a crane, bigger than a bowling ball, with this huge, case hardened lock tying it all together. I couldn't believe it. "That Mother fucking K.O., that sneaky son of a bitch! Fuck, I thought you guys were watching these fucking bikes?" I started to laugh and thought better of it. By this time, Chief's screaming had brought everybody out of Bill's house. Chuck ran down the steps to us. Neighbor's lights were coming on because of his screaming, and that's when I could see where someone had pissed all over the seat and bike. That's when Bill and another member came down to calm him down. Then you could see everyone grinning, including me, as we were all ready to break out laughing. It was a picture perfect crank played on Chief. Chuck and I got our asses chewed out, me for the first time, as my apparent virginity was over. Chief told us to get that fucking thing off his bike and finally went back up stairs. Chuck told me that Chief and K.O. had been pulling this kind of shit on each other for a long time. He told me that one of Kenny O's favorites was to piss all over Chiefs bike, to really piss him off. That was the last time I can remember that one of us didn't almost have to sit on the bikes first.

Chief was really a natural "wanna be" leader, but dangerous in his daring. I remember when we had Church at Father Jack's in Richmond, California. Chuck, Luck, and I all rode our bikes there and had them all parked and lined up in a row in front of the house. We were hanging out there, on guard duty, just waiting for Chief to show up. He finally rode up on his bike and asked us, "Where the fuck is all the Member's bikes parked at?" We told him that everybody was here and they all had shown up in cars, and then we pointed out some of the Lincolns and Caddies. He started to throw a fucking fit, cussing and kicking shit as he stormed up to the front door. I had never seen him get that mad before. "We'll see about this fucking shit right now, because this is a Goddamn Motorcycle Club, not a fucking car club!" He walked into Church and started yelling so loud that we could here him outside. We were really digging this, as for once it wasn't our asses getting chewed, and the Members were.

The next week Church was at Teddy Bear's house, and all the Members showed up on their bikes to that one. I guess he had gotten his point across pretty damn well. After Church was finally over, we all packed our noses first and then our bikes, and headed out at about midnight for our titty bar in Vallejo. We were all feeling high and enjoying our strength and camaraderie as we pulled up and stopped at the stop light. Everyone was revving up their bikes and doing little burnouts and shit on the main drag, it was beautiful! There were probably 18 to 20 bikes in all, riding two abreast. The noise was deafening at times, with all the straight pipes belching our favorite music of no finer noise into our ears. I will never forget when Chief, up in front, turned to the pack at the next stoplight and yelled above the noise with a big grin, "Keep it down, boys!" Everyone all revved their bikes in unison and the noise was deafening. We were looking good that night. As the light turned green, Chief took off and did a burnout and we all did the same. We flew down Vallejo's main drag and through the business district. Most of the time, we snuck around the alleys to avoid our enemies and the cops, but not that night. I was so proud that night to be part of our crew, as this happened right after I got patched and back from the U.S.A. Run. That ride was as I had always dreamed of! We were the Outlaws from hell, and living and loving every minute of it! We never even got pulled over that night, which was unusual for us. I guess Chief made his point that night, that we were still a Motorcycle Club.

Besides Sonny and Deacon's Oakland Chapter and maybe Sandy's New York Chapter, the Nomads were one of the badass Crews at that time. Our Chapter had dove into the meth amphetamine market and the money and problems it would bring. I knew only one Member who held a steady job in our Chapter at that time and that was Mike K. Everyone was proud of him though and not just because he held a job. No, it was because he worked for the U.S. Army Depot, a man who new weapons and worked with them daily, imagine the implications of that! He also carried a lot of respect as an old school Member that was fast with a knife. I had never seen anyone as fast with a butterfly knife as him. With in a blink of an eye and a blurred movement of his arm that knife was opened and ready to use. Mike was mostly a drinker as he always loved his beer more than anything else, fair and evened tempered and respected by all. He never really fucked with the Prospects to go get this and go get that. I would watch him and when I saw that he needed another beer I would be standing there with it, he didn't even have to ask. I respected the guy totally, as he showed nothing but respect to us.

To give an example of Mikes speed and reputation as a much respected Member. The first time I met Mike was in Sacramento. The Sacramento Chapter had a Turkey shoot going and they had invited The Gladiators along with the other local Clubs. Mike had come down from Vallejo to Sacramento to participate. The SAC Chapter had some property out in the sticks complete with a small Clubhouse. About four of us Gladiators showed up and it was an honor to be invited. Before we had got there Stretch our President at the time told us all to keep a tight group. No LSD or reds, just stick to the crank, pot and beer only. In other words let's keep our shit together. I was a new nineteen-year-old member and I listened to what he said. We did a bump of some crank and I got too admit I had a few butterflies flying around in my stomach when we pulled in. We paid our entry fees and rode in with style. Stretch pulled up right in front of their Clubhouse right in the middle of the shit. Everybody's eyes seemed upon us from all the different Clubs and bikers there. This is when you hope you do everything just right. Back the scooters in of course against the curb. Don't slip, get your kickstand down right, whew were all being cool so far! Lonesome was then the Sacramento President walked right up and shook Stretch's hand followed with the biker hug, and then he proceeded to do the same respect greetings with the rest of us.

This was all going pretty well and as I looked around I could spot the other Clubs that were there. The Misfits was one of them, they were a one-percent Club made up mostly of younger street thugs that were really more experienced at staying in and out of jail for stealing bikes rather than riding their motorcycles. I believe their still exist in California and have no idea how strong they are today. We wondered over to the Clubhouse bar and grabbed some cold beers socializing as we did. The skeet shooting was just getting started. They had shotguns there that you could use if you were shooting in the competition shoot. I grabbed a Winchester model thirteen that my Dad had trained me on as a kid hunting quail and pheasants. That was the first model shotgun I had ever shot, so I was right at home with it. They had set the shoot up in a series of heats, as they would eliminate the lesser of two shooters in each heat. Given four shots each it was going to go on for hours. I was hanging in there although this was my first time shooting skeet in competition. It finally came down to the finalists which was gonna be Lonesome and me and with Mike K shooting against another Member. While Mike was shooting first Stretch pulled me aside "You know it would be best for us if you lose!" I told him I didn't think I had a chance against Lonesome and his fancy expensive shotgun. "Well I'm just telling you for the good of the Club," Stretch said.

Mike K won so that just left Lonesome and me to see who would have to shoot it out with him. Stretch was pretty good friends with Mike and he introduced me to him. Lonesome was using this fancy Browning Automatic shotgun that was all carved and inlaid with gold, a very expensive shotgun. We went through all four rounds and neither of us missed a bird. I was really amazing myself as nervous as I was, it was like I just couldn't seem to miss. So then we had too have another final elimination round. Taking turns so that if one misses and then the other hits you're all done and you got a winner. Lonesome started talking to me and getting a little personal with shit like "So you're from Placerville? You have joined a great Club and have got some good Brothers," Lonesome went on. I knew he was trying to distract me as we had drawn the whole crowd now to watch the show down. About our fourth strait round is when he got me. "Hey do you want too try my fancy shotgun, have you ever got to shoot a Browning?" The hook was set. "No I always wanted to," I responded. Hell I hadn't even held one before. So I traded him guns for the next round and when the bird flew, boom, I missed the fucker. Lonesome had conned me good.

It was his turn next and if he hit the bird he would win. I asked him if he wanted to try the pump I was using, he just grinned at me and said no thanks he had his gun dialed in. Lonesome hit that last bird and won our heat. Mike had unbelievable been winning all the heats with a little sawed off twenty-gauge pump shotgun. The gun being a smaller, less powerful weapon with a shorter-range shotgun round, usually used by women in skeet shooting. Here's all these thousand dollar shotguns with their adjustable chokes and fancy shit and here was Mike kickin ass with this small little sawed off shotgun that's short barreled and less powerful. How he was doing it was when they said pull, Mike would blast the bird up close before it hardly started flying. His speed once again was incredible and with the widespread of the sawed off barrel he just couldn't seem to miss. Mike and Lonesome went at it for six or seven more rounds until Mike finally won it and Lonesome was just pissed, as he wanted the trophy to stay on with in Sacramento with his Chapter. It was amazing how fast and deliberate Mike was with his hands and that butterfly knife that looked like it was flying with wings when he opened it.

We Gladiators hung around and partied and had a good steak dinner. I also met Chuck briefly that run that would prove to be in invaluable later on and become one of my close Brothers and allies. He was a Sacramento boy too that was hanging around the Hell's Angels then trying to join the Club. It was the beginning of a short but intense friendship. A bond would later form a necessary alliance for the survival of two young men in a most dangerous occupation we both had chosen. A Sacramento Angel gave us all a generous bump for the road. I needed it as Chuck and I had smoked some badass weed as we were finishing our last beers. It started getting dark as we finally fired up our bikes for the long ride home. I had a little third place trophy from the 'Turkey Shoot' as I started to stuff it in my saddlebag. Stretch stopped me and told me to show some class and tie it on my handlebars like Marlin Brando did in the Hollister movie so I did. We had showed a lot of face to the Angels and the other Clubs that day we were there. The Gladiators was struggling to keep our identity and our turf in a rapidly growing bike world. With the small club's were being absorbed or disbanded as some of the Angel's were seeking to gain control of all the turf that had profitable drug trade areas.

You never knew what was going to happen from day to day prospecting for the Nomads in those early days. Big Moose and I were hanging out over at Pete the Reb's house one day in the back yard. We were lying around in the grass being lazy, smoking grass and snorting some of Moose's meth, I had run down the street to the store and picked up a couple bottles of our favorite wino's wine, fruity Ripple. Moose was the only member that liked to drink that wine with me. For .69 cents a quart, a couple of bottles produced a good alcohol buzz. Reb come out and told me he wanted me to go make a drop for him, his old lady was passed out, and he would make it right with me for a mule trip. Later he laid a couple of lines and a joint on me for my trouble the cheap bastard. If I had got busted I would have probably had to do a couple of years in the joint for it. Well I told Moose that I had to go and he said, "Lets cap the jugs of wine, throw them in the saddlebags, and I will go with you. Maybe we'll get lucky and there will be some pussy over there!" Moose fired up his swing arm shovelhead as I got my scooter going and off we went down taking the maze of Vallejo's alleys. Standard practice if you're packing your 'heat,' which was almost always. We rolled in and out of alleys, crossing a few main drags. We finally got over to this cats house. This guy was a 'wish he could be' punk with a bike and a job. So like hundreds of others like him the Members used him to peddle their dope.

Big Moose and I pulled up to the curb in front of his house, backed in, and through down the kickstands. Moose said grab the wine bottles. We could here the music blasting and a party was definitely on. "Maybe I'll get lucky and find some pussy," Moose was a big, kind of rough looking member that had transferred over from San Raphael Chapter with Big Red Bryant and the rest. He was always looking for pussy and didn't have much luck at it, but he really had a good heart. You can't say that about a lot of R&W. I always tried to hook him up with a lady when I could. So we climbed up the stairs to the second story apartment. On the way up Moose says, "This is the guy that has all the fucking snakes, I hate them fucking things," I couldn't agree more. This punk opens door and the cloud of weed smoke almost choked us. Wow the young biker says, "I didn't know you were coming over Moose." "I just come over to check out and see if you got any pussy you don't need lying around," he declared loudly. "Sure come on in" as he paraded us through the front door. There were four chicks in there hanging and getting fucked up, one of them was the punk's old lady. A couple of his 'biker' friends were hanging that looked like they were scared to death of us. We sat down and Moose gave me the nod, and I spooned a little meth up everyone's noses, about three times as much to the ladys and the punk.

His two buddys started spinning on the uncut shit I had gave them, so then they got paranoid and made some stupid excuses and split. Things were going as planned for Moose and me. Well Moose gets up and plops down in between a couple of these chicks and with a wink at me I handed him a joint. Do you see how this works? A Hell's Angel didn't break out any dope, pass it out, or provide to under age girls any narcotics to really anyone, the Prospect did. The Member gets the credit for it but the Prospects protect the members at any cost. Well those chicks were all ready spinning as that uncut dope was doing its work. "Wow I haven't ever had any of this kind of speed before." Yea you have, it's just this little punk stomps (cuts) the same dope with so much shit that you wouldn't recognize it". While Moose was being entertained I thought this would be a good time to make the drop. I finally got the idea into this now fucked up punk. So we went into his bedroom and took care of business. All around us were aquariums and reptile tanks, there were snakes everywhere. Pythons, coral, rattlesnakes, you name it and he had them. I got to admit it made me a little uneasy too. "Hey you want too watch this python eat this mouse," the punk asked. I kind of watched as I counted out the cash he gave me. "What do you think," I told the punk that was cool man.

So we went back into the living room that also was surrounded in cages. So we hung out partying and polished off our morning jugs of ripple wine. So the punk offers us some beers. Everybody sucked them down for a while and I handed Moose another joint. It looked like Moose had this one chick in the bag. I was trying to relax and have some fun, but this place was weird with all the fucking snakes. Then the punk asks if we want to see this real rare snake he had. Moose kind of grunted disapproval, but the chick told him that she wanted to see it too. So he walks all of us into the bedroom and points at this glass cage that had a large towel covering it. So he tells us we need to get real close because once he pulls the towel off it will hide and you won't see it. So we get our faces up close to the glass. The punk pulls the towel and we are staring eye to eye with a King Cobra snake. It was all flared out and spit that poison at our eyes. Well that poison hit the glass as Moose and I jumped back about six feet with out our feet not touching the ground. I don't think I could jump back like that if I had to again, and Moose was an awful big dude to do that.

The punk was laughing as Moose planted one right in his mouth, blood flew all over all of us. This all took about a second as the punch had split his lip open. He pounced on top of the punk and began wailing on him. I kicked him in the side as I grabbed his old lady who was launching herself on Moose to protect her man. So I threw her into the rest of the chicks that were screaming. Moose had his knees on the guy's chest on the floor as he just kept punching him. I looked back and kicked the punk in the ribs again. Then here come his old lady again, I had my hand full covering Moose's back. I turned back and he was sitting on his chest and short punching him in the head. There was blood everywhere with all the chicks screaming. With every punch I could here Moose saying "Don't you ever pull that shit again," as he would punch him. Finally Moose got up and the punk was out cold and bleeding like a pig. He looked at me and said, "He shouldn't have pulled that shit on us!" I told him I agreed. He looked at the girls as they were all sobbing and told them that he shouldn't have done that because it wasn't funny. Moose tried to grab the girl he was hitting on and she just pulled away, sobbing with the rest of them. He looked at me and said "Fuck it Prospect, lets blow this zoo!"

I couldn't have agreed more. I was hoping the people down stairs didn't call the law with all the screaming and thumping. We slipped down to the bikes, on the way Moose said, "That stupid punk, I was gonna get laid, fucking stupid shit, what else could I do? He insulted a Hell's Angel, and nobody gets away with that!" I could tell Moose was depressed, he wanted to fuck, not fight. We fired up and split on our bikes. On the ride back to Reb's house I thought how lucky we were that no cops had showed up. Then it dawned on me that Reb might be pissed because we fucked up one of his dealers. We got there and told Reb what happened, Moose said he had no choice, he insulted a R&W. Reb just rolled his eyes and said he would take care of it "Yea you rightly fucked him up cause he shouldn't have disgraced our colors," Reb said. I gave him the money. Moose looked at me and said "I kind of liked her, I thought I was gonna get some." I tried to console him by agreeing that she absolutely had really liked him. Then I told him, "She will probably be all right with it after awhile, she seemed to love the product, and I'll bet you can still get in her pants." That cheered him up as he said, "Fuck it, let's ride down to the Titty Bar and have some beers and check out some tits." This all seemed like a movie and I was just playing my role. The afternoon once again was looking up, another day in the life as a Nomad in Vallejo.

Moose and I always had weird things happen to us wherever we went. He and I were taking care of some Club business one time. I will just say it wasn't a drug deal. We had our cuts rolled up under the front seat with our pistols. We had borrowed a truck and were heading down the freeway, somewhere between Vallejo and San Francisco. It was rare for either of us to be in a cage as neither of us owned one. Myself being the Prospect, of course I had to drive. We were shooting the shit and had just smoked a joint as we had packed our noses before we had left Vallejo. All of a sudden about a half a mile ahead of us this big accident happens in front of us. Were all stoned going wow, look at that man! It was quite a show, reminded me of high-speed bumper cars playing on a freeway. Everybody's standing on their brakes, including me screeching to a halt. There were two cars ahead of our pickup and five or six behind us when the carnage all finally stopped. The one car involved in the accident that was directly in front of us only crossways across the double lane freeway facing us. It was a smaller car and the driver's door was ripped open and barley hanging on its hinges. The driver was a pretty young girl with short hair slumped over the steering wheel. Bruce says, "Wow, look at that chick, she's all fucked up."

The car was all smashed as you really couldn't even tell what the model of the car was, just a mangled piece of shit now. But there in the middle of the mangled metal sat this chick wrapped around her steering wheel. This dude in front of us jumps out of his car and runs over to the chick. Moose said, "Look at that asshole running over there, and were staying out of this as the cops will be here soon." This dude runs over to my side of the pickup and starts beating on my window. I rolled it down and he started screaming at me, "I need your help to save this lady!" I looked over at Moose while he rolled his eyes and got out of the truck. We ran over to her with this dude to her smashed up car. The lady was breathing, more gasping as she moaned. Blood was running out of her nose, the corner of her mouth, and ear, with visible contusions. You could see her arm and both her legs were broken and twisted up in the metal. This dude is screaming at her, "We'll get you out!" He was panicking and yelling and turned to us. "Help me get her out!" Moose looked him in the eye and told him "No, her legs are pinned in there to bad to move her. The fire department will probably have to cut her out of there." The guy started arguing and yelling at Moose that he had to help him.

He then told him that "If you move her you'll probably kill her and I am not getting sued over this, lets just wait for the ambulance!" The guy kept screaming at us to help him, and finally yelled, "I'll do it myself!" We watched him grab her shoulders and tried to pull on her. I was watching her face and as he pulled on her she contorted in pain and she gasped for air one more time. Her eyes opened widely and then her chin fell to her chest, she died. It struck me as so final, death had found her and nothing could be done. The good citizen kept pulling on her saying she was going to be fine. We watched as he dragged about half her body towards the street, I could here her bones grinding as her broken mangled trapped legs stayed in the car. I will never forget the blank look on her face or the sound of the bones crunching when he moved her. By this time there was a crowd forming around the scene. I could here sirens and yelling and confusion all at the same time. The citizen was still messing with the lady when Moose finally said, "Why don't you leave her alone, you already killed her, she's dead man!" The dude jumps up and started to get in Moose's face yelling "You chicken shit," boom he punches the guy right in the nose.

Down the guy went bouncing of the street, as he was falling a couple dudes in the crowd started to go for Moose. I shoved one of them back into the crowd as he squared off with the other. Right then a cop finally appeared and got between them and us. "What's going on here, everybody calm down!" The dude stood up about then pointing at Moose and saying "He hit me!" Blood was running out of his nose. The cop turned us and asked if he had hit him, Moose said he had to cause the guy was panicked from killing that girl when he moved her. He then told

Moose and me to go stand by our truck and wait. I was amazed that he didn't try and throw the cuffs on us, but he was by himself and traffic was backed up etc. As we walked away I could here the dude telling the cop he wanted Moose arrested for assult. We watched as the tow truck as it moved the car enough to open a lane to get traffic moving. By now there were cops everywhere, interviewing people, measuring, checking Id's, taking names, and taking pictures. Finally that same cop with a couple more come over to us, he told Moose that he should arrest him for assult. "But after hearing the story from the witnesses it sounds like the asshole deserved it, now get out of here." I thought to myself, for once we done the right thing. Every now and then, I see that woman die and crunching noise again and again in my memories as it's hard to forget something like that!

Running with the Nomad crew in those days was not only dangerous, but also an easy way to end up in jail. One fateful day that would be the beginning of changing the course of my life forever. That day I was just hanging out with Kanuck over at Lucks house working on bikes. Luck used to have a radiator shop there at his house so there was a lot of garage space so a lot of Members would work on their bikes there. Most Members didn't have a shop or garage with tools at their houses. That's one reason why Lucks place was so popular with his air tools and shop equipment. So I was helping Kanuck wrench on his bike and talking about tearing apart my top-end cause he thought I had a noise going on, I told him I couldn't hear anything. Finally after a lot of chitchat Kanuck decided he was hungry and he would buy us some lunch so away we went to go eat a burger. So we came out of Lucks front door to go to the café around the corner. There across the street were three black dudes drinking wine and hanging with some black chicks, they all appeared pretty wasted and were eye fucking us. Kanuck yelled, "What the fuck are you looking at?" "Fuck you white boys this is our neighborhood!" I knew right then that this was gonna be a fight. Kanuck not a very big man but was strong and fast with his hands and had boxer training so he could handle himself. I would find that out later personally. I always respected him because he always had his shit together. He would almost always get some sleep and eat. His old lady worked and he hustled but you would never catch him over abusing anything.

I followed him as he charged across the street towords the one loud month that was trying to show off for this young black chick standing there. The dude suddenly whips out a chain and confronts us, "You white Mother fuckers want some shit?" Kanuck stopped just out of range of his chain and turns to me and says in a low voice, "Prospect get me something quick!" Neither one of us had our guns as we had put them on the bench when we were wrenching and had let our guard down. To this day I don't know why I didn't hand him my Bowie knife but I'm probably glad I didn't. I turned and saw a broken piece of wood lying in Luck's yard by the gutter. It looked like a good club so I grabbed it and quickly handed it to Kanuck as the two started to square off. The black man swung the chain first and Kanuck grab it with one hand and then hit him over the head with the make shift club. Blood started flowing down the guys face as the fight was on. I tagged the dude next to the other one with a right as hard as I could and it spun him pretty good. My hand felt like it exploded in pain, yes it's true he had a hard head. The other one that was standing there jumped right into it as we all started swinging. The one guy almost got me with his wine bottle that I barely ducked away from when Kanuck hit him with the club too. Then I saw more of them coming out of the house behind them running to join in. But by now we had a few Bro's with Sweet Phil in the lead running out of Luck's place yelling that they were coming to help us out.

The fight was starting to turn into a pretty good brawl until a cop car pulled right into the middle of us. It was two of Vallejo's finest that we always called Batman and Robin. These two cops's always acted like our friends whenever they jacked us up to the point of being ridiculous. They hated all the blacks almost with a passion. Like one night when they had pulled three or four of us over on our bikes, they jumped out of their patrol car all jazzed up. You could see the wild look in their eyes and the excitement in their voices. "Hey did you guys hear what we did earlier tonight man, we killed a nigger! Yea I got him with my twelve gauge shotgun as he was trying to get away over this wall. Man I hit him square with 00 buck, he just kind of exploded with blood and chunks' going everywhere, Batman was almost screaming in his excitement. They figured we would be proud of them, as they were as predacious as they get and figured we were too. Soon as they got there they jumped right in with their batons out and swinging and started beating the blacks off us and separating all of us. By this time we had woken up most of the predominately black neighborhood that surrounded us. It looked like we had the beginnings of a first class race riot. That stick I had handed Kanuck was covered in blood; he had dropped it when the cop's had showed up. Batman had called for back up when they had first gotten there. All kinds of cop's had started showing up thank God, the fist fighting had stopped with everybody yelling and screaming back and forth.

Batman comes over to Kanuck and me and says that the chick that was with the black dude had said we had started the fight by attacking her boyfriend with a board. "She picked you two out of the crowd and wants to press charges, so there's not really a lot we can do unless we want to start a race riot. Let me put the cuffs on you guys and haul you off so this will all die down and go away," Batman gave us this reassuring wink. Kanuck said at first, "Fuck no we didn't do fucking nothing!" With that we had a few more of the cops started paying attention and backing them up by surrounding us. "Come on guys help us defuse this situation," Robin pleaded. "Ok but were not going to the station," Kanuck replied. Personally I thought it was an easy way of getting out of there with our asses in one piece as we were still out numbered. Looking around it looked like by now about twenty to one against us with what looked like more coming. They cuffed us and put us in the back of their patrol car as promised. We watched, as another cop picked up that stick and put it in a plastic evidence bag and then walked over and handed it too Robin at the side window. Kanuck and I looked at each other's eyes, this wasn't looking so good. What did they need evidence for if they were going to let us go? The black's had already wisely policed up the chain and gotten rid of it, I guess they weren't as drunk as they seemed.

They drove us a couple blocks and turned like they were heading towards the direction of the jailhouse. Kanuck asked, "What the fuck is up? I thought you guys said you were gonna let us go?" Batman says, "Oh we will but first we need to go down to the station and make out your statements to make it look right." Kanuck looked at me and rolled his eyes again. "Why didn't you guys pull out your guns and shoot them niggers," Robin asked? We arrived at the Vallejo jailhouse, which was my second visit to that police station. They led us in with our cuffs on into the booking area where we got patted down for any counter band. We were left alone for a few minutes in our little holding cell "Were fucked now, remember don't say shit about nothin'", Kanuck stated. They come and got us and took us into an office where there were two detectives sitting there with the bagged bloody stick that said evidence on it. They started to question us and immediately Kanuck says, "It was self defense, just ask Batman here and I want to talk to my lawyer right now!" I knew enough to shut up and let Kanuck do the talking. Batman immediately gave Kanuck a hard look and went on, "When we got to the scene there appeared to be a race riot going on. There was a confrontation going on between the Hell's Angels and the local blacks on their block. There were weapons involved and some injuries!" The detective told Batman and Robin to go fill out their incident report and when they had completed it to bring it back to him.

"Gentlemen you are being charged with a felony count each for assault with a deadly weapon, do you understand," he asked. Kanuck immediately said yea we understand and asked again for a phone call to get our lawyers. Then the detective read us the Miranda act bullshit and asked us if we understood. Then the other detective tried to pull one and said he would send a police unit over to Kanuck's house to let his wife or girlfriend know what was going on. This is a standard cop trick because it gives them probable cause too s reasonable cause to knock on your door unexpectedly and get their foot inside. If they smell some weed or the chick's dumb enough to let them in to check your shit out. They'll try anything to try and bust you. "No thanks were split up, fuck the bitch," Kanuck declared. From there they took us back too another holding tank and started to book us. The Club had us bailed out before we even got processed to a regular cell. I was hoping to get at least twenty-four hours lock up to get some sleep. Those expensive lawyers they retain already had our bail reduced! As I was being processed through the jail system, I was being escorted to the holding tank. I looked over and saw Chief sitting opposite the head detective at his desk laughing and talking, then he saw me watching as the cop moved me further down past the door. I could only imagine what that was about. Chief had his hand in everything! I had just finished paying the Club back from my last beef, and now I was going back in debt again. Just another fucking beautiful day prospecting in Vallejo!

Once Kanuck and Jungle Jim and I rode over to Santa Rosa / Sonoma Co wine country area. They were looking for this 'used to be' prospect that owed them some money. We finally found this guys old pickup in a parking lot after riding to every bar in town and finally cornered the dude in a small bar. We walked in and I could see the blood draining out of his face as he was scared shitless. He glanced around for a way out but he had nowhere to run, you could see his eyes kept glancing around for an escape route as we had all directions covered. We all slowly moved forward from each direction both the front and rear entrance to surround him as he started babbling hellos and excuses about the money he owed. He stated in a cracking voice that he would gladly pay up when Kanuck busted him right in the nose and he hit the floor. That was Kanucks style, we all immediately took up our positions, and I covered their backs. Jungle and I backed off a couple of his buddys as Kanuck picked the guy up by his collar and got right in the guys face. "I'll get your money," the guy kept pleading. "No doubt, but that's not all of it. You think you can steal from a Hell's Angel and just get away with it that easy," Kanuck punched him again. The bar tender started to pickup the phone, I told him he didn't want to do that, and he stopped and hung it back up.

Jungle got in one of his buddys faces, "You want some of this too?" "No, no, I didn't do anything, that's his problem not mine," his buddy wisely said! I watched him take another blow, to the head. "I'll pay you twice what I owe you, please, please don't kill me!" "That not enough, you have insulted my Club and my Brothers too," Kanuck yelled as boom he threw yet another punch. "I'll triple it, anything, don't kill me," he pleaded! "Then give me the money now," Kanuck yelled. "I'll go get it, I promise," the guy cried! "Fuck that, you think I'd let you go so you can run away again, I'll kill you right here and now if you don't go get the moneys now," Kanuck yelled! He let the guy up and he made a couple frantic calls begging for money to "Save my life!" His third call was to his girlfriend who apparently agreed to come down and pay. We drank a beer and finally his lady showed up with an envelope in her hand. She handed it to him and he quickly passed it to Kanuck and then she hung around nervously as if to protect this guy. If you are stupid enough to ever owe an Angel some money, I do suggest you pay it no matter if it's even just a few bucks. See what people don't get about the R&W is that it's more about power and respect than it is the money. Hell's Angels demand respect of the other Club's and its Members, or anybody or anything else or they will fuck you up to get it!

One day I went over to Kanucks house to check in with him and see what was up. Harry the Horse was with Kanuck out on his back porch and a Hang Around from the Chicago area. This Hang Around we'll call Charlie was a real rough talking 'tough guy' attitude dude with full-sleeved arms and his body all covered with tattoos. He was the 'street type' of hard-core bikers who claimed to have done some time back in Joliet Prison. Charlie was pretty young say in his mid twenties and had done some weight lifting as he had some pretty good guns on him. He rode into our Titty Bar on his pan head one day and just hung out after that. I had helped him with a place to stay the first night and he hooked up with a local chick for a place to stay after that. I had overheard a couple Members talking about how they thought he might be a paid snitch or informant or maybe an Outlaw spy. When I walked up on them in the back yard it looked like there was a fight going on between Harry and Charlie. Harry the Horse was an old Frisco member who had transferred over to the Nomads just before I started hanging around. A big Irish or Scottish man who was known to run on meth most of the time, and smoke a little weed too.

It was said he had done way too much LSD in the early flower children days in Frisco. He generally was a bitch to be around as he always was complaining about everything. But worse was when he started drinking, he would get moody and mean and would light anybody up that he could pick a fight with. Personally I had to agree that he had done way too much LSD as he seemed like he was searching for that total high and rush that he just couldn't find. Harry started yelling at Charlie with Kanuck listening but not saying a word. I could tell Harry had been up all night cranking and drinking and knew he was about to explode. He cold cocked Charlie, which sent him flying of the porch and on to the ground. As Harry jumped off the porch he had grabbed an old Harley stock muffler pipe and swung it like a baseball bat hitting Charlie in the side of the head. The first blow with the pipe knocked him back to the ground where Harry kept on beating him with the pipe. I had jumped off the porch and just kind of stood there like I was standing guard watching the beating. Then Kanuck stepped in and beat on him with his fists a few blows and then he turned to me.

"What the fuck you waiting for Prospect," Kanuck yelled! So I jumped in and started beating on Charlie some too. That's when Harry and Kanuck just stopped and stood back and watched me go to work on him. He Momentarily looked up to me like why are you doing this to me? He wasn't fighting back as he wisely chose to just cover up his head for protection. I tried to just hit him in the back of the head where hopefully I would do the least harm. Both of my hands were hurting and swelling from the multiple blows I had thrown. Harry and Kanuck would both give him an occasional kick as they watched me beating him. This seemed to go on forever as Charlie just kept covering up with his hands to try and fend off the blows to the head. All of a sudden I realized he stopped moving as I now had both my knees in his back pining him face down on the ground as I continued too beat on the back of his head. I finally stopped as he wasn't moving anymore, I had knocked him out. Harry finally says "That's enough, but you ever hesitate again it will be you getting the beating and then I'll kill you, you got it!"

This was one of those basic lessons in the process of the training of a Prospect for Membership. Brotherhood is supposed to be about loyality and trust, without it you have nothing. What bothered me was in the Club I had been in before I wouldn't have hesitated for a second. I would have jumped on top of the guy in an instance, why was it that I had to be told? The automatic reaction to protect my Brothers blindly didn't go off. I knew I hadn't made any real points with these two Angels. As for the Hang around, he eventually woke up and sat up and looked me in the eye and asked me "What happened?" "He had bumps and lumps everywhere and bleeding, but his first concern was "What did I do?" I told him I didn't know what he had done but you must have fucked up, or maybe it was a mud check, which seemed to make him feel better. About a month later he disappeared, the cops came over to Sharon's house asking about his disappearance. I never saw him or his bike again. 'He ain't around no more,' as the saying goes.

The worse I have seen of Prospect abuse by a Club was up in Wyoming while I was dealing drugs with a Club called 'The Grim Reapers.' A Bro of mine had joined this Club which was actually a fairly large MC out of the mid-west at the time. I had met Jerry through an old Bro of mine named Spyde. Spyde had a good soul but was a California boy that had a serious problem with heroin because he couldn't get enough of it. He was burning this guy Jerry who was new too the bike world by selling him a piece of shit pan head. He had sold it to him for big dollars and split on him without finishing the deal by getting it running. I was living in Denver at the time when Jerry shows up at my door one Memorial weekend with this pan head in the back of his truck. Well Jerry was a coal miner and had plenty of money and asked me to fix it for him. I felt sorry for the guy, as I knew what Spyde had done as he had bragged to me about it. So I fixed it for him and we became pretty good friends and he always felt he owed me because I had gotten his first Harley going for him. Years later I was on a drug run when I called him up in Rawlins Wyoming and asked if he needed any drugs. I had heard that he had joined a Club and I wanted to make some business ties with them. So I went up and partied with him and his Club Brothers for the weekend.

The Reapers had a party going at their Clubhouse and it was wild one. I met a bunch of their Members and was introduced to their President named "Mad Painter". So I'm digging the sales, as I had sold off all of my dope to them and decided to stay and party. I have never seen Prospects being treated as bad as this though. They were pretty much human punching bags for the Membership. Shit like "Hey Prospect go get me a beer!" They would jump and run and fetch and would hand the Member a beer and boom, the Member would cheap shot him, knocking him on his ass. I watched as the party progressed in disgust as these Prospects just kept getting more and more lumps and bleeding as the party continued. I finally asked Jerry if they were trying to impress me or if they always treated their Prospects like this. He said "Yea we figure if they will take this kind of abuse and keep coming back for more then they were men and really wanted to join." I told him it wasn't any of my business but I had never seen nothing like this before. "Dam Jerry I would think you would drive away any good Membership material by knocking all their teeth out before they can even join. Sure you want their respect but they have to respect what they're joining." Jerry gave me a funny look and I figured I should probably shut up. I wasn't impressed at all, what kind of Membership is a bunch of human punching bags going to make? That is not what Brotherhood is or should be about.

In Vallejo I was over at Lucks house one day working on some bikes. Harry was there and had been up all night drinking and snortin, which was nothing unusual for him to be hammered at eleven o'clock in the morning. There was these two young chicks there were drinking and smoking with Harry. They were hanging around fucking Members to get free speed and booze and maybe some thrills at seventeen years old. I was told they would really spread their legs for any downers but especially for reds, which can be a good way for them to end up getting turned out. Some chicks were actually looking to get turned out to fulfill some sexual fantasy. One of these chicks was named Beth, I would eventually move in with her for a place to live. They had started drinking and doing drugs with Harry, laughing and partying. I don't know what the bigger gal had said or refused to do but Harry started to come unglued on her. He was slapping her around a bit when she made the near fatal mistake of doubling up her fist and taking a shot at Harry. He instantly went into a boxer's stance and proceeded to punch her out.

I guess Harry figured if she wanted to fight like a man then so be it, as he literally beat the shit out of her in front of me and Beth. I wanted to stop it but knew if I tried it would be me that Harry the Horse that would be punching instead of her. She was bleeding pretty well as Harry drug her off by her hair into a bedroom inside the house. Beth just hung out in the shop with me and was shaking all over as she clutched her beer. I told her to be cool that I was sure her friend was going to be all right. When she finally came out and not looking to bad, then Beth and her friend split. I guess they had both learned a lesson about hanging around and teasing

Hell's Angels, a lesson I expect they would never forget. The two chicks kept coming back for the drugs and to party. After that she always took care of Harry in the bedroom no matter what. Was I proud of what happened, No? I felt like I belonged to something that was out of control, or at least out of my control. Before that though, I always would have just figured she had it coming as my Brothers always come first.

Eventually I ended up living with Beth for a short time when I really just needed a place to stay. I had about as much feelings for her as I did for any woman in those days, not much. She was nice enough but she really wasn't a moneymaker yet, she was young and a little innocent but had no problem fucking for drugs and booze. I did have some respect for her because she was pretty cool for her age and wasn't a total nose candy whore yet. But really she was just ok on the looks, just looking to party and wasn't old enough to work at the Titty Bar yet. When she got old enough she would turn into a real asset for somebody as she did eventually. One night a back east Angel showed up for a visit and Moose was showing him a good time. So he takes this heavy weight ugly old Angel over to Beth's to get him laid. I was at the bar when Moose and our guest come up and told me of their plans for the evening. "I know your living with her and all but she's not your old lady or nothing. She's been one of our young party things since before you came here so I am gonna take the Brother over there to get him laid," Moose explained. I knew there wasn't anything I could do to stop it, but I really wished there was. So they split and I tried to forget about it. It wasn't long and Moose called the bar and got a hold of me and said he needed me to get over there quick.

So I jumped on my bike and jammed over there. I walked in and saw that Harry the Horse had joined the party and they had Beth cornered on our bed, she was half naked and crying with a red cheek where she must have gotten slapped. Moose says "Prospect you tell her that it's all right for her to give this Brother and us some pussy, she thinks she just belongs to you now!" Beth looked at me with tears rolling down her cheeks with her mascara smeared and this look of help. I hated what I had to say, "Beth you were a Club party girl before I knew you, so there's nothing I can do. You better do what they tell you." She looked at me with hurtful crying eyes that broke my heart. That ugly Angel grabbed her hair and pulled her down to get some head as I turned my back on them and went outside. I felt bad inside and knew I had let her down. I tried to convince myself that she's the one that had been playing this game before me, the Brothers come first above all, but it still didn't help my depression. I went back to the bar and got drunk and didn't go home until the next afternoon. Years later I found out that after she got old enough to work at the bar that Harry made her his old lady. Of coarse she got into the meth real bad and heard she was dancing, playing tricks, and dealing to support them. I also heard that Harry had eventually made President of the Chapter also. One day they were both found in their apartment shot to death. She was probably twenty-three years old or so when she was murdered, like so many of us she had chosen the fast lane and rode it into hell!

Life with the Hell's Angels always kept you on your feet as something was happening all the time. That day we had another funeral to go to over in the San Francisco area. A Member had died that I really didn't know personally. We were supposed to meet up at our Titty Bar, but of course most of the Members were late. Like always everyone was going to ride their bikes, but that's always at the night be fore's party. All of us Prospects were hanging around, on time and gassed up as usual. Big Moose was one of the first members to show up. It started to rain, one of those gloomy bay area days that was going to be wet all day type, you could tell. We got some calls and a few Members showed up in their cages and made their excuses why they couldn't ride. This was no big surprise, I would have bet money on it as shitty as the weather was. Even on a beautiful day most of the Members would get out of it somehow. We finally got all packed up with who was going too ride with who, and finally got down the road with about four Members and the rest Prospects. It rained the whole fucking way over the bay bridge, we all were as soaked to the bone as you can get.

We finally got to the meeting place in Frisco where there weren't a lot of bikes in that weather. We solemnly joined the procession too the graveyard as we all somberly road two a breast in the rain. There were plenty of people that had showed, a funeral any of us could be proud of. Some kind words were said, a couple of the deceased member's old ladys had a little interesting tussle. Some members broke up the catfight as I guess he had a few too many lovers that his old lady apparently didn't know about. I hate funerals, I have had to go too two too many of them in the bike world I live in. To this day that's still true as I hate to attend them no matter who they were. We all paid our respects that day, and then we all gathered up in the parking lot. The bag was passed around and everybody started feeling a little better, drowned rat's comes to mind. We all fired up our bikes and off to the predetermined bar for the wake. We rolled up and Moose took me and the other Chapter Prospects across the street. There we met up with Chief, he said to follow him, and up a set of second story stairs we went.

We finally got to the end of the stairs which brought us to an empty second story apartment and there at the front window were some other Prospects with scoped rifles watching the bar out the opened window to the street below. They had the two big windows which they had slid open and taken out the screens, which made it kind of damp and cold. Chief walks right over there and picks up one of the rifles, checks the clip to see that it was fully loaded. Then he hands it to me, it was a scoped 30-06 semi automatic rifle. He asked me if I know how to use it, yea, I told him, it was just like my Dads. Chief explains that they think the Outlaw Motorcycle Club might be gonna try and make a hit on us. "We are all grouped up after a funeral in this bar and the bastards know it, and are gonna try and hit us," he said. "If anybody shows up that don't look right, start shooting the shit out of them, got it? Watch for a car or truck that tries to park close to the bar too and then walks away from it in the opposite direction of the bar because they might try to bomb us, okay?" Yea we told him, "We got it."

"I better not come back up here and find you guys partying or sleeping as this is serious shit. We spotted a couple of Outlaws this morning, their going make a hit all right, so keep your fucking eyes open," Chief said. Then he pulled me aside and said "Make sure you shoot them Outlaws first for the Chapter, ok?" With that he was gone. We talked to the other Prospects and they were all concerned as we were. We all sat there in the cold in our wet leathers for a couple of hours. There was a hell of a party going on down at the bar where at least somebody was having some fun.

As it started getting dark we all got colder and colder, we actually discussed trying to start a little fire on the floor somehow for warmth, but decided against it as it would give us away. We would watch Members come in and out, pass a bag and bullshit and go back in. From where we were you could see everything. We counted how many times we would see cop cars go bye. If any Outlaws had showed up, it would have been a shooting gallery.

One of the Prospects said he wished they would show up so he could cap one. Chuck and I looked at each other and both gave each other the same look. Thank fucking God they didn't show up, this was premeditated murder. It was a fucking ambush with high-powered scoped rifles for Christ sakes. Finally one of the Members came up to check on their Prospects and Moose had come up with him. We asked if one of us could run down and get us some sandwiches and some beer and sodas. They let a couple of us go while they waited. After that we all felt a little better with a few beers and a joint with some food. We did what Prospects always do, we started shooting the shit on Club news and who had got patched and who didn't as it helps pass the time. Remember there's not a Member in the Club that didn't have to put in some sort of Prospect time no matter who they were, even if it's just a token short period. We were up there shivering for around eight hours until our crew finally decided to go, Big Moose come up and told us to get our asses down to the bikes. After we said our goodbyes we finally fired up our bikes and made the cold wet ride back to Vallejo. It was one miserable ass ride I mean to tell you. At least the members had gotten a chance to dry off and get warm for a while in the bar but we were still wet to the bone The Outlaws never showed up that night thank god, if they were around they had left us alone to bury our dead. There was always the standing rule though, if you see one, kill him! The HAMC have their enemies for sure.

There were good times as well as the bad, unfortunately not always in a very even per portions. We were told after Church one day that we were going over to visit our Frisco Brothers that coming Saturday. We were being hired by the Grateful Dead Band to do security for the Grateful Dead's last concert they would ever have, and that it would be held over at the Winterland. That's what we were told anyway, it wasn't their last concert for sure as the real last one was in July 1985. I believe they wanted it to be, but like everyone else, sooner or later no matter who you are, you always run out of money. We all gathered up on a bright beautiful Saturday morning to ride on over to San Francisco. I actually was really looking forward to this, not just a free concert and all, but just one of those beautiful mornings that you just want too ride. I had spent my unusual night with my whore from our titty bar that Chuck had given me. So I had a pocket full of money and had packed my nose early and then got the fuck out of there. I had got her a three-day supply of crank so she would be dancing and playing tricks with them sailors all weekend for more money to get some more dope. You never gave them more dope than that as you wanted them saving their money and wanting to see you to get some more shit, that's how the game was played. Really it just made it easier to keep track of them on the drug leash so they didn't stray off, that was their life.

Big Moose showed up in an old pickup, I made the mistake of walking over there and shooting the shit with him. I asked where his bike was and he said it was broke down so he had borrowed this truck to go to the concert in as he didn't want to miss this one. That's when Chief coming riding up and strolled up to us. Moose explained about the truck and Chief said that might be good anyway, we might need a chase truck and he also wanted to bring a couple of shotguns just in case. That's when my bike ride went to shit, Chief decides we can't have a Member driving the chase truck or be by himself now can we. Fuck I thought why me, so sure as shit Chief says I got to drive Moose to Frisco in this truck. I didn't mind that much because I always liked him and he was always good company. I was missing a beautiful ride though, but business is business and as the saying goes, "That's Prospecting!" Sidecar Larry use to always say that "Don't ever let them make you a Member because it's more fun being a Prospect. You're always in the middle of whatever is happening and you're the first to get into the booze because you always got to go on the beer run!" I don't think I totally agree with that one. We followed the pack over to a Frisco Members house for a visit and to have a pre-party and wait for the concert to start. The truck turned out kind of handy for picking up the beer and all at the liquor store, except Frisco's streets are a real bitch and I always got lost there.

We hung out snorting, smoking, and a drinking as the afternoon passed bye pretty quickly. Some of them Frisco Angels called up some old hippie type party girls they were so famous for and they put on quite a show for us up in his apartment, Frisco always had the girls. We entertained ourselves as best we could until it was time to go. We followed some of the Frisco Angels who had kept showing up all afternoon so they could lead our pack to Winterland. Everybody was excited as they ever got cause we knew this was gonna be a happening. I had one hell of a time keeping up with the pack while driving through traffic in that truck. When we got there we had a hell of a hard time finding a parking spot for the pickup anywhere, the place was packed. Then Moose and I walked through the crowds and finally the gate, all the hippies just parted that were in our way. We finally made our way to back behind the stage and ran into Billy Graham, he explained what he hoped was a good security plan. He wanted a group of Angels at the gate and a group in front of the bandstand to keep the people off the stage. Then after everyone had entered he wanted the ones up front to comeback and help to maintain the back stage area to keep anyone from getting in there. I thought I got lucky cause I drew the behind the stage detail with Moose. Chief was dividing us up when Moose said he would take me and hang there behind the stage until the ones up front could join us as he gave me a wink out of the corner of his eye.

I was lucky as hell, Chuck had to go man the front gate until the show got started and then they would come help us protect the stage and the Dead. All the Chapters that were there split up like that, which I thought was fair. We went on a beer and alcohol run for our area, and you could feel the electricity in the air. We looked out at the crowd that was building up from behind the stage. I could see why musicians got scared of the crowds on stage at live performances, as it was pretty scary. Everybody looked as fucked up as they could get. When the Dead come walking bye headed for their dressing room they stopped and started shaking all of our hands, thanking us all for being there to help. As I shook Jerry Garcia's hand he said he wanted to make sure we were all coming to the Dead's last after concert party the band was throwing after the show. "Make sure you all come, I promise we got some real good treats. You are all are welcome of course to any of the snacks and drinks we have for everyone in there," Jerry pointed to a room with this grin. He was as cool as everyone said he was, but you could see a worried feared look about him. He looked into your eyes when he shook your hand firmly, which I really respect. Then Garcia said something weird with complete fear in his voice, "If any of them come at us on the stage, please for God sakes stop them cause their all crazy!" He was assured that wasn't gonna happen by Moose, but looking out over the crowd while we were there I wondered, remember Altamont?

After we had met them all and bull shitted a bit they went off to get ready. Moose and I walked over to the stage entrance again. Moose said, "I see what Garcia means look at them!" He was right as the crowd looked crazy and delirious on the party favorite of the Grateful Dead, LSD. I mean it was in the air, you could feel the electricity in it, all crazy and uncertain like. Moose said, "If they get past the Brothers in front of the stage, we can charge into them from both sides of the stage entrances!" He looked down at my Bowie knife and nodded. I remember what happened at the Altamont concert with the Angels doing security for the Rolling Stones. An Angel Prospect had stabbed and killed a black man at that one. I was there but stoned on some killer purple haze acid and missed the stabbing. Viewing what was out in front of us, I could see how things could get out of hand in an instance. I was at a Jimmy Hendricks concert years before in Sacramento tripping on some acid when that concert had turned into a full-blown riot, people got hurt and trampled. I could see why Garcia was scared too hell as I now understood why he was quitting.

The lights dimmed and the concert started with the psychedelic lights started pulsating, it was really kind of beautiful, but different than being on the other side of the stage in the crowd. It was getting scary as hell after the beginning band left the stage as the crowd wanted the band, then here come the Dead from behind us all ready to go, Garcia took a deep breath and winked when he looked over at us as he went on stage. Personally I felt for all of them, they might be millionaires, but what a scary way to make a living. They started playing and the crowd went ballistic, I was sure glad the Hell's Angels reputation from Altamont would prevail to save us all. After a couple of songs Moose wanted to step back into the rear area and we smoked a joint, I was right on him, that was my job, and I was grateful. We fired up a 'dubie' and a group kind of formed around us to get high as we passed joints around in a small circle. The lights were blinking and pulsating in the Jello and paisley effect they used to do in the acid days. So these lights were dancing around all over the people and walls, it was definitely psychedelic.

Well I took a hit and passed it to this dude standing next to me as he leaned towards me a little and took it from my hand. That's when the lights lit up his face for a second, and I recognized this famous movie actor, at least I thought that was who it was. I don't want too get sued, so I will just give you his some initials, M D. He wasn't quite as famous then as he is now. After a couple of joints we moved on, as we walked away I asked Moose if that was who I thought it was, he said yea, M D. That kind of blew my mind that I was blowing a joint with a cop actor, but that wasn't nothing like I had in store for my mind coming up. We went from there to where the beer was. Chuck and some of his group said the gate was pretty dead and they had been sent up to see if we needed any help. Moose was digging through the cooler and said he couldn't believe we were out of beer already. So Chuck and another couple of Prospects were sent to get some more cases of beer. I had cotton mouth bad from the weed, and after they left, I some how wandered into the snack and food room. I was delighted to find all kinds of fruits and vegetables, melons, juices, all health food shit. What I thought was kind of strange was it all looked pretty much untouched.

My lucky day, this will kill my case of cottonmouth. The juices were pretty bad without any vodka, but the watermelon and fruits were delicious, I ate my fill. I came out and saw that Chuck was back and with Moose standing with some other Angels sucking up the newly arrived beer. I dove into the ice and cracked one and Chuck asked where I had been. I told him I went over and wolfed down some fruit and shit. Chuck's eyes got big as he pointed, "You ate some of that shit in there?" Yea I told him, they said it was free and to help ourselves. "Yea, but this is the Grateful Dead man, that shit is laced with some bad-ass LSD" Chuck yelled over the noise! "Well fuck I didn't know that, I just ate some cause they said to help ourselves, are you sure about that?" "Yea I am fucking sure, you are gonna get really fucked up Bro," Chuck warned me. I told him I had dropped a thousand hits of acid since I was a kid and I was sure I could handle it, "But let's not tell anybody." "Shit man Chief and them are gonna know, you not going to be able to maintain enough to hide it," Chuck added.

"Man we got to, thank God you aren't on your bike, we are gonna have to tell Big Moose, he likes you, he'll have to help cover for you", Chuck said. We went and told Moose what had happened and he agreed we shouldn't tell anyone how stupid I was. As I was listening to this I felt that beginning creeping feeling of some good LSD coming on. Dam if Chuck wasn't right, it looked like I was going to be taking a free trip compliment of the Grateful Dead, the 'Dead head' way! Within a half a hour I was off, that's pretty fucking fast as a normal dosage would be take about an hour, all depends how good and fresh it is and how much you take. The light shows were just getting better, and as I was looking out into the crowd they were getting scarier. I was really tripping my ass off now as Chuck and Moose kept eyeballing me while keeping me between them as best they could. This went on for an eternity, probably about an hour but I was having the time of my life. The concert that was blazing away was starting to wind down to the end, thank God!

We had a bunch of Angels in front of the stage keeping the people off and the rest behind the stage with a bunch of reinforcements on the sides in case they were needed to storm the stage. One Angel said the chicks were getting out of control in front, lots of LSD, "You can grab all the tits and ass you want, some of them are stripping naked on their own, you ought to go out there!" Normally I would want to check the chicks out but no fucking thanks tonight. I have done a lot of LSD in my time and the only reason I stopped is you couldn't get a hold of any decent shit that didn't poison you or make you sick. I can think of only a couple of times it was this strong and good. I would have enjoyed it more if it weren't for the circumstances. I was supposed to be Prospecting and looking out for the Membership, not flying high as a kite. Inevitably Chief came strutting up. He was talking to us about something, and I just pretended I knew what he was saying. I tried not to start grinning and give myself away to

Chief, but if you have ever been there you know that is almost impossible if it is that good of shit. You get that grin on your face you just can't get it off.

Moose tried his best and told Chief that maybe he and I ought to go a head to where the party is and make sure everything was cool, but basically he wanted to get me the fuck out of there. That's when Chief asked me "What the fuck are you grinning at." I said nothing really I'm just stoned and smiled. He then asked "What the fuck are you on?" I told him I had some fruit and pointed toward the room, even he knew about the famous LSD lacing thing. For once to his credit he half ass understood my mistake. He started laughing his ass off, and then of course he had to tell a couple other Angel's about it. He told Big Moose to baby-sit me, and to get me out of there and over to the party when the concert was over. Of course we needed to stop and get some rum and coke and some more beer. We really never needed the booze later because the Dead had any thing your heart could desire, or so I was told later. As we started to split the concert was ending with screaming and banging as the crowd tried to get another song out of them. They did get another one and we watched them from behind the stage do the 'Truckin' song. It was complete chaos, but the Angels in the front of the stage only had problems with intoxicated women, nothing really got out of hand like Altamont.

The chicks were buzzed and kept trying to get on the stage to get a piece of the band. The lights kept beat to the music and I was having one of the best trips of my life. The band finally came off the stage and I could feel their energy, fear, and relief. I finally had some idea of what being a rock star might be like. Garcia was jazzed with energy, as was the whole band. They were milling around shaking hands and trying to calm down. Their entourages handed them all towels to dry off as they were all sweating from the heat the crowd had generated. They were working their way towards the dressing room shaking hands and telling people they would see them at the party. Garcia's comes by us as we were manning the door out towards the dressing room. He shook our hands and when he looked into my eyes as he grinned at me and said, "You liked the fruit didn't you" and gave me a tired grin. Only a fellow acidhead knows what tripping is really like to know when a fellow 'head' is high on it! You could tell he was like most intelligent people, he feared HAMC but he also felt safe and protected with them, a wise man in my book.

Moose led me out of there to the truck as I couldn't care what we did because I was flying so high. I was a total mess and could barely talk, it was one of the best edge running trips I have ever took. The color's and patterns were so intense and the product was clean. The lights of Frisco were almost frightening, Moose asked me if I was gonna make it. I told him I would be fine but probably shouldn't be around the public. At that point I really didn't know how high I was as I was floating in the world of LSD. We finally got parked after driving around trying to get near our packs of bikes. But there were so many vehicles everywhere that we just ended up a long way from the bikes. Moose said lets go, I tried but I just couldn't move. The inside of that truck seemed like the only safe place in the universe. "Come on man, this is a party of a lifetime, you don't want too miss this one!" I just couldn't make myself start moving as I was way too fucked up to move. Moose didn't know what to do, it is best not to leave anyone alone tripping if you can help it. I have seen people lose it and never really come back the same. I told him not to worry that I was going to watch the truck, I remember petting the dashboard as we talked because it was swirling paisley.

Moose shook his head and said "Man I wish you could watch the bikes as that would look better for you, but you're too fucked up huh! Well try and watch them and don't forget that I tried to get you in there, what are you grinning about, is my face melting?" I told him it was swirling in a paisley design and how did he know that? "I've been there before myself Bro," and with that he left. I never got out of the cab that night except to piss. I remembered the Frisco city lights all swirling and moving for my enjoyment. I watched the sun come up and remember thinking that I was having more fun than anyone in the whole world because I was the only one getting to see it. It was daytime or sometime, who cared, and then Moose finally showed up. "Did you spend the whole time in here? Man you missed one hell of a party, chicks, cocaine, LSD, you name it, and it was all there and plenty of it!" I told him I had to piss once and he just started laughing his ass off. As we were crossing the bay bridge I started to finally come down from peaking, it had lasted almost ten hours. The only other time I could remember peaking that long was when I took some 'white lighting' in Berkeley, fresh of the press, 'better living through better chemistry' has always been my motto!

I was pissed at myself for being so naïve, I love tripping on good LSD, but was glad when I finally started coming down from one wild trip. I made the concert but missed the party of the decade. That was one of the real bummers of the whole thing, which might have been 'The Party' of my young ass life. I was hoping I hadn't let the Chapter down, and I waited to get my ass chewed out. I guess everybody had enough of a good time to let it go while cause I only got a few wise cracks like "Our acid boy" from Chief. I didn't really give a shit but of course we all know the Grateful Dead went back to playing for a long time after their 'last concert.' But I have always felt privileged for the brief encounter with Garcia and M D because it's cool to know that they shit just like us. The amazing thing to me was that the respect and obvious curiosity they had for the Red & White. The Rolling Stones and Janis Joplin to name a few that had also used the R & W for security needs, and I believe also that they were curious too. Like I said I was at Altamont and saw the Stones whose use of R&W turned ugly, but I wonder what would have happened if they weren't there?

I saw Janis Joplin in concert, but there wasn't but a few R&W that were there when I saw her in Sacramento. Even the famous were curious and wanted to use them, if you were behind that stage as I was, you would understand some of the fear these musicians feel. Security guards, they just have a paycheck attitude, R&W has a reputation to up hold, even at a cost of their lives. Little Mike was one of the smallest Angels I ever met. But he carried a ball penne hammer inside of his cutoff under his arm pit. Big Angels wouldn't even fuck with him as he was known to be ferocious with his hammer at knocking anybody that fucked with him in the head. Hell's Angels don't miss a fight, no matter with who it is or what the odds are. If I was on that stage I know whom I would hire too protect my ass, the feared organization of men known as The Hell's Angels! I can think of few organizations that inspire the common fear and notoriety that they do, and believe me when I say they deserve it. They are some badass dudes and have earned that right. If you don't like to fight, stay away. This is no game to them, not a one-time thing at all as this is the way they always are. Honor for themselves, fear for everyone else. Believe me when I say they won't lose a fight, they just won't cause the fear of repercussions is what gives them their real power which is fear. You can't beat them, as they will be back with as many Bothers or weapons as it takes to win. If they have to pay the ultimate price for power, even if it means their death, they will gladly. Their symbol is the Death head, think about that. They are living the ultimate game you can play, life or death. If you join that world, you except that your fate is to probably too die or rot in prison for your beliefs and for the Club. The funny thing is you are more than willing to do so because you have already sold your soul to Red and White. You can't be a Hell's Angel if you're not ready to die if necessary for the Club. Once you put that Red & White patch on its usually forever, there's no going back because you have already passed through the gates of hell!

THE VACATION

Chuck and I spent countless hours riding all over the country while we were prospecting together. We were Brothers, as well as best of friends who helped each other to survive. We split the costs for places to live, and hustled and stole shit together to support ourselves. If we had one joint left between us, I knew he would share it with me. More importantly though, was that we watched each other's backs to try and survive the rough game we had chosen to play in the world of the Hell's Angels MC. Fate had drawn us together by chance, and to this day I miss him dearly. He started prospecting for the Nomad Chapter in Vallejo way before I did. The first time I met him was at the Sacramento Hell's Angels First Turkey Skeet Shoot, and I was in The Gladiators Club. Our next encounter for Chuck and I was at Big Bruce's house in Placerville. Big Bruce was a Hang Around wannabe. Bruce was one of those big tree trunk types. He had hung around the Clubs for a while. He started out mostly around The Gladiators. He was a trucker with his own Peter built truck, so he always had plenty of cash. He dealt drugs a little, but mostly just played with them for his image and to keep the chicks around, and he did always have a lot of them hanging around his place, doing whatever or whoever it took to get high. I got to know him better by keeping his truck supplied with tires and parts. I had procured him a bitching stereo and a turbo for his Peter built truck one time. He would case the shit out that he wanted and then he would tell me what and where to get it. "There's this bitchin' scanner in the red truck parked over at such and such place, and I'll give you a hundred for it, but make sure you get the brackets, too." He would ask for shit like that and I'd go get it for him. Burglary at the time was a specialty of mine, and not just for the money, but also for the thrill of doing it. Bruce would simply call me up and tell me that he wanted this part off the number three truck that was parked here at this address. He always paid in cash or dope. We got along pretty good personally, but more so for the crime and drug dealing connection. He probably tried to act too intelligent for his own good, because he wasn't. I always thought he was an arrogant fuck that you couldn't trust to watch your back, as he just seemed worried about his own ass. He was too good for The Gladiators, and we didn't want him anyway. Like Doc had said, "Use the fuck for what we can get out of him." We all did just that, as often as we could. He had his sights on Red & White anyway for the power, women, and money it would bring him. They let him hang around awhile as they played him as much as they could. I think he finally figured it out and got tired of being used, as he eventually drifted away from the scene.

I believe Bruce enjoyed it when the Hell's Angels shut The Gladiators down, as he was sore because we had never approached him about joining our Club. I don't think he really ever got it, you have to approach bike Clubs about joining because they won't approach you. The Clubs have pride of course, but it's also a good way to see if a Prospective Member had any brass balls or not. Wild Bill had called Stretch and said he was riding up from Vallejo and asked him to tell me to meet him there. He said this cat named Chuck, who was a Prospect for the Nomads, was coming with him, as he had a beef going with Bruce. I didn't put together what Chuck he was talking about, so I was surprised a little that he wanted me to meet them there. Bill was trying to get me to start hanging around for the R&W, but like I told him, I was happy with my family in The Gladiators, even though they had shut us down. I got there a little early and kind of surprised Bruce, as he was acting a little nervous and wanted to know why I had showed up there. He knew I was just kind of hanging around the Hell's Angels a little then, but he was always very nosey and suspicious. He probably figured I was going to help them fuck him up or something. Since we had just been shut down, I wasn't really sure what I was going to do, as my old Club Brothers told me to wait awhile. "Don't go Red & White yet, because you aren't even 21 years old yet! Don't let the sound of your own wheels drive you crazy," Triple Jack had told me many times. I told Bruce that I was at his house to party and because Bill said he was coming up for a visit, and had told Stretch that he wanted me there as he needed me to do something. That wasn't exactly true, but it seemed to make Bruce get a little more nervous. He knew I was tight with Bill and he asked me if I was friends with this Prospect Chuck dude. I told him that I didn't think I knew him, and he seemed to be relieved and relaxed a little. Then he started telling the whole story on how this Chuck had fucked him. "Red & White or not, this guy Chuck isn't gonna' burn me" he boasted. He went on to tell me that Chuck had disrespected him by fucking one of his babes that was dealing a little for him. To add insult to injury, he took some of *his* drugs from the broad and she had spent some of *his* money on him. She had claimed to him that Chuck had sort of forced her, because she didn't want to say no to a Hell's Angel. I told him that I didn't really see a problem about the fucking part, but nobody should steal drugs. That seemed to appease him enough to make him feel better about my presence.

Wild Bill and Prospect Chuck finally showed up about two hours late. Bruce and I had just did a little of his bump and drank some of his beers while we waited. We had just burned a fat joint when they showed up, and it definitely had calmed Bruce's ass down. Then we all sat down in the living room. Bill started to introduce me to Chuck, when he spoke up and said we had met before at Folsom Lake, a while back. As fate would have it, this was going to be the beginning of a short but intense Brotherhood between us. We kind of took to each other right away, as we were so much alike. I sat in on the confrontation between them, with Bill sort of being the judge while he listened to Bruce first, then to Chuck's side of the story. If you knew Hangtown Bill, which was his new Red & White nickname, you were a lucky guy to know such a man. When he was President of The Gladiators, he was called Wild Bill and had done a lot in leading and building that Club. Bill commanded respect and the best from you, as he was just that kind of guy. Being a very large, confident, strong man, he portrayed the perfect Angel that nobody, wisely, wanted to fuck with. He was both a man of intelligence and leadership, and a bad motherfucker for sure. He would rarely use his power in the Club because he could handle anything himself. He carried a two shot .357 magnum Derringer in those days. In the middle of a brawl one time, at a party at Poncho's house, Bill capped one off in the ceiling. Everyone froze and stopped immediately in their tracks, ending the scuffle. Bill was a man to be feared and reckoned with by his own right, which made him a natural Hell's Angel. So this incident with Big Bruce turned out to be over the usual women, dope, and money. Bruce explained his story of his house mouse's explanation, or excuse. Then it was Chuck's turn to defend himself. He said that she gave him the dope and had bought him dinner, and she was the one who wanted to fuck. The bitch didn't say she had an old man or Daddy, so how would he know to keep his hands off? "I'm not turning down some good pussy and a good meal, and if the chick wants to give me free dope, who wouldn't take it! If Bruce needs to go outside to even up the score, then I would be more than happy to oblige." Bruce didn't know what to say about that, especially with Chuck's willingness to fight and the fact of him being a Hell's Angel Prospect, which meant he wouldn't lose. Chuck was smart though, he had thrown it all back in Bruce's lap, with a "you want to go outside and fight about it?" That being the usual biker's way of settling disputes with each other, such as with these two.

Bruce backed down, as gracefully as he could. I admit that I was enjoying seeing Bruce's humility as he squirmed out of it. What was he going to due? If he and Chuck started to fight, he knew Bill would have to jump in. He probably figured I would, too. Again, the power of the Bike Club's code, you fuck with one of us, you get them all. So Bruce went with the old, "Out of respect to the Red & White, I'll let it go as long as Chuck doesn't let this shit happen again." It was the only way he could save face without getting his ass kicked. So Bill said, "You both need to shake hands for me and hold no grudges, as this problem is over." Then the confrontation was over and we all started partying again. Chuck and I got a chance to get to know each other a lot better. He was from Sacramento too; he had just run in different areas and with different bikers. We both remembered that we had bumped into each other over at a Folsom Lake party a couple of times, but we had just really eyeballed each other. I had actually heard of his reputation before, through a mutual friend. That was before the Turkey Shoot meet.

He had an old L.A., California Highway Patrol Shovelhead. It was still black with a few of the white lines left on it. There were a lot of these bikes out there. Chuck never really gave a shit how fancy his bikes were. He would trade any of them in for the most reliable one, and didn't care if it wasn't the prettiest. He just wanted to ride them, like me it was his only transportation that he had, usually. He told me once that when he got patched that he was going to put together a badass bike. I know I used to average 30,000 to 40,000 miles a year on my Pan-Shovel back then, and he was the same kind of guy. We both lived out of our saddlebags and off of our wits and charms. I guess that's why we both became such good Bros and we had so instantly hit it off with each other. Bruce's had turned into an all night party with lots of chicks and people. Stretch and Gentle Jim had come over to join the party and visit with Bill. We all packed or noses. Drinking beer, smoking weed, snorting the product, and fucking with Bruce's harem of women, which he didn't appreciate, was how it turned out. When the sun came up, I went and had breakfast with Bill and Chuck. They were going back to Vallejo after breakfast and wanted me to ride along. I told them I was too financially broke at the moment, but Chuck and I did talk about when I came down to start hanging around the Nomads, we could maybe get a place together.

Chuck had already been prospecting for about six months. I new all this would be good for me, if I went down there. He knew the area and all the local hustles. I rode with them as far as Sacramento, to Lonesome's shop, where we parted ways with the promise that I would be down soon. Teddy Bear would be the one to finally coax me down a few months later. It looked like my destiny was to go and that was what I had always wanted anyway.

When I got back from Sacramento, I rode over to Stretch's house. I figured him and Jim would still be partying. They were just doing a line and asked me if I wanted one. I took a bump as we started bullshitting and smoking some Humboldt badass weed, and drinking some brews. Stretch's old lady was a beautiful and caring Indian woman, who I used to call Mom. I called her that because she always took care of me, I didn't even have to ask. She would treat me like a son and cook me breakfast, not unlike that morning, and she would get my dirty socks and t-shirts out of my saddlebags and exchange them with some of Stretch's. He never said anything, but I don't think he really appreciated it. But that was the way she was, and I always loved and respected her as a second Mother. We all briefly talked about me going Red & White over breakfast, and how much we all missed The Gladiators.

When I finally moved I stayed at Teddy Bear's house where I became an official Nomad Hang Around. I decided I should move out of Bear's place, as he had been busted for a machine gun rap that was still on the Judge's table. First, I moved in with a welfare chick and stayed there until I had gotten voted in as a Prospect. Chuck had been living with one of the strippers from our titty bar and she had moved out and let him have the place. He couldn't keep up with the rent by himself, as he was working hard for his Colors and didn't have any time. You're put in the position of supporting yourself without a job, while you serve the Club and its Members about 24/7. You had no time for a job even if you wanted one. So if we shared all the expenses as we always did, it was cheaper for both of us. It was a three bedroom place and quite expensive for us unemployed bums. The first month we burned a Shovelhead to cover the rent and shit. Chuck was getting more depressed as he had been prospecting for a long time and getting discouraged, as everybody did. He decided he needed to quit the meth habit, as he felt some of the Membership was leading him around by the nose. I explained that I didn't know how he could do that and keep up, as meth was the crutch to help keep up the pace. How else do you stay up with all the Members that are doing the product? He decided he would go on a health kick and try to get some regular sleep. I laughed about any kind of sleep and went to bed. The next morning I got up and he was just getting back from the gym. He said that he had joined a health club as he was mixing up some protein drink. He went on to further explain his new plan. He figured he would get healthy, quit dope, stand up against his enemies, dazzle them with his strength and then maybe he would get his beloved Patch. "Look at us Bro; look how out of shape and skinny we are!" I looked at myself and had to agree. "Fuck it then, let's get in shape and stand up to these motherfuckers. They're just pushing us around because they got us acting like zombies!" I said, agreeing with him, as we needed to show our mud or we were never going to get patched.

I was feeling so puny and shitty after about a two day speeding stint that I asked Chuck, "What are you making to drink?" Chuck said it was half and half, with some protein mix that he had bought, and did I want one? I figured if it was good enough for Chuck and got him so jazzed up, it must be good enough for me. So that's what we did, we cut the booze and the drugs out almost entirely. We started pumping iron every day at the gym, smoking a little weed to get by. I had been raised pumping iron with my Dad and knew the ropes. The old man used to be a professional boxer and had taught me not only how to build up my body, but some boxing skills as well. My old man gave me about the best start in life for the whole 14 years I had lived with him.

We kept drinking half and half like beer, and started eating a couple of meals a day. The Membership didn't know how to take our straight asses. I do know that after a couple weeks of training, our confidence improved and we started sticking up for ourselves. You have to remember that the Hell's Angels of the time we were running with were older than us, and had more experience at almost everything. Also, they were the boldest and baddest motherfuckers on earth that I have ever found. So you had to stand up and be a man and prove yourself to them, that you had the heart and the attitude to become one of them. Until you did, they would use you to do any chicken shit thing they could think of. I finally confronted my pain in the ass, named Pete the Reb. Chuck also stood his ground on some old fights with a couple Members. In about five weeks, we were buffed up and had started settling things. Nobody seemed to be so anxious to push us around anymore, so let's say we had regained our confidence in the Membership as men. The next Church was held over at Bear's house, where they called Chuck into the meeting. The rest of us Prospects continued doing security outside, wondering what Chuck could have done. Then finally Chuck came strutting out, wearing a brand new shiny Death head on his back; he had gotten patched! Of course we were all jealous, but this was Chuck's moment we all had been waiting for. The celebration began as we headed for our bar with Chuck, wearing this grin on his face for the whole damn night. While I was buying him a beer at the bar, Chuck asked me if I was ready for our vacation.

When Chuck got patched, he told all the Members that he was taking a well deserved vacation, and wanted to go show off his Colors. He was going to go see some Sacramento Members and visit some people he hadn't seen since he had started. He wanted to fly his new Patch in the wind and I didn't blame him. I was standing there when he told them that he and I were planning on Bogarting him a new bike before we hit the road, and hopefully we would leave next week. Chief asked Luck if he could go with Chuck on his "The Vacation," as he called it. Luck said no, he already had something he had going with another Member. Ronnie was over in Santa Rosa at the time. You could tell Chief didn't want Chuck and me going together, as he thought we were too tight, or for whatever reason, as he always tried to split us up. Chief finally said all right, go ahead and take me because somebody had to protect him. Chuck winked at me. "You two better not be gone more than a week though, because we might need you both," Chief commented. Wow, a legal vacation from the Club, I just couldn't believe my luck. I was running with just my Brother Chuck, and I couldn't hardly fucking wait!

What a blessing it was going to be, now that Chuck had finally gotten patched. We immediately started making plans after we got out of Church and away from everyone. First thing was that we had to get Chuck a better bike. His old police Shovel was starting to hammer and smoke. I still don't know what was holding his transmission together, but that was Chuck's luck. He usually had an old, worn out rat bike as long as I knew him. So he told me about this wannabe that he had been watching for a while, and that he was going to Bogart his bike. The plan was to invite him to a staged Chapter barbecue on Sunday. Chuck had talked one of the other Brothers and his old lady into helping him set up the stage for the scam. The plan was to lure this guy to the BBQ, where we would all be friendly and get this guy to let his guard down while we all got him cranked up and drunk. As soon as he got fucked up enough, I was to break out some of the badass Humboldt weed we had, and get him totally fucked up. After the joint and while he was still spinning, a Member would come over with his old lady and a bottle of whiskey. The con was to then accuse him of insulting his lady, who knew what was happening and would play it up by slapping him in the face. Then everyone would play their roles out to scare the shit out of this guy. You needed to pick the right kind of guy for this kind of mark. First, he needed to be so scared to death of the Club that he wouldn't go to the cops after it was over. He also had to be a coward in his heart, as you didn't want him coming back with a gun on you later, after he realizes what had happened. That and he had to be pretty fat with the money and insurance so he could recover from his loss easier, which this guy was a boss in some company, so he made good money.

Fortunately for us, everything went perfect. This guy was playing right into the scam, better than we had expected. I kept feeding him beers and bullshitting about how everybody liked him, and he ought to try and join our Chapter. Then Chuck would come over with a jar of whiskey and we would all take our turn and have a shot and then get him to take one, too. After the first couple shots, we were all tonguing the bottle so we didn't get drunk, all the while telling him how cool he was and yeah, everybody liked him. We all thought he would make a good Prospect and shit. This guy wanted to be in the Club, but was too scared to ever try and join. This went on and Chuck gave me the nod. I went over and asked the dude if he wanted a few hits of some good weed. "Yeah," he says. He was already pretty polluted. We all let him smoke most of it by taking tiny little hits and passing it back. One of the Members told me to go get something, and I saw Chuck and that Member and his old lady kind of corner him. After about 20 minutes of chit-chat, I watched him get knocked on his ass. Of course, everybody ran over and jumped all over him. After yelling and installing the fear of God into him and he had plenty of lumps, Chuck dragged him up off the floor. Chuck was playing his role as well as any Hollywood actor could have, as he had this guy terrified. "You insulted my Brother's old lady, my Club, and my Patch, you're going to die!" Chuck then told me to go get the car pulled up to the front and open the trunk, making sure the mark heard him. "We're going to take this disrespectful lump of shit to the marshes. Does anybody have some plastic?" Charlie yelled. As I left I could hear him start pleading for his life, "Please don't kill me! I got messed up and don't now what I did, I didn't mean to insult anyone. I'm sorry, I apologize!" By the time I got back, the guy was ready to give Chuck anything to save his life. They took the dude over to his apartment, telling him the only way he could save his life would be to sign over the title of his bike to the Club. I followed them on my bike. There at his own kitchen table, he signed the back of his title over to Chuck, who had kept his gun pressed against the guy's head. Once everyone figured we had enough fear in the guy, we were firing up Chuck's new Shovelhead. The plan was that Chuck and I would ride away and go stash the bike to see what the mark would do. We had a guy watching his apartment all the rest of that day and night to see if the cops showed up. After we left, we would call from Sacramento to find out if our mark had gotten in his car Monday morning and left for work. So we figured we might be home-free, as apparently he wasn't going to call the cops. This used to be called Bogarting back then, and was frowned upon by some of the Members, as they wanted it to be tabooed because it created a bad reputation for the Club.

Chuck's new Shovelhead was another L.A. police bike, but in good shape with some extras on it. It had 154,000 miles on it. That means the previous owner had only put 4,000 miles on it since he had bought it. The L.A.P.D. would get them brand new, and then do a top-end after the first 50,000 miles. Then they would do the top end and bottom end again, at 100,000 miles. Then at 150,000, they would do another top-end on it and then auction it off. This thing still had the black and white L.A.P.D. paint job on it. They took off the emblems from the tanks. The cop sirens, lights, and radio are all removed, which turns the bike into a stocker basically. I asked Chuck if he was going to take the fiberglass side compartments off, as he had his old leather bags. "No, I'm gonna' leave it like it is. I want to get the fuck out of here quickly and get on the road! You never know what that guy I Bogarted is gonna' do when he sobers up and thinks about what happened to him," Chuck replied.

The choices the dude had were to go to the law and file charges, or come after us with a gun to try and get it back. But with the fear of the Club's reputation of reprisals, they usually don't do anything, out of fear. He'll probably go buy a Honda if he ever rides again. We changed the oil and the plugs, and loaded up our tools and shit. We were on the road and out of Vallejo in about an hour and a half. It felt good for a lot of reasons.

For one, we didn't have some pissed of dude shooting at us. Best of all though, Chuck and I were free of the Club and were started on our needed and well deserved vacation. No "Prospect this and Prospect, get that." It was Chuck and me in the wind. This was the trip he and I talked about on our way back from the U.S.A. Run in that fucking U-haul truck. The wind in my face felt free, no worries, just freedom. Then it dawned on me, was the Club turning into a job for me and taking away my beloved freedom?

We headed up through Sacramento, and didn't even stop at Lonesome's or at his shop, California Chopper Supply. We rode up around the Garden Valley area to some people Charlie hadn't seen since he started prospecting. He was going to show off that bright, new, shiny Patch he had earned with the legendary Death head. He was proud and I didn't blame him, I envied him! You don't realize what it takes to get one. From the moment you put it on, the whole world changes and people look at you in a different way. The God like power you feel is incredible. When you walk into a store to pay for your gas, everybody in there stares at you. It takes some getting used to. If you have never worn one, you can't possibly know. Sometimes it can really bug you. But you are so proud of it that really doesn't matter. Your life has changed forever after you put one on, fuck the straight world.

We partied with all his old friends and felt comfortable at hiding out in his old stomping grounds for a while. Chuck hooked us up with some babes. We spent a week up there, just riding around and partying. We biked all over that beautiful Northern California countryside we both had been missing. Everybody Chuck knew treated us like kings; it was a great time. Chuck knew we had to check in and he finally made the call to Vallejo. Chief wanted us back, of course. I overheard Chuck saying he wasn't ready yet, he had some more visiting to do. I thought that a boy, you're a Member now, you can throw some authority back. I couldn't wait to get my Colors, because then we could do this all the time. But for now, prospecting and my Patch could all wait. I needed this break, and so did Chuck, as we had earned it. He had spent about three years of hanging around and prospecting to get it. We did some needed cleaning and wrenching on the bikes and decided we would leave the next day. Chuck said it was my turn, and asked where I wanted to go? What a Brother! I told him I knew of a beautiful ride up through Coloma, and I knew some old Gladiators that we could hang with. Chuck's friend gave him a present of a matching set of black leather gauntlets, all riveted up and looking bad. As soon as we departed and got down the road, he gave me one of them. Later on I would give it as a present to Hangtown, as he kept drooling all over it from the first time he saw it.

After a memorable, beautiful ride through the back roads, we finally arrived at Poncho's. He was happy to see us. He had a new, foxy welfare lady that was paying his house payment for him. Living on her welfare commodities for basic food allowed him to live real well. Things hadn't changed for him at all, as he was still the same hustler as always. He still had the dog kennel to discipline his welfare kids. He would straighten them right up, or he would punish them by putting them in the kennel whenever they misbehaved. Believe me when I say that after a week at Poncho's, they were the best behaved kids you have ever seen. "Go get us some more beers," and off they would go, happy to be fetching. He would keep them fetching and carrying, doing yard work for him. He really would whip them into shape. To Poncho's credit, he would reward them with little candies. Personally, I believe he was good for them. Most of these welfare chick's kids sucked. Not only wouldn't their Mothers discipline them at all, but they were being spoiled by both parents. When I was living with Poncho in my younger years, I had to go pick a welfare chick and move her in to cover my share of the rent and eats. I had this chick and her two boys living with me, and she was divorced from a biker/drug dealer. I had met her ex-husband while fencing hot shit in Sacramento in the early days with Fat Ray. Anyway, I remember Poncho sending this chick's two boys to The Pin. Crying all the way up the path together holding hands, they went in and closed the gate behind them. They were little angels after a few trips to The Pin. Unfortunately, later, she had bought this big old 1.5 ton box commercial van. She wanted to fix it up to live in and make a hippie wagon out of. Poncho had told her the brakes were bad and not to drive it until we could fix it. I had taken off on my bike to do a little business and partying. She throws her kids in it and decides to take off and go to town. Down the Chili Bar grade she went which was a steep grade with winding curves that went to town. The brakes failed as predicted, and she rolled it. The kids weren't seat belted in, so it threw them around inside like dolls, amongst tables and all the other crap. It killed the one boy, and seriously injured the other. After the funeral she left and got a house in town. I moved in with her for a while, but I got clipped and had to do six months in the county jail. She came to visit me with one of my old buddy's, Chubby. They explained how they were sorry, but they were fucking and he was moving in. I don't know why I don't trust women much.

After Chuck and I got all settled in at Poncho's and everybody was comfortable, I made a call to Princess Red, a chick I used to run with every now and then. The problem was that she was five years younger than me. So when I turned eighteen, she was definitely jailbait. She brought up one of her cute underage girlfriends for Chuck. The party was on, as we took them on a few short bike rides in the backcountry. To get pulled over with them was jail time for sure. So when we got bored we still snuck around on our bikes a lot on the back roads. Poncho broke out his party weed and we had plenty of meth. Poncho sent his old lady to the store with her food stamps and we gave her some money for some booze. The party was on for a week and it was a good time for all. Those two chicks had to run away from home so they could hang with us, and to our stupidity we wanted them to. We partied, told stories, and laughed, and on and on. About the third day, Poncho broke out some good acid. We all dropped together and what a trip we had. It was some good old California shit that really peaked well. That's when Poncho had to start telling Chuck the story of my most famous wreck. Back then I never brought the story up to most people, because I guess I was a little embarrassed. But Poncho proceeded in telling Chuck and everyone about me launching my trike into the canyon, and like always, after a while I joined in on the story.

The canyon wreck had happened about three years before, when I was having a blast prospecting with The Gladiators, as they were my family that I hoped to get patched out with someday. The Club bylaws said that you had to be 21 to join. My eighteenth birthday was about a week away. My problem started because the Vietnam War was going on while I was prospecting for The Gladiators. So by the laws of the draft at the time, I was supposed to sign up for the draft. While I was in Stretch's garage doing the usual snorting crank, drinking beer, and working on bikes, I told Stretch, our President, my problem. I was going to ride down and sign up for the draft. He asked me if I was sure that I wanted to do that. I told him I had to or go to jail. "No, you are just a draft dodger if you don't. You just sign up the day before your nineteenth birthday. What are they gonna' do, send you to Vietnam?" Stretch says. I told him that I always figured I was going there anyway. "So why don't you wait a while and ride that Panhead around with us, and until then, they are gonna' send you there anyway," Stretch said. I thought about it, and it sounded cool to me because I would just be going in a year later.

I was used to taking my Brother's advice, as all of them were at least 10 years older than me. I was the kid. So I took their advice and partied on my bike for another year. Then on the day before my nineteenth birthday, I went down and signed up. The lady told me I was going be sent to Vietnam for sure, because I was a draft evader and they could put me in jail. I told her I had forgotten to sign up because I had been too busy riding my Harley and I was sorry. That didn't go over very well. So then I told her that I had lost a lot of high school friends in the Nam already. I was good to go in the draft all my young life, since as a boy I had been watching the news on TV with my Dad and listening to the daily body counts. She sneered at me as she handed me a piece of paper, telling me where to go to get my physical, and that I had better show up or there would be a warrant issued. I showed up to the bus and went through the medical exam and passed my physical and was classified the then famous 1-A. I've got a 1-A death sentence with a one way ticket for the Nam is what I told everybody. I have often wondered if that was the reason I had lived life so recklessly? Then, a week before I was supposed to report to the bus and go to boot camp, the Club was having Church, and said they were going to have a farewell party for me.

That farewell party was really my planned Patching Out ceremony and celebration as I got my Full Patch and became a Member in The Gladiator Family. Then we partied all night to celebrate my Patch, and a goodbye and good luck party as I was headed for Vietnam. During the party on the second day, my Dad called Stretch up and said he had a registered letter for me. I had used his address since I didn't have a home, and had given him Stretch's phone number for emergencies. I told him to open it and read it to me. He told me it was from the draft board. It read, "You are to stand down and await further orders," my Dad said. "It looks like they don't want you right now." I was so excited that I had a reprieve that I told Stretch and the Brothers what had happened and everybody was so happy for me. We all had lost somebody we knew in that damn war. My Dad told me he heard on the news that Nixon was stopping more troop deployments. Stretch's and the Brother's advice had probably saved my life.

We had to keep partying now, for sure, as my freedom was another good excuse. So we stayed up all Saturday and Sunday night doing all of our usual party favors, and Doc broke out some Yellows (Nembutal), which are heavy downers, and gave me a bunch of them. That would turn out to be a bad mistake. By Sunday night, my Patching party and the not having to go get killed in Vietnam party was coming to a close. I was drinking some sloe gin and had eaten too many of the Yellows. All the Brothers that had to go back to work and deal with their shit all went home. I didn't have any responsibilities, so I just kept partying with the few that were left. I finally left the party and rode this chick over to her house to continue celebrating there. I rode my trike that had an eight inch over wide glide front end, done with screw in slugs. It had a trick King/ Queen seat set up that Carl had built, and some cool mag rims and tires that I had stolen. Brother Carl had also done the paint for me as a present, with a purple paint job with a swastika on each side of the fat bob tanks. I never did get the generator to work. It had a big battery box that I had built that would hold about any sized battery. It was a 6V system, and would last up to a week on a full charged car battery if I didn't ride at night too much. So when it started to backfire because of lack of juice, I would either head over to a Brother's house that had a charger or just go steal another battery. I would always leave them my old one in its place; I never really thought of it like it was stealing. I procured another one that night down the street from that chick's house in an alley. I left this chick's house Monday morning because I couldn't really stand her anymore, and decided to go home and talk Poncho into eating some Yellows and getting drunk again with me. I knew he had some speed too, and I definitely needed some more of that because I had eaten two much Yellow candy. I'll be the first to admit that I was a mess, just being a little too happy about my new Colors and a reprieved life.

I was riding up the curvy grade known as "chili bar grade" and had already crossed the river on my 45 trike towards Poncho's, where I lived most of the time then. I came around a corner a little wide and was cheating in the other lane a bit. I was heavy on the throttle, speeding a little too fast as it was pushing the trikes ability to hold its own traction on sharp corners. I met a car coming around the corner at me and attempted to swerve back into my lane. But after I just missed the car, I had one rear wheel up in the air from turning so quickly to return to my lane and miss the oncoming car. So when I came down on the rear tire, the ass end bounced and I attempted to correct with the front end and I lost control of the trike. At least that is what I think happened, as it is still a real blur to this day. I remember it happening sort of in slow motion. So the trike and I launched straight off the side of the canyon's edge, at probably 40 mph. I remember flying through the air and thinking I was dead, then I felt the trike reach its peak of momentum, and then it just started dropping like a rock as I let go of the handle bars.

The smart thing to do in this scenario is get away from the trike, which I did, out of motor function or pure luck. Weight and gravity took it and I was flying in midair, slowly dropping behind the trike, as it was heavier and flew further through with the weight momentum. This is one of many stupid and dangerous wrecks I have lived through in my life. People who have known me for very long figure I am about half cat and half rat they say, because I have lived nine lives and always end up crawling away. I don't remember much of the wreck. I remember trying to crawl up this hill in the dirt. I kept sliding. The next thing I remember is Poncho talking to this guy and I looked down at myself and saw dirt and a lot of blood. He was trying to tell Poncho where he had found me lying in the road. The local said that he had figured I was on my way up to his house. No, the Good Samaritan said, he didn't know how long I had been there or how I had gotten all tore up. "Looks like he fell out of a moving car or somebody tried to kill him and left him for dead," the guy said. Poncho thanked him for bringing me there and would appreciate no calls to the law. I was slow coming to because of the Yellows and booze, along with my head injuries.

My brand new Gladiator patch was shred into pieces. I had big knots on my head with road rash and bruises. I was a mess. Poncho kept asking me what happened. I finally remembered saying that I was riding my trike and partying. "I know that damn it, where's your trike?" he asked. He finally started putting together what had happened. He called some of the other Brothers that weren't at work for some fast help, and they were all up there in a flash. They all kept questioning me while a couple old ladies were cleaning off my blood. I remember them saying that they had better take me to the hospital, especially because of my head injuries. "No, he's young and tough, he can't pay for that shit anyway, and they'll never let him in the hospital. We'll watch him for awhile and keep him awake in case he has a concussion." So what do they do, shove some crank up my nose to wake me up. Talk about caring for a Bro's ass! At least in my yellow Nembutal alcoholic state, I wasn't in as much pain as I could have been. Boom, all of a sudden I'm awake. Yeah, I told them, I was riding my trike? "We'll then, where the fuck is it," Poncho asked? "Fuck if I know," I told Poncho. "Well it wasn't on the road up here or we would have seen it," one of the Brothers said. Finally they decided that where the neighbor had found me was their best option to start the search for my missing trike.

They put me in one car, and some more Brothers in others. We set out as search parties. We finally spotted where I had launched off the curve that had a 1,500 foot drop off into a canyon. The trike was about 180 foot down the cliff, where the rear end had hooked around a tree that had stopped it from going on down to the bottom of the canyon. There was a couple of cut down, small trees, which had been sheared off by the impact, that had slowed it's descent down. It was that one last tree that had stopped her from going all the way down to the bottom of the canyon. The front end had sheared off at the slugs, which had happened before. The front end hadn't went down as far, with the logic being it snapped off as I had launched. We split right away to avoid any unwanted law involvement. After we had gotten rid of all our stash and guns and shit, we gathered up to go back.

We got one Brother's four-wheel drive truck that had a wench on it. We grabbed some extra cable, ropes and chains. They lowered a Brother down with ropes. It was a real bitch, because everything was sliding in the loose dirt on the steep incline. If the law showed up, our cover story was that a car had run me off the edge, which was kind of true. One of the Bro's that had been riding with me would be my witness in case it got ugly. Luckily, they never showed up. They finally got it hooked up and started to try and wench it. It was dragging the truck down. So then we chained another vehicle to the truck, and still no good. We chalked all the wheels and then we hooked a snatch block to give us more pulling power and she finally came up. We left what was left of the front end, as it was mangled from impact. We finally got what was left over to Poncho's. They found the spot that they figured I had landed on, which apparently was where I touch downed after I went airborne and let go of the handlebars. The trike being heavier, it fell faster and further. So I hit about a 120 feet down, they figured. The trike had went further and touched ground about 150 feet down. Then it started hitting the small trees, which slowed it down. The one tree hooked the rear end and the tire and lodged it and held at about 180 feet. If it hadn't, we wouldn't have been able to retrieve it. It would have gone clear to the bottom in a mangled mess. Nobody could believe I had lived through this one. They all figured what saved my ass was that I was so fucked up. Like a drunk rolling down the stairs. They figured my Patch had gotten shred in the rocks as I slid down the canyon. They could see where I had snail crawled a trail up to the road. We never had an exact time on how long I was knocked out and lying there, or how long it took me to crawl up the hill, or just how long until that citizen picked me up out of the middle of the road. As the lore or story goes, it was conceived that I had launched about nine or ten in the morning. I was knocked out and crawled up that hill, got picked up, and brought to Poncho's by about three thirty in the afternoon. From the accounts of information given them by that chick, they could guess when I had come through there. Until the time I got delivered to Poncho's, it is generally agreed upon that about five hours elapsed. No one really knows any more for sure, and I was too fucked up to know. I do know that I have recurring dreams of flying through the air and letting go of the handlebars and having this helpless, flying sensation. It started about the right time in the scheme of things. I do know that I had an angel that must have been riding on my shoulder in that one, too. None of my old Brothers that witnessed what they found left of this wreck believed anyone could have survived it. It must have been one of my dead Bro's riding with me then. I would like to believe that it was one of them that had saved me. I should not have survived that one, but there was plenty more to come.

For a long time, people looked at me in disbelief of my mortality and now after my last wreck, they still do. I have no explanations for what I have lived through. I know it is probably hard to believe. On my Mother's dead soul, it's the God's honest truth. That story from my past and some others lasted almost until that next morning with all of us sitting around Poncho's campfire until L.S.Crazy finally left our brains. Chuck asked me if that wreck was a no shit story. I was a little embarrassed, but told him that yeah, it was real. He said, "Would you mind showing me where it happened, Bro?" We loaded the chicks and rode down the grade and I showed him the spot. He just shook his head as he looked over the edge, "Bro, you shouldn't be here!" We hung out at Poncho's for another week. Chuck called into Vallejo, and word was that Chief was getting pissed. Chuck gave me the bad news. Neither of us was ready to go back yet, we were having too good of a time. We had a couple of young 'uns to keep us warm, and Chuck was love bitten with his little "pup." We had all the comforts of our world that could be given us, and we were free from the Club and our responsibilities to it. We both knew it would have to end soon, as our world in the Club was calling us back. But our dream was happening and we were sad to leave our vacation, as it would all quickly come to an end. We blew some meth up our noses early that morning and smoked a joint to ponder our demise.

Once we got amped up, we started to try and come up with a scam to tell Chief to extend our vacation. If you knew him you would know that wasn't very easy. We ran a few ideas back and forth, but none fit. Finally Chuck said, "The only thing Chief considers an excuse is business." Okay let's work on that one. We knew we couldn't safely hang for more than another week, because these underage chicks were dangerous. But fuck it, we thought, let's try for one more week of vacation. It finally hit me; a drug deal! That Chief would buy, if it would make him or the Nomads money and I knew about everyone around that county. I remembered a biker dude that used to have some pretty heavy connects in Tahoe. I jumped right on it and made some calls, and located the dude by phone. I hung my neck out a little and talked a quantity deal. It wasn't a ground shaker, but gave us some time. It was only a two Z deal, but enough. Chuck told Chief we had to hang so that we could get the bucks, straight up. Our plan of extending our vacation worked, and we got almost another week. We just kept playing the same games and hanging out with the young 'uns.

Some of my Old Bros kept coming by, visiting and seeing Chuck, as we all were so proud of him and his new patch. I was probably more elated than anybody, because I knew the pain and work it took to get it. I told him at one moment during the party that it was definitely the prettiest Death head I had ever seen. We played it all out the whole week. We barbequed, drank, smoked weed, snorted, and fucked our little hearts out. We rode all the back roads we could find. Chuck's Bogart, which I was calling her now, was running strong, even for an ugly bike. Chuck would end up putting endless miles on her, as she had found a good home. Poncho's old lady showed up with some good blow. The cocaine train was now running in us, with what turned out to be some pretty pure shit. Those young girls were getting an education, but unfortunately, also spoiled. When Poncho's old lady checked around in town a little, our two little ladies needed to go home to their Mommies and Daddies. We rolled the Z's out of Sacramento, and then we moved them up to Tahoe and collected our money. We said our goodbyes, and then threw a little product to our host. Poncho laid a cool blade on Chuck for getting patched. It was an original Nazi piece.

I didn't know if I was going to get Chuck to leave that young chick behind or not. He was in love with the little puppy. We ended up staying one extra day, because he wanted another night with her. The next day he was starting to talk about bringing her back to the Bay Area. I told him he was fucking nuts, and to quit thinking with the little head. He finally agreed, with the promise that we would be back in a couple weeks. We got Poncho's old lady to drop the young 'uns off in town to cover our asses.

We finally rolled out and hit highway 50. We got to puttin', and then Chuck blew my mind as he turned onto highway 49. We were gonna take the long way back to Vallejo. I knew I was gonna be in some deep shit with Chief. But I also now had a patched Member as an ally. We rode at a pretty slow pace, with neither of us wanting to get back. Chuck was starting a whole new world for himself. Me, I was going back to the wonderful world of prospecting. Looking back, this would be our best time together. If I could only live a few weeks again with Chuck, these I would choose. Chuck was a great man as a Member, and he never really got Patch Fever. A lot of them do, and if you have ever been there, it's really a hard thing to not do.

When we went through Sacramento, we decided to stop by Lonesome's shop. Chuck wanted to show off his new Patch. Everybody had heard about it and all the respectful hugs were given. You could see that it meant a lot to Chuck. He was planning on transferring to the Sacramento Chapter. Lonesome said, "I can only imagine what you two have been up to, as your Chief called here asking if I had seen you two." He never missed anything. I heard in the later years that Lonesome had gotten killed in a strange drag boat accident. The world lost one righteous Angel. The first time I saw him was when I was about ten. In retrospect, I wish I had gone with the Sacramento Chapter too, who Lonesome was President of. I know things would have turned out different. They weren't into the drugs like the Nomads were. Like I said, the Nomads were a tough crew of cranksters. We got invited to hang out for the night and decided Chief could wait. At the shop, we bumped into Michael Mouse, and it was great to see him.

A Teddy Bear favorite, Mouse was already a well liked and respected Angel of six years. We shot the shit a bit. I asked him if he had seen our mutual friend, Mike D. He said he had and that Mike was doing well. "Finally got him a real bike," Mouse commented, as everybody kidded Mike about riding a Sportster. I asked about how Joe N. was doing. "Crazy as ever," he said. All these Angels were in the Nomads at one time. Now they were all Sacramento Chapter. These guys didn't live on drugs. They all had jobs or businesses, a real together Crew. I was learning to respect them more and more. It was good to see them all. I wasn't asked to do any real prospecting while I was there, and I was enjoying myself, as I still felt like I was still on a vacation.

We rode over to another Angel's house, named Gino. He was a big Italian that had prospected a little with Chuck. Gino and Chuck used to run together before they got involved in the Club. Back in the old days, I used to see them together at Folsom Lake. A lot of bikers used to spend their afternoons hanging out in this one parking lot at the lake. It was a good place to swim, drink, take drugs, and pick up women. A lot of young chicks would hang out, all dressed up in their little bikinis, wanting to get high and drunk. They always wanted to go for rides on the bikes. The party usually started slow in the morning, but was usually a big one by late afternoon. I had seen Chuck and Gino there, but I really didn't get to know them very well. Chuck said they all used to get a chuckle when they saw me take a bar of soap and jump in the lake a couple of times. Chuck said, "You bathed in the lake every time you showed up. We figured you for a hard core, biker tramp motherfucker for sure!" Gino said he saw me washing my socks and putting them on rocks to dry, and we all got a big laugh over that one. I hadn't realized that they were watching me. I was literally living out of my saddlebags then, while I was prospecting for The Gladiators. We all laughed about the old days and our stories. We bullshit about the Turkey Shoot we had all attended, what seemed so long ago. Gino asked how all the old Gladiators were. I told him they were all doing good, and missed our Club. Gino mentioned that he thought we had all gotten a raw deal, and I held my tongue. I told him that it was a good Brotherhood, and thanks for the thoughts. He asked Chuck if he was gonna stay with the Nomads or transfer back to his Chapter in the Sacramento area. Chuck said he didn't know when for sure, but that he wanted to. He was tired of some of the cranksters and drug abuse in Vallejo. I know he was thinking about how quick he could do it and get away with it. I asked how Earl was doing since his wreck, and he said amazingly well. Earl and I had been friends before either of us went Red & White. An old lady had run him over on his bike and had pinned them both under her car. But the real damage was when she kept backing up and then going forward, trying to get off Earl and his bike. He was really fucked up and barely survived the wreck. Gino said that with his lawsuit money he was going to buy a scooter shop. We talked and talked, and it was a good visit for all of us. We split from there and Chuck wanted to go see a chick he used to know. She was surprised to see his new Patch. She was happy for him, and wanted to celebrate. She had a friend she called and we all went out to some of their favorite old haunts. We partied until the bars shut down. We ended up back at her place. We all slept in until about 10:00, then we all went and had breakfast. We said our goodbyes and headed for the highway.

As we got closer to Vallejo, my mind was thinking of what lay ahead. The vacation was going to end and I had relaxed so much. It had felt good to roam free like the old days. Chuck and I had talked and dreamed of this for so long. Even though we were flying our Colors, which keeps you on your toes, those weeks went by without any of the problems. We were heading back into the shit now, as there was trouble brewing in our Chapter and we knew it. The cops had been on our ass like stink on shit. I had that assault case coming up in court. I needed to raise some cash for that. We were about tapped on the money we had left, even counting the change from the deal we had done. We stopped and got some gas and sat on our bikes as Chuck was smoking a cigarette. He asked me if I was feeling like he was. We were both feeling the blues. We talked about it all for a while and then he said he already missed Sacramento. We finally looked each other in the eyes; fuck it, let's smoke a joint; always our answer. We did, and we both felt a lot better. We gave each other a big hug. "Brothers forever," I told him, as I was sure glad his getting patched hadn't changed us. "Wait until you get yours, which will be our next vacation, only then we can go as long as we want!" I told him, "Brother, I wouldn't have it any other way!"

WE'RE GOIN' TO WAR!

Sonny B was in jail in the early '70s when the Nomads Chapter almost went to war with the Oakland Chapter. When I say almost went to war, I mean we went to the mattresses, which sounds like mafia shit, but that's what happened. It all began after I had rode over with Pete the Reb to Sonny's place on Golf Links Road in Oakland. I wasn't digging this much at all, because Pete and I didn't really like each other that much. Matter of fact, we hated each other, as I had moved in with one of his ex-old ladies when I first got to Vallejo, for really no more reason than I needed a place to eat and stay. The trouble started when, as I mentioned before, Sharon received some cash from a settlement from a car accident that had happened before I had even met her. I had been busted riding a Member home from the titty bar, who was a little drunk. That bust ended up with me getting nailed for a felony that cost me bail and lawyer's fees, which the Chapter had covered for me. I was trying hard to pay the money back, as I had just gotten my Prospect California Bottom Rocker, and was trying to get my Full Patch. Sharon was probably taking our relationship a little too seriously, but all she wanted was a Hell's Angel, and was willing to pay for it. She gave me the cash to get paid up on the bail and lawyers money that I owed the Club. The problem was that Reb had been boning her on the side, and was living with her as his old lady when the accident occurred. He never figured she would get any money out of it and had dropped her and went elsewhere for hustling money and entertainment. Sharon was different than most of the women hanging around the Club at the time, and she really didn't do a lot of speed, so she wasn't even a good customer or dealer for him. That was one of the few things that I *did* like about her. But that's where all the trouble started between us, was because Pete figured he should get the money because he was dating her when the accident occurred. My side, of course, was she was my hustle now, as I was living with her, and what was hers should be mine. Now, Pete's a Full Patched Member and I am just a lowly Prospect, so he figured he could bully me. He went so far as to leave me a note that he had written onto Sharon's bed's headboard in a felt pen, basically letting me know he could still fuck her. This being done for my benefit, to piss me off, hoping that I would throw a punch at him in front of the whole Nomad Membership. I wouldn't fall into that trap, but it would all eventually come to a head at a Church being held at Teddy Bear's.

He came out during a break in the meeting and walked up to me and asked if I wanted to smoke a joint? I immediately thought this was one of two things, he either wanted to say no hard feelings, or he wanted to get me spinning so I would be easier prey. As we bullshit and had just about finished the joint, I knew it was coming. So in front of most of the Chapter, he started talking loud about me taking his money from Sharon, as it was his because he had never stopped fucking her. We were standing face to face and I could see the veins that were popping out of his neck because he was getting so pissed. I knew he was going to try to cold cock me, as his earlier plan hadn't been working, and he also knew that I had Sharon's money in my pocket. I planned to turn the money in after Church, and I wasn't sure what the Membership would do. Chuck and I had discussed this on guard duty, and we had agreed that I had only a few choices. One was to go talk to my sponsor Big Red, but I knew that was worthless, because he didn't give a shit. So Chuck and I agreed that my second option was that I had to stand up to him. We both had been on a health kick and working out in the gym, just for this kind of situation.

As a Prospect you have to walk a very thin line dealing with the different Members. Remember the Club bylaw that says when one Angel fights, they all do. You don't really want to get into a fist fight with them, but you can't let them run over you, either. In short, you have to be a man and handle it, is what both Chuck and I agreed on. So, in front of most of the Membership watching, Reb and I stood toe to toe as I stuck up for myself. "I can't see how it is your money Reb, as I have been living there and putting up with her and her two kids that drive me nuts for months now." Reb yelled back in my face, "That fucking accident happened when I was fucking her and she was my girlfriend, so I deserve all the money instead of you!" I told Pete and everybody, "Pete, I think I've earned that money at least twice over, and besides, I was living there when I got busted taking care of Club business! I am gonna' give the money to the Treasurer after Church to clear me of my debt with the Chapter!" I could see in Pete's face as the muscle in his arms flinched, that he was moving to throw a punch at me. I grabbed both of his wrists as hard as I could as his arms started to rise. I wasn't going to let him cold cock me, and I thought this was a better move than getting into a punching match with him. He started yelling at me to let go of him, as he struggled to free himself of my grip. I held on as he struggled against my hold, and then he just started screaming like a little kid to "Let go of me!" "Pete, I not gonna' let you hit me," I said calmly. That's when I could here Kanuck, Moose, and some other Members start laughing behind me, which just aggravated Pete more. "Goddamn it, you let go of me now," Pete yelled! I calmly told him, "I am not gonna' let you go if you're just gonna' punch me over this bullshit, Pete!" As his eyes darted around at the onlookers, Pete said, "I'm not gonna' hit you, just let go of my arms!" I was amazed at how weak he was as he tried to twist free of my grip, and I was thinking that I could easily kick his ass.

I let go and jumped back, expecting to start boxing as I put both arms up fast into a boxing stance. But he just turned and started explaining to some of the Brothers what was going on, like it was no big deal, and trying to defuse the confrontation. I think he felt my strength and just didn't want to fight me. After explaining the situation, he finally turned to me in front of everyone and said that if the money was going to the Chapter, that of course he didn't have a problem with it. We didn't fight, but I made a life long enemy. Some of the Brothers kidded him about what a Prospect had done to him, which just aggravated him even more. I had humiliated him in front of everyone and had made a serious enemy. But if I had fought one on one with him and kicked his ass, it would have been worse. I never trusted him again, and I knew that one day he was going to try to pay me back in spades. I did turn in the money and paid off my debt to the Chapter.

When I was told by Chief to ride with Reb over to Sonny's place, I knew I had to go, and orders are orders, no matter how we felt about each other. So we both just ignored the fact that we couldn't stand each other. We pulled up to the chain link fence gate as I remembered how the place looked a lot like a fenced in security compound or a prison. I had only been there once in my life, which was about six years earlier. This was when I was a young kid and lived in Oakland, going to school. We had driven by in curiosity of the then already famous Hell's Angel leader. He had been on the news about then for being busted in a car with two terrified men in his trunk, supposedly being taken up into the mountains for a one way ride. Everyone in Oakland knew, even back then, exactly where the famous leader lived. I had lived and worked near the Montclair Golf Course, which was in the same area known as the Oakland Foothills. This was right before I got busted that summer for felony drug sales and starting a riot in Berkeley. As we pulled up, Sharon, Sonny's famous wife at the time, came out on cue and called off the watch dogs and then met us at the door with a smile. I was told that we were picking up some bike parts, which usually meant we were picking up some dope. We went inside and Pete introduced me to Sharon, and she was very polite and welcoming as she shook my hand. There was a little chitchat and then Pete kind of cut it short. He told me to go outside and do security, in his best bossy attitude. I went out by the bikes and waited as told for about an hour, pacing around the driveway on the usual security duty. I smoked about ten cigarettes out of boredom and was kicking myself for not throwing a jug of wine into my saddlebags. I finally heard that all too familiar sound, "Prospect, where's that fucking Prospect at!" I found them waiting in the garage for me. Sharon was smiling and being nice as she thanked me for waiting and asked if I would like something to drink? I immediately thought of asking her for a cold beer, but then Pete butts in, "No, we don't have time for that shit, we have to get going, and he's alright!" I spoke up and told her that I was sorry they had Sonny in jail on those chicken shit charges, as I really didn't know what else to say. She began telling me about Sonny's legal fund and started to go into his update on his trial, when Pete sort of cut in and told me that I was going to be looking for a certain Panhead transmission, as he was pointing to an opening in the ceiling above the garage. I crawled up there as told, into the attic above the garage, and for a second thought that I must be in a scooter shop or gone to Harley heaven. There was fucking Harley parts everywhere you looked! You name the Harley part and it was up there. I would guess that there was at least four bikes worth of parts up there. I showed him a couple of trannies through the opening until I got the right one. I handed it down to Pete's skinny, outstretched arms. I climbed back down to the garage floor. I kind of glanced around and saw Sharon's beautiful bike parked there, next to Sonny's bike, I guessed.

I remember seeing her name embossed on the primary cover. I commented to her that she sure had a beautiful bike, and she agreed and bragged about it for awhile. Pete told me to grab the tranny, and we all walked outside to our bikes. Pete told me to pack the tranny on my bike, which I knew he would. Then he told me to wait there and to watch and if anybody showed up, no matter whom it was, to come into the house and yell for him. I had opted to tie the transmission onto my passenger area of the seat, with it against my chicken bar. I put some of my rags under it so that the studs wouldn't tear holes in my seat. I had two good bungee cords that I wrapped around it. I also broke out my thin rope that I always carried and tied the shit out of it, until I wondered if I wasn't tweaking on it a bit too much? Finally satisfied that the tranny would make it back to Vallejo, I broke out a joint to relieve the boredom. After detoxing for what seemed like a very long time, I was thinking how good a cold beer was going to taste, when Pete finally came out of the house and said, "Let's split." We left Sharon and Sonny's place in Oakland and rode back over to Vallejo with me packing the damn tranny. It never moved.

The next day I was sleeping it off at home after getting back from Oakland and a late drunk from being down at our Strip Bar, prospecting with the Club. I was awakened by Sharon at eight o'clock that morning, as I had a phone call. I cussed at her and asked why in the fuck she would wake me up when I was sleeping, and she said calmly, "It's someone from the Club!" I jumped up and ran to the phone, wondering what fucking

Member would be up this early in the morning. Luck told me, "Get your ass down to the titty bar, quick, condition red, and for God sakes, don't forget all your heat!" Most Members don't even get up until noon, so I asked, "What the hell could be going on this early in the morning?" "I don't know yet, but you know the drill, and I think it is something big!" Luck responded. I did a line to get moving and to clear my head from the night before. I had gotten home only about three hours before the call. The line helped me blast through a quick shower, but then I butted heads with Sharon as she wanted some attention. Sorry, bye. Of course my bike didn't want to start. I think she wanted to rest some more, like me.

I rode up into the parking lot with my free hand on my gun in my waistband, not knowing what to expect. It looked cool enough, because it looked like most of the Chapter had already showed up. They were all milling around and had kind of worried looks on their faces. There they all were, gathered up around Chief, who then came right over to me immediately and asked to see my piece. I then moved my cut enough so that he could see the pistol in my belt. We hardly ever used holsters then because if you had to throw your piece and they patted you down for weapons, how do you explain an empty holster, and where the gun that goes in it is? Chief said to go hang out by the nightclub entrance door and to leave it open! Then he said not to let anybody in, except our Chapter Members only. Then he went on to say something even stranger, "I mean not even anybody from the rest of the Club!" Now I really didn't know what the fuck was up, but it sure seemed like something big!

Everyone's face showed a concerned, worried look of fear, something you did not see often. These are Outlaws that I lived with almost every day, who feared nothing, as nothing seemed to scare them. Chief seemed all excited, but I caught a few other Members looking around in disbelief. This was all too weird for this time of day, or anytime really, especially because most of the Members didn't even get up until noon. Then Luck showed up packing his pistol, and I asked him if he knew what the fuck was up yet? He said that he heard we had some trouble going with Oakland and that's all he knew. I relaxed a little as I figured the Outlaws were here for a fight or something. Now that's a real problem, you are either going too probably die, or go to prison for life. But Oakland, I thought, we're all in the same Club, right, I mean how bad can that be? Our few missing Chapter Members kept showing up and rushing inside, that's when I started thinking too much about what Chief had said, don't let anybody else in from the Club. Finally, after an hour or so, they came out and Chief told us that we were hitting the mattresses; we were at war with the Oakland Chapter!

Chief told us to go stash our bikes and a vehicle would pick us up. "Take the alleys home boys, and watch your asses, nobody's bringing bikes!" The alley system in Vallejo was extensive, you could get anywhere by them and we used them to sneak around. I was good at alley cruising because I used them all the time to get around town. You wouldn't usually pick up any cop tails that way, and I just always felt that they were safer for some reason. I always figured if there were any of our sworn enemies of the Outlaws MC around, they would never find me. If you did it just right, you only had to cross a few main streets, which I would vary my routes home to. I zigged and zagged around with Chuck to the pad he had rented, and stashed our bikes inside the kitchen, all chained up to each other. So we waited for the cage to come by and pick us up, and nervously smoked a joint. A pickup finally came by and as we jumped in, I saw plenty of guns and ammo everywhere inside. Bruce handed me a loaded 12 gauge pump shotgun and said, "Let's be careful, okay, your ridding shotgun? Do you guys have your guns?" That's when it really hit me what was going on, holy shit, we were really going to have to kill our own kind, why?

We ended up driving way out of town into the sticks, which was our destination, to a retired Nomad Member's house, I was told. I didn't know this retired Member at all, but he was one big dude, though. He had all the Club tattoos and a lot of scars to prove who he was. I could hardly believe the size of his guns, meaning his huge, muscled weight lifter arms. I figured he must have done a lot of time in the joint and spent the dead time bodybuilding. I thought the prison theory made sense and that's why I hadn't seen him before, because he was probably out on parole, with a non-association tag on his condition of parole. I figured I'd ask around with some of the other Prospects later and find out. He was really friendly though, and greeted us with a smile as if we were arriving for a party or something. He hugged Members and reached out and shook my hand with a smile that made you feel totally welcome. Chief and a couple other Members went upstairs with him, just about the same time as another carload of Members showed up and came in.

The atmosphere still seemed tense, but most of us were a little more relieved and felt safer there. About then, Chief and the Members from upstairs came down and Chief walked over to me and handed me a B.A.R. with a couple of loaded clips. "That's a 30-06 Browning automatic rifle and is a very powerful, fully automatic military machine gun," Chief instructed me. One badass motherfucking weapon if put in the hands of someone who knows how to use it. Some of the other Members handed out the same to the other three Prospects, explaining that this was some heavy firepower. Chief proceeded to sit all of us Prospects down and produced a bag of speed and told us all to pack our noses and don't be afraid to ask for more whenever we started getting tired. "I want you guys to be alert and on your toes," and then he started to give us a crash course on "his babies," as he called them. This problem was apparently getting as serious as it gets, fast!

First he asked if any one of us had any experience with the B.A.R.? I said that my Dad had a semi-automatic 30-06 clip fed rifle that I had been trained on. Chief said, "Good, you know how much they kick then. This was John Dillinger's favorite weapon and mine too!" He showed all of us how to pop the clips in and out to load it and shit. They are very heavy guns, especially with a full extended magazine in it. So then he told all of us to go outside with him, and he would show us our defensive positions. They basically put one of us on each corner of the house, hidden in the bushes and shit. Chief said, "Orders are that nobody gets in, nobody! If a car tries to ram the building, you open fire and don't stop shooting. Those clips are loaded with military armor piercing rounds, so they'll go right through a car and its tires. So if they try ramming us, try to shoot the driver first and then kill the rest of them." They said that they would back us up from the house with some more firepower. "If they pull in all peaceful and shit and stop, tell them to stay in the car and don't move around. Whatever you do, don't expose yourself any more than you have to, and for God sakes, don't take your eyes off of them!" Chief said.

This was getting out of hand I thought. I still couldn't believe that they were talking about us shooting our own people. I mean the Outlaws MC; okay they were strangers, and we were already at war with them. I didn't think I could shoot Pie because he was my friend that I looked up to. Chief ended our orders with that, and he meant every word he said. Then they all went inside, and had a meeting to try and straighten shit out. They would be calling Oakland soon, but we weren't backing down. "Remember the Nomads are your family, the other Chapters are just relatives, no matter what happens," Chief said! He went back inside as we all looked each other in the eyes in awe and went to our positions. Like I figured, it wasn't five minutes until one of the Members popped his head out the door saying that two of us were gonna' be making a supply run. So once we had the list we left one guard in front and one in back, while the other two jumped into a pickup to go fill the list of booze, food, mattresses, blankets, and all kinds of shit. For once, all of us wanted to go on the supply run, as it just seemed safer!

There were no old ladies on this trip, also we were told not to call anyone or tell anyone where we were at. This is where our Chapter was going to hang for as long as it took. I thought that this would probably be our Alamo, if you will. Chief was definitely in his element, as you could tell that he was enjoying the shit out of himself. Some members seemed indifferent, but some seemed really fucking worried, and yes, that would be me. After the supply run, it wasn't very long before everybody got the party going. After some drinking, smoking, and snorting, all I started hearing was "fuck this and fuck them," as their moods seemed to be getting worse. There were some calls made back and forth to Oakland after they finally got Chief's black box set up. It was all kept pretty much all hush hush from us. We would hear, "Them motherfucker this," and, "Who do they think they are?" I was really starting to get more worried about this whole situation, as it was really bothering me that we might even consider going to war with our own people. Like I say, I liked some of the Oakland Members, and what kind of Brotherhood was this anyway? I considered them like distant family members, cousins if you will. I started feeling better after Chief had us go pick up some women for them to party with, which I figured would calm everyone down.

After awhile, it did seem to relax everyone, sort of defuse the situation. When we got back from another supply run, I had to pull fucking guard duty right off, and as expected, to say that I was a little more nervous than usual is probably a real understatement! Later that evening, I was relieved for a short break. I was hoping against hope that they hadn't eaten all the sandwich shit we had bought. As I was putting together some of the leftover scraps, Luck walked over and asked me if I needed a bump, which was a little out of character. So up the nose it went, because I didn't want to be nodding off on duty, as trouble could be around the corner tonight. I could barely choke down that sandwich and finished it with a big guzzle of my second beer. Chief came walking over to me in the kitchen with a chick in each arm. He explained that he was taking these two fine babes upstairs to the bedroom for a little personal party. "I don't want to be disturbed by nobody, and I mean nobody, you got that, or it's gonna' be your ass! You don't let anybody up those stairs, nobody!" "Yeah, Chief, I got it," I told him. I thought this was kind of weird, because Chief had never been that picky about sharing his women before, as he really didn't like them except to get laid.

So I grabbed another brew and put one into my cut pocket so I wouldn't have to leave my post. I jammed over there to the bottom of the stairwell thinking this was weird, but better than being outside and being the first one shot! I thought I noticed Members kind of watching me out of the corner of their eyes, and decided the crank and current events were making me paranoid. So I popped my second beer out of my cut and took a big pull to get that dope taste out of my mouth. All of a sudden, here came the big, retired Member who owned the place. He started to go right by me and up the stairs. I didn't really know how to say it as I touched his shoulder, and he was already about three stairs up. "Hey man, I am sorry but I can't let you go up there and disturb Chief," I stated as politely as I could. He just ignored me and kept on trucking. I thought to myself how I could tell this giant, older Member what to do in his own house.

He got up to the top landing of the staircase and I kind of spun him around and sort of pleaded, "Look man, I know it's your pad and I am real sorry, but it's my ass if I let you go in there, you know what I mean?" He shoved me straight back with both hands in my rib cage and yelled, "It's my fucking house and I will go wherever I fucking want!" I tried to plead with an, "I guess he just don't want to share," and I smiled when I said it. "Fuck you," he screamed! Before I knew it, Members had surrounded us both. Then he had his finger in my face screaming, "This is my fucking place and I don't give a shit about you or what you say!" With that, he shoved me aside and started for the bedroom door that Chief was in. My first thought was he's right, it is his fucking house. Then it hit me, this must be a mud check. No matter what I thought, I have got to stop him, now! I'll admit that I was one scared hombre.

This was definitely the biggest man I had ever squared off with by myself. These thoughts jammed through my head in probably a split second. I had no choice but to stop him. I grabbed him by the shoulder to spin him around and threw a punch into his stomach with everything I had. To my surprise, he gasped for air a little, and I thought, he's not a machine. I decided right off that I wasn't going to hit him in the face, as I would probably just piss him off! I hit him with another gut shot and he puffed some more air out. He threw a roundhouse at my head that I dodged, just as my old man had showed me as a youngster. He groaned as I started rabbit punching his kidneys and mixed in a solar plexus shot, or two. My old man's training as a professional boxer was saving my ass, as he used to tell me, "Son, no matter how big a man is, he can't fight if he can't breathe! Take the air out of them and you can take him." He had won a professional fight at the L.A. Gardens once just that way, but he also had pissed blood for two weeks himself. His opponent had whooped him with body blows, but he had luckily landed a head shot in the last round, which was his last pro fight.

Dad had also taught me that especially with a big man; you have to watch their shoulders as they would "Telegraph their punches every time." He was so big, that when he went to throw a punch, I could read it coming, just like my old man had said. I kept up a flurry of rabbit punches as we went back and forth with blows. All of his were headhunters, because he knew that if he connected, I would be knocked the fuck out. I had felt someone grabbing at my side, which I had no idea who or what that was. We kept going back and forth with blows being thrown at my head, with one catching me, but really just grazing me as I rolled my head. I kept up the rabbit punching on his guts and kidneys. I never once threw at this guy's head, which was totally keeping him off balance, as he kept covering his head. I knew my only chance was to not let him connect or get a bear hug on me, or was I a goner. My only shot was to knock the wind out of him. There wasn't one moment of this fight that I thought for a second that I wasn't fighting for my life. I'm sure the speed was part of it, as that shit was definitely pumping through my system.

This giant was getting frustrated with his near misses and I was starting to get winded, too. I just kept up the rabbit punching, as it was my only choice, and dodging his punches. I have always found that bigger men throw slower punches due to their size and bulk muscle. A true boxer trains with using lighter weights, with three times the repetition. That doesn't give you bulk muscles, but rather faster, snappier muscles. The baddest man in the world is a man with big natural muscles, and fast hands. You run into one of them and you pretty much have your hands full. I kept up my attack of dodging and trying to knock the air out of him, with mostly gut and kidneys shots, as that seem to hurt him the most. He lunged forward, trying to grab and pull me down. I knew that was coming and if he did get a hold of me, I was dead meat. I spun out of that one and jabbed a kidney on my way by. He recovered and turned and lunged again, as I tried to spin out of his grasp, but he had gotten his arm around me as he started to take me down to the floor with him. On my way down was when I glimpsed an outstretched hand that I grabbed. It was Kanuck's hand, and he pulled me out from his grasp, leaving him falling to the floor. I stayed up on my feet as he went down to the floor, face down. I immediately jumped, landing with both my knees into his lower back and kidney area, when I then saw his entire air blow right out of him! Then he struggled to try and get up as he was gasping for some air.

I wasn't going to give him any chance to recover his breathing. I grabbed some of his hair on the back of his head and started slamming his head down on the floor, as hard as I could. The adrenaline and speed were flowing, as I fought like I was fighting for my life. It seemed like I slammed his head down a dozen times or more, as I was panicking, trying not to let him recover and get up. The next thing I know is I'm being grabbed from behind and pulled off. "Come on, that's enough," someone said. I admit that I had gone into a frenzy for survival, as it took three or four of them to pull me off of him. It's not an easy thing to just turn it off when you get in a fighting rage where you almost turn into a senseless wild animal, being controlled by a natural fighting instinct to survive. I remember hearing Chief say, "I told you he could fight!" I flashed to the realization that he had popped out of the bedroom to see the fight. This confirmed to me that I had been right, that they had set this fight up as a mud check. Some Members were trying to get the big guy up onto his feet, as he was trying to get his breathing back to normal, and they kept us both apart.

We momentarily made eye contact and he gave me a wink, like its cool. That was a tremendous relief to me, as I had been lucky and didn't want any more of his ass. That was the biggest man I had ever fought by myself! I remember one of my first thoughts was that I didn't shit my pants. Members were all over me, slapping me on the back and shaking my hand, congratulating me as the pandemonium started dying down. I felt someone pulling at my side again, and as I looked, one of the Members was putting my Bowie knife back into its sheath. I found out after that, when they planned this mud check, they told one of the Members to grab my knife, as they didn't want me to stab the guy. I was known to be handy with it because I always wore it and used to quick draw it and play with it a lot. I always figured it would intimidate people and make them reconsider wanting to fuck with me. Apparently, that was working well enough, as a lot of survival in the bike world is intimidation. With all the Members surrounding us they coaxed the big man and me into shaking hands. I started babbling that I was sorry about slamming his head on the floor, but I had orders from Chief and… He sighed and said, "Don't worry about it, you did alright kid!" We shook hands and he gave me a hug, which I was relieved about, when he let me down. He was grinning as he did, and I about melted down, as the fight was over! Everyone was still taking turns shaking my hand and shit, telling me what a good fight it was. The only one I really looked in the eyes and thanked from my heart was Kanuck. Without that hand to grab, it probably would have been a different outcome altogether.

After everything calmed down and I slammed about four beers in a row, everyone went back to partying. I went into the kitchen, talking with everybody about the fight, and as I went to the fridge to slam a couple of more deserved beers, I could hardly breathe. Luck came over and said to me, "You looked like you were fighting for your life!" I said I thought I pretty much was. Then Luck says, "Why didn't you hit him in the fucking head right off?" I told him the truth that I didn't want to piss the big man off! He laughed and shook his head, saying that he would have. I told him it wasn't my first mud check and he seemed like a good old ex-member. I really had been through the mud check thing before, in The Gladiators. All Clubs do it as a matter of necessity, as it just has to happen. Brothers need to know for sure if you'll fight, because their lives may depend on it one day!

After that first night we held up there for a couple more days as negotiations went on. Oakland would call and everyone would get excited. Then our Members would have a meeting after the call, and then after a couple hours of discussion they would call Oakland back. Us Prospects didn't really know why or what this beef was really all about, but I thought I had a good idea. The party and guard duty for us continued on. Chief loved it, besides having some chicks that seemed to move in to do his bidding. He was acting like some kind of General and enjoying every minute of it. He would come out to inspect his troops every once in a while. Everybody else was growing tired of the whole thing. I know that some of the Members were starting to be disgruntled, complaining about missing their broads, and all the moneys they were missing. I know that I was out of money, because I couldn't make any calls to keep my shit going. This whole thing was becoming bad for business. I know that I was getting on edge thinking too hard about a car load of Angels rolling up and having to start shooting at them. This whole thing stunk and I was hoping it would end soon. I think a lot of the Members were feeling the same way. Finally Chief announced, "The war is declared over." It had lasted a total of about four days, without a drop of blood being spilled, except the big man's and mine. I know for sure that Pete the Reb was in the middle of the whole thing somehow. I think that anyone might be able to do the math on that one. Oakland was the number one badass Hell's Angels

Chapter in California, as they had been running the show as the Chapter with supreme power. Even with Sonny locked up, they still held the reins of power within the Club.

The Nomads were right in there, in second place as the growing Crankster Chapter of crime. If Chief had his way, he would take the Nomads right to the top of the pile if he could. This incident only increased the Nomads rep at the time. I hate to think what could have happened if it had come to a shootout. You would have had a bloody mess on both sides, because neither would have chickened out. I don't know what Oakland had, but we had enough firepower for a bloody massacre. I have wondered often what affect that would have had in changing the future then, or the present modern day world of the Hell's Angels; that one could only be speculated on. But I am sure that it would have been devastating, with the effects lasting forever. I am glad it didn't happen, for all concerned, and damn sure for me. In those times, the drug trade was becoming what seemed to be the route of all evil for the Clubs. There was big money involved and at stake, and the power that comes along with it.

Attracting some unwanted Membership that would just be in it for the money and crime would eventually hurt the Club's image. The bulk of the Membership in the Club as a whole was not involved in drug dealing. But in certain Chapters, this was the way some of the Members had started making their fortunes. The Membership was beginning to be set up in a pecking order consisting of importance measured by the wealth from their drug manufacturing and sales. A Hell's Angel's free, careless partying lifestyle almost demands that he make his living without working. It is different from the origins of the original Club, where they were broke and poor most of the time. Everything was changing with the times. With the endless pressure of the law and the bogus charges, such as the Rico act, and continued pressure from the law, being a Member was now a full time job, with access to making enough money to support the bondsmen, lawyers, and courts, if you played the game. The war had started me thinking about what this Brotherhood was really all about and where it and I were going.

AWOL

"Three can keep a secret if two are dead." This is an old biker saying that unfortunately, some Bikers truly believe in. You can't dismiss the logic in it, but you don't want to believe that someone would actually do it. To kill to stay out of jail or trouble has probably been going on since the beginning of time. There is that kind of evil in this world absolutely, I have felt it and seen it. Sometimes you can see or know too much for your own good. Some things you just have to take to the grave with you in order to survive. Why did I leave the HAMC, my childhood dream? Obviously from reading this book, it was the life that I had chosen and thought was my destiny. I wanted to be a Hell's Angel since the first time I saw them as a kid. So how come after all that I went through to be one, did I decide to split, just as I was about to get my full Patch? That is a complicated question for me, and to try and understand why I left, I will have to tell you what I can that led up to my decision. Few men get to be where I was, because it almost took a lifetime of commitment back then, as the Angels were very selective on who they would let fly their beloved Death head, as it should always be.

Back in 1972, no cops had really ever penetrated the Hell's Angels organization. I stated in a previous Chapter on how and why the Angels were so successful at keeping their organization from being infiltrated. But what they did have was a few chicken shit members that rolled on them when they got busted on some serious beef with the law, and were looking at long prison sentences. The original Members would never have dreamed of doing that, so all went well for a long time. But with the drug movement and the abuse of drugs, and fast money that could be made by selling them, some Members would finally change all that forever. George Wethern, who joined the HAMC in almost the beginning, would become the first Angel I had heard of that rolled on his Brothers. Not only did he testify against some of his Brothers and help the law put them behind bars, he also came out with a poorly written book, *Wayward Angels*, exposing a lot of unknown secrets about his Brothers and the HAMC that no one really knew of at that time. Drug abuse to the point of insanity, and selling drugs, would be the contributing factors leading to his demise, as well as others.

George had bought a ranch in California with his drug money, which the law would end up finding three murder victims buried on. Whenever I heard Angels talk about him years after that, it was, "That snitch needs to die, someday we'll get him!" "His time is coming," and, "He needs to go away." In the world of the Angels, when they say, "He ain't around no more," that means just what it sounds like, he's dead. During my time and after I had left the Angels in '74 (no, not a seventy-four cubic inch Harley), the meth market was big business and still growing with what seemed to be endless boundaries. That's when they would get infiltrated by an enemy, but not by cops, but by something worse, cranksters, who would turn out to be just as bad or worse for the HAMC. These members would join the Club for all the wrong reasons, and when cornered by the law, they would snitch their own mother's ass off to stay out of jail. They used the Club for their connections, power and protection. Who is brave enough to snitch on an Angel? Only a few phony Angels that somehow had impersonated themselves into Membership. "If you can't do the time, then don't do the crime," is an old 1% saying. But in fact, it has been a law since the beginning that no one snitches on a Member, no matter what. Another rule is that if you were ever a cop, probation officer, guard, or anything to do with law enforcement, you can't become a Member in the HAMC. Military police, security guard at Macy's, applied to be a meter reader cop and didn't get the job, you can't join the Club. I always believed that is the way it should be, as it just makes sense. Another 1% saying was, "Once a snitch, always a snitch," and they meant it. You only get one chance in their world and that's it! I had been in and out of jail a lot during my young ass life then, doing over two years locked up, and was always prepared to go to prison for my lifestyle and crimes. Which I just knew that some day I would, because of the crimes I committed and the reckless lifestyle I was living. Besides, my Mom always told me that I wouldn't live to see 21, which I really did believe, because my Mom never lied. Death or incarceration being the price, you must be prepared to pay if you live a criminal life in the fast lane, with such a notorious group of badass men.

I believed then and now that it should be a death sentence if a Member snitches on his Club. This snitch is trying to put my Bros and me in jail and take down our world, so he's got to go. I was totally consumed and programmed to believe in that world, with its often harsh rules of survival. Up until a month before I split, I had spent my entire knowing life, and all my energy to get into that Brotherhood. I would have killed to protect it if needed, without any hesitation.

So what would change all that for me? I loved motorcycles and the unrestricted freedom to party and ride with others that were just like me; it had always been my thing. Brotherhood is what it has all been about for me, and always will be. Without the Brotherhood, flying Colors doesn't matter to me, and to some it does. The daring, adrenaline flowing lifestyle was what I wanted, to party and be respected in my world with my own kind, to belong to the ultimate biker world of men and Brotherhood. I enjoyed making a free living so that I could live unimpeded in my lifestyle. A careless and wasteful short life it would be, but I didn't care. I was in it for the rush and the glory of being part of "the life," and the only place I felt I could find total freedom was with my Bros.

As with a lot of the Outlaws of the past, I could not just live some mundane existence as we were suppose to. As Jimi Hendrix put it, "Let me live my life the way I want to, fall mountain, just don't fall on me!" I believe in a man's right to have and pursue the total freedom to live the way he wants, and to this day I still do. The world is closing in on those of us who believe in our own laws and destinies. They are closing in on Outlaw Motorcycle Clubs in general, for the good of all. The Great Society is going to save us from ourselves once again, whether we like it or not. The laws generated by our society are doing their best to stop anyone from living free. Laws that I feel unjustly trap an individual, laws that will put him in a cage that society has built and has waiting for him. They would rather pay to have you locked away for the good of all, as to better their ideas of a perfect society. No, they can't let Outlaw individuals live on the street to inspire any more kind of individualism. No, the great society must protect us from others and ourselves with our radical thinking and ways. Janis Joplin sang, "Freedom is just another word, for nothing left to lose!" Jesse James and John Dillinger would not be subdued by society, and they had to die for their sins. This has been the way for Outlaws throughout history. It has taken society a lot of time and money to stop Outlaws, which are just that by definition, men living Outside of the law. To me, living the Outlaw's life is where I found the freedoms I sought. Why does America have such an infatuation with its Outlaws? Simple, we are what they are too scared to be. They can only dream of what living an Outlaw's life would be like. They want to know every detail of an Outlaws life, so they can read and imagine what it is like. Citizen's curiosity and the need to know drives them to somewhat idolize the Outlaws from both the present and the past. That's the only reason why a book like this might sell, is the need of the straight people of society to try and imagine or understand what its like to live such a lifestyle that they fear. That is why America loves their Outlaws, and holds on dearly to their memories. That's why the *Easyriders* movie of '69 caught Joe Public's interest and imagination. For me that movie fit what I had already dreamed of doing for years, and only reinforced the idea to me.

What changed my life in the California Bike Club scene after fighting my way almost to the top, which I had lived and fought for to be my destiny? It would be a series of events that forever changed my world. I couldn't help it, but I had begun to have a conscious and started contemplating the results of my actions. First, I not only had gone against the Club a few times, but had also felt remorse for some of the Member's and my own actions that I was involved in. Why I started feeling these things, I would even surprise myself. I had let that turnout chick escape at the U.S.A. Run by turning a blind eye on our orders. After that incident, I ashamed myself by letting the girl I was living with get turned out by three Members against her will, and did nothing to stop it. Then I had let that rich girl that could have been the best meal ticket I would ever find go because I didn't want to hurt her and put her through my lifestyle of drugs and crime. How many lives had I poisoned by using women and drugs to support myself before that? Then I would throw these women away when they were all used up. I had felt pity for a Hang Around's senseless brutal beating, for the crime of being there, and was shamed of my physical participation.

Being a One Percenter always seemed to be so natural for me, until some of my actions and the destruction of lives started to bother me. This would be the first time I would start having a conscious in a career that would span 28 years, in which I would sell drugs and use meth and women to support my life. But turning weak willed people onto meth and getting them strung out to take all their money and valued possessions, for the first time, had started to bother me. The good side of my soul seemed to be struggling with the evil side, which had taken over since I was a kid and seemed all too natural for me. I do not know to this day what had started the good side to come out and change me. As I neared getting my full Patch in the Hell's Angels that I had always dreamed of, I questioned myself as to whether or not it was really what I wanted. I had lost the heartless cruelty, but more important than anything else, I felt that I had lost the most important thing, Brotherhood. After almost "going to war" with our own Club Brothers from the Oakland Chapter, things were beginning to unravel in the Nomads. Greed, drugs and power were taking over the Brotherhood. Drugs and money became more important to the Membership than anything, including Brotherhood. My one regret to this day was not going for the Sacramento Chapter instead of the then famously crazed Nomad Chapter of the Hell's Angels.

As I neared getting my Full Patch, I would be mud tested to prove myself to the Brotherhood. It started when I was still a Red & White Hang Around and I was up in my old stomping grounds partying. I was out hustling some drugs and trying to invite some chicks over to a party for Teddy Bear that we were having over at Sidecar Larry's, in Coloma. We had planned to party for a couple days there, because Larry, Teddy, and Tran had been busted on a machine gun rap together. Disguised as a party, the three of them needed to talk about the bust and planning their defense for the lawyers. I bumped into this Mexican chick that I used to party with in traffic. She pulled me over and we talked a bit and she said she really would like to go to the party. She had her little girl with her in the front seat. So the plan was that she was going to meet me there, as I had explained where it was and that I was going to haul ass because I was running late. I took off and had hit the real curvy part of the road to Coloma, and saw her in my mirror following me and right on my ass in her little Volkswagen bug. She was doing damn good at keeping up with a Harley through those tight curves. I came into this one curve that was almost too much, even for my bike, as I dragged my front foot peg and barley made the corner myself.

I looked in my mirror and saw the Volkswagen flipping in the air. I watched as it started to slide on its side down the road. I stopped and jumped off my bike and ran up to the car, as it had finally stopped. I forced open the bent up door and helped her get out and then her daughter, as both were bloody and screaming. I finally got them to calm down, and then I wrapped up her daughter's bleeding wounds with my dew rags (handkerchiefs). I jumped onto my bike to haul ass to get to a phone to call 911 for help. I'll never forget as I looked back as I pulled out and she was sitting there with her little girl in her arms, both crying and bleeding. I have always felt bad about the whole thing, but I didn't know she was so stupid to try and keep up with a bike on that curvy road. I felt bad that I didn't pay attention enough in my mirror and notice that she was trying to stay up with me sooner. I could have slowed down, and wish I had. Being the shit I was then, I was too scared to go back to the accident scene after I had called 911, because I was holding dope and was afraid I would get busted. The little girl survived but was scared pretty bad for life, and I heard that they had to wait until she reached a certain age before they could do any plastic surgery. The girl's Father was an older, local drug dealer that I had done business with in earlier days. He put out the word on the street that he was going to kill me for what happened.

This all went on for over a couple of years as I had moved to Vallejo and had gotten my Prospect Rocker. Finally, some of my Red & White Brothers had heard about it. Jungle Jim and Kanuck, both Members of the Nomads, had patched in from the Sons of Hawaii MC. Jungle was a stone cold, crazed Club Member who was too loose even for the Hell's Angels. Eventually the Club had to do something about him. Both were experienced, hard core, old school, bad motherfucker types that you would hope that you were on their good side. Jungle was also known for his unique paint job on his bike, which I thought matched his personality. His rigid frame Panhead chopper was painted orange on one side and black on another. When you looked at it, there was a centerline that had been drawn right down the middle of the bike, from the front fender to the rear fender. It was trippy, because from the one side it was bright competition orange, beautiful paint, and the other a glossy black.

To me it was the same as Jungle's personality. The orange side of his bike was his bright side of a crazy, fun loving, prankster, and partying type personality. The black side of his bike was his dark, evil, cruel Member that he was most of the time. Jungle Jim was one complicated dude that as I said, our Chapter, and eventually the Club, would have to deal with. Kanuck, on the other hand, was almost the opposite, the solid and cool Vice President type that had his shit together. They looked like blood brothers, but were both just about opposites, except their beliefs and loyalty to the Hell's Angels. I had learned to respect Kanuck a lot, as he was a smart man and Angel all the way. So they heard about this guy threatening my life, as he had been shooting his mouth off to some biker that they knew. When they questioned me about it, I told them not to worry about it, as the incident had happened long ago. That's when they schooled me up that it wasn't my problem anymore, it was the Hell's Angels problem.

"Nobody threatens the Hell's Angels without paying for it, and you better learn that right now! This fucking guy is gonna' pay for shooting his fucking mouth off and threatening the Angels. Get your shit packed as you, me and Jungle are going to find him and take care of this mouthy motherfucker and shut him up for fucking good. Besides, we also got some money we're gonna' collect in Sonoma County," Kanuck said. I'll admit that I feared how far Jungle would take this whole thing right away, because he was fucking crazed on meth in those days.

We packed up our saddlebags and rode up there in a couple of hours.

They told me to go find us a home base that we could operate out of while we found this guy. Then they went into a coffee shop and waited for me, and I knew this was another mud check, as they wanted to see how good of a hustler I was. I knew the best home base would probably be Poncho's house, as being my old Club Brother and mentor that I had lived with before. Poncho and I were always tight and back then he was my Brother to the bone that I could trust with my life, and whom could handle anything. Not only had he helped me with my first Harley, but he had taught me the fine art of surviving in the crankster world. Right or wrong, we had the bond of Brotherhood.

He happened to be gone when I got there, but I knew where the key was. I rode back and picked up the boys and led them over to Poncho's, who still wasn't there, so I let them all in anyway. I was sure he wouldn't mind, which would turn into being a big mistake. Being the Prospect and my hometown, they sent me immediately after women and booze. They had brought crank, weed, and Reds, which always started a party in El Dorado County. They also told me that when I was on the street finding them some women, to find the drug dealer that had threatened me. I had no problem finding anything in my town, as this was my old stomping ground. Especially the women, as the county was filled with old, addicted Red whores. I sent a carload of them out as soon as I hit town. I also found out where the dude we were looking for lived. I figured with the broads and the booze, they would forget all about it.

The guy was my enemy for sure, and I liked the idea of getting him off my back. But I also was worried that maybe they might go too far, and I didn't feel he deserved that. This wasn't a game anymore, because nobody disrespects Hell's Angels and gets away with it. I really didn't want to see the confrontation happen, but on the other hand, I would lose an enemy. I decided to wait and see if I could kind of blow it off, and just send a message to the guy through these girls or something. I went and got the booze and started heading back, with two cases strapped to my chicken bar, and another case straddled between my legs. On my way, another couple of chicks pulled me over, as they had heard that there were Reds around, and they wanted some. So I loaded the booze in their car and told them to follow me to Poncho's house. When we got there, I told the girls these men were Hell's Angels, and if they didn't want to deal with that, they should leave right now. Like the other Red whores that were already there, they said they didn't give a shit and that they would fuck them all for some good Reds. I said okay, and had the girls haul the beer in with us. As we entered Poncho's I could see that the party was well on its way. When we came through the door, everybody was naked, except for the R&W Patches being worn. Jungle was nailing one, and Kanuck had two going for himself in Poncho's bedroom. I handed the other three chicks some Reds, and then gave a couple of the girls that had been there a snort of meth, as they looked like they were going to pass out. We partied into the night, with everybody drinking, eating Reds, snorting meth and smoking weed. Everything went fine, until Jungle came out of Poncho's bedroom with his old Gladiator patch in his hand. He yelled at Kanuck and said, "Look what I found, this will look good on the Clubhouse wall, or in my cut!" Old School Clubs would sometimes sew confiscated Club's Colors inside their own cutoffs, sort of a prize or coup of bravery. Jungle then threw the cut to Kanuck, and I stepped between them and grabbed Poncho's Colors, and yelled, "Hey, that's my Brother's cut!" Boom, Kanuck hit me so fast I never even saw it coming. I hit the floor and bounced right back up. I remember thinking how I always thought, that he would have hit harder.

He threw another punch at me again that I blocked, but I got punched with his other hand almost at the same time. I only fell backwards on that hit, as it was thrown off set, and his boxer training showed. The girls had scattered out of our way, as they were mostly naked and screaming and freaking out. "We are your Fucking Brothers, and no one else! You better learn that right now Prospect, and learn it fast! You have no other Brothers or friends, you just have Hell's Angels, and we are your only fucking family until you're dead!" Kanuck yelled. Jungle Jim popped up behind me and hit me with a chicken shit blow in the back of my head, which knocked me down to the floor again. It really didn't hurt and I stood right back up again. Then Jungle yelled, "Don't forget it, Prospect"! I wouldn't, as when you join the Hell's Angel's, they are your family and your only family forever. I knew this was a lesson that they were going to teach me, one way or another. I was receiving some of my final lessons before getting my full Patch. I started realizing that this whole trip was about this and had been planned, and that was all right by me, but it wasn't over yet. I looked Kanuck in the eye and said that I was going back out with the bikes for my security shift. "Yeah, you better watch them all night, Prospect!" Kanuck yelled.

When their all night orgy ended the next morning, I got rid of the women and came back inside. They were milling around and laughing and both turned and looked straight into my eyes. "Did you find out where this loud mouth asshole lives?" Kanuck asked. "Yeah," I told them, "He's not around." "Well, where the fuck is he?" Jungle asked. "I was told he was in jail," I lied. All the previous night while on duty, I had contemplated what to do and had decided that I would try this white lie and save the loudmouth's ass. But I would be lying to two Club Members, and that bothered me. "Ah fuck, we will have to come back here to get him. Find out when he's getting out so we can come back and take care of this asshole for good," Jungle said. As I suspected, they were going to take this further than I wanted, which would make me an accomplice to "making your bones," as the mafia would say. Of course the guy wasn't in jail, as I just didn't want to get involved in this. The guy was being stupid by telling people he was going to kill me, but I am sure he wasn't that serious, he was just being protective of his daughter. A loudmouth drug dealer yes, a loudmouth asshole yes, he needed a good ass whopping, yes, but did he deserve to possible die, no. But the Hell's Angels were serious, they were dead serious, this is how they stayed alive by their code. "Well, lets get our shit rolling, we got some more business over in Sonora," Kanuck said. That's when I noticed a lot of shit was missing off of Poncho's wall.

He had a large collection of real Nazi memorabilia. That included knives, daggers, medals and shit, all authentic and worth some bucks. He was very proud of his collection and cherished and valued it. I asked, "What happened to all of Poncho's shit?" "Were taking it for expenses, he's not in the Club, so he's a nobody," Kanuck said. They had taken down most of his collection, and all the good shit was laying on the counter in the kitchen. Poncho's Gladiator Patch was there too, which was lying beside the pile of memorabilia. I thought this wasn't right, I should have never brought them over there, and they were purposely making a point of disrespecting Poncho for my benefit. They were burning the bridges of my past with another Club and my former Brothers, making a point to me and my old Brothers of where my loyalties now lay. My jaw still hurt a little from my earlier lesson. I knew there wasn't anything I could really do. If I tried to take the stolen shit back, I would just get my ass kicked. I knew that the old Colors meant the most, so I played my only cards. "Yeah, that's some cool expensive shit, and we'll get some good bucks for that. I always wanted that Nazi Mother's medal award... I thought it would look good on my cut."

They seemed surprised that I was joining in on their scam, as if I was passing the test where the wrong answer would have meant another thumping, like before. I made it appear that I had learned my lesson and I was with them no matter what they did, as I had blindly been before. They both were looking at the Mother's medal because of my interest. "Yeah, they gave that to Mothers of the German Reich that had lost more than one son in the war." They were really eyeballing it and were going through their booty. I grabbed The Gladiators cut and turned and walked back to Poncho's bedroom and put his Colors back under his bed, where they were. I knew I was taking a chance on getting another ass whooping, but I had always fought for those Colors and was willing to do it again to save them. The fact was that Poncho was a true Brother and had saved my ass many times, and I just couldn't let him down. Even though Poncho was a criminal and probably stole the shit, he wouldn't have went to their house and pulled this kind of shit. I missed the true Brotherhood and respect that I had been a part of in The Gladiators. The Nomads at that time were more like a pack of wolves, they would fight in a pack for sure, but everyone of them were out there for themselves, for that bigger piece of meat. This incident happened just before I left the Club for good, as they had really lost some of my respect.

The next big incident happened that had turned me off on the Nomad's Brotherhood, and helped seal my fate. One old time key Member of the Chapter had gotten busted on two major busts, gun violations and drug dealing. He was out on bail as he went to court facing these charges that went on for over a year. The law had finally cornered him and not even the top criminal lawyers of the time could figure a way out of these charges and because of previous convictions, he was going to probably spend the rest of his life in prison. Some of his co-conspirators were getting paranoid and feared that he would snitch them off for a reduced sentence, or worse, the witness protection program. This was far from the truth, but in their drugged out state, they began to believe it. Paranoia and fear of Brothers snitching and prison was being taken to the extreme. Once in their minds, it all seemed to be a reality in their drug induced state. Once you suspect, or someone even suggests to you, that someone's a snitch, paranoia makes it seem real. So as his final court day approached, so did the trust of a few of the crankster Members of the Chapter's leaders and cohorts. As his court date neared, all of a sudden nobody saw him around. I rode my bike over to his house and his old lady said she hadn't seen him since the day before, as he had left saying that he had to meet someone and take care of some Club business. I rode over to the bar and asked around and nobody had seen him. Then two Chapter Members were saying that the word was that he had gone on the run!

The story was that he left the country for good to stay out of prison and that sounded good to me. He had confided to me about running before, and that he thought it might be his only option and he would do it if he had to, because he wasn't going back to the joint for life. I was actually happy for him, just as everybody else, because we wanted to see him free, even if it was in a non-extradition country a long ways away. He was very much admired and loved by most, having been a long time Member. But he also had made a few enemies, as he was President of the Chapter for a long time and been dealing drugs. I wanted to believe he ran so badly, but there was a flaw in it. Yes, I believe he would have tried to run, who wouldn't? But I also knew the man well enough that I knew he wouldn't leave his old lady and kid behind for good; he had told me that. When I asked about that, I was told that he would have them joined up with them later, after he had gotten settled in somewhere and had let the shit cool off. The cops and the bail bondsmen were hot on his ass. I know that I was supposed to shut up and follow orders, but this whole situation upset me a lot and still does. I went and visited his mom and his old lady and kid again. They all knew nothing and couldn't understand his leaving without their knowledge either, but they were waiting for him to contact them.

Nobody has seen him anywhere since then that I know of. This whole situation had upset me then, and still does. I feared the worst, and could feel the tension between the different Members in the Chapter. It was almost like sides were being drawn in an inner Chapter struggle of power, money, loyalty, and leadership. I was confused by the fact that we had almost had a shooting war with our own kind from a different Chapter, and now it seemed like there was a deadly struggle going on in our own Chapter. Chief and some of his henchman seemed like they were right in the middle of it. My love for the missing Member seemed to be endangering me, also. Chief confronted me on why I went to the Mother's house, looking for information. "I told you, he split out of the country, and that's that, so stay the fuck out of it, because he ain't around no more," Chief angrily told me. Why was he mad about me doing the natural thing of finding or checking on my Bro's safety and whereabouts? I knew he would do the same for me out of our loyalty for each other.

Then all of a sudden, after a short time, Chuck moved in with his old lady, to help her out. Somehow, this whole thing didn't seem like Brotherhood to me anymore, something was real wrong; this was just unacceptable to me. I couldn't get it out of my head, what if what I suspected was true. My dream and expectations of the Club had diminished, as I thought about where the honor and trust had gone? Was this what you got when you devoted your life and soul to this Brotherhood, and was this the fate that lay in store for me, and then, should I wait around to see if I was right?

Later that week, after Chief's warning to me to stay out of it, I was told to get over to Luck's house, A.S.A.P.! As I rode my bike over there, you can only guess what was on my mind, as this was driving me nuts. I threw down my kickstand as Chief immediately walked up and told me to leave my bike there and get into Hangtown's cage. "We need to go over to San Rafael to see Big Red, to pay your sponsor a visit and take care of some business." Chief then handed me his bag of speed and told me to take a whiff. Chief and Brett looked like they had been tweaking for about a week. What was strange to me though, was that Hangtown was going to drive, which normally the Prospect does. But stranger yet was that I was told to sit up in the front seat with Chief sitting directly behind me, with Brett next to him, putting both in the back seat of the cage. Chief told me to find some music on the radio, which surprised me again, as he usually just wanted to talk and talk. I had never seen him listen to music, he just liked crank and talking shit. The route took us through some marshy, unpopulated land on both sides of the highway. This area also had been known to have dead bikers turn up once in a while in the past, being found rotting away in the swamp-like environment; this I knew as a fact.

As we were driving through that area, my mind was convincing me that maybe I was being taken for a one-way ride. Like I said, once you're suspicious or paranoid, your mind just creeps and imagines things. I had my reasons why I thought this was all wrong, that I wouldn't ever talk to anyone about. I was waiting for what seemed like hours for that bullet in the back of my head. I told myself that I had no one to blame but myself for being in this position. As I waited, it was like déjà vu, as I could see it all happening in my mind like it had already happened. Then I tried to convince myself that I was just paranoid and tried to relax. Then my mind would wander again as I waited for the bullet, when all of a sudden, a gun goes of behind me, bang, bang, bang. I jumped in my seat and spun around to see Chief grinning at me, with his pistol hanging out his side window. "Damn thing keeps jamming," he said at me, with a shit eating grin. "The fucking thing is supposed to fire the whole clip at once after Jim Jim worked on it for me. I thought that fucker knew what he was doing. It's supposed to fire one round at a time on the fire selection and the whole clip on safety," Chief explained to us. I turned back around and bang, another round went off.

My heart and blood pressure were just pounding in my body and I could feel each rapid beat. Bang, another round went out the window. I turned around again in my seat to see Chief and Brett grinning at me. I turned back around and looked at Hangtown, who was driving, and the only person in the car that I trusted. He just looked at me with a concerned look on his face. Bang, another shot fired, and I jumped again in my seat as I heard Chief giggle. I contemplated pulling my piece out and trying to take them both with me to hell! I put my hand on the butt of my pistol in my belt and stared at Hangtown, who just stared back. I could not decide what to do. My hand was on the trigger of my piece by then, when I heard the next shot and in that split second, I would cock the hammer back, and was going to pull my gun as I turned around to go to work! I kept thinking that I am not going out like this, like a punk, without firing a shot. That next second I hesitated, as I saw in my head turning and shooting Chief first with two shots, and then Brett. I thought, I can't panic and shoot all seven rounds, as I needed to save at least one to confront Hangtown. I started to move and briefly hesitated, thinking that I just couldn't shoot Bill, I didn't have it in me.

That thought had stopped me for probably another two seconds of hesitation. Then Chief reached over the seat and I felt him grab my shoulder and say, "You have to loosen up and hang in there!" Those seconds of hesitation over Hangtown probably saved all our lives! After he said that, those next minutes seemed like hours in a lifetime; that was definitely the longest drive I have ever been on, with my heart pounding in my chest and my mind reeling on my fate. It was a living daytime nightmare. We finally got over to Big Red's house and Chief did his drug deal with him. I got out of the car with my legs almost buckling, as I gladly, for once, took up my security position outside, thus ending the longest, shittiest, nerve wracking drive in a cage in my life. I felt lucky to be alive and knew that Chief was making a serious point to me, and believe me, I got the message. I had asked Bill if I could drive back to Vallejo, thinking that they can't shoot the driver too easily, when he just looked at me and grinned. It was a long trip back to Vallejo that day sitting in the front of Hangtown's ride, but I relaxed as I convinced myself that if I was going to get capped, I knew it would already have happened!

By that time I had paid back the Club for my lawyer and bail money from my last bust again, so I was square financially with the Chapter. But, I had pulled a bad crank deal back home to get the last of that money, and that's when things turned real bad for me. I luckily heard there was a warrant going out for my arrest back in my hometown. My old girlfriend had heard accidently through a cop's wife about it. I had broken the cardinal rule of dope dealing. I had sold a quantity of meth to a stranger on someone else's word, whom I hadn't checked out enough. The charges would be at possession, and possession for sales of dangerous drugs, at least. Of course, with me being an R&W Prospect, they would attach another couple charges; this was called "growing branches on the tree." It was an old jailhouse expression, portraying how the law trumps up a bust with all the felonies they could, so that if you plea bargained out, you would end up with at least one felony for what you really did. With my previous drug busts as a juvenile, and my busts as an adult, I would get some long time. Of course, the Club would bail me out and I would automatically get a Club retained lawyer, the most expensive kind. So I would go back into debt with the Club. What really bothered me though were current events in the Chapter, Members disappearing, and tensions mounting between different fractions of the Chapter's Membership, and my warning car ride. Also, what about Kanuck and Jungle Jim's trip to find the guy that was saying he was going to kill me, what would be the outcome of that?

With the missing Member that I had idolized mysteriously gone because he was facing for sure a life sentence, the cards all seemed to be stacking up against me. I was torn between loyalty and my life's ambitions, and my own self-preservation. I knew that if I stayed I was definitely going to prison, which I had always expected, but that didn't seem as bad as a bullet in the back of the head. Up to that point, I never feared dying, I expected it. I figured a bar fight, doing a burglary, stealing someone's bike, a shootout with the Outlaws, wrecking my motorcycle, but not executed by the hands of my own kind, like some punk rat. The thought of that bothered me a lot, as I could see I was also getting as paranoid as the Membership was. It seemed like a real waste of my life and my efforts and loyalties. I felt let down by the Nomad's Brotherhood, almost betrayed, so should I go to jail or take a bullet? As soon as I bailed out, I again would be trapped in debt to the Chapter, but also, what about what I knew? Would the same out of control Members trust my loyalties, or assume that I would take the easy way out and snitch? Now remember, "Three can keep a secret, if two are dead." I was close to getting my Patch, as I had put my time in and would be voted in soon. But what about now? Since I would be arrested, would I be trusted? I knew too much probably for my own good. Would the same crazed thinking be my demise? Would all my Chapter Members trust me not to snitch, that was the question. Or was I simply having drug inspired paranoia from my own drug abuse?

I could see that car ride happening all over again in my head, but this time it would be blackness and an eternity in a lonely, dark swamp with no end. Honestly, at my young age, I would have rather run until the law caught me than go to prison! The only person I could really talk to about this had maybe already met his fate. Then there was Chuck, who was patched by then and enjoying his well deserved prize. He had told me that he was gonna' put in for a transfer to the Sacramento Chapter and go with Lonesome's crew. "Fuck these crazed, drugged out motherfuckers, I have had enough of this gangster shit," Chuck had told me. We had quit doing as much crank at that time and had been eating better, sleeping, and weight lifting to get back into shape. So we both had cleared our heads some, and our mutual missing Brother had vanished, which had changed both of us. I trusted Chuck with my life, but I would fuck things up for him if I had asked him for help. I just couldn't put Chuck in that position, no matter what. I thought of Hangtown, but realized that he was Angel all the way and was up to his neck in the Club's business, so could I trust him with my life? No, I was caught in a no win situation, how could I get them to trust me not to snitch? I felt that those few crazed Members might decide to not take a chance. This sounds like the mafia, doesn't it?

I knew that I was running out of time and if I didn't make a decision soon, it would be made for me. The law would figure out where I was soon, or I would get stopped and they would run a check on my I.D. and I would get arrested. From that moment on, I would have no control over my fate, because once I bailed out, I would be trapped for sure. I knew I wouldn't snitch, I would do my time like a good soldier, but those few that had a lot to lose wouldn't know that for sure, would they? No, I decided, I had no choice but to run and give up my dreams, but at least I might be in control of my destiny. Once I ran, there would be no way back that I could see. If I did go on the run, how could I pull it off, was the next problem? I didn't want to put anybody in jeopardy that I didn't have to. I didn't have enough bucks to finance my escape. This bust happening right in the middle of my Chapter's inner power struggle had sealed my fate. Some of the Nomad's Members were nervous and I couldn't trust them to be sane. Even if I survived that, I would be doing at least ten years in the joint for drug sales. It seemed my only choice in this life or death situation was to go rabbit and RUN, and far!

One of the ways I could raise the money to boogie was to do one hell of a bunch of burglaries, but I didn't have the time to fence it all. Besides, that would have caused the Clubs suspicion, as they would hear about it. I could rip off a bunch of Harleys, but once again, too slow. I thought of trying to set up a major drug deal but didn't really have a big enough clientele, and once again, the Chapter would know. The only quick criminal act I could pull off for fast cash to get away quick was an armed robbery. I considered that as my last desperate move. I needed the money now, as I had all kinds of other problems, one being a fake I.D. I couldn't drive or ride without one, because the first time I got jacked up, it would all be over with my fugitive felony warrant. At this time, they had just combined the law's computers to interact between California and Nevada, sharing a warrant database. They said within the year that Colorado and New Mexico would also be combined. This would now make it hard to disappear or get a Nevada drivers license. The whole thing seemed nearly impossible to get away with, that's why I would eventually settle in Wyoming, because they were behind in the computer age. Then I finally came up with a plan, probably the only one with a chance of working. Who was the one person with the bucks that would give a fuck enough to change my fate? Maybe my Dad...?

Even though we weren't close, he might give a shit. I would have to eat a pile of crow, but my parents were my only hope, as I had no choice. I made the call not knowing what their reaction would be. After all, I was probably their biggest disappointment in their lives, but through it all, they still loved me, even for what I was. My Father opened up his heart and his wallet, to my surprise. He didn't ask about all the particulars on any of it, as long as I was leaving the Hell's Angels. He then asked me to call him back in an hour, so he could think about it and see what he could figure out. I called him back almost to the second, and they had a plan. He would set up my train tickets for three days from that night. I would head back east towards our relatives. The slow train ride across country would give us more time for planning a future, as he put it. His plan was after dropping me off, he would return home, as they hoped that they could have their house all shut down and they would leave that same day in his Cadillac for back east, too. They remembered Teddy Bear's remark all too well, and they wanted to disappear too, for a while. So it was arranged, and I almost thought of calling it off because of the risks of them getting involved, but I hung up the phone. I contemplated any different possible ways to escape, but agreed with my old man, his was the best. I did feel a lot of guilt about possibly risking my parent's safety.

I figured that once everyone knew I had gone rabbit, they would be after me. The law had a warrant sworn out by then for my arrest, and were definitely looking for me. I made my first mistake already, as Sharon was trying to listen in on my conversation with my Dad on her phone. She immediately started questioning me on who that was and what was going on? I tried to brush her off, but she was way beyond nosey, as I would find out. The next morning I went out on my same routine over to Luck's, as always. I saw Chuck and asked if he could cover for me the next day and I would probably hook up later at the bar with him, as I had some personal shit to do. I figured that would give me an excuse as to where I was, so that I could split and get a head start to make a break for the old man's. So I threw a few things in my saddlebags that next morning trying not to raise Sharon's suspicions. I was abandoning a lot of shit, but didn't really care. As I was getting ready to make the ride that would take my putt and me back to my hometown, changing the course of my life, Sharon came right up and jumped me on what was happening, and why I was loading my saddlebags? I explained that I probably wouldn't be back that night, as I had some Club business I needed to take care of. I didn't really think she would give a shit, as Ronnie, another Prospect, had been sleeping on the coach for most of the last two weeks. She was sneaking in there early in the morning and screwing him when I was asleep. She actually said, "If you're leaving, take me with you!" She had heard enough on the phone with my Dad, "Please take me with you," she pleaded.

I had no choice so I told her, "Okay, but you need to be ready and waiting early the next morning to haul ass, and you had better pack light!" She thanked me and said she would do whatever I asked, "But please, don't leave me behind!" She said that she would drop her kids off early at her folks and would be ready. I remember thinking, how could she just dump on those two kids that I had secretly grown to care about? There was no way I was going to take that good looking, two timing bitch anywhere, to abandon her kids. I had enough of all these California whores, money or not, especially one screwing another Prospect behind my back! She loaded up her kids in the old Chevy Impala that morning and said she would be right back. "We're gonna' start a new life together, I love you," Sharon said. After she left, I hurriedly finished packing my same two leather saddlebags once again, with everything I owned, and all I ever really wanted. I thought of how ironic it was that I was leaving Vallejo with almost exactly what I had came with, two saddlebags full of socks, t-shirts, and tools. As I rode out that morning, I left Sharon behind with her kids, and I watched Vallejo disappear in my rear view mirror for the last time.

I made the two hour ride to my hometown as I watched the people in their cars eyeballing my Colors, and was enjoying what I figured was my last ride with my Colors. I knew I was taking the chance of getting picked up on my warrant, but had decided to cast my fate in the wind. As soon as I hit town, I went right to the local biker/drug bar where I used to do business, for my last time to fly my Red & White Colors, in a bar that I was known at by reputation. Bikers and everyone treated me like a king that night, as I didn't even have to buy a drink. Dancing and partying, I was the center of attention with that Red & White Patch on my back. I enjoyed seeing all the local bikers and chicks that I had known, or had grown up with. I was going to miss being the local celebrity Hell's Angel Outlaw biker that I had become. But I felt that I had no choice, and that tomorrow was going to end one nightmare, and possibly begin another. When closing time came at the bar, an old high school sweetheart that wanted to take me home to play kidnapped me. I enjoyed myself for the rest of the evening with her and left the next morning early, as I knew this would be my last ride on my beloved chopper for a long time. Riding down the back highways, my mind wondered if I would ever be free to ride my old home stomping grounds again.

Once I arrived at my Dad's, we hurriedly hid my bike out in the bushes with a tarp, and as we worked, my Dad told me that we had to move fast.

He explained that they had received a weird phone call from a girl in Vallejo that insisted on talking to me. "I told her that I hadn't seen you, so she said she needed to leave you a message. They're on their way up," she exclaimed to my Father. He said that he thought he heard her talking to someone that was listening, as my Dad kept insisting that he hadn't seen me and didn't know where I was. We got my poor bike into the deep bushes where my Dad had made a platform out of some wooden pallets. We then laid her on her side and covered it with a canvas tarp, as I watched the gas run out of it. We stacked some old wood around and over it, and then covered it with a bunch of branches he had cut. It was a sad moment for me, as not only was I burying my first love, I was also burying my whole life. I already felt empty and alone and began doubting my decision already.

I finally felt safe once I was in my parent's car and mixed into traffic on the freeway, as they drove me out of California and into Nevada, where they would put me on a train headed for back east. In the bathroom of the train station, the old man finally got his wish, as he took a pair of scissors and whacked off my long, blonde hair. I believe he enjoyed that more than me quitting the Club and the California bike scene. I wanted it cut to change my appearance anyway, as I was running from the law, which had left me going A.W.O.L. from the Club, too. The plan was simple, I would meet them in Pennsylvania and we would hook up with some relatives until we could decide on a plan. It had been a long and dangerous road down the road into hell. I would come out of it with some scars. Some showed and some didn't, as they are deep in my memories, still. I felt rode hard and put away wet, and I never dreamed that this would happen to me. I believed that there was no other life for me after living in the fast lane. I was facing prison for sure, or would be dead if I got caught, and I was going to be running for my life. I felt anger toward myself for getting myself into this position and ruining my life's dream of flying the coveted Death head on my back!

I packaged up my beloved Colors, almost changing my mind, and then, with regret, mailed them back to the Nomads from the train station. I knew I was giving up my only chance to be an Angel. I owed the Club no money, we were square, but I was going to miss the old Gladiators

Brotherhood. What I would really miss of the Hell's Angels was Chuck, and some of the other Brothers, of course. That and the almost God-like feelings you get being with them and having their powerful army behind you. I would miss seeing the fear in people's eyes, and their fear-hidden curiosity of what we really were, and with no amount of money they could never be. The respect and connections I had earned in the biker world would be sorely missed. I wasn't just leaving the Club behind; no, I was leaving a way of life. I always felt that I was part of something larger than life, an individual.

My whole life's worth of connections and crime were behind me. I could get anything, drugs, guns, motorcycles, and whores. I was the man when it came to that. I was nothing more than a criminal biker who lived the easy life of preying on others weaknesses. I preyed on them for money, but sometimes in the process, I would destroy their lives. It was a lifetime of crime, and the only real way I knew of making money; it was my profession. I did it so that I could do nothing in life but party, use women, and ride my bike into hell. In my wake I had left a lot of misery behind me, with bad karma, for sure. I had ruined a lot of people's lives, but really still didn't feel a lot of regret for what I had done. I had been taught by some of the best criminals I would ever know. Between some of us, we often joked, but deep down believed that we would "Die with our boots on." For a lot of them it came true, and for myself, I would almost make that list. The life moved you so fast in that fast lane, that there was no time to contemplate remorse or regrets. So this would be the end of my ambition to be a Hell's Angel. What could I possibly do now? I would be permanently "Absent without leave."

Years after I left them, I talked to Hangtown Bill, as we were Club Brothers in two different Clubs together and I have trusted him all of my life. He was a mentor, silent most of the time, but always observing. When he talked to me I listened. I wished I had confided in him before I had left. About two years after I went rabbit, he called me when I was living in Colorado, through one of our old Gladiator Brothers. Stretch talked to me first and asked if I wanted to talk to Bill. He reassured me that Bill didn't know my phone number or location. I said sure, and he put Bill on the phone. I had been sleeping with a gun under my pillow since I had left, and still do. Living in fear all the time is not much of a life, but the one I have chosen, and it's stressful to say the least. But dead or in prison I would be if I had stayed with the Nomads that I do know. Our phone conversation meant the world to me, as I was nervous and did not know how Hangtown had taken my A.W.O.L. I asked Bill how he was doing, as I really did care, and had been worried about him. He said that he had survived and was doing great, and he told me that he had his own airplane and a lot of toys, and was doing well. He was living on a small ranch in our old stomping grounds. I knew then how much I had really cared and had worried for his life, as when I had left he was involved in the Nomad politics and with the drug dealing cranksters that were totally out of control.

I asked Hangtown, "So, how's Chief?" "He ain't around no more," he said. Bill also said, "They had gotten rid of some bad blood!" I was happy and proud that somehow Hangtown had survived the Nomad's purge, as I had prayed he would, even if it was like surviving Stalin's regime in Russia. Any organization can and will get bad people, like I have said, it happens. But they had policed up their own crew of the undesirables, as always. The Hell's Angels have to get rid of some of the evilest men on earth as they infiltrate and give them a bad name. These men con their way in, and then become evil monsters, even to the Hell's Angels standards. I feel that there are evil men and women that do not deserve to breathe our air. Child molesters and perverts are not tolerated in motorcycle clubs, especially around the HAMC. They see any of that perverted shit happening, or hear about it happening in their neighborhoods, and they take care of it. They wouldn't think of involving the cops, they would rather do it themselves. Young chicks though, that consent to attending any of their parties/orgies, are mostly accepted as alright.

Hangtown said that he missed me and he felt that I had gotten a bad deal. He said I could comeback anytime and all would be forgiven, and I should have never left in the first place. I explained to him that I was still on the run from Johnny Law on those old California warrants I had to split over. "Come visit me anyway, or at least call me collect once in a while, so I know how you're doing." I said I would, but I still couldn't find the trust in myself to take that chance. Unfortunately, that would be the last time I would speak to Hangtown Bill. Thirty years would go by before he died of prostrate cancer. Cancer can kill men that men can't kill. All who knew him would miss him dearly, and many loved him, as he was one of the great Angels of our time. He had a large funeral in our old stomping grounds that I decided to miss, for my own sanity. Some of my Club Brothers attended and filled me in on it. He would have been proud of all the bikers, Clubs, and women that showed up to pay their last respects. Bill and I had attended many funerals riding together over the years, and had discussed death on occasion. I know he never dreamed that he would go out the way he did. We had both agreed long ago that there was no other life for bikers like us, as we both knew we would die by the gun or be killed on our bikes, "with our boots on!"

THE LONG RIDE INTO HELL

To all beginnings, there must be an end, or so I am told. I wrote this book mainly about my early years of growing up in the late '60s and early '70s, of living and surviving in the fast lane with the 1% Bike Clubs of California. I felt it necessary in this last chapter to share what physically happened to me through my entire biking lifestyle, up to the present. I feel that I have lived more lives than most, with more excitement and vigor than I could have hoped for, or expected.

I was still running hard and still playing with the bad boys when I turned 50 years old, as I still felt like a bulletproof King fucking Kong. I flew like an eagle, and soared in the wind on my motorcycle, fearless of anything. I had cheated death so many times that I felt almost invincible; nothing could stop me. I had the back of a 70 year old, with 11 broken bones at that time, all due to motorcycle accidents. Nothing had stopped me from my passion, and my life of riding motorcycles as much as I could. Not my parents, the law, other drivers, mechanical failures, bad roads, Motorcycle Clubs, nor their wars. Vietnam, drugs, alcohol, money, showing off, pushing the limits of my machines, my ex-wife, raising children, accidents, absolutely nothing stopped me, until my life almost came to a deadly end at 50 years old. I had finally run out of luck, or karma caught up to me, or I had ignored (or forgotten) some of my knowledge and skills.

All my motorcycle riding life I had one fear, as I am sure all motorcyclists know, the fear of coming around a blind corner and finding a car in my lane. I've had many near misses, and had learned to always come around the corner as far over to the outside of the center lane as I could. I had picked up the bad habit of riding on the inside, with my wife or Club Brothers, as we always rode two abreast, with the leader being on the inside, next to the centerline. That day I was by myself and was riding in the middle of my lane, and I fucking knew better. It seems partly my own stupid-ass fault, because I should have been further to the outside. Many times as a Road Captain I used to warn other riders of this, especially when one breaks formation and goes single file, or while riding solo. You should always expect the worse and you might have more of a chance of survival. Motorcycling is a dangerous way of life, as I have ended up now with 29 broken bones, all from biking, so it's hard to survive even if you do everything right.

Let's start in the beginning and see some of my fuck-ups as I grew up in the Motorcycle Club world. I think you will see arrogance and impairment due to substance abuse, as these were major factors that contributed to my demise as I took my "ride into hell."

My first serious injury in a motorcycle accident happened when I was 13. As kids, we had trails and dirt roads connecting us briefly to paved roads to visit each other, go by girls' houses, and get to the schools, restaurants and stores. We would ride through people's property with no respect for their fences or signs. This was our way to be cool and ride everywhere, because we were too young for driver's licenses. One such owner had about 40 acres that we would cut through daily, as his property bordered the high school. To his credit, he had tried signs and fences, and even approached our parents regarding us hellions trespassing. We cut the fences and ignored everyone's pleas. One day the owner had enough, and he drug an eight inch, round culvert across our trail where we had cut his fence. My buddies and I had just smoked a joint and decided to head over to the high school pool to jump the fence and go for a swim. I was riding a Honda dirt bike as we came around the corner doing about 50 mph, with me unfortunately in the lead. The trail led through a dense oak tree stand. I made the curve and saw a large pipe in the trail, too late, and tried to slam on the brakes, but still hit the culvert head on. I flew through the air and landed on my head and shoulder, and rolled to a stop. I had broken my right collarbone, a compound fracture. I had to ride my bike back to my parent's house for about four miles in great pain, to get to a doctor.

I remember sitting on the gurney with the doctor examining my collarbone. I was watching my Mom's face contort, as she would always pass out when it came to blood. About a year before, I had gotten shot in the cheek in a BB gun war, and I squeezed my cheek and the BB hit the floor and rolled, then boom, my mom passed out and hit the floor. I didn't want to get whooped by my Dad's belt again for hurting my mom, so I told the Doc to tell me before he was going to set the bone back in place, because my mom might pass out.... Snap, the Doc jerked my shoulder, and to both of our surprise, that did it. My mom's eyes rolled up in the back of her head and down she went. Yeah, I got whooped for that one too, for my Mom's grief that I had caused, just like I figured.

From then on, until I was 18 years old, I did a lot of riding and unfortunately, some jail time. I rode various bikes, anything I could get my hands on, but Harley Davidson's were always my passionate choice. I had many wrecks and close calls, but mostly road rash was the worst of it. After I got my full patch as a Gladiator, I had one of my most famous of all my many wrecks. I flew my Harley trike off of a cliff and into a deep canyon. That one should have killed me for sure! After that is when I got my beloved 56 Panhead. She could really go too fast, enough to fuck up on, and I did. One of my first tricks that I mastered on it was popping wheelies, which I did often, until I had to replace the chains and sprockets a few times from the mechanical abuse.

Danny the Duck and I were drinking tequila sunrises at a downtown bar in Placerville one night. This wannabe dude says that he will buy all we can drink, and back then we could drink a lot. After drinking for hours and what seemed like 40 of those tequila sunrises, we started to leave on our bikes. That's when the dude asked me if he could go for a ride on my bike. "We don't give men rides on our bikes," I explained. Then Duck and I glanced at each other and grinned. "Can you pop wheelies with this?" the dude asked me. "Sure," I said. "Hop on the back and I'll show you," I said to the wannabe, so he did, and I was drunk enough to let him have it. I told him to lean back on the chicken bar and relax, that I was gonna' take him for the ride of his life! I still don't know why I did it; well, yeah I do, I was high and drunk. I dumped the clutch and launched my Panhead straight off the curb. My front wheel went straight up in the air and the bike just kept rolling over until it came right down on top of us. We had made it about three feet from the curb. Duck helped pull the bike off of us, and it didn't hurt the bike, but it wrenched my neck. I would forever feel the gravel effect in it. The dude was scraped up and bleeding with a big knot on his head. He kept saying, "What happened?" while Duck and I franticly got my bike started again. We got the fuck out of there as we didn't want a DUI, or be responsible for a vehicle injury. We left the dude lying there in the street, bleeding and holding his head, moaning. I never heard anything more about it, but that dude definitely got the shortest ride I ever gave.

The next broken bone came when I was riding again in Northern California. Fat Ray and I had ridden our bikes down from Colorado to visit old friends in California. Ray had been in prison for a long time. Actually, since I was a kid working in his criminal empire. We had a dream back then of riding coast to coast on our Harleys, before he went to prison. So that summer, which was nine years later, we were finally fulfilling our lifelong dream. I had left my pissed off, first wife at home to keep my drug dealing business going. We were selling pot and chocolate mescaline; the mescaline was really just good ole' LSD that I used to mix with strawberry or chocolate Nestle Quick to make pounds of it. The accident actually happened on Ray's and my second trip that summer, as we had enjoyed the first run so much. We had ridden back to get more money so we could do it again. My ex-old lady didn't appreciate *that* much, to the point of she was going to leave me if I went. But once was just not enough, when you were having a careless gypsy tour of your life. We both had been strung out multiple times on speed and Reds and were the wiser. Ray and I had tripped on LSD together many times. We both still smoked dope, but mainly we drank hard liquor at that time, to get our buzz for riding.

We were both easily drinking a quart a day each, and sometimes two, of cheap whiskey. We would ride for an hour or so and then stop to buy a couple cans of soda to mix our whiskey into, to get our fix, as we called it. Then we would smoke some weed and have another fix, then smoke cigarettes and ride on. One trip took us two weeks, just to get from Colorado to California, a 24 hour straight through normally. It took us six days in our drunken stupor to get back. We would throw our sleeping bags out in KOA campgrounds, or any level spot that we landed at. I could write a whole other book on our experiences that summer. Ray and I would kid each other that we were living the Easy Rider lifestyle, complete with selling dope to finance our wanderings. The ultimate freedom of riding the open road on our Harleys, with no time tables to keep, was a thrill. We always found something to do to entertain ourselves.

We bought a bunch of bottle rockets in Wyoming and had learned to shoot them out of our hands, and we got pretty good at it. Once, we got so drunk on whiskey in Battle Mountain, Nevada that we got into a bottle rocket war at their Main Street Park. Ray and I shot rockets at each other, up and down the main drag for an hour or so, until our alcohol buzz wore off. We wore ourselves out and ended up sleeping it off in the park, and not even one cop fucked with us.

We finally made it to Modesto, California to visit an old Bro named Danny B. He was a drug dealer we had both known and done business with from the old days. We hooked up with some chicks and decided to ride up to Oroville and visit Herby and his brother, Sidecar Larry. We partied all weekend and went to all the bars with them. We got up Sunday morning and after a couple of fixes, we decided to head back to Modesto, as the girls had to get back. We asked Herby if he knew any cool back roads we could take, as we had already started drinking and wanted to do some more. Of course he did, and so with his directions, off we went.

It was a beautiful, curvy, old county road and we were definitely taking advantage of it. As we pushed our riding skills to the limit with our morning whiskey buzz, we hauled ass around the corners jamming while accelerating hard. With Ray in the lead, we came around a long corner at about 60 mph, with no way to slow down in time for what lay ahead.

There in front of us was an old bridge, which was more like a jump ramp. When we hit it, we both immediately went airborne, launching us at probably 45 mph. As we launched through the air with Ray about two bike lengths ahead of me, I remember seeing Ray hit his rear brakes, as his brake light came on and his rear wheel stopped spinning in midair in front of me. I thought that was pretty funny and pointless; he was braking in mid-air! What it did though, was spell disaster. We were both traveling through the air, Evel Knievel style. We cleared the opposite side's ramp and landed probably five feet past the end of it. As Ray landed first and still had his foot on the fucking rear brakes, the bike began to skid to a stop, pulling slightly sideways when it touched ground. I'm in midair and gaining the distance between the two bikes. I saw Ray glance back and his eyes widen, as he realized what he was causing. Ray finally let off the brake and started to accelerate and straighten out of the skid, but it was too late for me. My front wheel just hit Ray's rear tire and fender, along with the brake light, and forced me to land with my front end and wheel turned sideways, and down the girl and I went.

I rolled once and then ground on the pavement sliding straight, following Ray's bike, as he was accelerating just enough to stay ahead of us. I finally came to a grinding stop. I remember sitting up and turning to look back at the melee. I saw the chick that was riding with me lying there with her hands out in front of her, laying flat on her stomach, and then I could see my carburetor lying out in front of her. She started to stir as she slowly sat up, holding her one hand with the other. I could see blood running down her arm from her hand that was severely cut. Ray and his old lady had stopped and ran back to help us. "Are you okay," Ray asked? I told him I thought that I broke something, because I felt like I was going to puke, and that's how I can always tell. Yeah, I puked and sure as shit, I had broken my other collarbone this time. The chick had a deep cut that went clear across the palm of her hand, which would need a lot of stitches. Ray picked up my bike and pushed it to the side of the road. Ray was feeling guilty and went and grabbed my carburetor and he broke out the tools and miraculously put it back on. We wrapped a handkerchief around the chick's hand to stop the bleeding.

I was coming off my adrenaline rush and hurting. The bone didn't pop out of the skin this time, which helped. We did the only thing we could for my pain; we pulled our bottle of whiskey out of Ray's saddlebag and took a couple shots of whiskey, straight. Ray started my bike for me and off we rode for the nearest hospital. It was about 40 miles away. With my left shoulder being broken, the only thing I had to do with it to ride was pulling in the clutch. It was extremely painful every time I had to shift gears. With the pain shooting through my shoulder constantly, it was a miserable ride. Ray had his union insurance card from working at the tunnels, and I pretended to be him to get medical treatment. I used to have one when I worked the tunnels, so it was easy to fake. They snapped my bone back in place and put me in a chicken brace. We called it that because it pulled your shoulders back, pushing your chest out. They had to stitch up the girl's hand, which we had to pay cash for. We would have made that aerial jump if Ray had not hit his brakes; that's biking though, because shit always happens.

The next major wreck came about due to substance abuse and showing off my favorite trick that some use to call "Harley surfing." I used to stand up on the seat of my bike while going down the road. The best part of the trick was letting go of the handlebars. "Look Ma, no hands," I would yell. This time, my favorite trick would end me up with a broken back and losing my beloved Panhead. I had been working on some condos up in Aspen, Colorado all the summer before and made good money. My little girl had just turned two in May, and my boy had just been born in February. He damn neared died when he caught a bug from the water at the trailer court, which was sucked out of the headwaters of the Colorado River. They also had their sewer effluent running into the river, too. It had taken all my money and savings and borrowing to save my newborn son's ass, and we had barley survived the winter layoff by selling drugs, mainly cocaine and pot.

A carpenter that I had befriended and I were dealing together, and as usual, we were making a drug run to Grand Junction, Colorado for a couple kilos of weed and to deliver some coke. Since all the construction workers, including us, were back to work after being unemployed all winter, we had money in their jeans, so we had to re-supply our drug business. It was a beautiful spring day in the Rockies, and the snow had pretty much all melted off. We decided to take our bikes to make the drug run, because up in the high country you have to ride every chance you can get, because you only get about a four month biking season in the high

Colorado Rockies. I was living between Aspen and Glenwood Springs in my travel trailer at the time. We had a beautiful ride down there, as we followed the road along the Colorado River into Grand Junction. We scored a couple pounds of weed from my buddy Frank, a rough neck oil worker who was my weed connection at that time. He would buy his cocaine from me, which would eventually ruin his family life. My buddy who rode with me had a stock bike and said that he would haul the weed in his saddlebags on his bike.

We delivered the coke and Frank gave us both a couple lines as we smoked weed and drank beers, and finally we left with a pretty good buzz on. As we turned off the freeway at Glenwood Springs towards Aspen, we were feeling no pain. We were enjoying the ride as we passed a car with a couple of chicks in it. We accelerated a bit ahead of them. Then I decided to show off with a trick for them. I jumped up onto my seat and planted my feet, while bending over and holding the handlebars straight with my hands. I'm rolling down the road at about 70 mph as I carefully let go of my bars and stood straight up. I was Harley Surfin'. But somebody had crossed the highway with a small utility trench. When I saw the bump coming up, it was too late. I quickly tried to lean back down and grab the bars. I didn't reach the bars in time, and the bump hit and it launched me right off the seat. I fell backwards and hit the pavement at 70 mph and I started rolling down the road. I believe that first impact as I hit the pavement is probably what broke my back. I started rolling and I instinctively tucked up into a ball, as down the freeway I went. What seemed like forever, over and over I rolled, until I slowed down enough that I finally just started sliding on my back, and then I finally came to a stop!

All I had on was a t-shirt and Levis, which offered limited protection. I was high, but not high enough for what was happening. I had gone into shock but really didn't realize it. I immediately jumped to my feet and looked down the highway and I could see my bike still going down the road. I had a dead man's throttle set up for doing tricks. That kind of throttle was originally set up for hand relief for holding your gas and speed steady, but it was also great for tricks. It was basically cruise control. I caught a glimpse of some cars pulling over as my bike was still going all by itself. I saw my construction buddy way ahead of it jamming down the road to get away from the scene and my rider less scooter. The two girls coming up behind me had to lock up their brakes to avoid running me over as I was rolling down the road. Luckily, that stopped any more traffic from running over me. As they pulled up next to me and opened the passenger door, I just stood there. They just looked at me in awe, and I didn't know what they were seeing or staring at.

I yelled at them to please give me a ride to get to my bike ahead of us, before it falls over! They said okay as I jumped into the back seat. By now, there were people who had stopped on both sides of the highway, watching an orange Harley with no rider on it going down the road. The dead man's throttle was slowly shutting her down. With my adrenaline flowing and the shock I was in, I really didn't feel my wounds. I glanced down the front of myself and all looked fine. As we neared my bike, there were more people out of their cars on the side of the road pointing at the rider less bike, as it had slowed down almost to a stop. All I could think was that the cops were going to bust me if I didn't grab my bike and quickly leave. When we just about caught up to it, it started to wobble from lack of throttle. I jumped out of the car running for her, just as she fell over. The old custom hummer tank took a severe dent on the side as it hit the curb. The slowing speed had killed the motor and it finally fell.

As I jerked her back up by the handlebars I felt a sharp pain in my back. People were yelling and pointing at me. I thought I heard, "Don't do it!" I figured what the fuck do they want me to do, get a DUI? I jumped down on the kicker and she amazingly sputtered back to life. I clutched her and dropped her into first gear and hauled ass, spraying gravel, as I wanted to get away from there as fast as I could. I had about ten miles to go before I'd reach my trailer in Basalt and the safety of my home. My partner who was holding all the dope was long gone, which was the smart thing to do. I hauled ass to try to stay ahead of any cops that may have been called, as the adrenaline was still rushing through me. A couple miles away from home I started feeling funny. I could feel my shirt flapping around behind me, and then I puked. I still didn't really put it all together that I was hurt, as I was just in fear of the law and jail, as always. I finally pulled up to my trailer and threw down my kickstand.

As I dismounted the bike I felt this rush of pain shoot through my back. It was making me dizzy as I stepped into the front doorway. My ex asked, "What the fuck happened to you?" That's when I am told that my eyes crossed and I fell forward just to land flat on my face on the living room floor. I woke up to my ex screaming in panic that she wanted me to get on the couch, and she would go call an ambulance on the trailer park's pay phone. She could see my back injuries threw the shredded t-shirt that ironically used to say on the back, "I don't have a drinking problem; I just get drunk and fall down, no problem." "No," I told her, "I'll be all right," as I crawled a few feet over to the coffee table where I laid flat on it on my stomach for some relief, as that was as far as I could make it. I told her to forget the ambulance and hospital, as we didn't have the money. "I can see your fucking back bone, it's not gonna' be alright this time!" my ex screamed at me. The pain from my back was becoming overwhelming.

My ex was freaking, as she said she could not only see my backbone, but it was ground down and bleeding bad. She said there wasn't much skin left on my back and it was bleeding badly, with gravel and rocks showing that were embedded into my muscles. I told her to call around and find a doctor who would make a damn house call then. She left my son in his bassinet on the couch in front of me, and grabbed our two-year-old daughter and ran out the door to the pay phone. The Doc showed up and took one look at my back and said immediately that she needed to call an ambulance, as I needed to go to the hospital now. My ex explained that we had no insurance or any money to pay for anything. He told her, "Oh well, try and make him lay here still and flat on the coffee table and keep washing and scrubbing peroxide through all his wounds to help get the gravel out and to stop infection." He strongly suggested that she at least take me down for x-rays to see if anything was broken. The bone she was seeing was one of my vertebrae that had ground down into the bone, exposing it. He held his hand out for his fee, then gave her a script for some pain pills, said good luck, and got the fuck out of there. I lay there for three weeks in extreme pain, only moving to eat soup and go crawl to the toilet on my hands and knees to go to the bathroom. After another week I had to go back to work or lose my job. I was still in great pain, but we were running out of food and the rent was past due.

I finally did what I thought nothing in this world could ever make me do. I had to sell my bike to my buddy Frank, with the condition that if he ever wanted to sell her that he would give me first option to buy her back, which five years later he did. But I didn't have the dollars at the time to buy it back, as he needed all the money fast. It broke my heart to sell her, but because of my stupidity, my kids were going hungry, and I wouldn't allow that at any cost. So that wreck cost me my favorite motorcycle that I ever owned. I worked there until summer's end and moved to Wyoming for a better permanent job for the winter, and to hopefully make enough to get another Harley going. I started dealing there and working two jobs, which took 15 hours a day to make enough for my family debts and to build another Harley. I decided to build a 74 inch Harley Davidson trike, thinking it would be easier on my back, as I was still in a lot of pain. I had purchased a brand new 1974 Shovelhead engine, still in the crate. I found an old '45 trike frame with a hydraulic juice rear end. I finally found a wrecked Shovelhead swing arm frame. So I grafted the two together, and flipped the axle over so the sprockets would line up. I had only seen one that someone had built that way. It was a real pain in the ass, having to make everything and adapt things to make them work. I finally got the bugs out of her and road it around for the rest of that summer. I wanted two wheels again and sold it to this pot dealing chick from Denver, for two pounds of Mexican bud and $4,000.

My next series of wrecks came about 15 years later after getting off parole. My back pain was constant and at one point in '84 I slipped a disk working and had to get some x-rays. That's when the doctor told me I had a back of a man twice my age. He said the arthritis and calcium buildup around where you broke your back is bad. I said I had never broken my back, so he showed me where I had on the x-rays. That was when I knew I had broken it for sure, from the accident in Colorado when I had rolled down the highway. He told me that if I didn't slow down and quit riding motorcycles that I wouldn't be walking when I retired. I tried to explain to him what motorcycling was all about, but they don't understand. After my major drug bust in '89, I started a legal business for once in my life, being I was on parole. While I was being a good boy, I saved up my money and spent about sixteen thousand legal dollars to build a custom 1976

Shovelhead. I had set her up for racing and had built an expensive suspension to help my back and to lift it higher for cornering. I was packing my new old lady and I was jamming back to our house because I had forgotten my damn money clip. We were meeting some people at a bar and now thanks to my dumbass, we were running late.

I was following this dude in a car pretty close, and jamming him a little. We both were running about 10 mph over the speed limit. All of a sudden, he throws on his brakes and tries to make a ninety degree turn into this driveway. I locked both disc brakes up, but skidded right into him. My right hand on my ape hangar handlebars hit first. The chrome wide glide front end just crumpled and buckled under as we hit. The impact threw my head through the rear window and the glass just exploded. My old lady, to her credit, had bailed off the back of the seat on impact. She helped get me off the back of the car without getting cut anymore by the glass. I pulled my fingerless glove off to look at my broken thumb. The bone was broken between the two knuckles and it was trying to poke out the skin. I pulled on it real hard and thought I had gotten it set back somewhat in place, but to this day it sticks out. I told the owner to not call an ambulance, and that we didn't really need the cops either, but he insisted on the cops.

I ended up having to fix my bike myself because the cop wouldn't site either one of us. The funny part of this story, as my wife likes to tell, is the aftershave lotion. We had been drinking before the accident and since we were waiting for the cops, I was worried about getting a DUI. So since the accident happened only about two blocks from our house, I told the old lady and everyone else I was going to go wash off the blood. I no sooner got there and inside when the cops were beating on my door. I tried to find something to kill my breath quickly, and finally in a panic I grabbed some aftershave and gargled with it twice, then swallowed some. It burned and tasted like shit! When I answered the door the cops took me back to the scene of the accident and wanted to give me a ticket for leaving the scene. While the cops and everyone were all talking and being interviewed, my old lady is cracking up, as I kept burping that shit up; she said I stunk *so* badly of it. I still think it was worth it though, because I didn't get a DUI.

The next bad, bone breaking wreck came when the old lady and I were out racing and partying on my Shovelhead. When I had to replace the wide glide front end from that fender bender, I got extended tubes to get the bike up even higher off the ground, for even better cornering. We had been jumping from bar to bar and racing on the curvy roads all day. We had stayed a little too long at one bar, as they had a good band jamming and we ran into some old friends. We all did some dancing and we were slamming some shots, just partying hearty. I'll admit that like always, when we left the bar I was wasted. From the time I left the bar, I don't think I ever left off the throttle until I was thrown from the bike. There was a series of curves on the way out of town, and as we banked them with my throttle wide open, my old lady was yelling and having as much fun as I was on that Shovelhead as the custom suspension bike banked into the corners.

I should have let off the throttle some, because we banked into this one steep curve so far that we had the bike buried into it. What happened next is called, "going over the high side," or "high centering" by bikers. The corner was too steep and the bike's rear tire lost traction when the derby cover started grinding on the road, and the bike started sliding on it instead of the rear tire. That's high centering; so away we went sliding through the oncoming lane. On the opposite side of the road, there was about a one foot high curb and then a sidewalk with a rail fence. The bike slid across the road and slammed into the curb and tried to flip over sideways. That launched my old lady and I in the air, this being the going over the high side part. We went over the sidewalk and even cleared the handrail in midair. From the other side of the hand rail the ground just dropped away for about 12 feet down. There below was someone's yard with grass, and a few trees. So my old lady sails about 15 feet past the curb and slams into this tree, which she then slid down with the branches breaking, slowing her descent to the ground.

I had gotten my leg smashed between the bike's outer primary and the curb, which broke it before it threw me like the old lady, about 15 feet through the air. The only thing that slowed me down was a realty sign that I took out with my back as I cleared the handrail. I finally hit the ground hard after flying over the rail and dropping the 12 feet to the ground. I remember shaking my head, as everything was spinning, to slow down the wheels in my head. I looked at my old lady about 15 feet away from me, in all these broken tree branches at the base of the tree. She wasn't moving, which totally freaked me out. I crawled over to her, yelling her name, but she didn't even stir. My first thought was that I killed her. I heard people yelling above me and turned and looked up at the sidewalk above, where people were pointing and yelling at us. I looked over at my old lady and that was the first time I really knew how much I loved her! I yelled at her in a panic, "Get up or were going to get a fucking DUI!" Her eyes flickered to life as she looked up at me, and I was so relieved that she wasn't dead. "Come on, we have to go Baby, now!" I grabbed her hand and we crawled on over to the wall, where people were leaning over the railing reaching down to pull us up. We stood up and this one good-sized lady grabbed my old lady's arm, and with panicked strength she unbelievably pulled her right up and over the rail and set her on the sidewalk. My old lady really doesn't weigh much anyway. Getting my ass up was another story, at 250 pounds. I grabbed some guy's hands as they tried to drag my ass up. I tried to use my legs to help scale the wall, and that's when I realized how badly I had hurt my leg. I finally get over the railing and grabbed the old lady from that broad that had lifted her. There's a crowd now of tourists gathering around us, and they all are trying to help and get us to stop and lie down and shit. I said, "No thanks, we have to go, we're okay." That's when Joe Citizen says, "Don't worry, I called 911!" I started yelling at him, "Why the fuck did you do that!" I panicked immediately, like I always do when it comes to cops showing up, as I hate going back to jail cells.

The bike had incredibly lodged up against the curb from where it had launched us. I grabbed the bars and drug my ass on, pulling my old lady on behind me. I hit the button on my first electric start Harley, and she jumped to life. I couldn't have kick started it if I had to; my electric leg proved its worth that day. I pulled in the clutch and tried to shift, but couldn't lift my left leg that high. So with the clutch in, I leaned down to shift it into gear by hand. The shifter was all smashed around the primary, so I managed to stop and get off again to bend the shifter lever free, so I could shift it with my bare hands. The adrenaline was still flowing. People were helping hold the bike up with us sitting on it, while my old lady finally got it into gear. Against the crowd's protests, and with a push from them to get us started, we took off. I needed to shift to second gear and couldn't. So I yelled at my old lady to shift for me, but she had injured her left leg on the same side. So we both had to lean forward as she reached down and shifted into second gear with her hand. After we got through the worst of the curves, we popped her into third. Then we just kept lugging the motor and trying to put some distance between us and an inevitable DUI arrest.

Miraculously, we made it down the curvy mountain road about five miles. I was starting to puke, as the adrenalin was wearing off and the shock was kicking in. I pulled off onto this little dirt turnout that at the end almost hid us from the road. I threw down the kickstand and we both hit the ground. We lay there for a few minutes, moaning and groaning. I remember telling my old lady how proud I was of her for getting back on the bike that threw her. Then we heard the sirens coming. "Oh shit, here comes 911," I said. We both pulled ourselves up, crawling up the side of the bike. Then we leaned against the bike seat, facing the oncoming fire truck, volunteer firemen, ambulance, and cops. I lit up a cigarette and handed the old lady one to try and hide the alcohol on our breath. She looked at me and said she might have to puke. I told her that I felt the same way, "But maintain!" They all rushed up to us, "Are you guys okay!" "Yeah, why?" I said, as cool as I could. "Well, you just were in a serious accident back there!" My old lady was still in a daze, but holding her own and didn't say shit. "Oh that, we just fell over and picked up the bike and left," I told the cop. So the cop says, "You can't leave the scene of an accident like that, it's against the law!" The EMT and firemen were eyeballing my old lady and me for injuries, like they wanted to grab us and check us out.

The cop took the lead, "You have illegally left the scene of an accident, and I am going to give you a ticket." I explained that I didn't know that if you fell down and there wasn't any damage and no one was hurt, that you couldn't just leave. "How was I supposed to know you were coming?" "Well, that's the law and there was a sign knocked down," the cop answered. I was starting to get my wits back; fuck, that ticket was better than a DUI, what the hell was I thinking, take the ticket and shut the fuck up. I mean, the cop felt that he had to do something, and his next step could be way worse. "You're right officer, that sign was damaged, and I deserve the ticket!" My confession worked like a charm, as he had won the confrontation with this patched Outlaw biker in front of all his peers. His back straightened as he glanced at his buddies, as if he had won something. As he wrote the ticket with all these 911 people milling around us, he kept asking my old lady if she was sure that she was alright. It was all I could do not to pass out, as the pain now was becoming overwhelming. I bit my lip. The cop handed me the ticket as he looked me in the eye and said, "You're not hurt, huh?" As best as I could I said, "No sir, we're both fine." "Well, I don't know about that. You could be in a lot more trouble here, but I think you probably have enough problems for one day." I knew exactly what he was saying, he could have given me a DUI and hauled our asses to jail, tow the bike, etc... "Thank you Officer," I managed to mumble. "Are you sure that you guys are gonna' be alright?" the fireman asked. "Yeah, we're both just fine, we're just gonna' relax here for a bit and have another smoke, but thanks for asking."

We watched them all turn around and waved goodbye at them as they headed back for town. As soon as they were out of sight, we both collapsed to the ground. I puked, and I knew my leg was broken for sure now. I did not know for sure about my lady's leg, because she couldn't put much weight on it. Now I was starting to wonder if I shouldn't have taken the help, as we were in bad shape. We finally pulled ourselves up and got on the putt, working together to shift as we rode the next 20 miles home. I've always said that a family that rides together stays together. I would pull in the clutch and she would hit the shifter. We did well at the lights and shit by slowing down and planning a way not to have to put our feet down and come to a complete stop. But at the last light before our house, the car ahead of us threw on his brakes on a yellow and we had to come to a quick stop, and fell over. The guy in the vehicle jumped out, "Do you need help? I'll call 911 on my cell phone." I thought what is it with this 911 shit? "No, please don't call Sir, as we are fine, please just help me get this damn bike up!" We got it up and to the side of the road. I waited as the guy took my old lady the six blocks or so to our house. She got her brother and he came back with the citizen dropping him off. We got the bike started and he rode me bitch back to our house. From there they got me in a car and off to the hospital we went. They put me on a gurney and up to a stall, where we waited for what seemed like hours. Finally, her Brother says, "If I were you, I'd start making some noise." So I yelled at the top of my lungs, "I need a beer!" I continued for a short time and I had all the attention in the world in about 30 seconds. The leg was broken in two places, I was in a lot of pain, but I was thankful that we were still alive and I wasn't in jail with a DUI beef!

My last big accident should have been my last, as it would almost kill me. The doctors brought me back from death multiple times, and a Catholic preacher would read me my rights of passage a couple of times. This wreck would change my life completely and leave me disabled forever. It all started as I went to work one Saturday morning. I worked a couple of hours and went outside to light up a cigar, and observed a beautiful morning in the making. I had celebrated my 50th birthday a couple months earlier, and had made one promise to myself. I was going to quit working so much and ride my motorcycle as much as I could. I felt that I was running out of time and wanted to enjoy the passion of my life more while I still felt good and was at the top of my game. So since it was a beautiful day, I decided instead of work, I was going to go riding. I went home and told my old lady of my intentions, when she informed me she had other things going on with her daughter. It was odd for her not to be going along, as she loves to ride her Harley as much as me.

I told her that I was going to do a 100 mile loop and would stop back by and see if she wanted to go on another ride when I got back. I put on my Colors, slipped a gun into my waistband, aired up the tires, checked my oil, checked my knife and off I rode. I rode fast and hard by myself, like I always do. I never get to do that much, as I usually ride in a pack with my Brothers and *always* with my old lady. I stopped by one of our favorite bars, which was about the halfway point on my loop ride. I drank one beer and chit-chat with the barmaid, who was a friend of my wife, and then I hauled ass back, proud to be flying my Colors and with my shit in the wind, with a grin on my face. I checked in at home and the old lady said she still wasn't going. I told her that I was going to make another loop. This one was on one of those real curvy bike roads that you love to race and haul ass on. I decided to leave my gun at home, thinking that I needed to get a new holster for that piece, as it was uncomfortable in my waistband. At a light I got a call from a Prospect, who said he wanted to play and that he would meet me up there at the bar, which was the probable turning around point if we decided not to go any further.

I soared with the wind and never let off the throttle until I pulled into that little remote tourist town. I threw down my kickstand and went in and ordered a beer in the famous biker bar. I talked to the bartender for a while, as business was slow with the band not starting for a couple more hours. Bikers hadn't really started riding through and stopping yet. I sipped a beer as I waited for the Prospect. I got so bored that I even cleaned out my cut. I did find about 20 pounds of shit in my cut, so now I knew why it was so heavy. I figured the hell with waiting and finished my beer. I would probably run into that Prospect on the way back. So off I went out the side door of the bar, which was when the Prospect and his old lady were walking into the front door. Funny how fate works, as a couple seconds either way would have changed everything. So I fired up my bike and off I went, banking corners and having a blast. I had forgotten the freedom of riding alone. I was really getting into the corners and enjoying the scenery. I was admiring my beautiful machine with her $4,000 paint job and she was running the best she has in her life.

I was in tune with her and the road and thinking how this was and always would be the only life for me. I thought of all the Harleys I had owned over the years and what a perfect lady I had between my legs now! We didn't know that what waited a few curves ahead would destroy both of us. Unfortunately, we came around a blind corner that fateful beautiful Saturday afternoon to meet our fate together. I had banked into a blind corner and was about three quarters through it, when I hit a Toyota Tacoma pickup head on. He had crossed the centerline into my lane, and I wouldn't find out the truth about that for almost two years. I T-boned right into his left front bumper and wheel. I don't really remember the impact or seeing the truck, I just remember banking the corner. Bang, I hit a brick wall that changed my life forever. So everything I tell you about this wreck is what I was told by the few witnesses and firemen that I talked to two years later. The police blew the accident scene, as they thought I was dead anyway. I was just another Outlaw biker lying in the middle of the highway, dying anyway.

The first vehicle to come up on the scene was an off duty EMT and her friend that also was an EMT. When they jumped out of their vehicle, what they said they found was the Toyota driver and his family screaming and freaking out. The Father, who was the driver, was out of the truck and was crying and sobbing that he was sorry for crossing into my lane, and saying it was his fault repeatedly. This is what the off duty EMTs both told me almost three years later. She said that my bike was lying in the middle of the road, stretched out, and I was about 25 feet away, in the same shape. The EMT ran up and put my head between her knees to try and hold me down. She said that I just kept trying to get up and was thrashing about. She said that I kept saying, "I guess I fucked up real bad," and that, "My old lady is gonna' be pissed." Then another biker pulled up and ran up to help hold me down, and I told him, "Please don't leave me, Bro." I lay there bleeding out, my back broken in three places, and my pelvis shattered into pieces. They call that an open book pelvis.

Since then, I've been told by just about every doctor that I have talked to that open book pelvis usually kills you. At best, you have a very low chance of survival. My left leg, from the knee up to my hip, was shattered, with that bone having multiple breaks, which pretty much destroyed the femur. The leg was ninety degrees to my side, barely being held on by muscle and skin. I had six broken ribs on my left side, with two of them puncturing my lung, and had broken two on my right side. My heart, liver, internal organs, had all been crushed in my twisted torso. You can easily imagine the cuts and contusions, with closed head injuries from the impact, as I lay there bleeding out, just as Monk had done 30 years before. No, I didn't have a helmet on, as I have never worn one, and never will if I don't have to. Both EMTs held me there as I just kept bleeding out and trying to get up. She claims the guy I hit moved his Toyota and was talking with his family, calming them down. Traffic was backed up on the two lane road in both directions.

The Prospect, after learning that he had just missed me at the bar, had

371

gone about five miles from the bar to get gas, and then retraced his steps, trying to catch up. The fire trucks and ambulances all passed him on his way to catch me. He feared the worse then and finally caught up to the scene, and did what he could. He picked up my bike and with some help, drug it off to the side of the road. His wife, being a nurse, helped to hold me down. It took 45 minutes for the law, ambulance, and fire trucks to get there. The EMT that I spoke with later, that was already on the scene, said the fireman immediately called for the flight of life, which saved my life. A year later, I would walk into the firehouse on crutches, and the fireman thought he saw a ghost, as he had assumed that I had died like most did. I was able to thank him personally.

They all had a hell of a time because of my weight, but finally got me onto a stretcher and moved me to a parking lot where they could land a helicopter. She said that they put me on the life flight chopper, and away I went to a hospital, still fighting for my life. "Everybody knew that they had done the best they could for you, but nobody thought you would make it," she said. She went on and told me that they all went back to the accident scene and the cops told everyone that wasn't in the accident to immediately leave. Both vehicles involved in the accident had been moved, so the accident scene had been compromised. Any witnesses besides the Toyota family were gone, without even making a statement.

I was in a coma for five weeks before I mentally woke up. My old lady stood by my side, restoring my faith in her gender. She is one of a kind and is the true love of my life. The doctors performed miraculous surgeries that saved me, a surprise as far as all were concerned, including the doctors that I lived. The good Lord apparently had something else left for me to do, because it was nothing short of a miracle at times that I kept breathing. I had no medical insurance and ran up over half a million dollars in medical bills. First, they tried to put my leg in traction, and with the first surgery they drove a titanium pin from my knee up to my hip, through the center of my leg bone. They had to drill the center of the bone out. Then they did another surgery where the specialist used titanium plates and bolted my pelvis back together. Later he confided in me that was the worst reconstruction he had ever tried, but he said that he "Got to use all my tools and thank you for the opportunity."

Next a back surgery specialist attempted to try and repair my broken back. During that attempted operation they lost me. I went into cardiac arrest, code blue, and then damn if they didn't bring me back. They decided to wait on the back surgery to see if I would live. To go on would have killed me for sure, and why waste the effort? They were also afraid that if they couldn't keep me from moving my back that I could paralyze myself permanently, but apparently it was the better bet to wait.

One of the biggest problems *was* they couldn't keep me still. They tried with morphine and shit, but it wouldn't slow me down. I continued to rip out my hoses and picks, trying to get up. They tied my hands and legs down with restraints. Then I got pneumonia, while I was laying there in the ICU. I was still tossing around and trying to get up and leave. With my back broken in three places and with ribs broken loose, they were afraid that I would create further damage for sure. They continued to find more ways to restrain me, as I was rubbing holes in myself, which were bleeding where the restraints held me. I kept begging everybody to untie me and let me go. I guess I offered booze, dope, and money, trying to trick someone into letting me go. When my Prospect was there, I demanded he let me go or he would never get patched. Everyone was warned of my cunning to get someone to let me go. I did talk my 90 year old Father into it, but my wife caught him. I guess I got pretty good about pulling out the tubes in me and being an obnoxious asshole.

They told my wife that they were bringing in the priest to read me my last rights again. I hung on for another 24 hours. Then they told her that I had developed a yeast infection and a staff infection, along with the pneumonia I already had. The Doc pulled her aside again to tell her that I wasn't going to make it. They brought the priest back in again, and he did the last rights thing. I'm a confirmed Lutheran, but to me it doesn't really make a difference. They figured that they were losing me. They explained all this to my old lady, but she wouldn't give up on me. The place was full of Club Brothers and their old ladies, as they kept up a vigil of sorrow as they all waited for me to pass, so she had people to keep her company, console her, and help her be strong. The staff couldn't figure out at first how one person could have so many Brothers in one family. The Bro's were all saying that they were my blood to get into the ICU to see me. My daughter came up and helped my old lady make all the necessary decisions, and help her through the ordeal. But to everyone's surprise I hung on. There must have been an angel or a Bro on my shoulder for sure. Or maybe God had one more thing left for me to do in this life before I go, probably both. I do know now that I have plenty of Bros up there looking out for me, and that's a good feeling.

The mood, I was told, was a gloomy one, with everybody waiting for them to walk out and say I was gone. I hung on despite their predictions. They finally put me in an incubator to help me breathe and all kinds of shit. So then the decision was made finally by my girls to put me into a coma, so that my body could rest, as I was still trying to get away and wouldn't relax and sleep. I had open sores that were bleeding from the bonds trying to hold me down, and I guess what came out of my mouth scared even the preacher away. Plus I had somehow gotten more infections, and it was bad. I hung on to life for some days until the doctors presented my wife and daughter with a decision. They could not do the back surgery and leave me in my now coma state for three months to let my back heal on its own, but that was a gamble and I would probable be paralyzed for life. Or they could go ahead with the back surgery and if I survived it I might be able to walk but would drag my injured leg for sure but would recover quicker. My girls decided to risk the back surgery as they knew I wouldn't want to live in a wheel chair the rest of my life. The odds weren't in my favor to survive the surgery, but they felt it was the only choice and thank God they did. Her hope was that I would survive at least with my mind, but she knew I wouldn't want be wheelchair bound. The doctors told her that with the back surgery at best I would drag my left leg for good. The bottom line though was that they saved me as I survived the surgery. You could write another book on what went on in those six weeks. My old lady and my doctors still say it's nothing short of a miracle that I am still alive. She is my hero though, as she stood by my side for six weeks, damn near living in the hospital. She went through my cardiac arrest code blue bullshit, and being told that I would die multiple times. It was a living hell for her. She wouldn't give up on me and she became my hero for life! The only memories of those six weeks of my head being spun was a faint, peaceful sensation of looking down at the earth and the feeling that I was rising into the air as I looked down. We figure it could have been the helicopter ride, or…?

The other memory was as real as I know that I am alive today. I was suddenly riding my old Panhead in my black leathers and flying my Patch, riding through these big, beautiful pine trees. I figured I must be around Lake Tahoe somewhere, but strangely, after some miles, there were no signs or any cars, which was beginning to bother me, so I just kept jamming down the road on my bike. Then there were some bikers on the side of the road up ahead, and as I got closer it seemed that they were all looking back at me. I checked my waist band and guessed I had forgotten my gun, but I had my trusty knife. They waved me over and all of a sudden, I realized that I knew all of them. They were all my old school Brothers of the past, who were dead. I started to throw down my kickstand after I pulled up to get some hugs as I asked, "What the fuck is happening?" They said, "No, not here, let's ride up to their camp, which is just up the road, and we could party there, as the cops might come by here." So I kicked my kickstand up and we all rode off. As I was trying to figure this out, I only had one explanation, I'm fucking dead! As we rode, I wondered what they meant about cops, if we were dead. We turned down a side dirt road and went a mile or so and came up to this big cave. There was a thin line of smoke coming out. We threw down our kickstands and I got excited hugs and shit. I got a real good look at their faces close up, and they were like skulls! I knew who they were, felt the love, familiar voices, leathers, Club cuts, everything, except their skin was gone. I swore that back there on the road when I had ran into them; I saw their faces and knew exactly who they were by name. I still did know them though, but their skin was all gone; how could this be? I started to ask what the hell when they knowingly said to come in, as we have a lot to talk about. So we walk into the cave and all stood around the fire, and I noticed there wasn't anything around, no gear, food, booze, sleeping bags, nothing!

I went and greeted each one of them with a hug, telling them how good to see them and finally asked what the fuck is wrong with their faces. They all laughed and smiled with their teeth and silver fillings showing saying, "It's not so bad, you'll get used to it, we're just glad your finally back with us." I'm starting to freak out now, but then for some reason, all of a sudden, I calmed down instantly. I felt at home and cool with them and with whatever was happening to me. I finally asked, "What the fuck is up Brothers, am I dead?" They just said, "You are here with us now." I couldn't believe the words that came out of my mouth next, "No, I got to go ride around until I find a cool spot for a Club Run were having. I'm the Prez now, so I can't just stay, some of the Bros are counting on me you know." They asked me if I was sure, that they had it good there. I told them yeah, I was sure, but I knew I would be back some day. "But I still have shit to do right now." They told me it must not be my time yet. We chatted about a couple old runs and party's we had been through. It all seemed like old times, except those damn skulls. They finally told me that if I was gonna' go that I had better go now, and then we all walked back to where our bikes were.

As I through my kickstand up, they told me not to worry, as they would be there when I came back. I gave my goodbyes and said sorry that I had to leave, with the promise that I would see them soon. They said they understood. I asked if they wanted to ride me back out to the highway like old times, and they said they couldn't. I kicked her to life and rode off, shaking my head. I remember getting back on the asphalt and heading back the way I thought we came, wondering what the fuck was going to happen to me next. The last I remember of this experience was riding down the road, feeling a strange peace inside me. Was this an out of body experience while I briefly died? Had I visited the afterlife and came back? Or maybe this was just a dream I remember while being on so much Morphine and Demerol. Maybe the head injuries caused this memory, or maybe it was a flashback from the LSD days. The strange thing is that with all the things they did to me, surgeries, traction, tubes in every orifice, being in the incubator, MRIs, CAT scans, being a human pin cushion, and all the countless medical procedures done to me, I remember nothing of all the discomfort and pain. I just remember this memory of my ride into hell, as I call it. It was vivid and real and really the only thing I can remember from the six weeks of the whole ordeal. To this day, I still feel that it really happened to me, I know it. I am more comfortable with death now than ever before. It's going to be beautiful there, don't fear it. I have a lot of Bros to see there, so I sort of look forward to that ultimate ride, someday soon.

This accident would change my life forever. After the five weeks, as I finally woke up, as my old lady calls it. It took a couple weeks until I finally talked them into cutting me loose to a hospital bed at my house. It wasn't too hard, after I told them I had no insurance and I had no money to pay anybody. My Doc said that they couldn't do that, as I still had rehab to go. The next day they must have looked at my records, because when I begged again to go home, the Doc said, "Yeah, I think your cookie jar has been broken for awhile." I already owed over half a million dollars, and had no means to pay it back, except maybe my net worth at the time, of which would have paid maybe half of it. I was headed for bankruptcy and they knew it. They finally cut me loose with the promise that from home I would start rehab right away. Unfortunately for me, my back surgery wound from the last operation done ripped wide open, full of gangrene the second day after I had came home and started rehab.

A hole two inches wide by five inches long had split wide open, and my old lady said that she could see some of my titanium plates on my spine. To try and save money and get good cheap help like always, I turned to my biker Brothers for help. I had a Prospect bring over a Vietnam Vet Special Forces medic we knew. It took them five hours to cut the gangrene out with no anesthesia. After that we constantly had to clean and re bandage the wound twice a day for months, while I remained bed bound. This meant that any rehabilitation would have to wait until that wound healed up completely. Unfortunately, it would take another four months to heal completely. When I finally got to start rehab, that time lapse had ruined my muscle tissue forever. I hated the wheel chair thing, and couldn't stand the walker. The cane isn't too bad, as I still have to use it today. I did gain one thing, and that's pity for anyone confined to a wheel chair, because it's nothing more than a frustrating nightmare. It would be 11 months to the day after my wreck before I could ride my bike again. My wife and a lot of my Bros wondered if I would ever get back on the horse and ride again. The thought of not riding motorcycles has never entered my mind. I can only ride about a third as far in a day, not 600 miles as I used to. I am left with constant pain, neuropathy, carpal tunnel, and degenerate nerve damage is eating away at my feet and hands. They tell me that the end for me will be in a wheelchair again. The doc said to quit riding motorcycles or, "You'll end up in a wheelchair quicker!" Doctors just don't understand anything about motorcycling, do they?

Have you ever hit a truck head on at 50 mph on a motorcycle? It fucking hurts! I strongly suggest that you don't, as it will change your life forever. The titanium that my body is full of is a constant reminder of what I have done to myself, as I am in a lot of constant, aching pain from it. The metal just aches and aches, especially if the weather is changing. My back is all bolted together and fused with titanium plates and screws, as well as the plates holding my pelvis together. The almost two foot long pin in my leg is titanium too, so it constantly aches and throbs. My hands, from having broken eight out of ten fingers at least once, take at least an hour in the morning to get working, with my right hand being the worse of the two from hitting people in the head too often. It's also from holding on to my Harley's throttle. All those decades of riding have left it almost useless. My nerves in my feet are slowly dying, and the damaged nerves ache to the point of being unbearable.

Most of the time my feet are on fire, as if someone is pouring hot water on them. To be honest, my lifestyle and all the damage I've done to my body has left me in a physical mess. Enough sniveling about it, because it doesn't do any good anyway. With 29 broken bones now, my hero, Evel Knievel, bless his soul, has nothing on me! The doctors tell me that I can't ride my bike anymore, as they just don't understand what biking is all about for me. It's my life, not just a hobby.

My lifestyle has led me to my current physical condition, as it never was the motorcycle's fault for me. No, it was my daring, living the Outlaw life, along with substance abuse. It's more my fault than anything for causing my current condition. At 55 years old now my mind is still strong, but my body is ravaged from my lifestyle and won't keep up. A couple of years after the big wreck, I ran into a biker I had known for years and he asked me a question that I'll never forget. He asked me, "How does it feel going from being the baddest motherfucker in town, to now being a cripple?" I wanted to knock the shit out of him but I didn't, because unfortunately for me, it was the truth.

I recently resigned as President of my Chapter, as I no longer can keep the pace of being the leader. I am a shadow of the man that I was, having lost a lot of weight and physical strengths, and I have had to learn to accept my fate. When I look at myself covered with tattoos and scar tissue, it all reminds me of the old times. Some good times and some bad ones, but all of them a sort of record of my life, if you will. I have Club tattoos showing my allegiances, and others showing my loves and beliefs. Harley wings and eagles show my love of riding motorcycles and of course, freedom. I have an early tattoo of a dagger through a rose, showing my will to never love, with another latest one of my old lady's name, meaning that I've fallen in love with a woman. Old School Biker's tattoos always tell their beliefs and the personal story of their life. The scars being reminders of the accidents and fights you have lived through and survived, all being my badges of courage, if you will.

I am glad to say that I only have one bullet wound, in my leg, along with all the scar tissue, which is almost a map of the different surgeries of putting humpty dumpty back together again. I live on pain pills, taking them to be able to stand the pain that I live through daily. I feel that I am left in this position with all this pain and discomfort because of my bad karma, for all the bad things I have done in my life. God is making me pay for my sins right here and now, on earth. There has to be a reason that he has kept me alive, or like I say, maybe it is to pay by the suffering of constant pain. Maybe here instead of hell, who knows? Or maybe I had something in my life that he wanted me to do or finish, and if that's true, it has to be this book. The fact is, I would never had have the chance or been able to have taken the time to even try and write this book if that dammed last wreck hadn't happened. Most of my kind from my era are all gone, and the few old school kick starters that are left mostly suffer as I do. Would I do anything different if I knew what suffering that lifestyle I had chosen had in store for me in my last years on this earth? I absolutely would not, as I wouldn't change the thrills of my life for anything!

I have ended this book when I had to leave California for good in the end of 1974 with the law hot on my trail. I have included some glimpses of how the future turned out, for a better ending to this book. I chose to quit the Clubs and the 1% life in California with the cops after my ass on those felony beefs. I started a new life as I had no choice, but my biking days were far from over, as I continued some of my old ways in the 1% lifestyle in other states, up until the present. My hope is to write a second book to finish my life story in the near future.

I would finally get caught for those California felonies up in Colorado, after almost four years of being on the run from the law. I fought extradition with a good lawyer, and unbelievably won. I was told by the D.A. that I should never come back to California again, as I was not wanted there! I continued to build and ride my Harleys and would go on to Father and raise two kids. I kept my hand in drug dealing and thieving until 1991. Then a major drug bust would keep me under the man's thumb for another five years, during which I applied my skills to something legal for a change, and became a successful small businessman to make my money and support my motorcycling lifestyle, until present. I became just what I always had detested in my youth. But I did get a sense of a certain pride that I could accomplish being successful in something legal in the citizen's world. Who would have ever thought? I ended up outliving my Mother, bless her soul! I raised my two kids, as best I knew how. I eventually joined another Motorcycle Club and have rode and lived in another country and five different states in the last 33 years. I have lived in Bandito, Sons of Silence, Vagos, Sundowners, Mongol, and of course, in Hell's Angel territory, and have rubbed shoulders with them all. But like it has been said, "That's another story." Motorcycles have always been my life and always will be. I hope after five plus years of writing my early memoirs, that you have enjoyed riding and living in the fast lane with me through this true autobiography, Memoirs of a Biker. Keep the shiny side up, as I'll see you down the road, somewhere.